Applied Linguistics Methods

Applied Linguistics Methods: A Reader presents the student with three contemporary approaches for investigating text, practices and contexts in which language-related problems are implicated. Divided into three parts, the reader focuses in turn on the different approaches, showing how each is relevant to addressing real-world problems, including those relating to contemporary educational practices.

Part One introduces the reader to Systemic Functional Linguistics (SFL) as an approach particularly well suited to the description of language and language-related problems in social contexts.

Part Two examines Critical Discourse Analysis (CDA) as a means of uncovering the relationships between language use, power and ideology.

Part Three presents ethnography (and linguistic ethnography) as a methodology for observing the use and significance of language in real-life events as they unfold.

The book begins by introducing the student to the tools of SFL, CDA and ethnography and explains how aspects of the three approaches can work in complementary ways. Each section is made up of theoretical readings reflecting the key epistemological and methodological issues of the specific approach, along with readings which centre on a specific language problem. Introductions to each section provide synopses of the individual chapters, making the reader highly usable on courses.

Applied Linguistics Methods: A Reader is key reading for advanced level undergraduates and postgraduates on applied linguistics, English language and TESOL/ TEFL courses.

Caroline Coffin, **Theresa Lillis** and **Kieran O'Halloran** are all currently at The Open University, UK. Caroline Coffi͏̈   Reader in Applied Linguistics and Theresa Lillis and Kieran O'Halloran are bo   for Language and Communication.

This reader, along with the companion volume *Applied Linguistics in Action: A Reader*, form part of *Investigating Language in Action* (E854), a course belonging to the Open University MA in Education programme.

The Open University Masters in Education

The Open University Masters in Education is now firmly established as the most popular postgraduate degree for education professionals in Europe, with over 3,000 students registered each year. It is designed particularly for those with experience of teaching, the advisory service, educational administration or allied fields. The Masters in Education (Applied Linguistics) is of particular relevance to teachers of English or educators who are interested in exploring the role of language in education. Successful study on the MA entitles students to apply for entry into the Open University Doctorate in Education programme.

Details of this and other Open University courses can be obtained from the Student Registration and Enquiry Service, The Open University, PO Box 197, Milton Keynes MK7 6BJ, United Kingdom: Telephone +44 (0) 845 300 6090, e-mail general-enquiries@open.ac.uk.

Alternatively, you may wish to visit the Open University website at http://www.open.ac.uk, where you can learn more about the wide range of courses and packs offered at all levels by The Open University.

Applied Linguistics

Methods

A Reader

Systemic Functional Linguistics, Critical Discourse Analysis and Ethnography

Edited by

Caroline Coffin, Theresa Lillis and Kieran O'Halloran

The Open University

Routledge
Taylor & Francis Group

LONDON AND NEW YORK

The Open University
Walton Hall
Milton Keynes
MK7 6AA
United Kingdom
www.open.ac.uk

First published 2010
by Routledge
2 Park Square, Milton Park, Abingdon, Oxon OX14 4RN

Simultaneously published in the USA and Canada
by Routledge
270 Madison Ave, New York, NY 10016

Routledge is an imprint of the Taylor & Francis Group, an informa business

© 2010 Compilation, original and editorial material,
The Open University

Typeset in Perpetua and Bell Gothic by
Florence Production Ltd, Stoodleigh, Devon
Printed and bound in Great Britain by
CPI Antony Rowe, Chippenham, Wiltshire

British Library Cataloguing in Publication data
A catalogue record for this book is available from the British Library

Library of Congress Cataloging in Publication Data
Applied linguistics methods: a reader: systemic functional linguistics, critical
discourse analysis and ethnography/edited by Caroline Coffin, Theresa Lillis,
and Kieran O'Halloran.
      p. cm.
   1. Applied linguistics—Methodology.   2. Functionalism (Linguistics).
   3. Critical discourse analysis—Methodology.   4. Sociolinguistics—
Methodology.   I. Coffin, Caroline, 1958–.   II. Lillis, Theresa M., 1956–.
III. O'Halloran, Kieran.
   P129.A68 2009
   418.007′2—dc22   2009002071

ISBN10: 0–415–54544–7 (hbk)
ISBN10: 0–415–54545–5 (pbk)

ISBN 13: 978–0–415–54544–0 (hbk)
ISBN 13: 978–0–415–54545–7 (pbk)

Contents

Illustrations

Figures

Tables

Acknowledgements

The editors and publishers would like to thank the following for kind permission to use copyright material:

Armstrong, E., Ferguson, A.J., Mortensen, L., Togher, L. and Equinox for 'Acquired language disorders: some functional insights', in J. Webster, J. Matthiessen and R. Hasan (eds), *Continuing Discourse on Language: A functional perspective*, Vol. 1, pp. 383–412, 2005.

Blommaert, J. and Cambridge University Press for 'Text and context', in *Discourse: A critical introduction*, edited version of pp. 39–66, 2005.

Coffin, C. and O'Halloran, K.A. and Routledge, Taylor & Francis Group (www.informaworld.com), for 'Finding the Global Groove: Theorising and analysing dynamic reader positioning using APPRAISAL, corpus, and a concordancer', in *Critical Discourse Studies*, 2 (2): 143–63, 2005. Reprinted by permission of the publisher.

Continuum International Publishing Group for Figure 2.1 'Extracts from a news story appearing in *The Nation*, October 26, 2004' reproduced from Knox, J.S. and Patpong, P. (2008) 'Reporting bloodshed in Thai newspapers: A comparative case study of English and Thai', in E. Thomson and P.R.R. White (eds) *Communicating Conflict: Multilingual case studies of the news media*.

Fairclough, N. and Wodak, R. and Sage for 'Critical Discourse Analysis', in T. van Dijk (ed.) *Discourse as Social Interaction*, London: Sage, pp. 268–84, 1997.

Hanrahan, M. and Wiley for 'Highlighting hybridity: a critical discourse analysis of teacher talk in science classrooms', in *Science Education*, 90 (1): 8–43, 2006.

HarperCollins Publishers Ltd for concordance lines from the Bank of English® within Coffin, C. and O'Halloran, K.A. 'Finding the global groove: theorising and analysing dynamic reader positioning using APPRAISAL, corpus, and a concordancer' in *Critical Discourse Studies*, 2 (2): 143–63, 2005.

Kim, M. and Cambridge Scholars Publishing for 'Translation error analysis: a systemic functional grammar approach', in D. Kenny and K. Ryou (eds), *Across Boundaries: International perspectives on translation studies*, pp. 161–75, Newcastle upon Tyne: Cambridge Scholars Publishing, 2007.

Moore, T. and Sage for 'The "processes" of learning: on the use of Halliday's transitivity in academic skills advising', in *Arts and Humanities in Higher Education*, 6 (1): 50–73, 2007.

Slembrouck, S. and Elsevier for the edited version of 'Discourse, critique and ethnography: class-oriented coding in accounts of child protection', in *Language Sciences*, 27 (6): 619–50, 2005.

The Sun/NI Syndication for 'Two Million Jobs in Peril', by George Pascoe-Watson in *The Sun*, 27 May 2003.

Widdowson, H.G. and Blackwell for extracts from *Text, Context, Pretext: Critical Issues in Discourse Analysis*, 2004.

Every effort has been made to trace copyright holders but this may not have been possible in all cases. Any omissions brought to the attention of the publisher will be remedied in future editions.

Introduction

Caroline Coffin, Theresa Lillis, Kieran O'Halloran

This book is a reader in applied linguistics. There has been a good deal of debate about the scope and nature of applied linguistics. Recently, however, a certain degree of consensus seems to have been achieved, that applied linguistics is concerned with:

> The theoretical and empirical investigation of real-world problems in which language is a central issue.
>
> (Brumfit 1995: 27)

This useful and concise definition of the field is now both widely accepted and widely quoted, and informs the thinking behind this volume and its companion. As a broad definition it has a number of distinct advantages. It differentiates applied linguistics from other branches of linguistics by foregrounding its orientation towards language-related problems, and it implies – though it does not explicitly say this – that work in applied linguistics can have some impact upon those problems, potentially influencing how decisions are made about them. It is also general enough to encompass the many disparate activities and areas of enquiry which call themselves applied linguistics, and it can unite approaches to language which are different, even incompatible. However, it also necessarily leaves many questions open and unanswered. Which theories are best suited to applied linguistic investigation? What empirical methods should be used? How are problems to be identified? Which problems should the applied linguist investigate? After these problems have been investigated, what action might be taken to impact upon them? What is the relation between theorising, empirical investigation and action?

The aim of this volume and its companion is to present the reader with a variety of answers to these questions through a selection of writings. The companion volume

Applied Linguistics in Action: A Reader (Cook and North, Routledge, 2009) focuses broadly on the questions: which theories? and which real-world problems? In contrast, this volume has a more specific focus. It offers three contemporary approaches for the exploration of, and intervention in, language-related real-world problems, namely Systemic Functional Linguistics, Critical Discourse Analysis and ethnography.

The chapters in the volume illustrate how these three approaches offer methods, that is, different tools of analysis, framings or perspectives for investigating text, practices and contexts in which language-related problems are implicated. In particular, they show how these constantly evolving methods are well-placed to engage with such problems through identifying, investigating, understanding or addressing them. The problems range from identifying how language can mislead and misrepresent in the interests of the powerful at the expense of the relatively powerless, to educationally related concerns such as how to develop national and international literacy programmes which meet adult learners' needs or to enhance scientific literacy. 'Method' within this framing of applied linguistics refers not only to academic methods and approaches for researching and analysing language in context, but also to methods of intervention, that is, how the three different approaches lend themselves to intervention in real-world issues. The authors in this volume take the view that a rich and systematic appreciation of the relationship between language use and its context is important in deciding upon the best course of engagement with language-related real-world problems.

There are three parts in the Reader, with five chapters given over to illustrating each of the three approaches. Each part begins with an introduction to the theoretical tenets and methods of analysis for each approach. In other chapters, you will explore recent developments in theory and method, different types of problem engagement, as well as critical perspective on methods.

Systemic Functional Linguistics

Systemic Functional Linguistics (SFL) is a theory of language which sets out to explain how humans make meaning. SF linguists are interested in the relationship between language and the brain, on the one hand, and language and society on the other. Michael Halliday, its chief architect, makes the analogy that just as language and the brain are co-created and can be co-damaged and co-destroyed, language and society also co-evolve and also run the risk of upheaval and disruption (Halliday 2002: 5). It is the relationship between these phenomena that the theory seeks to explain. This places it in a strong position to be of use to the concerns of applied linguists. Halliday sees theory as a strategic tool, a problem-solving device and a guide to action.

So, how does SFL pursue its aim? From a theoretical perspective, SF linguists have proposed a model that brings into relationship the following: meaning, function, grammar and context. From a practical perspective the model has developed (and continues to develop) by engaging with applied linguistic concerns. For example, with the problems that occur when processes of child and adult language development are disrupted through brain injury or educational disadvantage; when poor communication within health systems puts at risk patient well-being; when language is used in political coercion; and when poor translations from one language into another threaten the integrity of the original text.

Three types of meaning are distinguished in SFL and each of these relate to the three overall functions that Halliday argues language has evolved to serve. As illustrated in the chapters, they comprise the ideational metafunction (meanings to do with propositional content), the interpersonal metafunction (meanings to do with the exchange of perspectives and the expression of attitude) and the textual metafunction (meanings concerned with how the text is structured as a message). In contrast to traditional approaches to grammar, each of these dimensions of meaning map onto different grammatical elements. In SFL, such elements are labelled functionally. For example, consider the following two clauses to illustrate functional labelling (of ideational meaning) in contrast with traditional 'subject/object' labelling:

The army	*shot*	*and*	*killed*	*the demonstrators*	
subject	verb		verb	object	(traditional labels)
agent				affected	(ideational labels)

The demonstrators	*were killed*	*in a shooting*	
subject	verb	prepositional phrase	(traditional labels)
affected		circumstance	(ideational labels)

In the first clause, the cause of the demonstrators' death – 'the army' – is the subject of the verb 'killed'; 'the demonstrators' is the object. Cause is made explicit because the subject of the verb is also, in functional terms, the 'agent' of the verb. In the second clause, 'the army' as agent has been deleted; while 'the demonstrators' is no longer the object, it remains in functional terms the 'affected'. Another change is as follows: while 'shot' features as one of the verbs in the first clause, in the second it features as part of a circumstance, a different functional unit. Circumstances provide extra information in a clause – how, where, when (and are often realised by prepositional phrases). In the second clause, because the agent has been removed, and 'shot' is in the circumstance, there is no longer a direct link between who did the shooting and the killing. In this way, responsibility for the action is obscured. Since functional analysis is designed to keep track of meanings such as in the above changes, it is a powerful tool for articulating meaning – both presences and absences – in a more precise way than in traditional grammar.

SF linguists propose that choices in grammar both shape, and are shaped by, the contexts in which people use language – both the immediate situational context and the wider cultural context. In this way context is understood in terms of the linguistic meanings made and vice versa.

Critical Discourse Analysis

Critical Discourse Analysis (henceforth CDA) is another method in applied linguistics which engages with language-related real-world problems. It investigates how language use reproduces the perspectives, values and ways of talking of the powerful, which may not be in the interests of the less powerful. It focuses on the relationship between language, power and *ideology*. Ideologies are representations of aspects of the world which contribute to establishing and maintaining social relations of domination, inequality and exploitation, which CDA views as problematic and in need of addressing. Employing tools of linguistic analysis, often from SFL, critical discourse analysts seek to unpick these problem relations in order to illuminate how language use contributes to the domination and misrepresentation of certain social groups. Critical discourse analysts have not only looked at political practices where ideologies promote domination but educational practices too, such as how traditional, and thus dominant, teacher–student discourse may not enhance learning. A diagnosis of discourse in CDA is then a 'critical' one. There are many scholars working in CDA. It is multidisciplinary, with different scholars drawing on different theoretical models and methods. Among its principal architects are Norman Fairclough and Ruth Wodak (who feature in this volume) as well as Paul Chilton and Teun van Dijk.

The concept of discourse in CDA is crucial in how real-world language-related problems are framed. It usually encompasses two notions. The first is 'language in use' (or 'little d' discourse).[1] For example, for conversation, discourse refers to the whole of the meanings made in interaction with features of context which are deemed relevant by participants, e.g. tone of voice, facial movements, hand-gestures. For writing, discourse refers to how a text (e.g. a train timetable) is read, understood and acted upon by different readers – in other words, the whole communicative event associated with a text. In both conversation and writing, text is the linguistic trace of the discourse; in conversation the text would be its transcription from audio recording. 'Little d' discourse analysis, in principle, includes the analysis of the meanings/understandings/interpretations that readers/listeners make.

A second key meaning of discourse in CDA is one associated with the work of the French social theorist/philosopher, Michel Foucault. Foucault (1972) characterises Discourses as ways of talking about the world which are intricately bound up with ways of seeing and understanding it. For Foucault, Discourses define and delimit what it is possible to say and not possible to say (and by extension – what to do or not to do) with respect to the area of concern of a particular institution, political programme, etc. For example, different religions have their own Discourses which delimit explanation of natural behaviour. Some religions accept that the universe began with 'the big bang' (scientific Discourse) but that a deity initiated it (religious Discourse). Crucially for Foucault, there is a relationship between Discourse (or 'big D' Discourse) and those with power. This is because the powerful ultimately control Discourse.[2]

CDA assumes a bi-directional (*dialectical*) relationship between discourse and Discourse (which has parallels with how SFL perceives the relationship between language use and context). In other words, reproduction of unequal language use (e.g. '*man* and wife' as opposed to '*husband* and wife') can help to reinforce unequal social processes/domination and vice versa. Repeated reproduction of Discourse through language use can lead to a situation where people tacitly assent to a dominant perspective which may not be in their interests. Such a state of affairs – known as *hegemony* – is one that CDA has a particular focus on. Since analysts are often actively involved in contesting the hegemonies they investigate, CDA is thus a committed form of discourse analysis, and many of its practitioners have a commitment to a particular political or cultural position. It is, in the words of one of its major proponents, 'discourse analysis "with an attitude"' (van Dijk 2001: 96).

Ethnography

Ethnography involves the systematic exploration of the 'culture' – that is the beliefs and practices – of a community or social group. Ethnography thus stands in contrast to many approaches within applied linguistics in that its starting point is 'culture' rather than language. A key consequence of this for real-world problem engagement is that reaching an empirical understanding of context (based on observation rather than theorising alone) is central. Core aspects to an ethnographic approach therefore include: 1) the collection and analysis of empirical data drawn from 'real-world' contexts rather than being produced under experimental conditions created by the researcher; 2) a range of data and not only the more obvious 'language' types of data; 3) a commitment to making sense of events from the perspectives of those involved; 4) a recognition that meanings and functions of human actions mainly take the form of verbal descriptions and explanations, which in turn renders these descriptions highly significant in any act of interpretation (for overview discussions see Hammersley 1994, 2006; Street 1993). In seeking to define the nature of real-world language problems, ethnography explicitly values insider (*emic*- language users) as well as outsider (*etic*- academics/analysts) perspectives.

The importance of ethnography is particularly evident in two traditions of the study of language in context; *sociolinguistics*, where there is a predominant focus on spoken interaction; and *anthropological studies* of literacy. In sociolinguistics, ethnography has been prominent ever since Dell Hymes – a major figure in this field – emphasised the importance of ethnography for understanding what is going on and at stake in everyday uses of language, influentially calling for the establishment of an academic field of study, 'the ethnography of communication' (see Hymes 1974; Gumperz and Hymes 1972). Within this tradition, the work of Gumperz (1999), in what is often specifically referred to as 'interactional sociolinguistics' (IS), brought a dynamic notion of context to the heart of the study of spoken interaction; away from a notion of context as a rather static-like container, towards *contextualisation*, signalling that context is dynamically produced, achieved and sustained in the process of interaction. To take one example, which is explored in one of the chapters in this book (see Rampton), people's sense of identity – who they are and want to be – is not simply reflected in the way they talk but is enacted, or performed in moment-to-moment interaction with others. This foundational work in sociolinguistics and in particular IS has become highly influential in recent studies referred to as 'linguistic ethnography'. This is a term which is growing in use (for overview, see Creese 2008), particularly in the United Kingdom, to refer to approaches which explicitly combine approaches from linguistics and ethnography, while at the same time taking account of critical social theory in similar ways to CDA, including a concern with power and ideology.

The second highly significant tradition comes from anthropology and studies of the different ways in which literacy is used. In what are often referred to as New Literacy Studies (NLS), ethnographic studies of literacy practices in specific communities have been carried out and include both formal and informal contexts of learning (see, for overviews, Barton *et al.* 2000; Street and Lefstein 2007). NLS draws closely on key analytic tools from anthropology, notably the notions of *emic* and *etic* which are used as a way of acknowledging and working with both insider (typically language or literacy users) and outsider (typically the academic researcher) perspectives respectively. It is not surprising that literacy has figured so strongly in ethnographic studies of language. 'Literacy' is a ubiquitous yet highly contested phenomenon at every level of societal debate – from a parent's concern with a child's progress in reading and writing and how these should be taught, to the use of indicators of literacy 'levels' as a way of measuring and comparing the economic and development performance of nation states. In the context of globalisation with increased mobility (physical and virtual), recognition of different types of literacies becomes even more crucial, where what is valued in one context may be undervalued or challenged for its legitimacy in another with high stakes consequences for those involved (see Blommaert (2008) for discussion).

Both traditions are reflected in the ethnographically framed chapters across the book, at points intersecting and overlapping, and mostly converging on a core position: that ethnography should be viewed as an epistemology rather than a method. That is, ethnography involves a particular way of approaching and understanding the real world, and consequently attempting to intervene in the world, rather than being simply a set of methods or techniques. Key aspects of this epistemology, such as the need to avoid cultural bias when researching the practices of groups with whom the researcher is unfamiliar, are unpacked in the five chapters centring on ethnography in this volume.

Some of the chapters in this reader focus solely on one of the three approaches, some combine elements from each. So, for example, certain chapters on CDA reflect how it draws on SFL, the latter providing a key descriptive apparatus for identifying 'CDA-type problems' in texts, such as a skewing towards the interests of powerful groups; other chapters indicate how ethnography can be used in CDA. While some chapters illustrate the compatibility between the three approaches, others reflect tensions, particularly around the relationship between language – or 'text' – and context. Theorists and practitioners in SFL, CDA and ethnography give different kinds of weighting to text and context in investigation. Ethnographers are likely to emphasise context over text, or at least start with context and then move to text in their investigations. SFL usually moves in the opposite direction, as does the SFL-based CDA of some analysts, such as Norman Fairclough. Whereas SF linguists would say that to analyse and interpret text in context there needs to be an understanding of how its linguistic choices relate to a language system (such as English), many CDA analysts would argue that it is equally if not more important to understand the contexts of production and reception (how people understand texts and what they do with their understanding) and ethnographers would argue that it is equally if not more important to understand the system of beliefs and practices of a community or social group in order to understand language use – and hence language problems. Seeking ways of exploring the vexed relationship between language (text) and context is at the heart of all chapters, with each offering distinct methods for empirically and theoretically engaging with this relationship.

Notes

1   The expressions 'little d' discourse and 'big D' Discourse come from Gee (1999).
2   There is also another concept of discourse which has currency in linguistics: 'discourse'
     is also used to refer to language which is above the level of the clause or sentence,
     that is, stretches of text. This third meaning of 'discourse' is sometimes used in CDA;
     in other words, the distinction between 'text' and 'discourse' is not always sustained
     in CDA. SFL, frequently, uses 'discourse' as equivalent to 'text'.

Bibliography

Barton, D., Hamilton, M. and Ivanič, R. (eds) (2000) *Situated Literacies: Reading and writing in context*. London: Routledge.

Blommaert, J. (2008) *Grassroots Literacy: Writing, identity and voice in Central Africa*. New York and London: Routledge.

Brumfit, C. (1995) 'Teacher professionalism and research', in G. Cook and B. Seidlhofer (eds) *Principle and Practice in Applied Linguistics*, (pp.27–41) Oxford: Oxford University Press.

Creese, A. (2008) 'Linguistic ethnography', in N. Hornberger (ed.) *Encyclopedia of Language and Education*, (pp. 229–41). New York: Springer.

Foucault, M. (1972) *The Order of Things*. London: Tavistock.

Gee, J.P. (1999) *An Introduction to Discourse Analysis*. London: Routledge.

Gumperz, J. and Hymes, D. (eds) (1972) *Directions in Sociolinguistics. The ethnography of communication* (pp. 35–71). Oxford: Basil Blackwell.

Gumperz, J. (1999) 'On interactional sociolinguistic method', in S. Sarangi and C. Roberts (eds) *Talk, Work and Institutional Order* (pp. 453–72). Berlin: Mouton de Gruyter.

Halliday, M.A.K. (2002) 'On grammar', in J. Webster (ed.) *Language and Education*. London: Continuum.

Hammersley, M. (1994) 'Introducing ethnography', in D. Graddol, J. Maybin and B. Stierer (eds) *Researching Language and Literacy in Social Context* (pp. 1–17). Clevedon/Milton Keynes: Multilingual Matters/OUP.

Hammersley, M. (2006) 'Ethnography: problems and prospects'. *Ethnography and Education* 1 (1): 3–14.

Hymes, D. (1974) *Foundations in Sociolinguistics: An ethnographic approach*. Philadelphia, PA: University of Pennsylvania Press.

Street, B. (1993) 'Culture is a verb: anthropological aspects of language and cultural process', in D. Graddol, D.L. Thompson and M. Byram (eds) *Language and Culture* (pp. 23–43). Clevedon: BAAL and Multilingual Matters.

Street, B. and Lefstein, A.S. (2007) *Literacy: An advanced resource book*. London: Routledge.

van Dijk, T.A. (2001) 'Multidisciplinary CDA', in R. Wodak and M. Meyer (eds) *Methods of Critical Discourse Analysis* (pp. 95–120). London: Sage.

PART ONE

Systemic Functional Linguistics

Caroline Coffin, Theresa Lillis, Kieran O'Halloran

Introduction to Part One

Part One of the reader aims to show how Systemic Functional Linguistics (SFL) is an approach not only suited to the description of language in social contexts but suited to the investigation of language-related problems and in some cases their amelioration. The first two chapters focus on SFL theory and the subsequent three on problem engagement.

For those readers unfamiliar with SFL's core concepts and premises the first chapter – *Language, register and genre* – provides an introductory overview. In this chapter, Jim Martin first discusses why linguists develop theories in order to make 'the invisible visible' and explains how systemic functional linguists differ from those working in other traditions. He goes on to introduce the main theoretical principles and concepts of SFL, including the following:

- Language is viewed as a large network or system of interrelated options from which speakers unconsciously select when speaking/writing.
- Language utterances can only be made sense of in relation to the context of situation and the context of culture.
- Register accounts for the systematic relationship between language and context of situation.
- Meaning can be categorised into three broad areas – ideational, interpersonal and textual, each of which relate to a cluster of language systems.
- Genres are seen as having distinctive goal-oriented staging structures.

Martin makes the point that whenever we write or speak we have to use enough signals of register and genre to ensure that our listener or reader can see where we are coming from but that, because these occur probabilistically (i.e. they are likely to occur but do not have to), they allow the individual considerable freedom in determining just how they are to be expressed. Thus, from a genre perspective, not all fairy tales begin with 'Once upon a time' (although many of them do!).

Although language and indeed any social conventions or norms usually develop for functional reasons, this does not mean that they remain functional or effective, particularly if there are changes in the surrounding social and cultural context. Thus genres may evolve and add or lose stages over time. In Chapter 2 – *Online newspapers: evolving genres and evolving theory* – John Knox explores genre and language change and the consequent need for theoretical innovation. The context for Knox's exploration is contemporary news media and in particular electronic, multimodal newsbites. Knox argues that like all texts, newsbites reflect the practices and interests of the institutions that produce them. Thus, owing to commercial pressures, together with changes in the readership and the nature of events reported on, news reports now tend to foreground the climax of the report both verbally and visually. These changes require changes in the SFL approach to modelling the structure of news genres. Knox argues a 'Nucleus–Satellite' structure more closely models contemporary news genres than does a linear stage-by-stage approach. Furthermore, analytical tools which take into account the verbal–visual interaction are also required: newsbites enter into different visual relations with other elements on the 'page' (or screen) than do longer news reports.

Chapters 1 and 2 introduce key SFL tenets and tools of analysis and discuss some of the implications for how these can be used to engage with real-world problems in various professional contexts. Martin makes the point, for example, that one of the aims of SF linguists is to provide a perspective on learning which challenges and complements that drawn from cognitive psychology in educational research. Knox also argues that SFL genre research can be useful to educators: functional descriptions of how new media texts work provide a basis for 'informed explanations and effective pedagogy' (p. 33). The main focus of Chapters 2 and 3 is thus SFL theory and tools of analysis. In Chapters 4, 5 and 6, the emphasis moves away from theoretical principles and methodological issues, with the practical uses and applications of SFL becoming central. Each chapter illustrates a different real-world problem and some of the ways in which SFL has been used to identify, investigate and address the problem.

In Chapter 3 – *The 'processes' of learning* – Tim Moore discusses three case studies which illustrate the academic writing problems experienced by Australian university students. He proposes that the analytical framework of SFL and specifically its functional categories of *participants* and *processes* (referred to as transitivity analysis) can ameliorate these problems by revealing some of the confusions that university students face when learning to understand and represent the world according to the demands of different academic disciplines. Moore's aim in the article is not only to elucidate the nature of disciplinary difference in how knowledge is construed and students' related difficulties in writing but also to show how Halliday's system can be applied in uncomplicated ways in teaching situations in order to address these difficulties. Moore's study demonstrates that SFL analytical tools, by evaluating the effectiveness of texts, are able to bring the domains of learning and language into a fruitful relationship including opening up space for students to critique pedagogical and disciplinary framing of knowledge. But this, he argues (following Halliday) is only possible by interpreting not only the texts themselves but also their context (both of situation and culture) and the relationship between the two.

Language disorder acquired through brain damage is the real-world problem illustrated in Chapter 4. As in Chapter 3, the authors emphasize the usefulness of SFL in providing a contextualised view of language use. Such a perspective, they argue, moves clinicians away from looking at patients' language purely in formal grammatical (often deficit) terms and focuses more usefully on how patients make meaning in context, i.e. how they participate in 'real-life' discourse as opposed to decontextualised language tasks and tests. As a result of this orientation to language disorder there is a focus on conversational partners (in addition to patients) and on their role in the co-construction of discourse. Elizabeth Armstrong and her colleagues explain that the use of SF tools to investigate a range of communication situations and partners, speaker roles and genres provides rich insight into how patients and their interlocutors use language to represent the world, interact with others and create cohesive and coherent text. This provides a firm foundation for addressing patients' communication problems through therapies and interventions that target not only those suffering from brain disorders but the wider community.

Chapter 5 focuses on the real-world challenge of translation. In a pilot study Mira Kim uses an SFL framework to diagnose some of the translation difficulties experienced by trainee translators. By adopting a metafunctional perspective (i.e. looking at the text from the perspective of the ideational, interpersonal and textual functions), she argues that she is able to articulate the nature of their translation errors precisely and constructively. Although her study is small scale, Kim is able to model how empirical data can be collected and analysed in a way that has practical applications for professional practice.

In sum, the articles in this Part demonstrate how the ever evolving analytical tools of SFL can be used to identify, understand, investigate and address a range of professional concerns and practices.

Chapter 1

Jim Martin

Language, register and genre

Without thinking

Everybody does things without thinking. People learn to talk and walk, drive cars, serve and volley, play instruments, and so on. And the point comes where what was once a slow and painful, often error-prone process becomes automated. It is then simply taken for granted – we forget about it. At least until something goes wrong. If we fall or stutter, have an accident, double fault or play out of tune, we may stop for a moment and think about what we were doing. But for the most part we carry on, functioning as members of our culture, doing what other people accept.

Towards the end of the nineteenth century, three famous scholars became very interested in the unconscious forces that shape our lives. These men, Saussure, Durkheim and Freud, were the founders of what is now known as social science. Saussure is the father of linguistics, Durkheim sociology, and Freud psychiatry. All were concerned with what it is that makes people tick, without their knowing that it does so. They were interested, in other words, not in physical, material things, as in anatomy or astronomy, but in human behaviour – in social facts. Taken together, these social facts constitute a system. These systems are set up to explain why people do what they do without really thinking about what they are doing.

For example, I am writing this paper in English, in English of a particular kind in fact. I am not using slang; I am not using double negatives (I don't write, though many speakers of English might say *I don't use no double negatives*); and I am not

An earlier version of this chapter was published in Christie, F. (ed.) (1984) *ECT 418 Children Writing: A Reader*, Geelong, Vic: Deakin University Press. The current version was revised for the second time in early 2008.

writing in French or Tagalog. Why am I doing this? I am not doing it because you cannot write about language, register and genre in French or Tagalog. I am doing it because I want to interact with you the reader. I know that you expect me to use English – that is the language we share. So, by convention, I use English. Or, to take another example, as I sit here writing I am wearing trousers. I am doing so because I am a male, working in Australia, and in winter this is what Australian males wear. I am not necessarily wearing trousers because of the cold. A number of females pass by my window from time to time, and many of them are not wearing trousers, but skirts or dresses. I, like them, am dressing the way I do by convention. I dress, without thinking about it, as people expect. I could, if I wished, think about it, and mutter to someone in Tagalog or put on a dress. But if I do, my behaviour will be taken as a joke, or considered asocial, perhaps even outrageous. If I break the rules, people will start thinking. Otherwise life simply goes on.

Now, the point of these remarks about the unconscious nature of language and culture is to try and give you an idea of what linguists and sociologists do. Their job is to discover the unconscious rules which govern our behaviour and to make them explicit – to make the invisible visible in other words. In order to do this they develop models for organising these social facts and theories about the best way to build these models (Culler 1976; Saussure 1915/1966).

Let me try and illustrate with regard to a small example the kind of description of human behaviour linguists and sociologists interested in social facts come up with. Imagine that you are an alien, that you have just landed on earth, and are standing at a pedestrian crossing. You notice that there is a set of lights, with green and red pictures of what appear to be men. The lights change in a certain sequence, first a green man, then a flashing red man, and then a red man which does not flash. This goes on repeatedly. You also notice that there are real people crossing the street and that their movements seem to be conditioned by the lights. When the light is green they walk, when the light is flashing red they walk faster or run, and when the light is red they stop and wait for cars to go by. Now, if you were an alien semiotician (a semiotician is someone who is interested in the systems of meaning or social systems which regulate human behaviour) you would jot down in your journal a brief description of the system you have been observing. The system would have three terms or options: 'walk', 'hurry up' and 'stop'. Each of these choices has a meaning: when people choose 'walk' they start to move across the street; if they choose 'hurry up' they start to run or walk more quickly across the street; and if they choose 'stop', they wait on the corner. In addition, each of these options has an expression – a way of communicating its meaning: 'walk' is expressed by (linguists would say 'is realised by') the green man, 'hurry up' by the flashing red man, and 'stop' by the red man.

The notes you have made are in fact a description of the semiotic system of pedestrian crossing lights. The description has three parts: (1) a statement of the meanings, in this case the socially significant human behaviour the system regulates – moving across the street, moving quickly across the street and not moving; (2) the choices themselves – 'walk', 'hurry up' and 'stop'; and (3) the realisation of the choices, in this case the lights – red, flashing red and green. An outline of this little semiotic system is presented in Figure 1.1, as it would be modelled in Systemic Functional Linguistics.

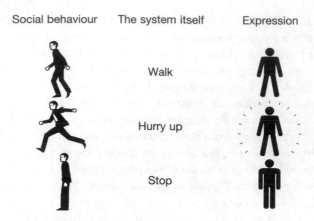

Social behaviour   The system itself   Expression

Walk

Hurry up

Stop

Figure 1.1 Pedestrian crossing lights as a system

Systemic Functional Linguistics

Systemic Functional Linguistics is one of the main functional theories of language developed in the twentieth century and which continues to evolve in this one. Its major architect is M.A.K. Halliday, formerly Professor of Linguistics at the University of Sydney (Halliday 1978, 1994); one of his main influences was J.R. Firth, the first Professor of Linguistics in Great Britain, who held the chair at the University of London (Firth 1957a, b). In origin then, the theory is a British one, with much stronger ties to European linguistics than to American approaches. The influence of Saussure (who taught in Geneva), Hjelmslev (who worked in Copenhagen), Malinowski (an anthropologist based in London), linguists of the Prague School and another of Halliday's teachers, the Chinese linguist Wang Li, combine to give the school its distinctive flavour (Hjelmslev 1961; Malinowski 1923, 1935; Mathesius 1964). Halliday moved to Australia in 1975, with the result that metropolitan Sydney became the main international centre for this research.

How do systemic functional linguists differ from linguists of other schools? First of all, they place considerable emphasis on the idea of choice. They view language as a large network of interrelated options, from which speakers unconsciously select when speaking. In more technical terms, their focus is on paradigmatic relations – on what you say in relation to what you could have said. Other linguists have a much stronger syntagmatic perspective – on what you say in relation to what you said before and what you are going to say next. Systemicists formalise these choices by means of systems (thus the name of the theory): for example, singular versus plural, active versus passive, declarative versus interrogative and so on. The way in which these systems bundle together in their grammars gives systemicists an insight into how language is related to the contexts in which it is used; this takes us to the second distinctive feature of systemic linguistics.

Second, then, systemicists, like Firthians before them, have taken a great interest in the relation between language and context. They have always argued, following Malinowski (1923, 1935), that you cannot understand the meaning of what someone says or writes unless you know something about the context in which it is embedded. Or, looking at this the other way round, if you understand what someone says or writes (a text in technical terms), you can also figure out a great deal about the context in which that text occurred (Ure and Ellis 1977). This idea about the relationship between language and context was taken over from Malinowski into linguistics by Firth (1957a, b).

Malinowski was an anthropologist who worked largely in Melanesia, studying the culture of people living on islands to the south and east of Papua New Guinea. Malinowski was what people commonly think of when they hear the word linguist: not someone who describes languages, but someone who knows a lot of languages and learns them easily. Malinowski believed that learning the language of the people you were studying was essential for an anthropologist, and he collected a number of texts, taken from many different aspects of the life of the Melanesians he was studying (note that anthropologists such as Malinowski are social scientists too, very closely related to sociologists in what they do, though tending to work on more exotic and less familiar cultures). When he was translating these texts into English, for the benefit of his English readers, Malinowski noticed that the translations he was producing did not really make much sense. This was partly because Malinowski was not a linguist in the grammar-describing sense of the term, and tended to give word-for-word translations which exaggerated the differences between Melanesian languages and English. But more importantly and this was Malinowski's point, no matter how good a translation he made, it still turned out that if you didn't know what the people involved in the text were doing, and didn't understand the culture, then you couldn't make sense of their text. In order to deal with this problem Malinowski introduced the terms 'context of situation' and 'context of culture'.

Let me try and give an example of what Malinowski was on about. Suppose you are sitting in a room, and hear someone yell: 'John, don't do it there mate!' (if you know another language, think about how you would say this in that language). Now, however faithfully you translate this sentence into another language, it will still be the case that unless you know what John was doing, you don't really know what the person talking to him meant. You don't know what John was doing, what he was doing it to, and where he was doing it. If however you had a translation of this sentence, and a description of the context of situation in which it was uttered (say John dumping a load of broken mud bricks into a drainage trough), then you would be able to understand the text. So, in order to explain the meaning of a sentence, you need both a description of that sentence and of the context in which it was used.

But Malinowski believed that even this would not be enough. Alongside a description of the context of situation, you also need a description of the culture in which the utterance is used. Suppose, for example, you are wandering down a corridor at Sydney University, and hear someone say 'Okay, now what we have here is a mental process rank-shifted into the Carrier of a relational clause'. (Try translating that into another language if you know one!) Suppose as well that you happen to glance through an open door and see a lecturer talking to a group of students and pointing to the underlined constituent in a clause such as the following written on the whiteboard: *what they want is unacceptable*. You have now heard the sentence; if you look closely at the whiteboard you can see which part of the clause the Carrier is; and you can see what the lecturer is doing and who he is talking to. But if you are not studying functional linguistics you will still be at a loss as to what exactly is going on. This is because you have not been socialised into the world where such a sentence makes sense. You are not a member of the subculture which goes around talking about language in this way. This is Malinowski's point about needing a description of the language, the context of situation and the context of culture in which a sentence is used. If you are not a member of the culture, you cannot understand what is meant.

Malinowski's ideas about language in relation to context of situation and context of culture were taken over by Firth and incorporated into linguistic theory. In sharp contrast to the goals of many of his American contemporaries, Firth believed that the purpose of linguistics was to explain meaning (American linguists such as Bloomfield felt that this was a hopelessly complicated goal). Firth did little to flesh out Malinowski's concept of context of culture, but he did take steps to outline those aspects of the context of situation which were relevant to linguistic description. This work was carried on by Firth's students, who adopted the term 'register' for the study of the relation between language and context of situation.

Firth's students were for a time referred to as neo-Firthians (many, following Halliday, would go on to develop systemic linguistics; Bazell *et al.* 1966). They developed a more sophisticated framework than Firth for describing register, making use of three main categories: field, mode and tenor (at first they used the term 'style' for 'tenor', but then, following Gregory, agreed to reserve that term for the study of literary texts; Halliday 1978; Halliday and Hasan 1985). Definitions of these three categories varied slightly over the years (Gregory in fact suggested splitting tenor into personal tenor and functional tenor in 1967 – this will be further discussed below; see Gregory and Carroll 1978); but in general the terms can be understood as follows.

Field refers to what is going on, where what is going on is interpreted institutionally in terms of some culturally recognised activity (what people are doing with their lives, as it were). Examples of fields are activities such as tennis, opera, linguistics, cooking, building construction, farming, politics, education and so on. When people ask you what you do when first getting to know you, you tend to answer in terms of field (e.g. *Well, I'm a linguist. I play tennis. I'm interested in popular music* and so on).

Tenor refers to the way you relate to other people when doing what you do. One aspect of this is status. Our society, like all other human societies we know of, is structured in such a way that people have power over one another. This power is of various kinds: mature people tend to dominate younger ones, commanding their respect; bosses dominate employees; teachers dominate students and so on. There is no escaping this, however nice we try to be about it. When you think people are bossy or 'above themselves', it is usually because they are asserting an inordinate amount of power over you. When you think someone is quiet, evasive and looking insecure, it is often because they are being overly deferential to you. And of course you can resist, as when feminists struggle to renovate the power relations between women and men. Renovation is hard work as we all know, and however democratic our ideals, there always seems to be a lot of power pushing us around.

Mode refers to the channel you select to communicate – the choice most commonly presented is between speech and writing. But modern society makes use of many additional channels: blogs, Facebook, YouTube, SMS messages, e-mail, telephone, radio, television, video, film and so on, each a distinct mode in its own right. It should perhaps be stressed here that writing is a relatively late development in human culture, both in terms of the history of our race and in the life of a child. Writing as we know it was invented just three times in human history – once in China, once in the Middle East, and once in Central America (although this tradition has not survived). In European and Asian contexts writing is only a few thousand years old; many languages still do not use a writing system in day-to-day life, and across cultures children have learned to speak much of their language before they put pen to paper. Interestingly enough, the emergence of writing systems has had a considerable effect on the structure of languages which use them. This is related to why speech and writing differ as they do, and why learning to write involves far more than using squiggles to make meaning instead of sounds. The choices you make from your grammar are themselves very different in speech and writing. It is for this reason that learning to write effectively takes so long.

Formalising the relationship of language and culture

In the late 1960s, after working for some years on formalising the choices relevant to clause structure in English, Halliday made a significant breakthrough as far as work on the relationship between language and context is concerned (Halliday 1973). He noted that the register categories of field, mode and tenor that he and his colleagues had developed earlier in the decade had striking parallels in the structure of language itself. What had happened was that as work on formalising clause systems progressed, it became clear that those systems were tending to cluster into three main groups. One bundle of choices was referred to in his early work by Halliday as TRANSITIVITY; this bundle of choices was concerned with the structure of clauses in terms of the way they map reality – the difference between verbs of doing and happening, reacting, thinking and perceiving, saying, and describing and identifying, along with the VOICE (active/passive) potential associated with each. Another bundle he referred to as MOOD, and was concerned with distinguishing statements from questions from commands from exclamations as well as expressing usuality, probability, inclination, obligation and ability. The third bundle, called THEME, has to do with the way in which speakers order constituents in a clause, putting first a theme which connects with the overall development of a paragraph or text, and last something that contains information which is new to the listener. Later, Halliday was to use more semantically oriented terms to generalise these three broad areas of meaning potential: 'ideational' for meaning about the world, 'interpersonal' for intersubjective meaning between speakers, and 'textual' for meanings relating pieces of text to each other and to their context (Halliday 1978, 1994).

Looked at in this way, in terms of the kinds of meaning involved, the three main bundles of systems were seen to match up with register categories in the following way. Field obviously correlated with ideational meaning. There was a connection between the institutional activities in which people engage and what they were talking about. Mode was most clearly related to textual meanings. The channel you choose has a big effect on the relationship between language and its context. And tenor was closely related to interpersonal meaning; power and solidarity are both implicated in whether you are giving or demanding goods and services or information and how sure you are about what you are doing. This correlation between register categories and functional components in the grammar is very important. It is this that enables systemicists to predict on the basis of context not just what choices a speaker is likely to make, but which areas of the grammar are at stake. Conversely it allows us to look at particular grammatical choices and to understand the contribution they are making to the contextual meaning of a sentence. This makes it possible for systemic linguists to argue on the basis of grammatical evidence about the nature of field, mode and tenor at the same time as it gives them a way of explaining why language has the shape it does in terms of the way in which people use it to live. Systemic grammar is often referred to as Systemic Functional Grammar for this reason (Eggins 1994; Fries and Gregory 1995).

This particular approach to language and context of situation contrasted with other perspectives on language variation in the early 1960s. Other linguists who looked at context at that time were more concerned with phonological and low-level morphological variation, and were studying the difference between the dialects of English spoken by speakers coming from different social backgrounds (sociolinguists inspired by William Labov were the main researchers in this area). But Halliday's approach did have obvious implications for applied linguistics and began to be used in work on the teaching of English (both as a mother tongue – the Nuffield Foundation project (Pearce *et al.* 1989), and as a second or foreign language – English for special purposes and functional–notional syllabus research), language development (Halliday 1975; Painter 1984, 1991, 1999), schizophrenic speech (Rochester and Martin 1979), stylistics (Birch and O'Toole 1988), ideology (Kress and Hodge 1979) and coding orientation (Bernstein 1973; Hasan 1990, 1996). Initially it was mainly in these applied contexts that register theory continued to evolve (Ghadessy 1988, 1993; Leckie-Tarry 1995; Matthiessen 1993).

Register

The particular model of language and register to be presented here was developed in the applied context of studying the development of children's writing abilities in infants, primary and secondary school (Rothery 1996). One important aspect of the model is the emphasis it places on treating register as a semiotic system. *Semiotic*, as I have already noted, is a term referring to systems that make meanings. *Register*, however, is a semiotic system which differs from semiotic systems such as language, music, dance, image and so on. This is because it is a kind of parasite. It has no phonology of its own. The only way it can make meaning is by using the words and structures of the semiotic we call language. The great Danish linguist Louis Hjelmslev (1961) referred to semiotics such as register as connotative semiotics, in order to distinguish them from semiotics such as language which can make their own meanings and are not dependent on the resources of another meaning system to express themselves.

What does this mean? For one thing, if register is a semiotic, then it should be possible to work out the choices open to speakers as far as field, mode and tenor are concerned. What exactly is the set of domestic, recreational, religious, professional or disciplinary activities in which we participate? What is the range of roles we can adopt with respect to other speakers? What is the nature of the channels we can use to convey our message? Another consequence of interpreting register as a semiotic system is that you have to be able to say how the different register choices, once selected, are realised. What in other words does it mean as far as language is concerned if the field of discourse is linguistics instead of sociology, tennis instead of cricket, and so on?

Another important aspect of the model is its focus on genre. This in fact goes back to Gregory's (1967) suggestion that tenor be split into personal tenor (concerned with status and formality) and functional tenor (having to do with purpose). The relation of purpose, or what a speaker is trying to accomplish, to register has long been an uneasy one. Over the years Halliday has tended to subsume purpose through his definitions of field, tenor and especially mode (e.g. 1978). We encountered three main problems with this conflation. First of all, it makes the correlation between register categories and functional components of the grammar less clear. Predictions about such and such a register choice being realised in such and such a part of the grammar are weakened. Second, it fails to give a satisfactory account of the goal-oriented beginning-middle-end structure of most texts (for example, the Orientation Complication Evaluation Resolution Coda structure for narrative suggested by Labov and Waletzky (1967)). Third, it makes it difficult to map relationships among genres in terms of the distinctive ways in which they combine field, tenor and mode options. In our work on children's writing we felt that a relation between register choices and metafunctional components would help us clarify the linguistic reflection of the stages a child goes through in learning to write in different registers. We also felt a need to give some more explicit account of the distinctive beginning-middle-end (or schematic) structures which characterise children's writing in different genres. And we wanted to be able to map genre systems so that we could design curriculum. So we took the step of recognising a third semiotic system, which we called genre, underlying both register and language. Like register it is a parasite – without register and language it would not survive.

In a sense this takes us back to Malinowski, who argued that contexts both of situation and culture were important if we are to fully interpret the meaning of a text. Informally speaking, we might suggest that our level of genre corresponds roughly to context of culture in his sense (culture as a system of genres in other words), our register perhaps to his context of situation. This means we are using the term genre in a far wider sense than that which it is used in literary studies where it refers to literary text types such as poem, short story or novel. For us, a genre is a staged, goal-oriented, purposeful activity in which speakers engage as members of our culture. Examples of genres as staged activities are making a dental appointment, buying vegetables, telling a story, writing an essay, applying for a job, writing a letter to the editor, inviting someone for dinner, and so on. Virtually everything you do involves your participating in one or another genre. Culture seen in these terms can be defined as a set of generically interpretable activities. The model of language and its connotative semiotics presented here is outlined in using co-tangential circles in Figure 1.2, where language functions as the phonology of register, and register (and thus language) function as the phonology of genre (Christie and Martin 1997; Eggins and Martin 1997; Martin 1985, 1992; Martin and Veel 1998).

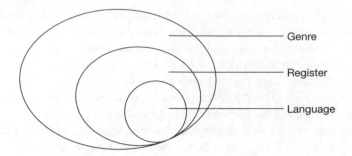

Figure 1.2 Language, register and genre

So much for the superstructure. Now let's come back to field, mode and tenor and see what they look like in more detail, given a framework such as this. First of all remember that field, mode and tenor make very general kinds of meaning. Even within language itself, grammatical meanings are more general than lexical ones (the TRANSITIVITY structure Actor Process Goal, which we might gloss as 'X does something to Y', makes a more general meaning than the wordings which might fill its roles, as in *Mary hugged John*, for example). And register meanings are more general still. Interestingly enough, once we leave language, an increase in the generality of the meanings involved does not seem to go hand in hand with invisibility. True, we cannot see them. But speakers are generally more conscious of the meanings associated with register and genre, once you point them out, than they are of grammatical meanings.

Field

This is probably the most daunting of the register variables we have to describe, simply because there are so many things people do. We may well get a workable description of tenor and mode in our culture long before we produce an encyclopedia of fields. Nevertheless, it is possible to sketch out here something of what we are on about, at least by way of an example. For purposes of illustration, let's consider the set of fields having to do with people in relation to animals. There are really two things to worry about here: first, what do people do with animals (activity focus)?; and second, what animals are involved in these activities (object focus)? Fields are about people interacting with their world, so they tend to be characterisable along these two dimensions: what people are doing and what they are doing it to. As a first approximation we might say that there are three main ways in which people are involved with animals: keeping them, using them and observing them. By 'keeping animals' I mean keeping them as pets. The main function of animals in this context is that of companionship. Some people are deeply involved in this field, breeding animals and taking them to shows. By 'using animals' I refer to two main areas: animal husbandry and sport. The main opposition here is between using animals for food and clothing and using them for recreation; hunting and racing being the principal leisure activities in which animals are involved. By 'studying animals' I refer to an interest people take in animals for their own sake. This interest may be focused in different ways: studying animals as a scientist, showing them off at zoos, preserving them in museums or observing them in the wild. This list of animal-related institutions is certainly not exhaustive, but it does serve to illustrate the activities which lie behind what people mean when they say 'I'm a naturalist' or biologist (or zoo-keeper/curator/punter/hunter/farmer/dog lover, etc.).

The other side of this picture is, of course, the animals themselves. We keep dogs, cats, fish and birds as pets; we farm cows, sheep, pigs and fowl; we hunt with dogs and hawks; we race horses and dogs; we study anything we can lay our hands on. I will not attempt to develop a folk taxonomy of animals here, or an analysis of their physical composition; but note that it is the nature of their involvement with people that would shape descriptions of this kind.

As noted above, register categories have no words and structures of their own; so in order to get realised they have to borrow linguistic ones. They do this in two main ways. The first is to make certain linguistic choices much more likely than others. The result of this is that as we listen to a text, certain patterns of choice begin to stand out in a non-random way. These patterns represent a particular register choice telling us it's there. The second way is for register categories to take over a small number of linguistic choices as their own. This type of realisation is indexical rather than probabilistic. The choice then functions as a trigger, giving away the register selection once we hear the word or phrase involved (phrases such as *I now pronounce you . . .*, *not guilty*, *let us pray*, *hit a boundary* function indexically along these lines). Obviously only a very small number of language choices can be taken over in this way – otherwise language would cease to exist as a system in its own right. The relationship between language and register is much more symbiotic than this.

As far as probabilistic realisation is concerned, field is realised by making certain experiential choices far more likely than others (lexical choices are more noticeable; grammatical choices are too general in meaning to transparently distinguish fields). Thus if you drop in on a conversation, it will take you a moment before you realise what people are talking about. You have to wait until you have heard enough of the mutually expectant lexical items to give away the field. Depending on your familiarity with the field, it may take you more or less time to catch on. When, for example, do you recognise the field of the following string: *boot*, *menu*, *algorithm*, *bit*, *storing capacity*, *program*?

The more you know about computers, the quicker you will catch on. Indexical realisations are also found. As far as field is concerned these are words, very technical ones, which tend to be used almost exclusively in a given field. If you understand the word, it almost automatically implicates the field. The word *morphophonemics*, taken from the field of linguistics, is one such indexical trigger.

Note that indexical items and sets of mutually expectant lexical items realise field; they must not be equated with field. Field is a register category, referring to one or another institution. Lexical items are linguistic categories, through which field is realised. At the level of register we are looking at field in terms of what people are doing with their lives. At the level of language we are looking at field in terms of how we know what people are doing. The two perspectives are distinct, associated with different semiotic systems – the one realising the other. For detailed studies see Coffin 2006, and Martin and Wodak 2003 on history; Halliday 2004,

Halliday and Martin 1993, and Martin and Veel 1998 on science; O'Halloran 2006 on mathematics; Schleppegrell 2004 on the language of schooling; and Wignell 2007 on social science. Recently, field has been further explored in relation to the sociologist Basil Bernstein's late work on knowledge structure (1996), a dialogue documented in Christie and Martin 2007.

Mode

On the surface, choice of mode looks like it could simply be specified in terms of channel: television, telephone, film, letter, notice, e-mail, SMS message and so on. But it is in fact necessary to go somewhat deeper than this if the effect which mode has on choices within language is to be fully appreciated. The best way to do this is to consider the effect different channels have on communication. One clear effect is that they affect the relation between speaker and listener by placing barriers between them. When compared with face-to-face conversation in this light, different channels can be seen to affect both aural and visual contact. Telephones remove the visual channel, while maintaining aural feedback. Television permits one-way visual contact, but removes aural feedback. Radios take away the visual channel completely. Considered along these lines it is possible to set up a scale ranging from face-to-face dialogue to stream-of-consciousness writing or thinking aloud at the other. At one end, speaker and listener are as close to each other as possible; at the other, the question of audience disappears completely. This scale is outlined in Figure 1.3.

The second thing that modes do is affect the relation between language and what it is talking about. This dimension grades language in action in relation to language as reflection. Consider, for example, a game of cricket. At one end of this scale we have the language of the players and umpire during the game. Next on the scale would be ball-by-ball commentary on the game. This will be somewhat further removed from language in action on radio than on television since on television the commentator and his audience can both see what is going on, but on radio only the commentator can. At a further remove from the action would be an interview with the players after the game, followed by a report of the game in the paper the next day. This is leading us towards the reflective end of the scale, where action is reconstructed, rather than commented on. Next we might place a book about cricket in a given year, then a book about cricket in general. Finally, is an even more abstract text, one which constructs rather than reconstructs reality. An example might be a philosophically oriented treatise on sport, fair play and cricket as symbolising the English way of life (no underarm bowling allowed). What is happening along

face to face	video conferencing	telephone	TV	radio	SMS message	letter	book	stream of consciousness
+ aural + visual	+ aural + mediated visual	+ aural – visual	one way aural & visual	one way aural; – feedback; – visual	minimally delayed written feedback – visual	delayed written feedback – visual (unless illustrated)	review feedback	audience = self

Figure 1.3 The effect of different channels on communication

this scale is that language is becoming further and further removed from what it is actually talking about, not simply in terms of temporal distance (distance from the scene of the crime as it were), but eventually in terms of abstraction as well. Abstract writing is not really about anything you can touch, taste, hear, see or smell, though of course, in the end, if what we write is in any sense material, it must connect with observable facts of some kind or other. This action/reflection scale is outlined in Figure 1.4.

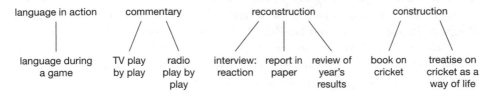

language in action	commentary		reconstruction			construction	
language during a game	TV play by play	radio play by play	interview: reaction	report in paper	review of year's results	book on cricket	treatise on cricket as a way of life

Figure 1.4 Action/reflection scale

Like field, mode has both indexical and probabilistic realisations. Unlike field, it is realised for the most part through textual systems. One clear set of indexical realisations occurs in greeting sequences at the beginning of texts: reciprocal *Hi* – *Hi* signals face-to-face dialogue; phone conversations begin with *Hello*, followed by *Hi* or some other greeting, and possibly some form of identification; newsreaders begin with a more formal greeting, to which there is of course no reply; letters begin with *Dear X*; books with a preface or acknowledgements, and so on. (Note that it is not the formality of the greeting which is important here, but rather the form of the greeting and its relation to a response if there is one. The formality of greetings is a feature of tenor.) Probabilistic realisations of mode focus largely on deixis, where this is interpreted broadly to encompass TENSE, IDENTIFICATION and THEME. Choice of present tense (*am doing*), first person (*I, we*), demonstratives pointing to the nonverbal context (*this, here, now*) and the selection of first or second person (*I, we, you*) Theme produces a pattern indicative of language in action/dialogue mode. Language which reconstructs events on the other hand prefers past tense and remote demonstratives (*there, then, that*). And reflective language often selects a simple generic present tense (*Braking distance varies with speed*), generic reference to whole classes (*Whales are mammals*), and favours abstract lexical items as Theme. Another crucial variable is the amount of nominalisation and embedding we find, and the consequences this has for packaging information in one part of a text or another (compare *braking distance varies with speed* with a less abstract translation as *the faster you go the longer it takes to stop*, and vice versa).

There is a great deal more to be said about the realisation of mode, based on knowledge about the grammar and discourse structure of English which cannot be assumed here. What all the different realisations reflect is the general concept of contextual dependency. Are the meanings of the text largely implicit, in the sense that unless we can see what the participants are doing we can't really understand what is going on? Or is the text explicit, independent of context, so that simply by reading the text we can understand what the text is about (assuming we know enough about the field that technicality is not a problem)? The more speakers are doing things together and engaging in dialogue, the more they can take for granted. As language moves away from the events it describes, and the possibility of feedback is removed, more and more of the meanings a text is making must be rendered explicit in that text if they are to be recovered by a reader, no matter how well informed (Biber 1988; Halliday 1985; Halliday and Martin 1993).

Grammatical metaphor (in relation to nominalisation and embedding), as outlined in Halliday (1994), is a key resource for developing abstract discourse at the reflective end of the action/reflection mode scale. Simon-Vandenbergen *et al.* (2003) present a number of key papers. Perhaps the most exciting recent development in relation to mode has been the emergence of multimodal discourse analysis, which focuses on texts which include images, sound and other modalities of communication alongside language. Joyce and Gaudin (2007) and Unsworth (2001) are the most accessible introductions to work on images, which is inspired by Kress and van Leeuwen (1996, 2nd edn 2006). Royce and Bowcher (2007) present papers at the cutting edge of this rapidly expanding field of inquiry.

Tenor

Tenor was discussed above with regard to status and formality; but it is actually a more complex issue than that. Alongside status, our relations with others are shaped by another factor: contact. This has to do with our feelings towards others – whether or not we like them, love them or hate them. These feelings themselves are somewhat volatile, depending in part on our emotions from moment to moment. We all have a tendency to treat our best friends as enemies after banging our heads or watching them break a prized possession. Alongside these dispositions is the question of how often we run into the people we are talking to. There are many people we meet quite frequently – for example, administrators, colleagues, newsagents, sandwich-counter attendants and sales clerks – without necessarily feeling much of an emotional bond with them.

This gives us two dimensions to worry about when considering tenor: status, which focuses on power relations (dominant or deferential roles); and contact, which focuses on our alignment and affinity with others (close and distant roles). It is always important to consider a text from both perspectives, since power and solidarity shape all the social relations we enact.

Tenor is for the most part realised through interpersonal systems. One of the clearest indexical realisations of tenor is found in the choice of vocatives or address terms. Reciprocal use of first names (*John/Bill*) signals solidarity, while non-reciprocal (*John/Prof. Brown*) is the sign of power. Similarly, *my little darling* indexes love, and contrasts with *you bloody fool* which does not. In addition, there are many probabilistic realisations of tenor. Indeed, English is probably at one extreme in this respect. Many languages structure tenor much more fully into their grammar and lexis than English does, indexing status and contact through verb morphology (Japanese) or choice of lexical items (in Javanese, for example, there are two or three words for every common English word, and you have to choose the appropriate one depending on tenor). English speakers express deference, for example, by favouring possibility as a modality (*possibly, maybe, may, might*), being indirect in commands (*Would you mind opening the door?* instead of *Open the door*), agreeing with their superiors, letting their superior initiate topics of conversation, avoiding expressing emotion and so on. Again, a full discussion of this matter depends on a detailed understanding of the lexicogrammatical resources of English uses in this area. The unifying theme of these resources is social distance. They show how close you feel to the person you are talking to – along the 'vertical' axis of power relations and the 'horizontal' axis of communality (Poynton 1985).

Inspired by Poynton's (1985) discussion of affect in relation to tenor, a number of functional linguists turned their attention to the development of a framework for studying evaluative language in discourse. This work is known as appraisal theory; Martin and Rose (2003) include an accessible introduction. Eggins and Slade (1997) consider appraisal in relation to tenor in casual conversation; and Martin and White (2005) present a more comprehensive framework, mainly illustrated from written texts.

Before turning to another important semiotic parasite, genre, it might be instructive to stop and consider for a moment what life would be like if register did not exist. It is impossible to find examples of recognisably human activity without register, although people often fantasise about what life without register would be like, thinking in terms of some kind of heaven, utopia or nirvana. A world without field would be one in which people didn't do anything with their lives. They simply wander around, eating grapes and berries as they run across them, in a sort of never-ending picnic (without the picnic basket of course). Without tenor, everyone would have to be equal – you would be on more or less friendly terms with everyone (no colleagues or enemies). You'd wander around visiting everyone, randomly in turn (no friends, no strangers, everyone is kin). Without mode there could be no media, not even writing of any kind. You would simply chat with your companions about what you were doing at the time – picking berries, eating fruit, taking a walk, whatever. Reminiscing or planning would just not be possible. Sound boring? A question of taste, perhaps. Whatever the case, humans as we know them do not live in worlds of this kind. The closest they get is perhaps the odd moment, relaxing with a spouse or close friend, job forgotten, kids asleep in bed, gender issues at rest, with memories of the past and tears for the future held in delightful abeyance. Transcendent moments to say the least? Inevitably, life (i.e. register) sweeps us away.

Genre

What about this other parasite, genre? Like register, genre has no phonology of its own. It makes meanings by shaping register – by conditioning the way in which field, mode and tenor are recurrently mapped onto one another in a given culture. This mapping tends to unfold in phases, and gives rise to the distinctive goal-oriented staging structure of genres. Consider, for example, a service encounter in a small shop. To begin you exchange greetings with a salesperson who will offer to serve you. You will then state your needs, perhaps helping yourself, or getting the salesperson to satisfy your requirements. When you get what you need, you will be told how much it costs. You then pay your money, say goodbye and leave. These stages can be set out as follows (cf. Hasan 1977, 1984; Mitchell 1957; Ventola 1987), using '^' to indicate sequence:

Greeting ^ Service Bid ^ Statement of Need ^ Need Compliance ^ Decision to Buy ^ Payment ^ Leave-taking

Some elements may be skipped; some may recur; and they do not always occur in this order. The important thing is that you get what you were after, using language to work your way through whatever steps are necessary. Note that these stages are culturally specific. In many cultures, for example, the price of goods is not fixed and you would have to bargain to establish a fair price before deciding to buy (Mitchell 1957). This is something that many travellers find difficult, because bargaining for small goods is not a 'matter-of-fact' part of the culture from which they come.

Consider now how the values of field, mode and tenor change as you move through the phases outlined above. Suppose that the field involves a small green-grocer's shop. During the Service Bid and Payment the focus of the text will be on the activity of buying and selling. But during the statement of Need, Need Compliance and Decision to Buy the focus will shift to the products the shop is offering. And the Greeting and Leave-taking are not really about anything at all. As far as mode is concerned, the text will tend towards face-to-face dialogue, language in action. But imagine that you are dithering over the avocados in the Decision to Buy stage. The greengrocer may well launch into a sales pitch, involving a more abstract monologic mode which reflects upon the merits of the avocados in question, speculates about how much you will enjoy eating them, makes suggestions for preparation and entices you with a special offer. A shift in tenor might be involved in this sales pitch as well, with the grocer carrying on as your trusted confidant. If you do buy you are likely to leave the shop you entered as a customer feeling more like the grocer's mate. If you don't, you may leave feeling a little less friendly than when you came in – perhaps reluctant to return in future. The register values shift around as they do in reaction to your goals. This is what genre is set up to explain: how you accomplish things, on a day-to-day basis, in a culturally specific way.

Like register, genre is realised both probabilistically and indexically. Let's take an example of a genre of a different kind to illustrate this – a narrative (Labov and Waletzky 1967; Martin and Plum 1997). Two of the best-known indexical realisations of narrative are the opening *Once upon a time* and the closing *And they lived happily ever after*. Once you hear these clichés, you know immediately what genre you are listening to (unless of course someone is playing a joke on you; the point is that you know it's a joke precisely because your expectancies are frustrated). Probabilistic realisations of narrative are also relevant. The Orientation which introduces the characters and sets the story in time and place will tend to include relational clauses (e.g. *Once upon a time there was a . . . He/she was a . . . the cottage faced . . .*) with associated circumstantial elements. The Complication will then tend to continue with a series of temporally related material processes (*She did this and then she did this and then she did . . .*) leading up to something unexpected – a crisis. At this point the temporal unfolding may be suspended for a moment while the thoughts and feelings of the hero and perhaps another protagonist are explored (*He felt . . . ; he thought . . . ; he said: '. . .'*). Then the Resolution carries on, much like the Complication in its realisation until the problem set up in the story is resolved, for better or worse. Finally, the narrator may comment on the point of telling the story in a *Coda*, often using a demonstrative *that* to refer to the story itself along with some expression of attitude (e.g. *That was a really close call*). Note that since both genre and register are realised for the most part probabilistically they allow the individual considerable freedom in determining just how they are to be realised. The patterns of selection by which we recognise a genre, or some field, mode or tenor, are distributed over a whole text; there are only a few local constraints.

However, this does not mean that register and genre can be ignored. They cannot. You have to use enough signals of register and genre to ensure that your listener can see where you are coming from. Otherwise, you will simply not be fully understood. But the notion of probabilistic realisation over whole texts does mean that genre and register are not mechanical formulae, which stand in the way of an individual's creativity or self-expression. It is perhaps a truism to say that you can't write if you don't first know language. But it is equally true to say that you can't write if you don't control the appropriate register and genres. Unfortunately, control of these systems is something that educators have too often taken for granted.

Like all semiotic systems, genre involves choice, and these choices bundle together into groups oriented to relatable generic tasks. In our culture, for example, there are many different kinds of story (Martin and Rose 2008). What they have in common is taking up a stance with respect to a temporally related series of events forming the backbone of the text. Perhaps the simplest form of story is the recount. In recounts, nothing really goes wrong, and this is what distinguishes them from narratives. Narratives are focused around relatively problematic or noteworthy events the narrator is making a point about. They may have a more developed beginning and end than recounts, with a more elaborate Orientation and a Coda which makes the point of telling the story explicit. This is because we usually tell recounts to people with whom we share a great deal of experience, whereas narratives are more public texts, needing to stand up in their own right. Labov and Waletzky (1967) suggest that one difference between narratives of personal experience (stories about something that happened to you) and narratives of vicarious experience (stories that happened to someone else or are made up) is that narratives of personal experience have some kind of evaluation at the crisis point, during which the listener is invited to identify with the narrator's feelings at this point in the story.

Specific kinds of story make specific kinds of point (Martin and Plum 1997). The point of a fable is usually made explicit in a moral. Parables make their point metaphorically, though they may be embedded in a religious discourse whose message they serve to exemplify. While sharing many aspects of structure, each of these story types differs somewhat in the stages it goes through and the precise nature of the stages themselves. This is because each has a different, though relatable purpose in our culture. Recounts review activities, narratives proper entertain, fables and parables instruct, and more literary narratives function as highly valued displays of verbal art. In order to achieve these different goals, the structure of the texts themselves must differ.

As with register, research into genre from a linguistic point of view is still developing. For significant developments see Christie and Martin 1997; Eggins and Slade 1997; Martin and Veel 1998; Martin and Rose 2008; Ventola 1987. Martin (2006, 2008) introduces recent perspectives on register and genre variation in relation to measuring the amount of meaning committed in particular texts and the ways in which discourse is used to negotiate identity in relation to community. The important thing as far as applied linguistics is concerned will be to determine which registers and genres consumers of linguistics are interested in, and to continue working on these.

In summary then, as Malinowski argued more than fifty years ago, you cannot understand a text unless you know something about the context in which it occurs. Because we are social animals, this context is a social one. It involves people doing things with their lives (field), interacting with other people (tenor), and making use of one or another channel of communication (mode) to do so. Beyond this it involves people engaging in purposeful goal-oriented activities (genre). The register categories of field, mode and tenor discussed here represent the attempt of one school of functional linguistics to come to grips with what Malinowski and Firth meant by context of situation. The discussion of genre represents a more recent attempt by students of the linguists working in this school to explore what Malinowski and Firth meant by context of culture. The strategy they are using is to interpret both register and genre as semiotic systems in their own right, but semiotics with the peculiar property of having no phonology of their own.

Both depend on language's words and structures to make meaning, alongside the meaning-making resources of other semiotics systems (such as image, sound, music, gesture or dance). Interpreted in this light, linguistics is the foundation not only of the study of human communication, but of social science taken in a very broad sense. The functional linguists adopting this extroverted stance are attempting to provide a perspective on learning which challenges and complements that drawn from cognitive psychology in educational research. For reviews of the contributions of what is often referred to as the 'Sydney School', see Christie (1992), Cope and Kalantzis (1993), Feez (1998, 2002), Grabe and Kaplan (1996), Hasan and Williams (1996), Macken-Horarik (2002), Martin (1993, 1997, 1999, 2000, 2007); Hyon (1996) and Hyland (2002) relate this work on language in education to genre-based research in related traditions.

References

Bazell, C.E., Catford, J.C., Halliday, M.A.K. and Robins, R.H. (eds) (1966) *In Memory of J.R. Firth*. London: Longman.

Bernstein, B. (ed.) (1973) *Class, Codes and Control 2: Applied Studies Towards a Sociology of Language*. London: Routledge and Kegan Paul (Primary Socialisation, Language and Education).

Bernstein, B. (1996[rev. edn 2000]) *Pedagogy, Symbolic Control and Identity: Theory, Research, Critique*. London: Taylor & Francis.

Biber, D. (1988) *Variation across Speech and Writing*. Cambridge: Cambridge University Press.

Biber, D. (1995) *Dimensions of Register Variation: A cross-linguistic perspective*. Cambridge: Cambridge University Press.

Biber, D. and Finegan, E. (eds) (1994) *Sociolinguistic Perspectives on Variation*. Oxford: Oxford University Press.

Birch, D. and O'Toole, M. (eds) (1988) *Functions of Style*. London: Pinter.

Christie, F. (1992) 'Literacy in Australia'. *Annual Review of Applied Linguistics* 12: 142–55.

Christie, F. and Martin, J.R. (eds) (1997) *Genres and Institutions: Social processes in their workplace and school*. London: Cassell.

Christie, F. and Martin, J.R. (2007) *Knowledge Structure: Functional linguistic and sociological perspectives* (ed. F. Christie and J.R. Martin). London: Continuum.

Coffin, C. (2006) *Historical Discourse: The language of time, cause and evaluation*. London: Continuum.

Cope, W. and Kalantzis, M. (eds) (1993) *The Powers of Literacy: A genre approach to teaching literacy*. London: Falmer (Critical Perspectives on Literacy and Education) and Pittsburg, PA: University of Pittsburg Press (Pittsburg Series in Composition, Literacy, and Culture).

Culler, J. (1976) *Saussure*. London: Fontana Modern Masters Series.

Eggins, S. (1994) *An Introduction to Systemic Functional Linguistics*. London: Pinter.

Eggins, S. and Martin, J.R. (1997) 'Genres and registers of discourse', in T.A. van Dijk (ed.) *Discourse as Structure and Process* (pp. 230–56). London: Sage (Discourse Studies: A Multidisciplinary Introduction, Volume 1).

Eggins, S. and Slade, D. (1997) *Analysing Casual Conversation*. London: Cassell.

Feez, S. (1998) *Text-based Syllabus Design*. Sydney: National Centre for English Language Teaching and Research (NELTR), Macquarie University.

Feez, S. (2002) 'Heritage and innovation in second language education', in Johns, A.M. (ed.) *Genres in the Classroom: Applying theory and research to practice* (pp. 43–69). Mahwah, NJ: Lawrence Erlbaum.

Firth, J.R. (1957a) *Papers in Linguistics 1934–1911*. London: Oxford University Press.

Firth, J.R. (1957b) 'A synopsis of linguistic theory, 1930–1955', in *Studies in Linguistic Analysis* (pp. 1–31) (special volume of the Philological Society). London: Blackwell. Reprinted in F.R. Palmer (ed.) (1968) *Selected Papers of J.R. Firth, 1952–1959* (pp. 168–205). London: Longman.

Fries, P. and Gregory, M. (eds) (1995) *Discourse in Society: Systemic functional perspectives*. Norwood, NJ: Ablex (Advances in Discourse Processes).

Gerot, L. (1995) *Making Sense of Text: The context–text relationship*. Sydney: Antipodean Educational Enterprises.

Ghadessy, M. (ed.) (1988) *Registers of Written English: Situational factors and linguistic features*. London: Pinter (Open Linguistics Series).

Ghadessy, M. (ed.) (1993) *Register Analysis: Theory and practice*. London: Pinter.

Ghadessy, M. (ed.) (1999) *Context: Theory and practice*. Amsterdam: Benjamins.

Grabe, W. and Kaplan, R. (1996) *Theory and Practice of Writing*. London: Longman (Applied Linguistics and Language Study).

Gregory, M. (1967) 'Aspects of varieties differentiation'. *Journal of Linguistics* 3: 177–98.

Gregory, M. and Carroll, S. (1978) *Language and Situation: Language varieties and their social contexts*. London: Routledge and Kegan Paul.

Halliday, M.A.K. (1973) *Explorations in the Functions of Language*. London: Edward Arnold.

Halliday, M.A.K. (1975) *Learning How to Mean: Explorations in the development of language*. London: Edward Arnold (Explorations in Language Study).

Halliday, M.A.K. (1978) *Language as a Social Semiotic: The social interpretation of language and meaning*. London: Edward Arnold.

Halliday, M.A.K. (1985) *Spoken and Written Language*. Geelong, Vic: Deakin University Press, republished London: Oxford University Press 1989.

Halliday, M.A.K. (1994) *An Introduction to Functional Grammar* (2nd edn). London: Edward Arnold.

Halliday, M.A.K. (2004) *The Language of Science*. London: Continuum (Vol. 5 in the *Collected Works of M.A.K. Halliday*, (ed.) J. Webster). London: Continuum.

Halliday, M.A.K. and Hasan, R. (1985) *Language, Context, and Text: Aspects of language in a socialsemiotic perspective*. Geelong, Vic: Deakin University Press, republished London: Oxford University Press 1989.

Halliday, M.A.K. and Martin, J.R. (1993) *Writing Science: Literacy and discursive power*. London: Falmer (Critical Perspectives on Literacy and Education).

Hasan, R. (1977) 'Text in the systemic-functional model', in W. Dressler (ed.) *Current Trends in Textlinguistics* (pp. 228–46). Berlin: Walter de Gruyter.

Hasan, R. (1984) 'The nursery tale as a genre'. *Nottingham Linguistic Circular* 13: 71–102 (Special Issue on Systemic Linguistics). Republished in Hasan, 1996, pp. 51–72.

Hasan, R. (1985) *Linguistics, Language and Verbal Art*. Geelong, Vic: Deakin University Press, republished London: Oxford University Press 1989.

Hasan, R. (1990) 'Semantic variation and sociolinguistics'. *Australian Journal of Linguistics* 9 (2): 221–76.

Hasan, R. (1996) *Ways of Saying: Ways of meaning* (eds C. Cloran, D. Butt and G. Williams). London: Cassell.

Hasan, R. and Martin, J.R. (eds) (1989) *Language Development: Learning language, learning culture*. Norwood, NJ: Ablex (Advances in Discourse Processes 27 – Meaning and Choice in Language: Studies for Michael Halliday).

Hasan, R. and Williams, G. (eds) (1996) *Literacy in Society*. London: Longman (Applied Linguistics and Language Study).

Hjelmslev, L. (1961) *Prolegomena to a Theory of Language*. Madison, WI: University of Wisconsin Press.

Hyland, K. (2002) 'Genre: language, context and literacy'. *ARAL* 22: 113–35.

Hyon, S. (1996) 'Genre in Three Traditions: implications for ESL'. *TESOL Quarterly* 30 (4): 693–722.

Johns, A.M. (ed.) (2002) *Genres in the Classroom: Applying theory and research to practice*. Mahwah, NJ: Lawrence Erlbaum.

Joyce, H. and Gaudin, J. (2007) *Interpreting the Visual*. Sydney: Phoenix.

Kress, G. and Hodge, B. (1979) *Language as Ideology*. London: Routledge and Kegan Paul.

Kress, G. and van Leeuwen, T. (1996) *Reading Images: The grammar of visual design* (2nd rev. edn 2006). London: Routledge.

Labov, W. and Waletzky, J. (1967) 'Narrative analysis', in J. Helm (ed.) *Essays on the Verbal and Visual Arts* (Proceedings of the 1966 Spring Meeting of the American Ethnological Society) (pp.12–44). Seattle, WA: University of Washington Press. Reprinted in *Journal of Narrative and Life History* 7 (1–4): 3–38.

Leckie-Tarry, H. (1995) *Language and Context: A functional linguistic theory of register* (ed. David Birch). London: Pinter.

Macken-Horarik, M. (2002) 'Something to shoot for: a systemic functional approach to teaching genre in secondary school science', in Johns, A.M. (ed.) (2002) *Genres in the Classroom: Applying theory and research to practice* (pp. 17–42). Mahwah, NJ: Lawrence Erlbaum.

Malinowski, B. (1923) 'The problem of meaning in primitive languages', supplement I to C.K. Ogden and I.A. Richards *The Meaning of Meaning* (pp. 296–336). New York: Harcourt Brace & World.

Malinowski, B. (1935) *Coral Gardens and their Magic. Vol. 2*. London: Allen and Unwin.

Martin, J.R. (1985) *Factual Writing: Exploring and challenging social reality*. Geelong, Vic: Deakin University Press, republished London: Oxford University Press 1989.

Martin, J.R. (1992) *English Text: System and structure*. Amsterdam: Benjamins.

Martin, J.R. (1993) 'Genre and literacy – modelling context in educational linguistics'. *Annual Review of Applied Linguistics* 13: 141–72.

Martin, J.R. (1997) 'Linguistics and the consumer: theory in practice'. *Linguistics and Education* 9 (3): 409–46.

Martin, J.R. (1999) 'Mentoring semogenesis: "genre based" literacy pedagogy', in F. Christie (ed.) *Pedagogy and the Shaping of Consciousness: Linguistic and social processes* (pp. 123–55). London: Cassell (Open Linguistics Series).

Martin, J.R. (2000) 'Design and practice: enacting functional linguistics in Australia'. *Annual Review of Applied Linguistics* (20th Anniversary Volume 'Applied Linguistics as an Emerging Discipline') 20: 116–26.

Martin, J.R. (2006) 'Genre, ideology and intertextuality: a systemic functional perspective'. *Linguistics and the Human Sciences* (Special Issue on Genre edited by J. Bateman) 2 (2): 257–74.

Martin, J.R. (2007) 'Metadiscourse: designing interaction in genre-based literacy programs', in R. Whittaker, M. O'Donnell and A. McCabe (eds) *Language and Literacy: Functional approaches* (pp. 95–122). London: Continuum.

Martin, J.R. (2008) 'Tenderness: relaisation and individuation in a Botswanan town'. *Odense Working Papers in Language and Communication* (Special Issue of Papers from 34th International Systemic Functional Congress edited by Nina Nørgaard).

Martin, J.R. and Plum, G. (1997) 'Construing experience: some story genres'. *Journal of Narrative and Life History* 7: 1–4 (Special Issue: Oral Versions of Personal Experience: three decades of narrative analysis; guest ed. M. Bamberg: 299–308).

Martin, J.R. and Rose, David (2003) *Working with Discourse: Meaning beyond the clause* (2nd rev. edn 2007). London: Continuum.

Martin, J.R. and Rose, D. (2008) *Genre Relations: Mapping culture*. London: Continuum.

Martin, J.R. and Veel, R. (eds) (1998) *Reading Science: Critical and functional perspectives on discourses of science*. London: Routledge.

Martin, J.R. and White, P.R.R. (2005) *The Language of Evaluation: Appraisal in English*. London: Palgrave.

Martin, J.R. and Wodak, R. (eds) (2003) *Re/reading the Past: Critical and functional perspectives on discourses of history* (eds J.R. Martin and R. Wodak). Amsterdam: Benjamins.

Mathesius, V. (1964) 'On the potentiality of the phenomena of language', in J. Vachek (ed.) *A Prague School Reader in Linguistics*. Bloomington, IN: Indiana University Press.

Matthiessen, C.M.I.M. (1993) 'Register in the round: diversity in a unified theory of register analysis', in M. Ghadessy (ed.) *Register Analysis: Theory and practice* (pp.221–92). London: Pinter.

Mitchell, T.F. (1957) 'The language of buying and selling in Cyrenaica: a situational statement'. *Hesperis* 26: 31–71. Reprinted in T.F. Mitchell (1975) *Principles of Neo-Firthian Linguistics* (pp. 167–200). London: Longman.

O'Halloran, K.L. (2006) *Mathematical Discourse: Language, symbolism and visual images*. London: Continuum.

Painter, C. (1984) *Into the Mother Tongue: A case study of early language development*. London: Pinter.

Painter, C. (1991) *Learning the Mother Tongue* (2nd edn). Geelong, Vic: Deakin University Press.

Painter, C. (1999) *Learning through Language in Early Childhood*. London: Cassell.

Pearce, J., Thornton, G. and Mackav, D. (1989) 'The Programme in Linguistics and English Teaching, University College London, 1964–1971', in R. Hasan and J.R. Martin (eds) (1989) *Language Development: Learning language, learning culture* (pp. 329–68). Norwood, NJ: Ablex (Advances in Discourse Processes 27 – Meaning and Choice in Language: Studies for Michael Halliday).

Poynton, C. (1985) *Language and Gender: Making the difference*. Geelong, Vic: Deakin University Press, republished London: Oxford University Press 1989.

Rochester, S. and Martin. J.R. (1979) *Crazy, Talk: A study of the discourse of schizophrenic speakers*. NewYork: Plenum.

Rothery, J. (1996) 'Making changes: developing an educational linguistics', in Hasan, R. and Williams, G. (eds) (1996) *Literacy in Society* (pp. 86–123). London: Longman (Applied Linguistics and Language Study).

Royce, T. and Bowcher, W. (eds) (2007) *New Directions in the Analysis of Multimodal Discourse*. Mahwah, NJ: Lawrence Erlbaum Associates.

Saussure, F. de (1915[1966]) *Course in General Linguistics* (eds C. Bally and A. Sechehaye in collaboration with A. Riedlinger). New York: McGraw-Hill.

Schleppegrell, M.J. (2004) *The Language of Schooling*. Mahwah, NJ: Erlbaum.

Simon-Vandenbergen, A-M., Taverniers, M. and Ravelli, L.J. (eds) (2003) *Metaphor: systemic and functional perspectives*. Amsterdam: Benjamins.

Unsworth, L. (ed.) (2000) *Researching Language in Schools and Communities: Functional linguistics approaches*. London: Cassell.

Unsworth, L. (2001) *Teaching Multiliteracies across the Curriculum: Changing contexts of text and image in classroom practice*. Buckingham: Open University Press.

Ure, J. and Ellis, J. (1977) 'Register in descriptive linguistics and linguistic sociology', in O. UribeVillas (ed.) *Issues in Sociolinguistics* (pp. 197–243). The Hague: Mouton.

Ventola, E. (1987) *The Structure of Social Interaction: A systemic approach to the semiotics of service encounters*. London: Pinter.

Wignell, P. (2007) *On the Discourse of Social Science*. Darwin: Charles Darwin University Press.

Chapter 2

John S. Knox

Online newspapers
Evolving genres and evolving theory

News texts are becoming shorter. In addition to the phenomenon of 'soundbite news' in broadcast media (Hallin 1997), the rapid rise of online newspapers has delivered home pages dominated by short texts consisting of a headline and lead, or headline only. Online newspapers engage readers for very short periods of time (Thurman 2007), and results of eyetracking research suggest that home pages play a central role in the reading practices of online newspaper readers (Barthelson 2002; Holmqvist *et al.* 2003).

Because online newspapers have quickly developed into a central element in the economic and discursive practices of individual news institutions and the mass media generally, the short texts which feature on their home pages pose problems for critical analysts of language and the media. How is it possible to analyse the ideological positioning of readers, the unfolding of an argument, and the development of meaning in a text of fewer than 25 words? What is the social significance of such short texts, with which readers engage on a timescale of seconds? And how can learners read such brief, 'factual' texts critically?

In order to address such questions, it is necessary to work with a theory that accounts for the relations between social processes and structures on the one hand, and the multimodal discursive activities by which they are played out on the other.[1] One such theory is Systemic Functional Linguistics (SFL), the principles and tools of which have been applied to studying a range of semiotic systems other than language (e.g. O'Halloran 2004; O'Toole 1994; Kress and van Leeuwen 1996; van Leeuwen 2005) and to online newspapers (Bateman 2008; Bateman *et al.* 2006; Knox 2007).

One aspect of SF theory which has been widely drawn on in examining multimodal discourse is the notion of genre (e.g. Baldry and Thibault 2006; Bateman 2008; Martin and Rose 2008; van Leeuwen 2005). Genre can be defined as the relatively predictable patterns of language and other semiotic resources (e.g. image, layout) observable across texts which are consistently used to achieve social goals. Individual texts can be identified as belonging to a particular genre, or as instantiating a mix of two or more genres (so-called **hybrid texts**).

Newspapers have always been multimodal, but the **newsbites** (headline-plus-lead-plus-hyperlink stories) and **newsbits** (headline-only stories) that feature on home pages are very, very short texts, and are all that a reader sees of a given story in many cases. Investigating the home pages and newsbites of online newspapers from a genre perspective allows us to consider their multimodal structure in relation to their social purposes. This is productive from two important perspectives: theoretical and professional.

Theoretically, new media pose fundamental challenges for existing theories of communication and language. The idea that language exists in a semiotic vacuum and makes meaning independently of other semiotic resources is no longer tenable. This means that description and theory need to evolve, just as new ways of communication are evolving.

Professionally, new media are an important site of social change: change in institutional practices of text production; change in the kinds of texts produced; and change in the social practices of text reception and use. Online media texts permeate personal, educational, and professional contexts, and educators need functional descriptions of how new media texts work in order to develop informed explanations and effective pedagogy. Professionals also need adequate descriptions to understand the roles that new kinds of text play in professional contexts, and the impact they have on professional practice.

The following sections of this chapter examine two newsbites which combine a number of semiotic resources, including language, image, and layout. The aim is to demonstrate what different tools from SF theory can tell us about these texts, and also how the texts raise questions for our understandings of what a text is, and how texts mean. Finally, the ways in which SF theory is evolving to account for new media are considered.

Newsbites: a linguistic perspective

The two texts discussed here were collected as part of a larger research project investigating the multimodal discourse of online newspaper home pages (see Knox 2007). Each is discussed in turn.

Text A: Verbal text of a newsbite from the Bangkok Post:

Perspective
Arrest of the 'ultimate mastermind'
Three years ago, terrorist suspect, Hambali was captured in his apartment near Bangkok.

Text A is taken from the home page of the *Bangkok Post* online <www.
bangkokpost.com> from August 11, 2006. Examining Text A from a purely linguistic
perspective, we can see that it has two headings. The first of these, *Perspective*, suggests
that the story is more reflective than other texts which might typically be found on
a newspaper home page or front page. The second (which is a headline), *Arrest of the
'ultimate mastermind'*, consists of a nominal group, and functions to predict for the
reader what is to follow in the text. In SFL, the element of a text that performs this
textual function (such as the classic 'topic sentence' in essay paragraphs) is known as
the **Hyper-Theme** (Martin and Rose 2007).[2] The main verbal text of the news story
– commonly known as the lead – is situated in past time (*Three years ago*) and in space
(*in his apartment near Bangkok*), and it is construed as an event (*Hambali was captured*).[3]

Taking a critical perspective on the text, we can say that the Agent of this event
– the one who did the capturing and arresting – is omitted by the use of nominalisation
in the headline, and passive voice in the lead (cf. Fairclough 1995; Fowler 1991;
Trew 1979). We can also say that Hambali is appraised negatively by implication.
He has been labelled as the *'ultimate mastermind'*, denoting high levels of intelligence
and/or skill. However, the fact that he has been arrested, and has been identified
by the newspaper as a *terrorist suspect* have a cumulative effect of portraying him
negatively, and construing him not only as a suspected terrorist mastermind, but as
the suspected 'ultimate (terrorist) mastermind'.

In this way, the reader is positioned by the text to view Hambali negatively.
Texts vary in the extent to which they are ambiguous and allow for alternate readings,
but it is common that a 'default', or 'naturalised' reading position is created in a
text, whereby a reader who agrees with the position of the author can read the text
as commonsense, while a reader who holds a different position can read the same
text as biased. So the existence of a naturalised reading position in which Hambali
is viewed negatively does not preclude readers from reading 'against' the text (see
Martin and White 2005: 95–7).

In summary, the brief, 'factual' reporting of the time, location, and the event
of Hambali's capture can also be seen as a vehicle for the newspaper to evaluate
him, and this reflects another important element of media discourse – evaluating
what happened and appraising who did it (or to whom it was done).

Text B: Verbal text of a newsbite from the People's Daily

China's Peaceful Rise
After 26 years of reform and opening-up, China has blazed a path of
development suited to its own conditions.

Text B is taken from the home page of the *People's Daily* online, English version
<english.peopledaily.com.cn> from September 2, 2005. The headline of this text
also consists of a nominal group, *China's Peaceful Rise*, which again functions as a
Hyper-Theme orienting the reader to the text. The lead of this story is also construed
as an event (*China has blazed a path*)[4] which is positioned temporally (*After 26 years
of reform and opening-up*).

China is construed as a social actor in this text: it possesses the *Peaceful Rise* in
the headline, and is the 'path blazer' (and Agent) in the lead. By implication, it is
peaceful, reforming, open, and trail-blazing, and, as with Text A, the cumulative

effect of these associations (particularly in the absence of any negative appraisal) is to naturalise a reading position: China is viewed positively.

A purely linguistic analysis of these two newsbites can tell us about how they work to construct a particular version of 'who did what, when, where and how'; how they construe certain value positions on the part of the authors; and how language is used to position readers in relation to the actors and events in the texts. Yet in isolation, these texts each present something of a puzzle. Why would anyone write nineteen words on the arrest of someone three years ago, or twenty-two words to tell a reader that China has developed in a manner of its own choosing? And why would anyone be interested to read these texts?

Newsbites: a historical perspective

Questions such as those posed immediately above go to the notion of genre – the social purposes of a given text, and the way it is structured in order to achieve those purposes. As with any text, Text A and Text B make meaning in part according to how similar and different they are to other texts. These intertextual relations are historical, and the verbal structure of Texts A and B is one which has evolved over time (cf. Iedema et al. 1994).

Texts A and B are news stories, and like all texts they reflect the practices and interests of the individuals, or in these cases the institutions, which produce them. Since the nineteenth century, news institutions have become more commercialised, the audiences of newspapers have broadened, and the nature of the social events typically reported on their pages have also changed. These social changes have contributed to a general move away from presenting chronological accounts of events written for a relatively limited audience, to writing stories which foreground the climax of the report both verbally and visually (Barnhurst and Nerone 2001; Iedema et al. 1994; White 1997), and a set of conventions has emerged whereby English-language news stories are structured in terms of importance rather than chronology. This structure is often termed the 'inverted pyramid', but has been described in SFL as an orbital, Nucleus–Satellite structure, which contrasts with linear, stage-by-stage approaches to modelling text structure (see Iedema et al. 1994; White 1997).

In the Nucleus–Satellite structure, the headline and lead (Nucleus) present the key elements of a story, and the subsequent sections (Satellites) expand on the information given in the Nucleus. Each Satellite refers back to the Nucleus, and does not depend on the other Satellites (Iedema et al. 1994; White 1997). This can be illustrated by what White (1997) calls 'radical editability', or the ability to re-arrange the order of the Satellites 'without damaging the functionality of the text' (p. 116). In Figure 2.1, the three Satellites can be read in any order, because each refers back to the Nucleus, rather than to preceding Satellites.

The 'distilling' of the climax of the news story into the Nucleus of print newspaper stories has contributed to the emergence of the newsbite as one of the primary news genres of online newspaper home pages. That is, by the time news-papers began to be published on the World Wide Web in the 1990s, the structure of hard news stories was already such that their purpose (i.e. to communicate the potential of an event to destabilise or consolidate the social order – Iedema et al.

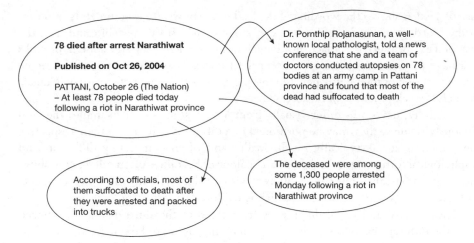

78 died after arrest Narathiwat

Published on Oct 26, 2004

PATTANI, October 26 (The Nation) – At least 78 people died today following a riot in Narathiwat province

Dr. Pornthip Rojanasunan, a well-known local pathologist, told a news conference that she and a team of doctors conducted autopsies on 78 bodies at an army camp in Pattani province and found that most of the dead had suffocated to death

According to officials, most of them suffocated to death after they were arrested and packed into trucks

The deceased were among some 1,300 people arrested Monday following a riot in Narathiwat province

Figure 2.1 Extracts from a news story appearing in *The Nation*, October 26, 2004 (cf. Knox and Patpong 2008). Reproduced by kind permission of Continuum International Publishing Group

1994: 107) was largely achieved in the headline and lead. This meant that the Nucleus of a story could appear on an online newspaper home page, and function as a complete text in its own right.

There are other factors which have contributed to the emergence of newsbites. Those related to the historical development of news institutions include the trend towards 'soundbite news', which has contributed to an acceptance (and perhaps expectation) of shorter texts by mass media consumers. In addition, it is common practice in print newspapers to split front-page stories in order to provide a number of entry-points for the reader, and to take maximum advantage of the 'prime real estate' of the front page. Thus, print newspaper readers coming to the web in the early days of online newspapers were already accustomed to 'following' stories past the front page when their interests so dictated.

Affordances of the medium of the World Wide Web have also played a role in the emergence of newsbites. For example, the need to make a number of elements of the home page visible on a single screen (and particularly the first screen) means that short news stories are suited to the home page. The reading practices associated with online texts – including the tendency for readers to scan the home page in search of stories to read in greater depth (Holmqvist *et al.* 2003) – are another related factor, as are the social contexts in which online newspaper reading takes place (Barthelson 2002).

As a result of factors such as these, many online newspaper home pages feature newsbites, and these short news texts differ in a number of ways from longer versions of the 'same' news story which may appear on a page 'lower down' in the website hierarchy.

Firstly, newsbites differ verbally from stories to which they hyperlink. For example, they sometimes include a superordinate heading – or **Verbal Frame** – not included in the longer story to which they hyperlink; and the wording of the headline and/or lead can differ from that in the longer story, sometimes completely. In the case of Text A above, the wording of the lead in the newsbite is completely different to the wording of the lead of the longer story to which the newsbite links. In the case of Text B, there is, in fact, no 'longer story' as such – the newsbite hyperlinks to a page (sometimes called a 'section page') that acts as a home page for a single content section of the newspaper. On this page, links to a range of stories on China's 'peaceful development' can be accessed.

Secondly, newsbites differ visually from longer stories. For example, they are obviously smaller; they may be positioned in a different column on their respective page; their image is typically much smaller and often completely different; and graphological features such as the size and colour of headlines often differ. Newsbites and longer texts also enter into different visual relations with the other elements on their respective pages, a point which is explored in following sections.

These verbal and visual differences are related to the third distinction offered here: the different purposes of newsbites on home pages on the one hand, and 'full-length' news stories appearing on dedicated web pages on the other. The purpose of a newsbite is to deliver the focus of a news story with both immediacy and impact, and to provide an entry point to the content of the newspaper for readers. Longer stories lower down in the website hierarchy 'unpack' the stories told in newsbites, and function more as 'terminal points' (from which readers often return to the home page) rather than entry points.

Their distinctive social purposes, and visual and verbal features identify newsbites as a distinct genre operating in online newspapers. Newspapers, in turn, are a macro-genre, or a genre of longer, more complex texts which combine a number of more 'elemental' genres (Martin and Rose 2008). The widespread use of newsbites on online newspaper home pages suggests that the demands of the news institutions and the readers of online newspapers are being addressed by the evolving genre of newsbites.

Newsbites: a multi-modal perspective

The preceding discussion argues that newsbites are visual–verbal texts, yet the earlier discussion of Text A and Text B considered them only as verbal texts. In this section, these two texts are considered from a multimodal perspective.

Figure 2.2 shows the 'Hambali newsbite' from the *Bangkok Post*, the verbal text of which has already been provided in Text A above. The use of the light-blue coloured bar across the top of the newsbite presents the *Perspective* heading as a banner. This, its larger font, and its centred alignment visually sets the heading apart from the rest of the text. Both this heading and the headline are hypertext. The banner heading links to a 'section page' where the reader can access different stories from the *Perspective* section of the newspaper, and the headline links to a single page featuring a longer version of the 'same' story. The image presents a close-up shot of the face of Hambali, an instance of what Royce (2002) calls **intersemiotic repetition** (see Figure 2.3), where a text includes two or more representations of the same thing using different semiotic resources (e.g. language and image).[5] The use of the definite article in the nominal group the *'ultimate mastermind'* can also be read as reference from the verbal text to the image.[6]

Figure 2.2 The 'Hambali newsbite' from the *Bangkok Post* online, August 11, 2006 (original in colour)

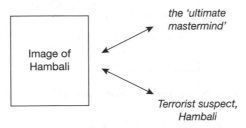

Figure 2.3 Intersemiotic repetition in the 'Hambali newsbite'

Clearly, there is also interpersonal work happening intersemiotically, and Hambali's image is associated with the interpersonal values expressed verbally as described earlier (cf. Knox 2008). The extreme close-up nature of the thumbnail portrait presents Hambali to the reader at an intimate distance (Kress and van Leeuwen 1996) construing a personal relation between Hambali and the reader not possible with words alone (Knox 2009a). In addition to this, the positioning of the image, its high visual salience, and the interaction between the image and the verbal text contribute to bringing Hambali to 'the front of the story', orienting the reader interpersonally to the story, and functioning as a visual Hyper-Theme (cf. Knox 2009b; Martin 2002).

Figure 2.4 shows the 'China newsbite' from the *People's Daily*, the verbal text of which has already been presented in Text B above. The headline is visually offset from the lead, and appears in bold, blue font, the conventional colour of hyperlinks on the World Wide Web. Both headline and image are clickable hyperlinks which take the reader to the same 'section page', where a number of stories on the development of China can be accessed as discussed earlier.

Drawing on Caple's (e.g. 2007) work on press images, the photograph uses the compositional technique of **serialising**, where an element in the image (in this case, the soldiers) is repeated a number of times. The edge of the red flag against the blue sky draws a vector between the soldiers in the image and the headline, *China's Peaceful Rise*. There is **intersemiotic meronymy** (i.e. part-whole relations between elements construed by different semiotic resources – Royce 2002) between the visual depiction of the Chinese military in the image (i.e. three soldiers standing

China's Peaceful Rise

After 26 years of reform and opening-up, China has blazed a path of development suited to its own conditions.

Figure 2.4 The 'China newsbite' from the *People's Daily* online, English version, September 2, 2005 (original in colour)

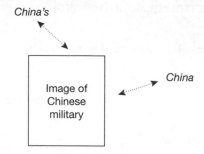

Figure 2.5 Intersemiotic meronymy in the 'China newsbite'

beneath the flag of the People's Liberation Army) and the lexical item *China*: the People's Liberation Army is a part of the 'whole' that is China (Figure 2.5).

While there is no mention of the military in the verbal text, image and text are presented to the reader as a single unit. Read as a single text, the newsbite presents the Chinese military as an integral element (arguably the key element) in China's 'peaceful' practices of *reform and opening-up*, a meaning completely absent from Text B as presented earlier.

As with the Hambali newsbite, there are interpersonal meanings construed in the visual–verbal interaction in the China newsbite. The positive appraisal of China discussed in the linguistic analysis of Text B affects our reading of the image. That is, the Chinese military is evaluated positively in this newsbite, and this is perhaps best illustrated by considering how the meaning of the image would change if the accompanying verbal text read, for example, *China Invades The Falklands*.

As discussed earlier, readers can always 'read against' a text. So although the China newsbite evaluates the Chinese military positively, a reader who has personal views contrary to this can, of course, read the relation between the image and the verbal text as ironic or flatly contradictory.

To summarise this section, newsbites do not make meaning verbally, nor visually. Rather, they make meaning multimodally, combining different semiotic resources (such as language, image, and layout) to mean in ways not possible using any single resource.

Newsbites: a page perspective

Online newspapers are non-linear texts – there is no 'default' order in which they are intended to be read. This is in contrast to linear texts such as films, which are created to be viewed (or 'read') from beginning to end. Likewise, pages of densely printed text:

> must be read the way they are designed to be read – from left to right and from top to bottom, line by line. Any other form of reading (skipping, looking at the last page to see how the plot will be resolved or what the conclusion will be) is a form of cheating and produces a slight sense of guilt in the reader.
>
> (Kress and van Leeuwen 1996: 218)

The linear/non-linear distinction is a cline, not a dichotomy, and home pages sit somewhere between the two extremes. On the one hand, they must be viewed a screen at a time – the bottom of the page cannot be seen before the top of the page. At the same time, each individual screen is a non-linear configuration, and it is possible to scroll down and up.

Newsbites contribute to the non-linearity of home pages and online newspapers. As multimodal texts, they make meaning by combining language, image and layout into cohesive wholes, and their verbal brevity accommodates non-linear readings of them. At the same time, as individual visual units on the page, they can also make meaning 'with' and 'against' other visual units on the page. That is, each newsbite on a home page is positioned relative to other newsbites, and texts of other genres (e.g. newsbits, advertisements, menus, mastheads). The positioning of texts on the home page of online newspapers is consistent over time; the page template is an ideological framework, within which individual stories are 'slotted' on a day-by-day, hour-by-hour, and even minute-by-minute basis. In this way, the values of the news institution are 'designed into' the home page template, and stories are crafted to meet the design strictures imposed upon individual newsbites according to where they are positioned on the page.[7] In the remainder of this section, the structures of the home pages of the *Bangkok Post* and the *People's Daily* are considered from this perspective.

The home page of the *Bangkok Post* online shown in Figure 2.6 is representative of the design of this page between August, 2006 and August, 2007. In the central column carrying the main news, the primary colour scheme is black text on white background, with large red font for hyperlinked headlines. Visually, this 'news column' (see further discussion below) blends the colour scheme of print newspapers (black text on white background) with the visual conventions of the World Wide Web (coloured font signifying hyperlinks). The overall design of the page also draws on other conventions of print newspaper page design, with the use of a masthead (which brings to the online publication the tradition and authority of the institution of the *Bangkok Post*), and the visual prominence of headlines in large font.

Consistent with what Kress and van Leeuwen (1996) describe as an 'objective perspective', the page is visually compartmentalised, and the use of a squared, componential design presents a factual and analytical stance visually. It would be possible to use an animated, circular design on the page with headlines and images rotating around the newspaper's logo, and/or with the use of sound and animation to highlight each story when rolled over with the mouse. Yet online newspapers consistently choose not to use such design features, and the squared, black-on-white design is widely used because visually it conveys a more 'serious' and authoritative stance, and draws in part on the tradition of print newspaper design.

Figure 2.6 Home page from the *Bangkok Post* online, August 11, 2006 (original in colour)

The authoritative, serious stance of the home page visually construes a particular kind of interpersonal relationship between the institution of the newspaper and the reader. The newspaper reports 'the facts', and the stories appearing on the home page are presented as impartial accounts of events and the actors involved in them (for discussion of the construal of 'objectivity' in the language of news stories, see Martin and White 2005). This contributes to creating a semiotic environment in which the stories on the page – including the Hambali newsbite – can be read as factual, objective accounts, and therefore where the alignment of the reader with the negative appraisal of Hambali (as discussed earlier) can be more readily achieved.

In addition to construing an objective and authoritative stance on the part of the newspaper, the design of the home page also constructs and categorises the 'world of the news' in a way particular to the *Bangkok Post*.

The main, centre column of news is broken visually by three pink horizontal bars with verbal headings: *General News*, *Business*, and *Sports*. Each of the newsbites in this column are roughly the same size and shape, and contrast visually with the newsbites across the bottom of the page, which are headed visually by blue horizontal bars, and verbally with the headings: *Outlook*, *Database*, *RealTime*, *Motoring*, *Horizons*, and *Perspective*. Drawing again on the work of Kress and van Leeuwen (1996), we can identify a visual–verbal taxonomy of newsbites as shown in Figure 2.7. The italicised categories in Figure 2.7 (namely *news*, *hard*, and *soft*) are **covert** categories, in that they are not explicitly named. In contrast, the categories on the lowest level of the tree are **overt** categories and explicitly named on the home page.

The taxonomy of news represented in Figure 2.7 is not obvious to the reader, as the home page is only ever viewed a screen at a time. Nonetheless, readers are presented the Hambali newsbite within this taxonomy (within the category *Perspective*), which is the way that the *Bangkok Post* online classified the world of news during the time period of this page design (cf. Knox 2008).

This way of categorising the events of the world is closely related to the organisation of the news institution, with different news desks (e.g. the Business desk, the Sports desk, the Outlook desk, the Perspective desk) having their own editor and staff, and therefore their own 'slice of real estate' on the home page. But the way the visual–verbal classification system works on the home page also goes beyond this. For example, Sport news is classified together with General and Business news, while Perspective (which includes commentary, analysis and investigative pieces) is classified together with Motoring and Horizons (the travel section) as 'soft news',

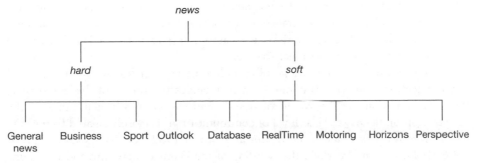

Figure 2.7 Taxonomy of news from the home page of the *Bangkok Post* online

despite the topical similarity between the content of the *Perspective* and *General News* sections of the newspaper. Further, the choice to position the Hambali newsbite on the home page as the 'Perspective newsbite' means that it must meet the particular visual and verbal design parameters which come with this choice.

In addition to construing the stance and authority of the newspaper, and the 'categorisation of the world of news', online newspaper home pages are composed in such a way that they function as cohesive wholes, taking into account the affordances and constraints of the scrolling screen. That part of the *Bangkok Post*'s home page which is visible when the reader first accesses the site – known as the **first screen** – features the masthead, a large banner advertisement, the main navigational menu, a large news image, and a table of breaking news. What is actually seen on different readers' computer screens varies according to factors beyond the control of the newspaper, such as screen size and browser settings. Nonetheless, the visual structure of the page takes account of the fact that the first screen – or **Head** of the page – needs to have visual impact in a way that is less important for the remainder of the page.

On some home pages, the difference is marked; on others, like the *Bangkok Post* at this time, the difference is less marked. Figure 2.6 shows that a line can be drawn across the page roughly at the bottom of the first newsbite (which is also roughly the bottom of the first navigation menu, and the table of 'Breaking News'). It is common (if not universal) that online newspaper home pages are designed in this way, with a **Head–Tail** compositional structure (Knox 2007).

This Head–Tail structure works together with the simple principle that stories closer to the top of the page are ranked as more important than those below them. The soft news on the *Bangkok Post* home page is compositionally valued as 'last in line', at the bottom of the Tail of the page.

Online newspaper home pages also typically have a horizontal composition pattern where a visually salient column of content (often the middle or left column) carries the **Primary** information on the page, and narrower columns carry **Secondary** information. Positioned as it is in the centre column at the bottom of the page, the Hambali newsbite is valued as Primary information (contrasting with navigational menus, advertisments, breaking news, and stock news positioned in peripheral columns).[8]

The home page of the *People's Daily* can be analysed using the same theoretical tools as applied to the home page of the *Bangkok Post* as described above. Figure 2.8 represents the home page design of the *People's Daily* between early 2004 and June 2007, and shows that similar to the *Bangkok Post*, it also construes a 'factual', 'objective', and 'authoritative' stance; constructs a visual–verbal taxonomy of news (which includes both overt and covert categories); and uses a Head–Tail and Primary–Secondary compositional structure.

As discussed above, the design of an online newspaper home page is an act of communication, and what is communicated includes the stance of the newspaper, the representation of 'the world of news', and the compositional value of the information on the page. This 'level of communication' is closely related to the way in which news is reported in newsbites at a 'lower level' (cf. Baldry and Thibault 2006: 144). As stated earlier, the wording of the Hambali newsbite and the China newsbite are unique: each newsbite has been written specifically for the home page.

Figure 2.8 Home page from the *People's Daily* online, English version, September 2, 2005 (original in colour)

But more than this, each newsbite has been written for a particular position in the ideological framework construed by the home page template.

It is not a new phenomenon that the stories appearing on newspaper pages are valued by the visual design of the story and the page (Barnhust and Nerone 2001; Kress and van Leeuwen 1998). However, the degree of regimentation in online newspaper pages is much higher than in their print counterparts, in part because the materiality of the print newspaper serves also as a navigational device, and the virtual nature of online newspapers means that a range of techniques – including page templates which are consistent across pages and over time – are necessary to aid navigation.

Overall, the discussion to this point has aimed to show that newsbites are short texts which can be analysed verbally, visually, and multimodally, and that they make meaning as individual texts, and in relation to other stories. Further, institutional structures and practices are realised in the multimodal structure of home pages and newsbites. In the next section, another dimension of online newspaper discourse will be considered: the dimension of time.

Newsbites: a temporal perspective

Online newspapers include many stories and many genres. There are extended news features, editorials, commentaries, hard news stories, video reports, audio reports, photographic essays, and slide shows, in addition to the newsbites and newsbits on home pages and 'section pages'. The home page of an online newspaper is, however, a crucial site where the news valued as most important in the value system of the news institution is carefully packaged for the reader, and therefore where the values of the newspaper are most prominently on display (cf. Fishman and Marvin 2003).

Newsbites are short texts, and may be read in seconds, or less. Online newspapers are typically read on a timescale of minutes. Yet one of the key functions of a newspaper is to build a loyal audience (Thurman 2007), and like their print counterparts, online newspapers depend for their survival on readers returning.

Letters pages, feedback through other media, blogs, and 'citizen journalism' mean that there is an ongoing dialogue between the institution of the newspaper and its readership. Viewed this way, each edition of a newspaper can be seen as one turn in a dialogue between the news institution and its readership – a dialogue which spans years, even decades (cf. Bakhtin 1986: 92; Lemke 2003: 141–6).

All newspapers are heteroglossic – the voice of the institution accommodates many voices, including the readers whose comments are published, the wire agencies whose stories are sourced, the photographers whose images appear, the sources quoted in stories, and the journalists, sub-editors, and editors who share authorship of news stories (Bell 1991). The audience is multifarious too, so features such as many-to-many interaction, the increasingly common updating of online newspapers on a minute-by-minute basis, the non-linear nature of online newspapers, and the attendant unpredictable nature of readers' pathways through the text at any given time, all combine to make the 'newspaper-as-dialogue' a complex, dynamic text.

Within this complex interaction, the structure of the home page allows the news institution to focus on actors and events they value as current and immediate, while keeping other issues valued as important simmering in the background of the readership's collective consciousness. This has long been a feature of print newspapers, but with the long-term tendency towards shorter texts and the Nucleus–Satellite structure, and the move to the medium of the World Wide Web, online newspapers have developed in such a way that news content (or experiential meanings) can be kept to a minimum on the home page, while the evaluation of actors and events (or interpersonal meanings) can be maintained. Newsbites are well suited to this semiotic environment, where readers are kept well informed interpersonally on a range of issues, but well informed experientially only with regard to those stories they follow to pages 'lower down' in the website.

Therefore, in addition to considering newsbites from the perspective of linguistics, multimodal discourse analysis, and page design, their role in the unfolding discourse of the newspaper-as-dialogue also needs to be understood. In order to do so, theoretical tools are needed that can account for texts with the features described above, and which unfold over a timescale of years.

Theory: a newsbite-inspired perspective

Two newsbites have been examined using a range of tools from SF theory. Aspects examined have included choices in lexis and grammar such as nominalisation, passive voice, and Agent deletion; choices in **discourse-semantics** (or meaning 'beyond the clause') such as Hyper-Theme and appraisal; choices in text–image relations; and choices in page design. One analytical perspective not explored here, but which is crucial, is the overall design of the website, including the relations between pages, and between elements on one page and elements on another (see Djonov 2007). Accounts of other genres in online newspapers are also needed.

In addition to these tools, researchers and professionals will benefit from applying tools which can account for texts such as the newspaper-as-dialogue which unfold over longer timescales. Issues such as terrorism (which features in the Hambali newsbite) are likely to feature prominently on home pages at some times, and trail off in others. This is also likely to be the case for stories dealing with national development. For example, at times when China is criticised internationally, we might predict that the *People's Daily* is more likely to include stories of China's development as hard news on the home page. At other times, 'News Features' and 'Highlights' allow the institution to keep such stories 'ticking over' in the discourse of the newspaper. Thus, the way that individual newsbites are written, and the configuration of values realised by the design of the home page template, are both less significant than the longer, constantly shifting mosaic of which they are part (see Lemke 2003).

SF theorists have long recognised the importance of texts unfolding over longer timescales. Examples include Fowler's (1991) account of the 'salmonella-in-eggs affair' in the British press; Christie's (e.g. 1997) descriptions of curriculum macro-genres; Coffin and K.A. O'Halloran's analysis (this volume) of the run up to European Union Expansion; Iedema's (2003) discussion of the resemiotisation of meetings into reports into plans into a physical building; and Henderson-Brooks' (2008) account of change in a patient over the course of psychotherapy sessions. Martin and Rose (2008) describe similar work by Jordens (2002), and Muntigl (2004) in other institutional contexts.

Such work is consistent with Lemke's (2003: 141) observation, that:

> There is a need for CDA [i.e. Critical Discourse Analysis] to enquire into [the] functional differentiation [of texts] with regard to timescales, and an important start on such enquiries is investigating the extent to which, say, shorter vs longer texts carry different functions and mediate different kinds of social organization across scales.

In order to understand texts as complex, dynamic and data-intensive as the 'newspaper-as-dialogue', and to be able to analyse and recognise the patterns which occur across longer timescales and which relate, therefore, to higher scales of social organization (Lemke 2003), mathematical modelling and visualisation of data are likely to become increasingly important (see O'Halloran 2005).

Conclusion

Home pages and newsbites provide the 'bare bones' of news stories, but at the same time their multimodal structure allows them to meet the institutional demands of the newspaper (to report on events; to evaluate events, people and institutions; to act as entry points to the newspaper) and the demands of readers (to be informed of current events; to navigate to those parts of the newspaper which draw their interest; to be engaged and entertained). For so-called 'digital natives', these hyper-media texts are as 'natural' as casual conversations, textbooks, television commercials, and comics. But new media genres challenge existing notions of text and communication, and are evolving rapidly.

This creates challenges for researchers and teachers working to develop informed descriptions of such texts, and pedagogical approaches that can teach learners to read and write them effectively. The pressure falls not only on the descriptions, but also on the theories informing them.

In such an environment, theoretical consistency and strength is vital if we are to avoid re-inventing the wheel at every new genre, in every new context. SF theory is one theory which has proved adaptable and useful in describing a variety of semiotic systems, and incorporating insights from different disciplinary fields. Building on solid theory which can explain texts systematically in relation to their social contexts of production and reception provides us with the best chance of developing sound and applicable explanations which can feed into pedagogy, and allow our work to remain relevant to current and future generations.

References

Bakhtin, M.M. (1986) *Speech Genres and other Late Essays*. Austin, TX: University of Texas Press.

Baldry, A. and Thibault, P.J. (2006) *Multimodal Transcription and Text Analysis*. London: Equinox.

Barnhurst, K.G. and Nerone, J. (2001) *The Form of News: A history*. New York: Guilford Press.

Barthelson, M. (2002) 'Reading behaviour in online news reading'. Cognitive Science Department, Lund: Lund University.

Bateman, J.A. (2008) *Multimodality and Genre: A foundation for the systematic analysis of multimodal documents*. Hampshire: Palgrave Macmillan.

Bateman, J.A., Delin, J. and Henschel, R. (2006) 'Mapping the multimodal genres of traditional and electronic newspapers', in T.D. Royce and W.L. Bowcher (eds) *New Directions in the Analysis of Multimodal Discourse*. Mahwah, NJ: Lawrence Erlbaum Associates.

Bell, A. (1991) *The Language of News Media*. Oxford: Blackwell.

Caple, H. (2007) 'Beyond reading images: how the textual metafunction is put to work in analysing the composition of photographs'. Paper presented at: *Systemic Functional Linguistics in Use: 34th International Systemic Functional Congress*. Odense, Denmark.

Christie, F. (1997) 'Curriculum macrogenres as forms of initiation into a culture', in F. Christie and J.R. Martin (eds) *Genre and Institutions: Social processes in the workplace and school*. London: Continuum.

Djonov, E. (2007) 'Website hierarchy and the interaction between content organization, webpage and navigation design: a systemic functional hypermedia discourse analysis perspective'. *Information Design Journal* 15: 144–62.

Fairclough, N. (1995) *Media Discourse*. London: Arnold.

Fishman, J.M. and Marvin, C. (2003) 'Portrayals of violence and group difference in newspaper photographs: nationalism and media'. *Journal of Communication* 53: 32–44.

Fowler, R. (1991) *Language in the News: Discourse and ideology in the press*. London: Routledge.

Halliday, M.A.K. and Matthiessen, C.M.I.M. (2004) *An Introduction to Functional Grammar*. London: Arnold.

Hallin, D.C. (1997) 'Sound bite news: television coverage of elections', in S. Iyengar and R. Reeves (eds) *Do the Media Govern? Politicians, voters, and reporters in America*. Thousand Oaks: Sage.

Henderson-Brooks, C. (2008) 'Interacting voices: "mother" as token and topic in psychotherapy', in C. Wu, C.M.I.M. Matthiessen and M. Herke (eds) *Proceedings of ISFC 35: Voices around the world*. Sydney, 35th ISFC Organizing Committee.

Holmqvist, K., Holsanova, J., Barthelson, M and Lundqvist, D. (2003) 'Reading or scanning? A study of newspaper and net paper reading', in J. Hyona, R, Radach and H. Deube (eds) *The Mind's Eye: Cognitive and applied aspects of eye movement research*. Oxford: Elsevier.

Iedema, R. (2003) 'Multimodality, resemiotization: extending the analysis of discourse as multisemiotic practice'. *Visual Communication* 2: 29–57.

Iedema, R., Feez, S. and White, P.R.R. (1994) 'Stage Two: Media literacy'. A report for the Write it Right Literacy in Industry Research Project Sydney, Disadvantaged Schools Program, NSW, Department of School Education.

Jordens, C. (2002) 'Reading spoken stories for values: a discursive study of cancer survivors and their professional carers'. *Medicine*. Sydney: University of Sydney.

Knox, J.S. (2007) 'Visual–verbal communication on online newspaper home pages'. *Visual Communication* 6: 19–53.

Knox, J.S. (2008) 'Online newspapers and TESOL classrooms: a multimodal perspective', in L. Unsworth (ed.) *Multimodal Semiotics: Functional analysis in contexts of education*. London: Continuum.

Knox, J.S. (2009a) 'Visual minimalism in hard news: thumbnail faces on the *smh online* home page'. *Social Semiotics* 19 (2): 165–89.

Knox, J.S. (2009b) 'Punctuating the home page: image as language in an online newspaper'. *Discourse and Communication* 3 (2): 145–72.

Knox, J.S. (forthcoming) 'Designing the news in an online newspaper: a systemic description', in A. Baldry and E. Montagna (eds) *Interdisciplinary Perspectives on Multi-modality: Theory and practice*. Campobasso: Palladino.

Knox, J.S. and Patpong, P. (2008) 'Reporting bloodshed in Thai newspapers: a comparative case study of English and Thai', in E. Thomson and P.R.R. White (eds) *Communicating Conflict: Multilingual case studies of the news media*. London: Continuum.

Kress, G. and van Leeuwen, T. (1996) *Reading Images: The grammar of visual design*. London: Routledge.

Kress, G. and van Leeuwen, T. (1998) 'Front pages: (the critical) analysis of newspaper layout', in A. Bell and P. Garrett (eds) *Approaches to media discourse*. Oxford: Blackwell.

Lemke, J.L. (2003) 'Texts and discourses in the technologies of social organization', in G. Weiss and R. Wodak (eds) *Critical Discourse Analysis: Theory and interdisciplinarity*. Basingstoke: Palgrave Macmillan.

Martin, J.R. (2002) 'Fair trade: negotiating meaning in multimodal texts', in P. Coppock (ed.) *The Semiotics of Writing: Transdisciplinary perspectives on the technology of writing*. Turnhout: Brepols.

Martin, J.R. and Rose, D. (2007) *Working with Discourse: Meaning beyond the clause*. London: Continuum.

Martin, J.R. and Rose, D. (2008) *Genre Relations: Mapping culture*. London: Equinox.

Martin, J.R. and White, P.R.R. (2005) *The Language of Evaluation: Appraisal in English*. Hampshire: Palgrave Macmillan.

Martinec, R. and Salway, A. (2005) 'A system for image–text relations in new (and old) media'. *Visual Communication* 4: 337–71.

Muntigl, P. (2004) *Narrative Counselling: Social and linguistic processes of change*, Amsterdam: Benjamins.

O'Halloran, K.L. (ed.) (2004) *Multimodal Discourse Analysis: Systemic functional perspectives*. London: Continuum.

O'Halloran, K.L. (2005) *Mathematical Discourse: Language, symbolism and visual images*. London: Continuum.

O'Halloran, K.L. (2008) 'Multimodality around the world: past, present, and future directions for research'. Plenary paper presented at: 35th International Systemic Functional Congress, Sydney.

O'Toole, M. (1994) *The Language of Displayed Art*. Rutherford, NY: Fairleigh Dickinson University Press.

Royce, T.D. (2002) 'Multimodality in the TESOL classroom: exploring visual–verbal synergy'. *TESOL Quarterly* 36: 191–205.

Thurman, N. (2007) 'The globalization of journalism online: a transatlantic study of news websites and their international readers'. *Journalism* 8: 285–307.

Trew, T. (1979) '"What the papers say": linguistic variation and ideological difference', in R. Fowler, B. Hodge, G. Kress and T. Trew (eds) *Language and Control*. London: Routledge and Kegan Paul.

van Leeuwen, T. (2005) *Introducing Social Semiotics*. London: Routledge.

White, P.R.R. (1997) 'Death, disruption and the moral order: the narrative impulse in mass media hard news reporting', in F. Christie and J.R. Martin (eds) *Genres and Institutions: Social processes in the workplace and school*. London: Continuum.

Notes

1   O'Halloran (2008) makes the important and useful distinction between *multimodal* (combining different modalities such as visual, aural, olfactory) and *multi-semiotic* (combining different semiotic resources such as language, image, and music). In this

chapter, *multimodal* (including its derivatives) is used as a cover term which includes the notion of multi-semiotic, as is common in the literature.

2   Following the convention of Systemic Functional Linguistics, function labels (e.g. Hyper-Theme) are indicated by using Initial Capitals, whereas class labels (e.g. nominal group) appear in lower-case.

3   One possible alternative would have been to construe it as a saying: . . . *authorities announced Hambali's capture.* For detailed discussion of the representation of experience in language, see Halliday and Matthiessen (2004); and Martin and Rose (2007).

4   One possible alternative would have been to construe it as a relation between *China's development* and the attributes of that development: . . . *China's development is suited to its own conditions.*

5   For complementary accounts of image-text relations, see Martinec and Salway (2005); and van Leeuwen (2005).

6   Q: What ultimate mastermind? A: The ultimate mastermind in the picture.

7   Like news*bites*, the meaning potential of news*bits* has been expanding recently, with some online newspapers using different font sizes, font colours, and also images with newsbits. The choices as to whether a story appears on the home page – and if so whether as a newsbite or a newsbit – are value-laden in themselves (Knox 2008, forthcoming).

8   The soft newsbites on this page actually break the main column boundaries, and it could be argued that this position at the very bottom of the Tail is actually outside the Primary–Secondary paradigm. The subsequent design of the *Bangkok Post* home page addressed this anomaly, and moved the soft-news newsbites to a Secondary column to the right of the page.

Chapter 3

Tim Moore

The 'processes' of learning

On the use of Halliday's transitivity in academic skills advising

Introduction

If one were to characterize the main trend in language studies over the last two decades it would be towards an activity that almost all linguists now do in some guise – discourse analysis. This reorientation has been due in part to a shift in interest from the single sentence to longer stretches of text as the key unit of analysis, but also to the emergence of a broad social interest in what Zelig Harris has described as the 'correlating of language and culture' (cited in Cook 1987: 2). The busy activity of discourse analysts over the last twenty years has been notable for producing a wide range of analytical frameworks – including, for example, Functional Linguistics (Halliday 1994), Rhetorical Structure Theory (Mann and Thompson 1989), Genre Analysis (Swales 1990), Critical Discourse Analysis (Fairclough 1995). These have been directed at a variety of analytical purposes: for example, to understand what makes texts meaningful, to demonstrate how texts achieve certain social ends, to show how they are implicated in the enactments of status and power in society.

Of the many uses of discourse analysis, one of the more significant is its educational applications – particularly how it can be utilized in the teaching of writing in the academy. To provide students with the tools to analyse texts in principled ways, it is argued, allows them to recognize broadly what might be required in meeting the demands of particular 'rhetorical situations', and thus to see how they might go about shaping their own work (Johns 1997). For some literacy specialists there is also an important social mission in this form of pedagogy. Cope and Kalantzis (1994:

Edited version of Moore, T. (2007) 'The "processes" of learning: on the use of Halliday's transitivity in academic skills advising', *Arts and Humanities in Higher Education* 6 (1): 50–73.

8), for example, point out that while some students, by dint of their social background, will have 'a comfortable ride . . . into the discourses of certain realms of power', others – especially those from 'historically marginalized groups' – will have experienced no such 'natural acquisition' and so these textual practices will often require explicit explanation.

But there is caution expressed in some quarters about discourse methods of instruction. John Swales, an applied linguist who has perhaps done more than any other to make the related concept of 'genre' accessible to students, urges a judicious approach to the way that discourse analytic methods are introduced in the classroom. There is a need, he suggests, always to draw a distinction between the practices of professional analysis *per se* and those which are directed at some pedagogical purpose:

> I see no good reason for believing that the kind of analysis that may best advance our understanding of discourse in general is necessarily the kind of analysis that will best advance the communicative competence of learners whose main interests lie outside the linguistic sciences.
>
> (Swales 1990: 18)

Freedman and Medway (1994: 12) are of a similar mind. On the one hand, they recognize the considerable potential of discourse analysis to 'demystify' university writing for students – to demonstrate, as they say, how the various forms it takes are neither 'arbitrary' nor 'arcane'; on the other, they lament that the effect is often only 'to make both the texts and the pedagogical issues look more complex than before'.

Of the many schools and methods of discourse, perhaps the most influential (at least in the Australian context) is that which stems from functional grammar, first developed by Michael Halliday and advanced by a number of scholars working in this tradition (e.g. Martin 1992; Mathiessen 1995). The original Hallidayan system has been described variously as 'catalytic' and 'revolutionary' in the way we have come to understand the social role of language (Cope and Kalantzis 1994), but the same caveats about its effectiveness as a pedagogical tool apply. Hunston and Sinclair (2000: 79), for example, note the complexity of its grammatical categories and are sure that its application should be restricted to expert analysis only: 'The difficulty that students experience when learning to use the terminology', they say, 'is evidence of its esoteric nature.'

In this chapter I wish to show not only that Halliday's system is able to be applied in uncomplicated ways to teaching situations, but indeed that if it is, it has the potential to reveal in significant ways some of the challenges and confusions that students face when grappling with writing in their discipline areas. I shall demonstrate this through three learning case studies, each taken from my work as an academic skills adviser. Common to each episode – involving students studying in three fields (history, art criticism, sociology) – was the student(s) having received feedback from lecturers that their writing was in some way inadequate for the task that had been set. In the subsequent assistance given, a form of collaborative textual analysis was conducted which was able to shed light on the nature of students' writing difficulties, as well as suggesting how the underlying processes of their learning could be adapted and developed. Before describing these cases, however, it is necessary to provide some detail about Halliday's functional grammar in general, and his sub-system of transitivity in particular, followed by a brief account of my teaching context as an academic adviser.

Halliday's system of transitivity

As noted, Halliday's functional grammar has had a considerable influence on linguistics in the last three decades. If we were to summarize the key principle underlying the system it would be akin to Louis Sullivan's famous dictum about architecture – that 'form follows function'. For Halliday, language is functional in the sense that it exists, and has evolved, to fulfil certain human needs, and the linguistic forms of which it is comprised necessarily reflect those basic needs. As Halliday (1994: xiii) explains: 'A functional grammar is essentially a "natural grammar", in the sense that everything in it can be explained by reference to how it is used.' He identifies three fundamental uses of language, or 'metafunctions'. The first of these is to make sense of the world around us, and to describe our place within it. This is the 'ideational' metafunction which finds expression in the formal system of 'transitivity' (subjects, verbs, predicates and so on), more of which presently. The second, the 'inter-personal', is concerned with relating to others and getting things done in the world, encoded in the formal system of 'mood' (indicative, interrogative, imperative, modality and so on). The third metafunction, the 'textual', is in a sense an executive system for the other two and is concerned with organizing ideational and interpersonal 'messages' – or 'breathing relevance into them', as Halliday describes it (1994: xiii). This function in turn finds expression in the formal system of 'theme' (clefting, ellipsis, reference and so on).

Some take issue with this particular tripartite dividing up of linguistic activity (e.g. Taylor 1980). In other such proposals, these functions are delineated differently. Popper (1979), for example, opted for a four-way taxonomy of functions ('the expressive', 'the signalling', 'the descriptive', 'the argumentative'); for Jakobson (1960) there were six ('metalingual', 'phatic', 'informative', 'poetic', 'directive' and 'expressive'). But, arguably, the achievement of Halliday's work has been to build a comprehensive grammatical description based on this basic presupposition: that the constituents of language are intrinsically 'semantic' and always involved in the enactment of certain social meanings. In the development of modern linguistics this was a significant departure from traditional syntactic grammars (such as Chomsky's generative grammar), the focus of which has been to describe language as formal structures – and then only optionally to consider how meanings are mapped on to these. Among other things, the reorientation to semantics meant that the perennial categories of traditional grammar (nouns, verbs and so on) would need to be set aside, and a different set created.

The contrast between functional and formalist terminologies can be illustrated in the range of sentences shown in Figures 3.1 and 3.2 taken from student assign-ments, all of which will be discussed in detail later. In Figure 3.1, these sentences are parsed according to the categories of traditional grammar; in Figure 3.2 they are re-analysed using Halliday's categories. Looking at Figure 3.1, we can see that there are two types of labelling: the syntactic classes of individual words (nouns,

	SUBJECT	PREDICATE	
Pattern 1			
	SUBJECT (NOUN)	VERB +	OBJECT (NOUN)
1.	*Britain*	*broke*	*its alliance (with Japan)*
2.	*I*	*will analyse*	*the events (leading to the formation of the alliance)*
3.	*Historians*	*have offered*	*very divergent interpretations (on this issue)*
4.	*Monet*	*used*	*a blush of atmospheric colour*
5.	*One*	*begins dividing*	*the composition (into three levels)*
6.	*There*	*is*	*a strong geometric element (in the work)*
Pattern 2			
	SUBJECT (NOUN)	VERB +	COMPLEMENT (ADJECTIVE)
7.	*The images*	*are*	*inviting*
8.	*These changes in women's position*	*are*	*very important*

Figure 3.1 Parsing of sample sentences (traditional grammar)

verbs, adjectives and so on), and the transitivity relations between words (subject, predicate, object and so on). In the analysis of these sentences the only salient distinction in patterning is a formal one – between those sentences whose predicate has a 'verb + object (noun)' structure (examples 1–6) and those with 'verb + complement (adjective)' structure (examples 7–8).

As mentioned, in Halliday's analysis of transitivity the distinctions proposed are not formal, but semantic. His starting point is the verb which, as the representation of some kind of 'going on' or 'process', holds the kernel of 'ideational' meaning in a clause. For Halliday, these 'processes', if investigated closely, are not of a single uniform kind but refer to different realms of experience. Some evoke the outer experience of actions and doings, categorized in his grammar as 'material' and 'behavioural' processes. Others, in contrast, refer to the inner experiences of reflection and speech, which he calls 'mental' and 'verbal' processes. A final realm is one that does not take in temporal processes as such, but refers rather to states of being: 'relational' and 'existential' processes. If we think of the category of verbs in this way – as covering a range of different process-type – then we need to think of the 'subjects' and 'objects' with which they collocate as exhibiting the same kind of variety. Thus, in a 'material' process clause (e.g. *Britain broke its alliance with Japan*), the subject will logically be some kind of physical, often volitional, entity – what Halliday labels an 'actor' (*Britain*) – and the object (that which is affected by the action), the 'goal' (*the alliance with Japan*). A mental process such as 'analyse' (as in *I will analyse events*) similarly suggests different types of participants, with the 'subject' typically some sentient being (a 'senser') and the object of this 'sensing', a 'phenomenon'. This principle produces an array of 'participant' and 'process' categories which can be seen in all their variety in the re-analysis of the sentences, in Figure 3.2.

PARTICIPANT	PROCESS	PARTICIPANT
Type 1: Material processes		
ACTOR	MATERIAL	GOAL
Britain	*broke*	*its alliance (with Japan)*
Monet	*used*	*a blush of atmospheric colour*
Type 2: Mental processes		
SENSER	MENTAL	PHENOMENON
I	*will analyse*	*the events (leading to the formation of the alliance)*
One	*begins dividing**	*the composition (into three levels)*
Type 3: Verbal processes		
SAYER	VERBAL	VERBIAGE
Historians	*have offered*	*very divergent interpretations (on this issue)*
Type 4: Relational processes		
CARRIER	RELATIONAL	ATTRIBUTE
The images	*are*	*inviting*
These changes (in women's position)	*are*	*very important*
Type 5: Existential processes		
Subject 'dummy'	EXISTENTIAL	EXISTENT
There	*is*	*a strong geometric element (in the work)*

Figure 3.2 Parsing of sample sentences (Halliday's transitivity)

There is no denying the complexity of this system. In fact, in the foregoing discussion, we have considered only the detail of one strand of the grammar – the ideational metafunction and its related system of transitivity – without venturing at all into the interpersonal and the textual metafunctions (see Coffin 2003 for an example of how all three metafunctions have been used in the analysis of student writing). Halliday was the first to acknowledge the 'extravagance' of his model, while at the same time insisting that such detail was necessary if the semantic potentiality of language is to be fully accounted for (Halliday 1994: xix). It is this evident complexity that has led some to feel that the educational applications of the grammar are limited. And such doubts have come even from those working within Hallidayan traditions of scholarship. Social and literary critic, Terry Threadgold, for example, cautions:

> There is a danger that the [grammar's] technical explicitness may become an end in itself and actually stop students and teachers from asking the questions that need to be asked to properly understand texts

(Threadgold 1994: 27)

However, as I hope to show in the case studies that follow, the use of Halliday's transitivity with students need not be overly technical and, rather than being an obstacle to the type of interrogations that Threadgold has in mind, has the potential to open up the writing practices of the academy to productive scrutiny.

Teaching context

Halliday's model of transitivity was applied in the work of the Language and Learning Unit in the Faculty of Arts at an Australian university, a type of unit found nowadays at many Anglophone tertiary institutions. These units, which have the broad role of providing language and academic support to students, have come into being in the last decades as a result of a trend towards increasing diversification among student cohorts – and a recognition on the part of institutions that many students now commence their courses without the familiarity and preparedness for university study that could once be assumed (Baldauf 1996). These students are sometimes referred to as 'non-traditional students' (Lea and Stierer 2000; Pelling 2001) and include in their number those from non-English-speaking backgrounds, students from disadvantaged socioeconomic groups, mature-aged students and the like.

In the activities of such units there is a need to have to hand certain analytical tools that are capable of bringing the domains of learning and language use into some fruitful relationship. The appeal of a functional account of language such as Halliday's is twofold. First, its focus on semantic content, as opposed to linguistic form, enables one to interpret in some principled way the meanings and understandings that students seek to express in their work. Second, its focus on specific instances of language use (or texts), as opposed to the linguistic system *per se*, gives us a basis to say something about the adequacy of these meanings – 'to say why a text is or is not effective for its own purposes' (Halliday 1994: xv). This latter evaluative goal, as Halliday explains, is hard to achieve: 'it requires an interpretation not only of the text itself, but also of its context (context of situation and of culture) and of the systematic relationship between the two.' In assisting students and helping them with their writing, then, there is a need always to have recourse to these contextual domains: the 'situational' (often the particular assessment task a student is working on), and the 'cultural' (the broad educational and epistemological practices of the particular discipline they are operating in). I now turn to the specific cases to which Hallidayan transitivity was applied.

Case 1: historical 'materialism' and 'non-materialism'

This case involved providing advice on essay writing to a first-year undergraduate History student (first language, L1: English). The student, enrolled on a part-time basis and returning to study after a period of full-time employment, had self-referred to the Language and Learning Unit after receiving what he thought was 'a disappointing result' (a low credit grade) for the first major essay written on a Second World War subject. The student was puzzled by his poor performance, believing that he had a very sound knowledge of the topic he had chosen on the origins of the Nazi–Japanese axis, namely:

> *Why did Japan and Germany become allies in peace and war?*

The lecturer's comments on the essay suggested that the student's knowledge of events was not really at issue. The essay was 'factually-sound in the main', the lecturer noted, but fell down by doing too much 'mere recounting of events', and for 'lacking the analysis and argument needed for a university-level history essay'. The support tutorial conducted subsequently was devoted mainly to helping the student interpret this assessment of his work, and to locate those elements in his text that suggested a lack of 'argument' and 'analysis'. Our work together in the session was assisted by having to hand an exemplary High Distinction essay on the same topic provided by the lecturer.

Our analysis was focused mainly on the introductory paragraphs from the two essays (see Texts 1 and 2). This was partly because the lecturer had singled out the student's introduction as problematic – 'for launching too hastily into the material'. But it was also apparent from a survey of the two extracts in advance of the session that the transitivity issues were particularly pertinent in this opening section, and able to show in relief the very different approaches adopted by the two students.

Initially, the analysis was focused on what Halliday calls 'thematized participants', defined as those participants occurring in subject position in a clause. The thematic element is 'that with which a clause is principally concerned' (Halliday 1994: 58). If one then considers thematic elements over a stretch of text, it is possible to see in effect 'that with which a discourse is principally concerned'. In the student's introduction (Text 1), it was noted that the text's 'principal concern' was the countries under discussion (*Japan*, *Britain*) or some attribute of them (*Japan's foreign*

TEXT 1 Student's introduction.

Japan's foreign policy from the beginning of the 20th Century until the early 1920's was principally based on its alliance with Great Britain. Although a partner of allied powers in the Great War, its role was not appreciated at Versailles. The Japanese were denied rights to migrate to the USA and Australia, their exports abroad were restricted and in 1921 Britain broke its alliance with Japan. These facts coupled with the decision of the Washington conference to reduce the Japanese Navy to 60% of American and British fleets developed not only bitterness in Japan but also a feeling of isolation. These were some of the underlying reasons why they chose to enter into an alliance with the Germans.

TEXT 2 Introduction from exemplar text.

Was Japan's alliance with Germany inevitable? On this question, historians have offered very divergent interpretations. Some have argued that the ideological developments in the two countries in the 1930's naturally brought the two countries together to form a powerful and aggressive alliance. Other accounts, however have viewed the creation of the axis as the consequence of the failure of Western diplomacy, particularly of Britain and the US. In this essay, I will analyse the events leading to the formation of the alliance and will argue that it was principally the West's disregard of the interests of an emergent Japan that more than anything else led to its fatal joining with Nazi Germany with all the tragic consequences this would subsequently have for the world.

policy, its role in the First World War and so on – see Figure 3.3, column 1). By contrast, in the exemplar text, we noted that beyond the first clause, the focus was altogether different (Figure 3.4, column 1). Whereas the student's text takes as its point of departure various real-world actors in this historical episode, the thematized elements in Text 2 are of a more 'abstract' nature (*historians* and *their accounts*): those who have been engaged in acts of reflection on these events. Significantly, an additional key participant in Text 2 is the student author himself, who is thematized explicitly in the two clauses of the final sentence.

Along with this difference in thematic participants, a corresponding variation was observed in the types of 'processes' these participants were construed as being engaged in. As can be seen in Figure 3.3, the processes in the student's text are mainly of a 'material' kind – the various acts in which a world power will engage in the conduct of its international relations (e.g. *forming alliances, granting or restricting rights* and so on). It is interesting to note in passing that, in most clauses in the student's introduction, Japan is represented not as the agent but as the recipient of actions, suggesting an historical interpretation, albeit an unstated one, of 'Japan as victim'. In the exemplar text, the 'processes' again relate to a different order of reality – not material processes, but the mental and verbal processes that characterize the work

Clause	THEMATIZED PARTICIPANT	PROCESS	OTHER PARTICIPANT
1	*Japan's foreign policy ...*	*was principally based on its alliance*	*with Great Britain*
2	*Japan's role [in WWI]*	*was not appreciated ...*	*[by the allies]*
3	*[Japan's] exports*	*were restricted*	
4	*The Japanese*	*were denied rights to migrate*	
5	*Britain*	*broke its alliance*	*with Japan*
6	*these facts ...*	*developed*	*bitterness in Japan*
7	*[Japan]*	*chose to form [an alliance]*	*with the Germans*

Figure 3.3 Transitivity analysis of clauses in student text (Text 1)

Clause	THEMATIZED PARTICIPANT	PROCESS	OTHER PARTICIPANT
1	*Japan's alliance with Germany*	*was*	*inevitable?*
2	*historians*	*have very divergent interpretations*	*[on the inevitability of the Japanese-German alliance]*
3	*some [historians]*	*have argued*	*that ... (proposition)*
4	*other accounts ...*	*have viewed*	*the creation of the axis as ...*
5	*I*	*will analyse*	*the events leading to ...*
6	*[I]*	*will argue*	*that ... (proposition)*

Figure 3.4 Transitivity analysis of clauses in exemplar text (Text 2)

of the practising historian (*interpreting* and *analysing events, arguing for a position*). The analysis was able to highlight how this second use of the process of '*arguing*' (final sentence) explicitly framed the writer's response in the exemplar essay:

> '[I] will argue that it was principally the West's disregard of the interests of an emergent Japan that more than anything else led to its fatal joining with Nazi Germany . . . .'

This happens to be a position not dis-similar to the one implicit in the first student's introduction ('Japan as victim') but is realized discursively in a different way. In the sentence just given, similar 'material' processes are present (*disregarding of interests, joining of countries*), but these are thematically subordinate to what is focal in the main clause: the act of arguing.

The comparative analysis conducted with the student was significant for allowing him to see how the same historical content could be conceptualized and written about in such different ways. These specific language differences suggested a number of implications for a general approach to learning and writing in the subject. First was recognizing how the study of history at university level might be more usefully conceived not as an unproblematic laying out of historical events (material processes), but more as a consideration of the way different scholars have tended to view these events (mental and verbal processes) – a transition described in the history education literature as a shift from 'narrative to analysis' (MacDonald 1994; Coffin 1997). The student thought that this shift in his understanding would have the greatest effects on his approach to reading in the subject, requiring not the assimilation of certain key facts but rather identification of 'the particular take' an historian might have on events. The second outcome was that the student was able to obtain a clearer sense of how he might view himself as a 'participant' in his writing. On this matter, he indicated surprise at the explicit self-reference in the exemplar sample (*I will analyse . . . and argue*), saying that this did not square with his understandings about the acceptability of first person 'I' in academic writing.[1] The focus in the analysis on those 'processes' collocated with the I-participant (*argue* and *analyse*) provided a perspective on this usage: that is, how the deliberate inclusion of verbal and mental processes can be used strategically in an essay to mount a position.

At the conclusion of our discussion, the student felt that the analysis of 'participants' and 'processes' in the essay samples had helped him to recognize underlying differences in approach. He was keen to point out, however, that nowhere was a preferred approach to the essay signalled in the essay topic itself, noting that the topic's wording (*Why did Japan and Germany become allies in peace and war?*) referred only to the countries in question with no allusion at all to the alternative participants (*historian and author*) found to be so prominent in the exemplar sample. The student presumed that his mistake was to subject the topic to too 'literal' a reading, but wondered whether essay tasks could be designed in a way that would make expectations clearer to students. A transitivity analysis such as the one conducted here, based on alternative essay responses, is one way in which such expectations might be clarified.

Case 2: the art of 'affect'

The second case involved a very different learning context; the discipline was art criticism, and the student from a non-English speaking background (L1: Mandarin).

The student was referred to our unit by her Art Theory and History lecturer who had withheld awarding a mark for the major piece of work she had submitted because the written expression was poor and because, as the lecturer explained, 'the student just seemed to have missed the point of the exercise'. The lecturer was also concerned that some of the material might have been plagiarized.

In contrast to the previous essay task, in this topic abundant detail was provided for students in a subject guide. In brief, the task required students to visit the local state art gallery and to write an interpretive response to selected works – described as the genre of 'personal report' in the art education literature (Barnet 2003). In the instructions to students it was made clear that these prompt questions were not to be answered in some simple literal way, but to be used as 'cues' to guide them in their viewing of the work (see Text 3 for sample). The exercise, as the lecturer stressed, was intended principally to be one of students looking intimately at selected works of art and giving an account of 'what actually happens when [they] look'.

Although the lecturer had mentioned problems of expression it was clear from an analysis of the student's writing in the support tutorial session that the more serious issues were at a macro-level, in the way the student had approached the task overall. A sample of her writing, her response to the Monet work referred to in Text 3, is shown in Text 4. These were the main language data considered in the tutorial. In the tutorial, we also had a reproduction of the Monet work on hand (Figure 3.5).

In our initial discussions of the student's passage, I explained to her that her work was overly-focused on the artist himself, on certain biographical details (*Monet's renewed interest in the Seine*) and on the processes of his creating the work (*dispensing with established technique* and so on). Greater attention, I suggested, needed to be placed on her individual response to the artwork. The student admitted to

---

TEXT 3 *Writing task in* Art Theory and History.

Claude Monet, French, 1040 1926
Vetheuil, 1878. Oil on canvas. Felton Bequest 1937

How readily does one begin dividing the composition into three levels, the water, the land and the sky? . . . But would you say there is a strong geometric element in the work?

Accepting that there are these essential divisions, what are the chief colours proper to each? How much interpenetration is there between the forms of these parts? . . .

Are the images of the scene such as the church and the houses inviting? Do we see the place as homely and comforting or is the image imbued with a gentle but impersonal spirit of objectivity? . . . Does the perspective make us feel cut off from the water?

Regarding the texture and mood, the painting can profitably be compared with another which normally hangs nearby: Alfred Sisley. French 1840–99. *Hills behind St Nicaise*, 1890.

TEXT 4 Student's written response to the task.

Student response
Vetheuil (1878) Claude Monet. French 1840–1926

As one of the traveller wrote on the Seine, 'Vetheuil is a sort of sleepy hollow'. Monet's interest in the Seine, which seem to have been waning in his last days at Argenteuil, had returned to him one more [sic].

The painting of Vetheuil is of secluded and peaceful place with no human presence to disturb it. The colour, even in the subdued world, is deep and sensuous. The accepted practice dictated that a painting should be worked from dark to light, but Monet has clearly dispensed with this technique altogether. Instead he used in his pictures including *Vetheuil* a mid-tone, a blush of atmospheric colour somewhere in between light and shade, and developed the picture from there. In its early stages the painting must have been simply an association of colours, with little form or definition of the landscape, analysing the colours more precisely and increasing the understanding of its form as he did so. The extremities of the picture, the highlights and deep shadows, were added last literally written onto the surface of the canvas, and with these finishing touches Monet explained the finer details of the scene.

Figure 3.5 Monet's *Vetheuil* (reproduction). Claude Monet, French, 1840–1926: *Vetheuil* 1878, oil on canvas, 60.0 × 81.0 cm, Felton Bequest, 1937. National Gallery of Victoria, Melbourne, Australia.

not entirely understanding the prompt questions, but felt that she had provided an adequate account of the painting. She also expressed scepticism about the idea of including herself personally in the description, believing, like the student in the previous case, that this was not acceptable academic practice.

To break this developing impasse, it seemed sensible to look closely at the two texts together – the task and the student's response – to see what account of the learning situation an analysis of transitivity might provide. The analysis was focused first of all on the structure of the prompt questions in the task (Text 3) and, as in the previous analysis, began with identifying 'sentence subjects' or thematic participants. Not surprisingly, many of these were found to be the painting itself, along with various components of it (colours, images, perspective):

> . . . **the painting** can profitably be compared . . .
> What are the **chief colours** proper to each?
> Are **the images** of the scene such as the church and the houses inviting?
> Does **the perspective** make us feel cut off from the water?

The analysis showed, however, that equally prominent in the 'task discourse' was reference to human participants, realized in a variety of pronominal forms (one, you, we, us) but all indicative of the 'viewer' subject:

> How readily does **one** begin dividing the composition . . .?
> But would **you** say there is a strong geometric element . . .?
> Do **we** see the place as homely . . .?
> Does [it] make **us** feel cut off?

In the student's text, there was also an aggregation of lexis around the art object, as one would expect:

> The **painting** of Vetheuil is of [a] secluded and peaceful place
> The **colour** . . . is deep and sensuous . . .
> The **extremities of the picture**, the highlights and deep shadows, were added last

But where the two texts were found to differ was in their respective representations of human agency. In the task questions, as noted earlier, the agency evoked is first- and second-person variants of the viewer; in the student's response it is the third person – the artist:

> **Monet's** interest in the Seine . . . had returned to him
> . . . **he** used in his pictures . . . a mid-tone, a blush of atmospheric colour
> **Monet** explained the finer details of the scene

This difference was also reflected in the associated processes depicted in the two texts. The student's response was constructed mainly around 'material' processes in past time, ones that typically describe the creative activities of the artist (*working* a painting, *using* colour, *adding* shadows and highlights). In the task text, by contrast, most are what Halliday would classify as 'mental' processes, rendered in present time – ranging from general acts of *seeing* ('Do we see the place as homely?') and *feeling* ('Does the perspective make us feel cut off from the water?'), to more specific techniques such as *dividing* the picture up ('How readily does one begin dividing the composition into three levels?') or *making comparisons* with other works ('the painting

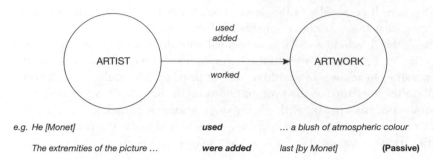

Figure 3.6 Principal transitivity relations (student response)

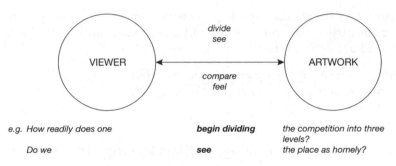

Figure 3.7 Principal transitivity relations (task)

can profitably be compared [by the viewer] with another which normally hangs nearby').

Out of this guided analysis, the schematic representations above of the two texts could be generated (Figures 3.6 and 3.7). For the student, these diagrams – in a more sparsely-labelled form than they are presented here[2] – showed in clear relief the basic incongruence between the task and her response to it, and this became the basis for some useful discussion. Firstly, the student wanted to stress that the approach she had adopted was based on the way she had learnt to write about art at school in China. She mentioned that, in 'the Chinese way', it was not possible to appraise a work without considering the artist who produced it, as well as the social and historical context in which they worked. Thus, she explained, one could get an 'objective' idea about the work in question. Such thinking about art is, of course, part of a long-established socially-oriented critical tradition (Barnet 2003) and in the context of Chinese education is readily associated with the foundational Maoist precept of art as ideology, such that any work of art is seen as necessarily reflecting 'an individual life within a given society' (Mao, cited in McDougall 1980: 75). Within this tradition, the eschewing of a purely 'aesthetic' appraisal of art (the approach manifestly prescribed in the *Art Theory and History* task) may account in part for the difficulties the student had experienced.

Another issue that emerged from the discussion, again related to the student's prior educational experiences in China, concerned her use of secondary sources. To pursue a broadly 'socio-historical' approach to an art work always requires seeking out background information, biography, social milieu and so on – the furnishing of a context that is not evident in the work itself. The student mentioned that she had done some preparatory reading, and that indeed this was unavoidable: 'I knew nothing about Monet, so I had to find out some things about him.' On this matter, it was necessary to point out the lack of documentation in her writing and to allude to the lecturer's concerns about possible plagiarism. This provided the occasion not only to clarify conventions of referencing in the discipline, but also to consider the broader issues of how sources might be used in one's written work, and how this will depend very much on the nature of the task and the types of judgements one is asked to make.

Perhaps the key learning activity in this episode, and the transferable skill to emerge from it, was the student's recognition that the writing tasks she needed to undertake in her course were now amenable to some analysis, rendering them less 'arcane' and 'arbitrary' for her. It seemed useful to point out to her that the two patterns of transitivity we had identified, in her writing and in the task on which it was based, correspond roughly to a first order distinction between broad 'productionist' and 'receptionist' orientations to art criticism (Barnet 2003: 20), and that it is possible to think of all commentaries on art (including those prescribed in writing tasks set for students) being slanted to some degree towards one of these two configurations. The transitivity analysis conducted was therefore useful in enabling the student to develop an understanding of variable epistemologics operating in the discipline.

Case 3: the sociological 'self' and 'other'

This final case, from the discipline of sociology, sees an application of transitivity not to the writing produced by students but to the analysis of essay topics alone. The outcomes of this teaching episode – an adjunct writing class for a group of mature-age first-year students (L1: English) – were perhaps significant not only for helping the students to recognize the particular epistemological frame they needed to adopt in the subject, but also for inadvertently provoking the beginnings of a critique of this frame.

The class was conducted at the request of a first-year sociology lecturer, who was concerned about his students' performance on previously submitted writing in the subject. Along with the usual comments about the quality of students' written expression and the lack of an analytical approach, the lecturer mentioned, interestingly, that his chief concern was that students were 'just too opinionated in their work'. When quizzed about this, the lecturer said he thought the real source of problems was students' failure to draw sufficiently on the sociological literature. Thus it seemed that the challenge in the writing class would be to help students tease out the differences between 'opinion' and 'analysis', and also to consider how they should go about integrating reading material in their writing.

The writing classes were focused on a major essay the students were preparing to write for which they had been given a range of topics, grouped under the various themes covered in the course (see Text 5). My preparatory work was to consider these topics and to work out what light, collectively, they might shed on the nature of sociological writing – or at least that required of students in the first year of their programme. Again, it was found useful to focus the analysis on the nature of transitivity relations.

Preliminary analysis of the topics suggested that a 'participant' common to all was what might be called a 'real-world phenomenon', and one that referred to the thematic content of the subject, namely: 'changes in women's position', 'inequality of women and men' (topics 1, 2); 'changes in family life', 'attitudes to marriage' (topics 3, 4); 'mental illness' (topic 5). But in a majority of the topics, juxtaposed with these 'real-world' participants was another type of participant – a more abstract mental or 'epistemic' phenomenon (see MacDonald 1994),[3] namely: *theoretical perspectives* (topic 2); *sociological perspectives* (topic 3); *sociological conceptions* (topic 5).

In the writing class, I began by asking students which topics they had selected to write on. Their choices were most interesting. Of the topics listed, the clear favourites were topics 1 ('changes in the position of women') and 4 ('attitudes to marriage'). When quizzed about the reasons for their choices some students mentioned their specific interest in these issues; others, however, suggested that these two topics would on the face of it be somehow 'easier to write on'. Drawing on the transitivity analysis above, it seemed that the students' intuitions about the relative difficulty of the tasks had some basis in the way that 'participant' roles were configured in the topics. Indeed, both of the preferred topics, as they are worded, can be distinguished from the others by their lack of specification of any epistemic phenomenon – that is, a 'theory', or 'perspective'. This difference can be seen clearly in a comparison of topics 1 and 2 below, the former being the most preferred by students and the latter eliciting no interest in spite of its coverage of similar thematic content.

TEXT 5 Essay topics in first-year Sociology subject.

Introduction to Sociology – Essay Topics

WOMEN, MEN AND MASCULINITIES

1. What are some of the major changes that have occurred in the position of women in Australia during the last 20 years? How important are these changes? What aspects of women's position are more intransigent? Why?
2. A number of different theoretical perspectives have been developed to account for the inequality of women and men. Which perspective do you find most persuasive? Why?

FAMILY AND MARRIAGE

3. Discuss the major influences on the changes in family life. Which sociological perspective do you find most useful in this discussion?
4. 'Marriage is as popular as it ever was in Australia'. Is this an accurate statement? Do we differ in our attitudes to marriage from countries like Sweden and the USA? If so, why do you think this is the case?

DEVIANCE AND SOCIAL CONTROL

5. Discuss the various conceptions of mental illness held by sociologists. How do these compare with 'common sense' conceptions?

1   What are some of the major changes that have occurred in the position of women in Australia during the last twenty years? How important are these changes? What aspects of women's position are more intransigent? Why?

2   A number of different *theoretical perspectives* have been developed to account for the inequality of women and men. Which *perspective* do you find most persuasive? Why?

On a literal reading of topic 1, we can see that the judgements students need to make are explicitly about aspects of the real-world phenomenon being considered (i.e. the 'importance' of changes in women's position; reasons for the 'intransigence' of some aspects of women's position and so on). In Figure 3.8, which shows the type of clause structure one would expect to see in an essay response to this topic, we can see the relatively straightforward way that judgements would plausibly be framed. The type of writing suggested by this configuration of participants can be characterized as an 'opinionative rhetoric' – a mode that students are largely familiar with when they enter the academy, and notably the type of writing the lecturer had identified in these students' previously submitted work. It is, for example, the rhetorical mode of many public forms of discourse, especially those relating to current affairs and social commentary (e.g. newspaper editorials, letters to the editor and so on). Interestingly, in the sociology literature it is this contrast with journalism that is often used to clarify sociology's distinctive epistemological outlook. As Willis describes it, journalism is concerned 'with more immediate aspects of social issues', and sociology by contrast with 'the underlying *theoretical aspects* of the processes of knowing about the social world' (Willis 2004: 133, emphasis added).

This focus on the 'theoretical' can be seen in topic 2, which requires a different order of judgement – in this case, one about the relative 'persuasiveness' of various theoretical perspectives on gender inequality. Here we can see that students are not being asked to give a view on the real-world phenomenon as such (the origins of gender equality), but instead to direct their thinking explicitly at what certain sociologists have written about this subject. The sample sentences in Figure 3.9 illustrate the additional discursive complexity involved in forming such a judgement: in effect, 'a judgement about a judgement'.

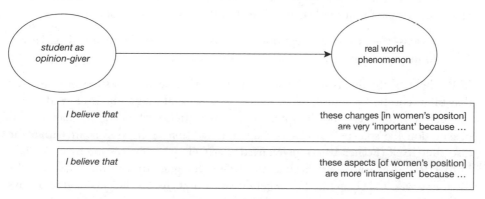

Figure 3.8 Sample content for essay topic 1 ('opinionative' rhetoric)

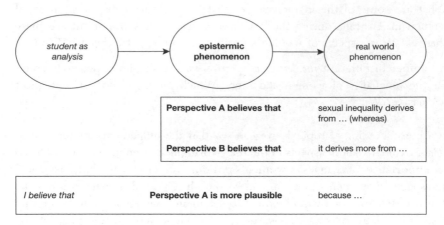

Figure 3.9 Sample content for essay topic 2 ('analytical' rhetoric)

As I have stressed throughout this article, in using transitivity analysis the purpose is not to train students in the methods of discourse analysis *per se*, but to use it in a strategic manner only – as a basis to help them better understand the nature of thinking and writing prescribed for them in their discipline areas. On the basis of the analysis conducted in this case, the main objective of the sociology support class was to help students grasp the essential differences between the two rhetorical modes identified, and to understand what implications these differences might have for the way they approached the subject matter of their essays (see also Wignell 1998, for a functional analysis of sociology texts).

Interestingly, these insights were also a spur for some students to begin critiquing the underlying pedagogy suggested by the essay tasks. For example, one student wondered whether it was realistic to expect students to be offering definitive comments about perspectives that 'we have only just found out about'. Wasn't this in itself a form of opinionated-ness, she wondered, that should not be encouraged: namely, the presenting of ill-informed judgements? A different, and perhaps more pointed criticism was the suggestion by another student that there may be something flawed about the discipline's apparent desire to separate itself from so-called 'common-sense' understandings. On this issue, she was particularly drawn to the final topic (topic 5) on the list, which makes this distinction explicit:

> 'Discuss the various conceptions of mental illness held by sociologists. How do these compare with "common sense" conceptions?'

In the light of the discussion she wondered whether such a question presupposed that the theoretical perspectives of sociologists were always to be preferred. If so, she believed this left the discipline open to criticism. Indeed, in making this observation the student had chanced upon a tradition of critique from within the discipline itself (Becher 1989), given particularly eloquent expression by C. Wright Mills (1959: 42) who as far back as the 1950s thought that a primary task for the discipline was 'to help grand theory get down from its useless heights' and find ways to 'describe and explain human conduct and society [more] plainly'.

This line of questioning from the students was an unanticipated, but most welcome one. From viewing subject matter in what the lecturer saw as a largely 'uncritical' way, some students were beginning to make the imaginative leap into what Ronald Barnett (2000) has called the realm of 'metacritique' – wherein the judgements that students make are less focused on disciplinary knowledge *per se*, and more on the structures in which this knowledge resides and the assumptions that inhere in them. These critical questions posed by the students in the writing class were ones that I, as a non-disciplinary specialist, was not qualified to answer, and which would need to be passed on to the lecturer. Arguably, it was in the micro-analysis of the language of the tasks given to them that these interrogations of the subject had become possible.

Conclusion

Recent research into writing in the academy emphasizes the great diversity of literary practices and forms across – and also within – disciplinary formations, taking in 'variations in knowledge structures, norms of inquiry, different vocabularies, differing standards of rhetorical intimacy' (Bhatia *et al.* 1997: 8). Reflecting on this diversity, Lea and Stierer (2000: 13) suggest that becoming a good writer involves a good deal more than just being able to reproduce ideas in accordance with universal writerly rules of 'grammar, usage and text organization'. Rather, they say, 'the whole process . . . involves making meaning in very specific academic contexts'. The considerable pedagogical challenge in the field of tertiary literacy then is to find ways to make these variable contexts comprehensible to students, or as Lea and Stierer suggest, to make explicit the ineffable 'ground rules' of disciplinary practices.

The method suggested in this article is one that begins at the most micro-level of analysis: the clause structure of key texts that make up the academic culture the students are seeking to enter. As I have sought to show, a focus on Hallidayan transitivity has the potential not only to clarify to students the immediate requirements of academic tasks, but also to help them understand some of the broader epistemological issues that may be at stake. These issues, which can be considered in relation to any writing task, can be summarized as follows:

- What is the principal 'participant' in a task – or what Charles Bazerman (1981) refers to as the 'object of study'? Is it for example a real-world phenomenon (like a work of art or the conduct of a war), or is it of a more epistemic nature (a critic's view of that work, or an historian's account of the war)?

- How is the student-author constructed as a 'participant' in the task? Explicitly or implicitly? And what types of cognitive 'processes' are suggested for them (seeing, arguing and so on)?

- What is the nature of the judgements ('attributes') that need to be made? And how do these judgements relate to 'the object of study'? – bearing in mind that the criteria for these judgements will be different, depending on which domain (real world or not) they are directed at (e.g. the *plausibility* of a social theory *vs* the *significance* of a social change).

- How is research constructed as 'participant' (or 'process') in the task, especially as it relates to the judgements that students need to make? Do students base these judgements on extant knowledge, on processes of primary research (like looking at a painting), on critical readings of secondary works and so on?

These were some of the issues that emerged from work with students within the sheltered confines of an academic support programme. The constant challenge for an academic adviser like me is to find ways to pass on these analytical techniques – both to students and staff – so that similar discussions might take place in the 'mainstream' context of their work together in the disciplines. It is to work towards this goal that the article has principally been written.

Notes

1.   The conundrum of creating an authorial voice in the student essay has been remarked on by a number of writers (Taylor 1989; Ivanic and Simpson 1992; Chanock 1997). As Taylor points out, on the one hand students are often encouraged to express their own point of view on a subject, but on the other hand may be told that nowhere should they have an explicit presence in their prose.
2.   For the purposes of this article I have included in the diagrams the specific Hallidayan categories for the contrasting transitivity relations (*Actor* ^ *Material Process* ^ *Goal* vs. *Senser* ^ *Mental Process* ^ *Phenomenon*); in the tutorial, however, such terminological detail was avoided. An important contrast between the two diagrams is the unidirectional arrow shown in the first diagram and the bidirectional arrow in the second. The latter configuration indicates the special nature of transitivity relations in the mental process clauses, such that the 'senser' (viewer) may be the principal doer of the action, as in *Do **we** see the place as homely?*; or alternatively it may be the 'phenomenon' (artwork) in this role, as in *Does **the perspective** make us feel cut off?*
3.   'Epistemic' phenomenon is the term used by MacDonald. The Hallidayan equivalent term is 'metaphenomenon'. For extended discussion of this concept as it relates to sociological knowledge, see Moore (2002).

References

Baldauf, R. (1996) 'Tertiary literacy policies: needs and practice', in Z. Golebiowski (ed.) *Policy and Practice of Tertiary Literacy: Selected proceedings of the First National Conference on Tertiary Literacy: Research and practice*, Vol. II (pp. 1–19). Melbourne: Victoria.

Barnet, S. (2003) *A Short Guide to Writing about Art* (7th edn). New York: Pearson.

Barnett, R. (2000) *The Limits of Competence: Knowledge, higher education and society*. Buckingham: The Society for Research into Higher Education/Open University Press.

Bazerman, C. (1981) 'What written knowledge does: three examples of academic discourse'. *Philosophy of the Social Sciences* 11 (3): 367–87.

Becher, T. (1989) *Academic Tribes and Territories: Intellectual inquiry and the cultures of disciplines*. Milton Keynes: Open University Press.

Bhatia, V., Candlin, C. and Hyland, K. (1997) *Academic Communication in Disciplinary Communities*. Hong Kong: Department of English, City University of Hong Kong (Mimeo).

Chanock, K. (1997) 'Never say I: the writer's voice in essays in the humanities', in Z. Golebiowski (ed.) *Policy and Practice of Tertiary Literacy: Selected proceedings of the First National Conference on Tertiary Literacy: Research and practice*, Vol. II (pp. 54–63). Melbourne: Victoria.

Coffin, C. (1997) 'Constructing and giving value to the past: an investigation into secondary school history', in F. Christie and J.R. Martin (eds) *Genre and Institutions: Social processes in the workplace and school* (pp. 196–230). Cassell: London.

Coffin, C. (2003) 'Exploring different dimensions of language use'. *ELT Journal* 57 (1): 11–18.

Cook, G. (1987) *Discourse*. Oxford: Oxford University Press.

Cope, B. and Kalantzis, M. (1994) 'How a genre approach to literacy can transform the way writing is taught', in B. Cope and M. Kalantzis (eds) *The Powers of Literacy: A genre approach to teaching writing* (pp. 1–21). London: The Falmer Press.

Fairclough, N. (1995) *Critical Discourse Analysis: The critical study of language*. London: Longman.

Freedman, A. and Medway, P. (1994) 'Introduction', in A. Freedman and P. Medway (eds) *Learning and Teaching Genre* (pp. 1–22). Portsmouth, NH: Heinemann.

Halliday, M.A.K. (1994) *An Introduction to Functional Grammar* (2nd edn). London: Edward Arnold.

Hunston, S. and Sinclair, J. (2000) 'A local grammar of evaluation', in S. Hunston and G. Thompson (eds) *Evaluation in Text: Authorial stance and the construction of discourse* (pp. 75–101). Oxford: Oxford University Press.

Ivanic, R. and Simpson, J. (1992) 'Who's who in academic writing', in N. Fairclough (ed.) *Critical Language Awareness* (pp. 144–73). London: Longman.

Jakobson, R. (1960) 'Closing statement: linguistics and poetics', in T.A. Sebeok (ed.) *Style in Language* (pp. 350–77). Cambridge, MA: MIT Press.

Johns, A. (1997) *Text, Role and Context: Developing academic literacies*. Cambridge: Cambridge University Press.

Lea, M. and Stierer, B. (2000) 'Editor's Introduction', in M. Lea and B. Stierer (eds) *Student Writing in Higher Education: New contexts* (pp. 1–15). Buckingham: The Society for Research into Higher Education/Open University Press.

MacDonald, S.P. (1994) *Professional Academic Writing in the Humanities and Social Sciences*. Carbondale and Edwardsville, IL: Southern Illinois University Press.

McDougall, B. (1980) *Mao Zedong's 'Talks at the Yan'an Conference on Literature and Art': A translation of the 1943 text with commentary*. Ann Arbor, MI: University of Michigan Press.

Mann, W. and Thompson, S. (1989) 'Rhetorical structure theory: a theory of text organization', in L. Polanyi (ed.) *The Structure of Discourse* (pp. 85–96). Norwood, NJ: Ablex.

Martin, J. (1992) *English Text: System and structure*. Amsterdam: Benjamins.

Mathiessen, C. (1995) *Lexico-Grammatical Cartography: English systems*. Dallas, TX: International Language Sciences Publishers.

Mills, C. Wright (1959) *The Sociological Imagination*. New York: Oxford University Press.

Moore, T. (2002) 'Knowledge and agency: a study of metaphenomenal discourse in textbooks from three disciplines'. *English for Specific Purposes* 21 (4): 347–66.

Pelling, N. (2001) 'A new approach to non-traditional student recruitment and retention'. *Australian Universities Review* 44 (1): 18–20.

Popper, K.R. (1979) *Objective Knowledge: An evolutionary approach* (2nd edn). Oxford: Oxford University Press.

Swales, J. (1990) *Genre Analysis: English in academic and research settings*. Cambridge: Cambridge University Press.

Taylor, G. (1980) 'The grammar of confusion'. *Journal of Literary Semantics* 9 (2): 55–72.

Taylor, G. (1989) *The Student's Writing Guide for the Arts and Social Sciences*. Cambridge: Cambridge University Press.

Threadgold, T. (1994) 'Grammar, genre and the ownership of literacy'. *Idiom* 2: 20–8.

Wignell, P. (1998) 'Technicality and abstraction in social science', in J.R. Martin and R. Veel (eds) *Reading Science* (pp. 297–326). London: Routledge.

Willis, E. (2004) *The Sociological Quest: An introduction to the study of social life*. Sydney: Allen and Unwin.

Chapter 4

Elizabeth Armstrong, Alison Ferguson, Lynne Mortensen and Leanne Togher

Acquired language disorders
Some functional insights

Introduction

The study of language disorder has historically encompassed a number of different perspectives. A significant amount of research has been undertaken using individuals with acquired brain damage as windows to brain function, e.g. from the studies which implied localisation of particular language function in particular parts of the brain based on aphasic individuals' performance on language tasks (e.g. Geschwind 1965; Goodglass and Kaplan 1983; Luria 1966), to the sophisticated studies currently being undertaken, focusing more on the complex neurological processes which might be occurring during language processing (e.g. Cao *et al.* 1999; Naeser *et al.* 2004). Another perspective involves what the breakdown of language might tell us about normal language function and indeed about the organisation of language regardless of neurological correlates. And yet another perspective involves the question of intervention – in finding out more about language disorder, can we learn better ways of facilitating language recovery or language improvement in the client or devise better ways to work with the person with the language disorder as well as assist their communication partners to overcome the social limitations they might encounter as a result of the disorder?

This chapter addresses the latter two perspectives, exploring a social semiotic approach to language disorder. It focuses on what happens when communication

Edited version of Armstrong, E., Ferguson, A. J., Mortensen, L., and Togher, L. (2005) 'Acquired language disorders: some functional insights', in Webster, J. Matthiessen, J. and Hasan, R. (eds), *Continuing Discourse on Language: A functional perspective*, Vol. 1, pp. 383–412, London: Equinox.

becomes difficult for adult speakers and their conversational partners due to one speaker having restricted access to linguistic resources as a result of acquired brain damage. Through the inspiration of Halliday and Hasan, the authors have explored this area for a number of years, with a clinical perspective the focus of our work. Coming to linguistics from speech pathology backgrounds, we are concerned with the nature of the language disorder, how it affects speakers in their everyday conversations and whether linguistic principles can assist in remediation of, or compensation for, the disorder. We have been particularly interested in the application of Systemic Functional Linguistic (SFL) theory to language disorder, as it offers a contextualised view of language rather than the decontextualised view offered by psycholinguistic models traditionally used in the field of speech pathology.

[. . .]

SFL: a different perspective

Traditional linguistic and psycholinguistic interpretations of language disorder come from an intrapsychological framework in which the breakdown is seen as a disruption to the linguistic rule system within the individual or in a blockage of access to particular modules of language within that individual (Caramazza and Hillis 1990; Ellis and Young 1988; Kay et al. 1996; Nickels 2002). Descriptions of aphasic language include such terms as 'lexical processing difficulties', 'a sentence processing deficit', 'a deficit in the phonological output lexicon'. In such a framework, language abilities are tested on a series of decontextualised language tasks, e.g. the naming of objects or pictures, for which specific processing abilities are proposed to be prerequisite. Little attention is paid to 'real-life' discourse in which meanings are exchanged for a variety of everyday purposes.

[. . .]

Instead of analysing language into simply formal categories, we have opted for functional categories which provide a means of analysing language in social terms; the SFL model has, thus, encouraged us to examine the wording from the point of view of meaning in context, allowing us to attend to both form and function in context.

[. . .]

A social semiotic approach has also encouraged us to examine the coconstruction of discourse between conversational partners and the way this is managed by speakers – an enormous move from the monologic focus of analysis and one that greatly enriches and yet complicates notions of brain and language relationships. Individuals with language problems often still manage to communicate. They can achieve particular meaning exchanges in a variety of different ways. This suggests that use of linguistic resources can be 'different' but still successful in realising a range of meanings and that contextual factors play an enormous role in listener interpretation of what is said in a particular context of situation. Not of least importance here is the 'other' participant's willingness and ability to contribute to making sense of the situation, bringing all shared information to bear upon the interpretation.

What has SFL shown us about language disorder?

Aphasia: the lexicogrammar from an ideational perspective

One of the most obvious characteristics of the speech of individuals with aphasia is the breakdown of the lexicogrammar. The transitivity system is certainly disturbed – nominal groups are simplified, lexical items are omitted (e.g. *I went to the . . .*) or substituted (e.g. *I ate the lemonade*) and word order is disrupted (e.g. *doctor . . . me . . . operation . . . have me*). While these disturbances were described in formal grammatical terms for many years, little research focused on the effects of such disturbances on overall text production. The application of SFL, with its insight in aspects of textuality, has provided some insight into such connections between the lexicogrammar and overall text structure and coherence (Armstrong 1987; Ferguson 1992; Mortensen 1992; Peng 1992). In an investigation into transitivity patterns, Armstrong (1997) examined the discourse of five 'fluent' aphasic speakers longitudinally over a 12-month period following their strokes and focused on the different process types the speakers used to convey a variety of meanings. On a recount task, discussing their most enjoyable holidays, two initially used almost only 'material' process clauses (close to 100 per cent) to describe the event. This led to an 'action'-based recount with few opinions, insights or descriptions of participants evident. An example is the following (with material processes indicated in bold) of an aphasic speaker (RD) at one month post stroke:

> That (–)[*] up the Gold Coast . . . good one yeah . . . pick on that one . . . what we **did** with the kids . . . Mum **did** . . . **went** and **played** . . . we **did** things . . . uh . . . **went** to . . . the pool **went** swimming and walks . . . **get** into things . . . we'd **get** I'd like the kids out and **make** 'em like kelevans . . . kids on kids . . . and they like to **get out** and **make** junks . . . **make** things **make** a giant (–) . . . **gotta get out** and do it . . . kids (–) we **get away** by ourselves . . . **go out** and uh . . . **play** silly buggers and **play around** a lot . . . we **have some fun** that way

Six months into this speaker's recovery, however, a different pattern emerged. As well as more content in general and more complex grammatical constructions, a greater variety of processes emerged as well as more specific verbs realising these processes. More mental and relational processes in particular were evident, leading to much more information on the speaker's and his family's feelings about the holiday and more description of participants, location and evaluations. The same aphasic speaker, RD, at six months post stroke (mental processes underlined below, relational processes in capitals, materials in bold):

Clinician: Last time you were telling me about the Gold Coast
RD: The Gold Coast . . . oh we **went** up there with the kids the last time . . . oh
CI: Yes tell me about that
RD: Uh that was the two boys over here . . . they WERE what fourteen and
   fifteen . . . fifteen sixteen something like that . . . and Mum and meself . . .

---

* (–) references an unintelligible lexical or grammatical item

uh . . . we **went** up there . . . we only HAD a week day seven days uh . . . ten days altogether cos we **went** up there for a couple of days seven days actually at the Gold Coast and uh . . . oh we **had fun** with the kids (–) Gold . . . Seaworld with the girls uh they could SPEND a full day couple of days there . . . not trouble to **get** it all and we went all places round [[they **went**]] . . . then we just HAD our days at the um . . . motel [[where we **stayed**]] we WERE right at the pool . . . ad they HAD it all <u>worked out</u> . . . twelve . . . looks . . . twelve . . . uh to **get** to 'em . . . just to **get** from out of her place into the pool (–) and you' RE in and for the kids that WAS good and we'd **go** down to the pool . . . we **did** our time up there . . . oh they <u>thought</u> it WAS good . . . they could HAVE anything [[they <u>wanted</u>]] they <u>thought</u> we WERE queens

[. . .]

Further examination of the process types used by these speakers compared to non-brain-damaged speakers (matched for gender, age and education) on the same tasks (Armstrong 2001) found relatively restricted use of certain process types in the discourse of two of the four aphasic speakers. As noted above, the aphasic speakers, in contrast to their non-brain-damaged counterparts, used fewer relational and mental processes, which resulted in more materially action-based texts, with little description, self-reflection or evaluation on the events recounted.

[. . .]

The interpersonal metafunction related to Traumatic Brain Injury

It is now well recognised that communication problems following a Traumatic Brain Injury (TBI) are distinctly different from those subsequent to a more focal lesion such as occurs in a stroke (or a penetrating head injury) and these require different approaches to assessment and remediation. This has come from the recognition that, due to the multifocal nature of TBI, there is a complex inter-play of cognitive, linguistic, physical, behavioural and organic psychosocial factors, which may contribute to the communication difficulties experienced. In turn, communication problems can have a significant effect on psychosocial outcomes. The ability to communicate successfully is crucial to being able to maintain relationships and to establishing vocational and leisure activities. It is therefore logical that by establishing ways of measuring and improving communication in these individuals, there may be a significant benefit in their everyday lives.

[. . .]

One of the key problems of people with TBI is difficulty matching appropriate language use to the tenor of the situation. Assuming that interaction is the most crucial formative factor in the enactment of social relations, the inability of people with TBI to use tenor appropriate to some social situation can have a profound effect when it comes to social roles such as father, husband or friend. Unfortunately the majority of studies of the communication of people with TBI have been conducted with speech pathologists or research assistants as the communication partner. In such situations, the tenor is fixed with a power imbalance in favour of the therapist/speech pathologist and a lack of familiarity between participants, thus limiting the contributions of the person with TBI, thus failing to measure the person with TBI in their everyday social roles:

To shed light on the real-life interactions of people with TBI, Togher and colleagues (Togher *et al.* 1997a, 1997b; Togher and Hand 1999) have conducted a series of studies investigating a range of communication situations, including a cross section of communication partners, speaker roles and genres. The goal of these studies has been to examine the contributions of the person with TBI, as well as the effect of their communicative partner on such interactions of people with TBI, so as to establish effective therapeutic guidelines for treatment. Given the reciprocal relationship between tenor and the interpersonal metafunction, a number of analyses have been used across stratal levels including exchange structure analysis (Berry 1981; Ventola 1987) and generic structure potential analysis (Hasan 1985) to examine the communication of people with TBI.

Results of studies into the communication of people with TBI have shown that genre and speaker characteristics (such as familiarity, status, power imbalance) are powerful determinants of the language options to people with TBI (Togher *et al.* 1997a). For example, in one situation, where a person with severe TBI was making an inquiry to a police officer on the telephone regarding the return of his driver's license, exchange structure analysis revealed that there were large discrepancies between his interaction and that of his brother (Togher *et al.* 1997a). Normally a request for information would be met with provision of that information. However, in this case, the policeman turned the request into a series of exchanges where he demanded the caller's name, asked for information that he already knew (see moves 24–25 in Table 4.1), and checked whether the caller had understood (moves 32, 25, 43). Consider the following transcript of this call (moves numbered):

Table 4.1 Interaction between person with TBI (S) and a police officer (P) regarding the return of a driver's license after sustaining a brain injury

11	K1	S: Actually I've had a bad car accident
12	Bch	P: Yeah
13	K1	S: I need to get my license back (unintell)
14	K2f	P: Right yeah.
15	K2	P: What's your name?
16	K1	S: R.C.
17	Cfrq	P: R.C. is it?
18	Rcfrq	S: Yeah
19	K2f	P: Right
20	K2	S: And if you could tell me if there are any other requirements I've gotta pass in order to get my license back
21	Bch	P: Right
22	K2	S: What I've gotta go through to get it back in other words
23	K1	P: Yep. Yep.
24	dK1	P: Do do you know what the Roads and Traffic Authority is?
25	dK1	P: The R.T.A. where you go and get your license from
26	K2	S: Yeah down at Kogarah
27	K1	P: Yeah right
28	K2f	S: Sure
29	K1	P: Um what what what you have to do is if you can um if you have to go to the R.T.A.
30	K1	P: They'll put your application in to get a license

31	Bch	S: Sure
32	Check	P: Right? If you can understand that
33	Rcheck	S: Yeah
34	K1-Fg	P: But prior to that, um what you have you have to go
35	Check	P: ah you know a driving school?
36	Rcheck	S: Yeah
37	K1	P: Right and they um have rehabilitation people that ah can ah put you through oh like your driving lessons,
38	Bch	S: Sure
39	K1-Fg	P: and then they decide whether you know
40	Cp	S: Whether you're capable
41	Rcp	P: Yeah whether you're then capable to go and get your license
42	Bch	S: Sure
43	Check	P: Right?
44	K2f	S: OK then

Key:
P = Police officer   S = Caller with TBI   K1 = Primary knower
Bch = backchannel   K2 = Secondary knower   cfrq = confirmation request
rcfrq = response to cfrq   K2f = follow-up   dK1 = teaching move
check = checking move   rcheck = response to check   cp = collocational prompt
rcp = response to cp   K1-Fg = fragment

Compare the above with the text in Table 4.2: interaction between the control subject and a police officer where the above speaker's non-brain-damaged brother (C) requests information from the same police officer:

Table 4.2 C making an inquiry to a police officer

2	K2	C: Um I just had to find out what the procedure is for obtaining a license
3	Bch	P: Right
4	K2	C: if it's been cancelled due to head injuries
5	check	P: Head injuries was it?
6	clrq	P: How how bad were the injuries mate?
7	rclrq	C: Um well . . . head injuries
8	bch	P: Right
9	rclrq	C: and it's still . . . well . he's not better yet and it's been four years
10	cfrq	P: Right it's been four years has it?
11	rcfrq	C: Yeah
12	K1	P: Right what has to what has to happen is he has to be ah go through rehabilitation um . . . by an approved driving school
13	bch	C: Ah right
14	K1	P: There are certain agencies to go through
15	clrq	C: So they de they determine
16	rclrq	P: Yeah go and speak to a driving school
17	rclrq	P: it doesn't really matter which one
18	K1	P: and just tell them ah you know the problem that you have

Key: P = Police officer; C = non-brain-damaged brother of Caller S; clrq = clarification request; rclrq = response to clrq

Here the information is given after some request for clarification (clrq) but without checking that C had understood. These differences reflect a larger picture of the interactional changes that frequently affect people with TBI. The role of the communication partner in these interactions (i.e. the police officer) had a significant effect on the communication options made available to S and C. Contrast this with a text presented in Table 4.3: an interaction between S and two school students where, as part of a community education program on safe driving practices, S in conversation with some school students is giving information about the effect of a TBI on a person's life. Note how this information is jointly construed between the interactants.

Table 4.3 Interaction between man with TBI and 2 school students, A and B, regarding having a brain injury

129	K2	B: So were you in hospital for a while or after the accident?
130	K1	S: About fourteen months
131	excl	A: Fourteen months!
132	K1	S: El-Eleven months I was in there permanently
133	bch	A: Yeah
134	K1	S: and then for the next five months I only used to go in just to the gym while my parents were in the hospital just spend the day there
135	bch	B: Oh yeah
136	K1	S: and sometimes long weekends in hospital
137	K1	B: long weekends – that's no good in hospital
138	K2	B: Did um – couldn't wait to get out eh?
139	K1	S: Yep – my most – the thing I enjoyed the most was standing on my own two legs for three seconds after the accident

Key: A and B = Students; S = man with TBI; excl = exclamation

In this text S was able to share information with the school students without having his contributions checked or questioned. This information was given appropriately and with confidence. The reason *why* S was able to do this lies in the context of situation (i.e. the field, tenor and mode) and *how* he did this can be described across at least three levels of language active in context. The difference between S's interaction with the police officer and the students was described with reference to the interdependent relationship between the different stratal levels of language. The three levels were genre (using generic structure potential analysis), discourse semantics (using exchange structure analysis) and lexicogrammar (politeness markers from mood and modality analysis). Applying this model to S's interaction with the students shows the interaction was an expert interview which was realised by S being primarily an information giver, with fewer politeness markers being produced than he did in an information requesting role. S's interaction with the police officer was a service encounter, where S was in an information requesting role, which was realised by an increased use of politeness markers.

The person with TBI was more likely to be asked questions regarding the accuracy of his information giving. The police officer pushed the burden of giving accurate information onto S and because S did not give this information in a ritualised manner, typical of official interaction, the police officer was also unable to play his role effectively. This is not surprising given that interactive roles are reciprocally constructed. In contrast when in a powerful teaching role with school students, where he was asked to talk about the experience of having a brain injury, the person with TBI had control over the information-giving therefore allowing him the opportunity to exercise language choices not available with the police officer (Togher 2000; Togher and Hand 1999) (see Table 4.3 above). If this person had been assessed with a routine clinical assessment of procedural, narrative and conversational discourse with the clinician, these observations would not have been possible. Being informed of a person's intact abilities in some situations (such as when giving information to school students) can assist the clinician to provide appropriate positive communicative opportunities (such as being involved in community education programs), where this would not have been considered an option based on his standard clinical presentation. Contrasting these two interactions highlights the effect of varied tenor and speaker role on the language produced by both the person with TBI and their communication partner. Information requests to a person of authority limits the discourse choices, whereas information-giving in a position of authority broadens them.

An important implication of Togher's work has been training communication partners to promote the person with TBI's communication abilities. The early studies showed that communication partners used a range of strategies to deal with perceived communicative ineffectiveness, which were deleterious for the person with TBI, thus making the interaction even worse (Togher et al. 1997a, 1997b; Togher and Hand 1998, 1999). This led to the evaluation of a training program, based on SFL principles, aimed at improving the communication of police officers during service encounters with people with TBI (Togher et al. 2004). Twenty police officers were randomly assigned to two groups (training or control). Prior to the six-week training program, participants with TBI made a routine telephone inquiry to the police officers. Training focused on specific aspects of telephone inquiries previously documented to be aberrant in service encounters of people with TBI. For example, participants were asked to analyse transcripts to identify the generic structural elements of a service encounter and to highlight areas of texts they thought were problematic and provide strategies to improve the interaction. Following the training program, police subjects received another telephone service inquiry. Service encounters were transcribed and analysed using generic structure potential analysis (see Hasan 1985; Ventola 1987).

Comparison of pre- and post-training measures indicated that trained police had learned strategies to successfully establish the nature of the inquiry, provide a clear answer to the inquiry and ensure appropriate leave-taking resulting in more efficient, focused interactions in the post-training telephone calls. People with TBI also altered their communication in the post-training calls with reduced episodes of unrelated utterances and an increased proportion of the interaction devoted to completing the service encounter. This appeared to be in response to the communicative options they were given.

Using the theory of SFL has significantly enhanced evaluating the communication of people with TBI. One of the key tasks facing a clinician working with a person with TBI is describing and measuring the communication problem in a way that reflects everyday abilities, which is meaningful for the person with TBI and their social networks and provides a guide to treatment. Families and friends are often devastated by a person's changed communication ability after a severe TBI and are keen to participate in the rehabilitation process. This has led to studies examining people with TBI with peers who also have TBI (Smith *et al.* 2004) as well as investigating the effect of interacting with a friend without TBI across a range of discourse genres (Togher 2004). The findings of these studies suggest that it is of paramount importance to look beyond the interactions of the person in the clinic room to their communication in a range of speaking situations, across distinct activities and distinct communication partners. Without information obtained from such examinations, we cannot claim to have a clear picture of the person's true communication ability, thus raising the possibility that treatment decisions may not be completely valid.

[. . .]

Treatment issues

Three primary approaches to language treatment exist – one based on a restorative model, one on a compensatory model and one referred to as a 'social' model. In the restorative model, the therapist works with the client to improve their impairment, e.g. naming skills, conversational skills. In the compensatory model, the focus changes to assisting the person to compensate for the disorder in some way, e.g. using cue cards to facilitate conversation, encouraging the use of gesture/intonation to add meaning to verbal attempts. The social model rejects the notion of disorder completely and suggests that the language impairment is not something that lies within the individual, for him/her to have 'repaired' or to even compensate. This approach reinforces the notion that communication is a negotiated process and that any interventions should involve certainly the individual's communication partners as well as the community at large, working on ways in which the person with the language difficulties can gain access to his/her social networks and participate in social life.

SFL principles can be incorporated into all of these models in some way. One of the most important premises of any therapy based on SFL principles is that language is used for a purpose, rather than being employed as a decontextualised set of items in an artificial task restricted to word or clause level. Different genres relevant to the individual's everyday life become the focus of treatment, with different systems targeted for improvement, e.g. transitivity, cohesion, clause complexing (see Armstrong 1991, 1993, 1995; Ferguson 2000). Semantic aspects such as generic structure can be 're-learned' or the principles of exchange can be taught to conversational partners (Mortensen 2000, Togher 2000; Togher *et al.* 2004). Conversely, the individual's strengths can be maximised, for example if their ideational resources are significantly impoverished, their interpersonal resources may be encouraged (Ferguson 1992).

Conclusion

The importance of exploring language disorder from the perspective of language in everyday contexts has been increasingly acknowledged in recent years (Holland

1982, 1991; Hopper and Holland 2002; Lubinski 2001; Worrall 1999). SFL has contributed significantly to investigations by providing researchers and clinicians with a theoretical framework in which language can be viewed from numerous angles – across different strata and metafunctions, as well as at different ranks. A change in focus from an intrapsychological approach to looking at disorder from an interpsychological viewpoint has enabled researchers and clinicians to examine breakdowns in communication as they occur in everyday situations. It has also enabled them to investigate the impact of the extralinguistic context on the use of linguistic resources, as well as the way(s) in which restricted resources impact on the construction of context for not only the speaker with an acquired language disorder but also for their conversational partners. Such advances in the field suggest that further applications of SFL to the investigation of language disorders of both acquired and developmental origin hold much promise.

References

Armstrong, E. (1987) 'Cohesive harmony in aphasic discourse and its significance in listener perception of coherence', in R. H. Brookshire (ed.) *Clinical Aphasiology* (pp. 210–15). Minneapolis, MN: BRK.

Armstrong, E. (1991) 'The potential of cohesion analysis in the analysis and treatment of aphasic discourse'. *Clinical Linguistics and Phonetics* 5 (1): 39–51.

Armstrong, E. M. (1993) 'Aphasia rehabilitation: a sociolinguistic perspective', in A. Holland and M. Forbes (eds) *Aphasia Treatment: World perspectives*. San Diego, CA: Singular Pub.

Armstrong, E. (1995) 'A linguistic approach to the functional skills of aphasic speakers', in C. Code and D. Muller (eds) *Treatment of Aphasia: From theory to practice* (pp. 70–89). London: Whurr Publishing Company.

Armstrong, E. (1997) 'A grammatical analysis of aphasic discourse: changes in meaning-making over time'. Unpublished PhD thesis. Sydney: Macquarie University, Sydney.

Armstrong, E. (2001) 'Connecting lexical patterns of verb usage with discourse meanings in aphasia'. *Aphasiology* 15: 1029–46.

Berry, M. (1981) 'Systemic linguistics and discourse analysis: a multilayered approach to exchange structure', in C. Coulthard and M. Montgomery (eds) *Studies in Discourse Analysis* (pp. 120–45). London, UK: RKP.

Cao, Y., Vikingstad, E. M., George, K. P., Johnson, A. F. and Welch K.M. (1999) 'Cortical language activation in stroke patients recovering from aphasia with functional MRI'. *Stroke* 30 (11): 2331–40.

Caramazza, A. and Hillis, A. E. (1990) 'Where do semantic errors come from?' *Cortex* 26: 95–122.

Ellis, A. W. and Young, A. W. (1988) *Human Cognitive Neuropsychology*. Hove, East Sussex: Lawrence Erlbaum.

Ferguson, A. (1992a) 'Interpersonal aspects of aphasic communication'. *Journal of Neuro-linguistics* 7 (4): 277–94.

Ferguson, A. (2000) 'Maximising communicative effectiveness', in N. Muller (ed.) *Pragmatic Approaches to Aphasia* (pp. 53–88). Amsterdam: John Benjamins.

Geschwind, N. (1965) 'Disconnexion syndromes in animals and man'. *Brain* 88: 237–94.

Goodglass, H. and Kaplan, E. (1983) *The Assessment of Aphasia and Related Disorders*. Philadelphia, PA: Lea and Febiger.

Hasan, R. (1985) 'The structure of a text', in M.A.K. Halliday and R. Hasan (eds) *Language, Context and Text: Aspects of language in a social semiotic perspective* (pp. 52–69). Geelong, Vic.: Deakin University Press.

Holland, A. (1982) 'Observing functional communication of aphasic adults'. *Journal of Speech and Hearing Disorders* 47: 50–6.

Holland, A. (1991) 'Pragmatic aspects of intervention in aphasia'. *Journal of Neurolinguistics* 6: 197–211.

Hopper, T. and Holland, A. (2002) 'Conversational coaching: treatment outcomes and future directions'. *Aphasiology* 16 (7): 745–61.

Kay, J., Lesser, R. and Coltheart, M. (1996) 'Psycholinguistic Assessments of Language Processing in Aphasia (PALPA): an introduction'. *Aphasiology* 19: 159–215.

Lubinski, R. (2001) 'Environmental systems approach to adult aphasia', in M. Mentis and C. A. Prutting (1987) Cohesion in the discourse of normal and head-injured adults. *Journal of Speech and Hearing Research* 30: 88–98.

Luria, A. R. (1966) *Higher Cortical Functions in Man*. New York: Basic Books.

Mortensen, L. (1992) 'A transitivity analysis of discourse in dementia of the Alzheimer's type'. *Journal of Neurolinguistics* 7 (4): 309–21.

Mortensen, L. (2000) 'Systemic functional perspectives on acquired language disorder: a strength versus deficit approach', in M. Hernandez (ed.) *Revista Canaria De Estudios Ingleses*. Special issue on intercultural and textual approaches to systemic functional linguistics 40: 209–25.

Naeser, M. A., Martin, P. I., Baker, E. H., Hodge, S. M., Sczerzenie, S. E., Nicholas, M., Palumbo, C. L., Goodglass, H., Wingfield, A., Samaraweera, R., Harris, G., Baird, A., Renshaw, P. and Yurgelun-Todd, D. (2004) 'Overt propositional speech in chronic nonfluent aphasia studied with the dynamic susceptibility contrast fMRI method'. *Neuroimage* 22 (1): 29–41.

Nickels, L. (2002) 'Therapy for naming disorders: revisiting, revising and reviewing'. *Aphasiology* 16: 935–80.

Peng, V. (1992) 'The use of reference items in aphasic and normal conversations'. *Journal of Neurolinguistics* 7 (4): 295–308.

Smith, V., Togher, L., Taylor, C. and Grant, S. (2004) 'The effect of discourse genre on communication opportunity in individuals with cognitive-communication impairment following traumatic brain injury'. *Brain Impairment* 5: 12.

Togher, L. (2000) 'Giving information: the importance of context on communicative opportunity for people with traumatic brain injury'. *Aphasiology* 14 (4): 365–90.

Togher, L. (2004) 'Assessing communication after traumatic brain injury (TBI): discourse tasks are not all created equal'. *Brain Impairment* 5: 13.

Togher, L. and Hand, L. (1998) 'Use of politeness markers with different communication partners: an investigation of five subjects with traumatic brain injury'. *Aphasiology* 12: 491–504.

Togher, L. and Hand, L. (1999) 'The macrostructure of the interview: are traumatic brain injury interactions structured differently to control interactions?' *Aphasiology* 13: 709–23.

Togher, L., Hand, L. and Code, C. (1997a) 'Analysing discourse in the traumatic brain injury population: telephone interactions with different communication partners'. *Brain Injury* 11 (3): 169–89.

Togher, L., Hand, L. and Code, C. (1997b) 'Measuring service encounters in the traumatic brain injury population'. *Aphasiology* 11: 491–504.

Togher, L. and Hand, L. (1998) 'Use of politeness markers with different communication partners: an investigation of five subjects with traumatic brain injury'. *Aphasiology* 12: 491–504.

Togher, L. and Hand, L. (1999) 'The macrostructure of the interview: are traumatic brain injury interactions structured differently to control interactions?' *Aphasiology* 13: 709–23.

Togher, L., McDonald, S., Code, C. and Grant, S. (2004) 'Training communication partners of people with traumatic brain injury: a randomised controlled trial'. *Aphasiology* 18 (4): 313–35.

Ventola, E. (1987) *The Structure of Social Interaction: A systemic approach to the semiotics of service encounters*. London: Pinter.

Worrall, L. (1999) *Functional Communication Therapy Planner*. Oxford: Winslow Press.

Chapter 5

Mira Kim

Translation error analysis
A Systemic Functional Grammar approach

Introduction

One of the most routine tasks for most translation teachers is checking or proofreading students' translations. The forms and methods of indicating errors may vary depending on purpose or individual teaching style. Some teachers may simply indicate "incorrect" parts with a wavy line and "correct but could be better" parts with a straight line. Pym (1992) and Kussmaul (1995) refer to the former as binary errors and the latter as non-binary errors. Others may correct every single error and suggest their own way of translating problematic parts of source texts. Either way, it is not easy to explain or articulate why problematic parts are identified as such. Classroom discussion is normally based on the teacher's opinions, if not judgements, which are based on his/her experience and intuition.

It is also true that even professional translators often find it difficult to defend their translation choices when a doubt is raised about their translation, as they may not have the vocabulary to do so. This situation may be explained by the fact that translation studies, and especially professional translator training, have a relatively short history, even though translation as a human activity has a very long history. As a result laypeople's understanding is to some extent that translating does not require any particular skills but can be done by any educated person who has a reasonable level of foreign language skills, which all professional translators know is far from the truth.

Edited version of Kim, M. (2007) 'Translation error analysis: a Systemic Functional Grammar approach', in Kenny, D. and Ryou, K. (eds) *Across Boundaries: International perspectives on translation studies*, pp. 161–75, Newcastle upon Tyne: Cambridge Scholars Publishing.

Recently, however, new teaching suggestions have been made by translator trainers. Kiraly (2000) suggests a social constructivist approach to overcome the problems of teacher-centeredness. Bowker (2000) and Pearson (1999) introduce a corpus-based approach to evaluating student translations as a tool that evaluators can use to provide objective and constructive feedback to their students. Pearson (2003) demonstrates that a parallel corpus is a useful resource to help students to handle translation difficulties. This study is not isolated from these new approaches but outlines how Systemic Functional Grammar (SFG) can be used as a tool to complement or even enrich them. For example, the social constructivist approach, which answers many questions about "how to teach", is very inspirational and can be applied in innovative teaching, but questions about "what to teach and/or learn from each other" still remain vague. The corpus-based approach is a useful tool to reduce subjectivity in evaluating translations when it comes to terms, expressions, collocations and semantic prosody, but the range of information that could be drawn from the corpus could be widened even further if the users' linguistic focus extended beyond the expression level to the systemic functional meaning-based level.

If the discipline of translation studies cannot explain translation-specific knowledge and skills and if the discipline of translator education cannot provide tools for future generations of translators to use, it will be hard to convince laypeople that translation is a profession rather than a useful everyday activity. This is one of the reasons why translation teachers or evaluators should be able to give explicit criteria for why and how one translation is better or worse than another. In order to be able to do so, professional knowledge of language, which is deeper and wider than non-professional knowledge, will be a primary tool. This chapter discusses empirical research and argues that SFG provides a fundamental basis for a comprehensive understanding of meaning. The following section briefly introduces a few concepts of SFG and its relations with translation studies. The chapter then describes the research design and method and concludes with a discussion about its application in translation teaching.

[. . .]

Systemic Functional Grammar and translation studies

SFG was initially devised by Michael Halliday in the 1950s and 1960s, and was influenced by Firth in the initial conceptual period. Williams (1994: 1) notes that it continues to be developed by Halliday and linguists such as Ruqaiya Hasan, Jim Martin and Christian Matthiessen. It has been applied to translation studies, and translation assessment in particular, by translation scholars such as House (1997); Baker (1992); Hatim and Mason (1990, 1997); and Trosborg (2002).

Systemic functional linguists regard language as a meaning-making resource through which people interact with each other in given situational and cultural contexts. They are mainly interested in how language is used to construe meaning. Therefore, language is understood in relation to its global as well as local contexts. This fundamental view of language is expressed through several strata or levels in SFL theory, as Figure 5.1 adopted from Matthiessen (1992) demonstrates.

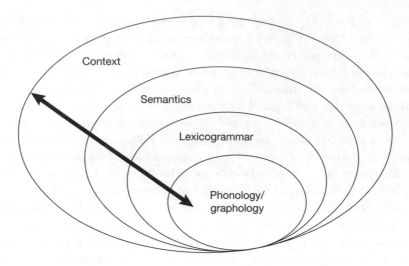

Figure 5.1 Levels of language

The levels depicted in Figure 5.1 are context, which includes both context of situation and context of culture; discourse semantics; lexicogrammar; and phonology/graphology. It can be said that a higher level provides a context for its lower level, and that a higher level cannot exist without its lower level. For instance, unless a word is expressed in a spoken or written form, we cannot talk about grammar. Unless an utterance is made at the lexicogrammatical level, we cannot create a text or discourse at the semantic level. Therefore, in SFL, it is common practice to study lexicogrammar, which is mainly concerned with meaning at the clause level, in relation to semantics, which is primarily concerned with meaning at the text or discourse level, and vice versa. This is one of the reasons for the strong relevance of SFL theory to translation studies. Translators cannot create a text without working on meaning at the clause level, and cannot produce a coherent text without working on meaning at the text level. In SFL, grammar is a way of describing lexical and grammatical *choices* rather than a way of prescribing a set of grammatical *rules*. The choices are interpreted as linguistic resources which the speakers of the language use to realize meaning. Halliday (1994: 15) states:

> One way of thinking of a functional grammar . . . is that it is a theory of grammar that is orientated towards the discourse semantics. In other words, if we say we are interpreting the grammar functionally, it means that we are foregrounding its role as a resource for construing meaning.

Two basic notions of SFG need to be explained: firstly, a distinctive meaning is construed through three simultaneous strands of meaning and, secondly, a clause is a unit in which these meanings are combined (Halliday 1994: 35). The meanings are referred to in SFG as metafunctions, and three such metafunctions are identified: ideational (resources for construing our experience of the world as meaning); interpersonal (resources for enacting our social roles and relations as meaning); and textual (resources for presenting ideational and interpersonal meanings as a flow of information in text). The ideational metafunction is split into two: experiential (resources for organizing experience as meaning) and logical (resources for expressing certain general logical relations as meaning).

SFG makes use of two types of grammatical labels: names of classes, including terms such as verb, noun, adjective, adverb, prepositional phrase, noun group, etc; and names of functions, including Participant, Process, Subject, Predicator, Theme, Rheme, etc. A constituent that is a member of a single class can have multiple functions in a clause. For instance, the noun group *my brother* has three functions in a simple clause like *my brother broke a window*: Participant, Subject and Theme. *My brother* is the doer of the action (Participant), the element on which something is predicated (Subject), and the focus of the message (Theme). (Following standard practice, labels for functions are written beginning with a capital letter in this article.)

The approach that SFG takes towards language is fundamentally different from traditional school grammar. Williams (1994: 5) explains that the most important difference between SFG and traditional school grammar is the metaphor of choice:

> Whereas school grammars have prescribed the correct form, functional grammar views language as a resource – one which makes semantic choices available to speakers and writers.

Research design and method

This study is based on an SFG-inspired error analysis of fourteen translations carried out by student translators who had completed the first semester of their postgraduate translation and interpreting studies in Korea. Most of these students had no or very limited experience of living in an English-speaking country and had not learned SFG-based text analysis. They were given one week to translate a 408-word English text into Korean. They were allowed to use any resources needed for the translation.

The source text was an editorial from *The Sydney Morning Herald* dated 13 March 2003 and dealing with the complicated issue of human reproduction technology and ethical issues raised by a particular case in Victoria, Australia. The selection of the text was motivated by my observation that newspaper editorials are one of the text types that student translators often find difficult to comprehend and translate.

As a first step, the source text was analyzed by the researcher, who divided it into forty independent, dependent, embedded and interrupting clauses. (For details of these clause types, see Butt *et al.* 2000: 166–71.) In general, a clause may be defined as a meaning unit that includes a verbal group that functions as Process. Each clause was then analyzed according to the three different metafunctions: ideational, interpersonal and textual. The ideational metafunction was further analyzed into two modes of meaning: experiential and logical. In order to understand experiential meaning, each clause was broken down into three functional constituents: Participant, Process and Circumstance. For the analysis of interpersonal meaning, Subject and Finite relations were identified and for the analysis of thematic meaning, Theme and Rheme relations were identified. (For detailed descriptions of these concepts see Butt *et al.* 2000; and Halliday 1994.) Each student translation was subsequently checked by the researcher and problematic parts in terms of accuracy and appropriateness were underlined and marked with *E* for an **experiential** meaning error, *L* for logical meaning error, *I* for an **interpersonal** meaning error and *T* for a **textual** meaning error, where possible. When all three transitivity constituents in a clause, namely Participant, Process and Circumstance, were wrong, it was classified as **mistranslation**. When a constituent was not translated, it was treated as a **constituent** error. For example, if the Participant was missing unjustifiably, it was classified as a **Participant** error. When a whole clause was not translated, it was classified as **omission**. Korean-grammar errors such as a space between words and spelling mistakes were identified but were not quantified in this research, not because they are less important but because they are issues that should be discussed in relation to L1 competence. However, **word-level equivalence** errors were quantified.

Data analysis

Table 5.1 indicates the number of clauses where each student made particular translation errors. For example, Student 1 made an interpersonal translation error in two clauses. The last column shows the average number of clauses that contain each type of translation error.

Table 5.1 Number of errors in the 11 error categories

Error types \ Students	1	2	3	4	5	6	7	8	9	10	11	12	13	14	Total	Ave
Interpersonal	2	1		1				1				1			6	0.4
Textual		2							2						4	0.3
Logical	2		1	1	5	2	5	2	2	2	1	2		2	27	1.9
Experiential:																
Process	2	4	6	3	4	6	2	3	5	5	2	5	2	6	55	3.9
Participant	2	6	5	4	4	7	4	4	10	5		1	3	3	58	4.1
Circumstance	2		3	1	1		3	3	1		2	4	4	5	29	2.1
Mistranslation		1		1	1	4	5	2	5	4			2		25	1.8
Modifier		3		2	2	2	1	2	3	1	4	1	2	1	24	1.7
Tense			1											2	3	0.2
Others																
Omission	1	2	3		1	2			2	2				1	14	1
Word choice		3	1	1	2	2	1	1	2	2				1	16	1.1
Total	11	22	17	16	20	26	18	17	35	22	9	14	13	21	261	

Discussions of errors within different metafunctions

In this section, some examples of translation errors or inadequate translation choices in each different metafunction are discussed. For each example, the source text (ST) analysis of the clause or clause complex is accompanied by the target text (TT) as well as my back translation of the target text (BT). (A back translation is a translation of a translated text back into the language of the original text.) A clause is indicated with double bars (|| ||) and a clause complex, which can be interchangeable with sentence in written text, with triple bars (||| |||). The problematic parts are highlighted in bold.

Example 1

ST: ||| || But if, <u>as in this case</u>, <u>a child</u> || <u>is born</u> || **to be loved**, || and there
                    Circumstance   Participant Process Process
<u>exists</u> || <u>a profound secondary value such as saving a sibling</u>, || <u>the ethical</u>
Process   Participant
<u>conundrum</u> || <u>dissipates</u>. || |||
Participant Process

TT: 그러나 앞선 경우와 같이 아이가 **부모의 사랑을 받고**, 출생과 함께

     부차적으로 형제의생명을 구하는 것과 같은 심오한 가치가 있다면 복잡한

     윤리 문제는 사라진다.

BT: But as in the previous case, **if a child is loved by the parents**, and, in addition to the birth, if there is a profound value exists such as saving a sibling, the ethical problem disappears.

In the part of the target text in bold, there are two metafunctional issues. One is that the main component of experience, which is represented by the Process *is born*, is omitted and therefore the experiential metafunction is misrepresented. The other issue is related to the logical metafunction. *To be loved* in the source text is a non-finite dependent clause which functions to provide the purpose for the previous clause. However, the target text fails to convey the logical relations. As a result, while the source text is talking about the purpose of the child's birth, the target text presents a conditional clause *if the child is loved by the parents*. An alternative translation would be 그러나 이번 경우와 같이 아이가 사랑받기 위해서 태어난다면 …, which means "But as in this case, if a child is born in order to be loved . . ."

Example 2

ST: || <u>All medical interventions against life-threatening conditions</u> **tackle** <u>fate</u>. ||
          Participant   Process Participant
TT: 치명적 질병을 치료하는 모든 의학시술은 운명을 거스르게 된다.
BT: All medical technologies to treat life-threatening illnesses **go against** fate.

In Example 2, there is a Process error which results in a shift in experiential metafunction. 거스르게 된다 means "go against", and has a much stronger negative implication than "tackle". Alternative translations would be 운명을 다루게 된다, which means "deal with fate" or 운명에 도전하게 된다, which means "challenge fate".

Interpersonal meaning errors are not prevalent in the translations of this text. One of the main reasons might lie in the nature of the source text. As it is a daily newspaper editorial, it of course expresses its view on the IVF issue but in a careful way so as to keep a balance between the pros and cons, mostly using declarative clauses (with relational Processes) but very few modal finites. Example 3 shows a shift in interpersonal metafunction caused by the student adding unnecessarily judgemental comments.

Example 3

ST: ||| **There is a temptation** among people of goodwill to dismiss out of hand

    Subject Finite Complement   Adjunct

ethical objections in such circumstances. |||

TT: 이번 사례와 같은 경우에는 윤리적인 이유로 시술을 반대할 수는 없다는

     생각이 충분히 들 수 있다

BT: In such cases, **people quite possibly can think** that they can't oppose the procedure on the ground of ethical issues.

In Example 3, the source text does not talk about whether or not they can dismiss ethical objections but just says some people have a tendency to do so. The translation adds a judgemental meaning in the expression "quite possibly can".

There are also some examples of errors of textual meaning. In the source text of Example 4, a marked topical Theme *at issue* is used to draw the reader's attention to a shifted focus of the following discourse. In the target text, the textual effect of the source text is not efficiently created as it has an unmarked topical Theme realized by a long nominal group although a textual Theme *here* is used to renew the reader's attention. Therefore even though this target text has no problems when looking at either the experiential or interpersonal metafunction individually, it needs to be revised to improve its textual meaning. (For a detailed discussion of textual metafunction issues in translation see Kim (2007a) and for a description of Theme in Korean see Kim (2007b).)

Example 4

ST: ||| || At issue is the purpose of conception: || do the parents conceive
        Theme   Rheme   Theme   Rheme
for the baby's sake or another's? || |||

TT: 여기서 바로 부모가 새로운 아기를 가지기 위해서 임신을 하는 지

     아니면 병에 걸린 아이를 치료하기 위해서 임신을 하는 지에 대한

     논란이 제기되는 것이다

BT: Here the issue of whether the parents conceive to have a new baby or whether they conceive to cure the sick child is raised.

Individual students' error patterns

One of the unexpected findings of this study was that individual students may have certain patterns of errors, which reveal areas in which they need to improve. Figure 5.2 shows the distribution of errors for Student 1.

Student 1 is one of the students who made the fewest errors in this translation assignment. As the graph in Figure 5.2 shows, she made two errors in five of the eleven categories: interpersonal, logical, Process, Participant and Circumstance, and one error in the omission category. In the other five categories she did not make any errors. What does this mean? Obviously her linguistic sensitivity and competence in those areas where she did not make an error is very high and reliable, at least in this text, but she may need to give more attention to expressing interpersonal meaning, as her two errors in the interpersonal meaning category were more than the average of 0.4 albeit in this small sample. In her case, comprehension does not seem to be a problem but she does not appear to be aware that the addition of judgemental comments actually results in a shift in interpersonal meaning.

In terms of logical meaning, Circumstance, and omission categories, the errors she made were roughly the same as the average (also see Table 5.1). It would be helpful for her to be fully aware that these are relatively weaker areas than other categories. Even though she made two errors in the Process and Participant categories, they do not seem to be major problems for her considering the average numbers are 3.9 and 4.1 respectively.

High average figures in a particular category can mean either that the source text presents difficulties in such categories or that the group of students is particularly weak in those areas. In addition, the repetition of the same patterns of errors by a group of students would be an excellent indicator for a teacher of areas requiring further explanation or practice.

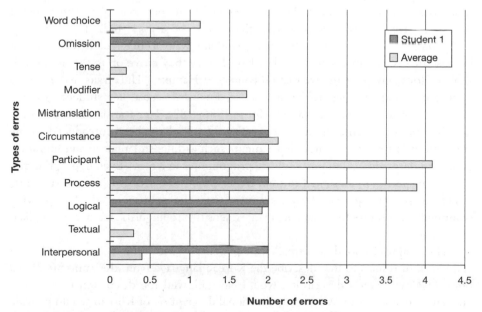

Figure 5.2 Error pattern for Student 1

Discussion and applications in translation teaching

This study found that it was possible to classify errors in target texts based on meaning using SFG. Errors were identified consistently at clause rank in this pilot research but it would certainly be meaningful to investigate beyond the clause in a follow-up study. Most of the errors identified were classified into different metafunctions, except for a small number of errors that were regarded as simple cases of selecting an inappropriate word, which was not a main focus of the research.

[. . .]

Teachers can use this knowledge to give systematic feedback on individual errors and to individual students. For example, instead of saying that "you should not add or miss anything in translation", they can actually articulate when addition or omission might or might not be justifiable, and also provide explanations for this by referring to what meaning is changed. This meaning-based approach to translation can empower students, for their part, to think critically and systematically about the translation options they have and articulate reasons for their choices, ultimately contributing to their development as independent professionals. This is due to the fact that feedback on their translation errors is not based on one's subjective judgement but on systematic, linguistic knowledge, which serves as a basis for students to make informed translation decisions, a practice they will then take with them in their professional lives. Particularly if their previous language learning experience has been focused on a set of rules of language instead of functions of language, and this experience unduly influences their translating, such a meaning-based, functional approach to language as a whole, and to translation in particular, can serve to broaden their conceptual horizons.

Using this classification, teachers can also give individual students systematic feedback on language competence, indicating their relatively weak and strong areas. One instance of translation might not be enough to detect areas of weakness but if repeated error patterns are observed, that would be a good indicator. Language competence is one of the areas that many students want to be given feedback about because that is an immediate need they have before they move on to the next level. Juliane House says that the translation courses at Hamburg University are designed to improve students' general proficiency in English because her students are not being trained to become translators (House 1986: 182). Her translation courses are not the only ones. One or more translation courses have been introduced to the curriculum of language-related departments such as English language and literature at both undergraduate and postgraduate programmes in Korea. Even in programmes which are specifically designed to train translators, there are always some students, if not many, who joined the programme with the primary goal of improving communicative competence and being more sensitive to linguistic features of English.

[. . .]

This chapter is based on a small-scale pilot study with limitations. One of them is the lack of resources that describe the Korean language from the same functional point of view. Such a description would have allowed the discussion to be more efficient and systematic. A systemic functional description of Korean would provide very useful knowledge for translators and language learners of Korean.

Another limitation is the small scale of data, which makes it difficult to generalize the findings at this stage. Follow-up research has recently been conducted to further investigate whether or not this translation error analysis based on SFG helps students develop translation skills and leads to improvement of translation quality (Kim, in press).

[. . .]

Research attempts like this small study that address theoretical and/or practical gaps in translation studies can eventually enrich both translation studies and other relevant disciplines.

References

Baker, Mona (1992) *In Other Words*. London/New York: Routledge.

Bowker, Lynne (2000) 'A corpus-based approach to evaluating student translations', *The Translator* 6 (2): 183–210.

Butt, David, Fahey, Rhondda, Feez, Susan, Spinks, Sue and Yallop, Colin (2000) *Using Functional Grammar*. Sydney: National Centre for English Language Teaching and Research, Macquarie University.

Halliday, Michael A. K. (1994) *An Introduction to Functional Grammar* (2nd edition). London/New York/Sydney/Auckland: Arnold.

Hatim, Basil and Mason, Ian (1990) *Discourse and the Translator*. London: Longman.

Hatim, Basil and Mason, Ian (1997) *The Translator as Communicator*. London/New York: Routledge.

House, Juliane (1986) 'Acquiring translational competence in interaction', in Juliane House and Shoshana Blum-Kulka (eds.) *Interlingual and Intercultural Communication: Discourse and cognition in translation and second language acquisition studies* (pp. 179–91). Tübingen: Narr.

House, Juliane (1997) *A Model for Translation Quality Assessment*. Tübingen: Narr.

Kim, Mira (2007a) 'Using systemic functional text analysis for translator education: an illustration with a focus on the textual meaning'. *Interpreter and Translator Trainer* 1 (2): 223–46.

Kim, Mira (2007b). 'A Discourse Based Study on THEME in Korean and Textual Meaning in Translation'. PhD dissertation, Sydney: Macquarie University, Sydney.

Kim, Mira (in press) 'Meaning-oriented assessment of translations: SFL and its application to formative assessment', in Claudia Angelelli and Holly Jacobson (eds) *Testing and Assessment in Translation and Interpreting*. Amsterdam and Philadelphia, PA: John Benjamins.

Kiraly, Donald C. (2000) *A Social Constructivist Approach to Translator Education*. Manchester: St. Jerome Publishing.

Kussmaul, Paul (1995) *Training the Translator*. Amsterdam/Philadelphia, PA: John Benjamins.

Matthiessen, Christian M. I. M. (1992) *Lexicogrammatical Cartography: English systems*. Tokyo: International Language Sciences Publishers.

Pearson, Jennifer (1999) 'Using specialized comparable corpora to evaluate student translations', in Barbara Lewandowska-Tomaszczyk and Patrick James Melia (eds) *PALC '99: Practical applications in language corpora* (pp. 541–52). Frankfrut am Main: Peter Lang.

——— . (2003) 'Using parallel texts in the translator training environment', in Federico Zanettin, Silvia Bernardini and Dominic Stewart (eds) *Corpora in Translator Education* (pp. 15–24). Manchester: St. Jerome Publishing.

Pym, Anthony (1992) 'Translation error analysis and the interface with language teaching', in Cay Dollerup and Anne Loddegaard (eds) *Teaching Translation and Interpreting:*

Training, talent and experience (pp. 279–88). Amsterdam/Philadelphia, PA: John Benjamins.

Trosborg, Anna (2002) 'Discourse analysis as part of translator training', in Christina Schäffner (ed.), *The Role of Discourse Analysis for Translation and in Translator Training: Status, needs, methods* (pp. 9–52). Clevedon: Multilingual Matters.

Williams, Geoff (1994) *Using Systemic Grammar in Teaching Young Learners: An introduction.* Melbourne: Macmillan Education Australia.

PART TWO

Critical Discourse Analysis

Caroline Coffin, Theresa Lillis, Kieran O'Halloran

Introduction to Part Two

Part Two of the reader shows how Critical Discourse Analysis (CDA) deals explicitly with real-world language-related problems. CDA accomplishes this through thorough descriptions of language data, often drawing on techniques of analysis from Systemic Functional Linguistics (SFL), which enables it to identify problems in language use. Together with detailed appreciation of the relevant context, this affords rich understanding of the real-world language-related problem in its specific context. On the basis of such rich systematicity, critical discourse analysts are then in a position to explain not only how certain use of language can maintain a status quo which, in effect, sustains the real-world problem, but also suggest ways to address the problem. The first four chapters in this Part engage with text data for these aims; Chapter 6 is more theoretically-oriented and Chapters 7, 8 and 9 more practically so, these latter three chapters all drawing on SFL. The last chapter provides some critical perspective on (SFL-based) CDA as well as SFL.

Chapter 6 comes from a classic statement of the aims of CDA by two of its best-known theorists and practitioners, Norman Fairclough and Ruth Wodak. They set out these aims by means of a CDA of a radio interview with Margaret Thatcher, the former British Prime minister (in office, 1979–90). In the interview, she sets out her political and economic philosophy which came to be known as 'Thatcherism'. The pronounced market-driven policies associated with 'Thatcherism', or 'Reaganomics' in the 1980s, continue to have influence on present-day politics, both in Britain and globally. (At the time of writing, though, there are expectations of a less laissez-faire global economy post the 'credit crunch' phenomenon.) Fairclough and Wodak show the value of CDA in investigating the problem of why the Discourse of Thatcherism achieved a certain level of hegemony. A reason for this, they argue, was because it restructured political Discourse by producing novel 'hybridity': a mix of traditional conservative Discourse (e.g focus on law and order, the family), elements of liberal political Discourse and economic Discourse (e.g. the focus on the independence of the individual) together with the discourses of ordinary life.

Within CDA, there has been ongoing interest in how texts position readers to view social and political events in a particular way. Traditionally, analysts have not examined how positioning is built up dynamically as a reader progresses through a text by tracing how earlier points of a text are likely to affect subsequent interpretation. Not doing so, however, can be problematic since it reduces the relevance of the critique of a text for the reading experience. In Chapter 7, Caroline Coffin and Kieran O' Halloran address this language-related problem. The chapter shows how APPRAISAL tools (as developed within the systemic functional tradition) can be usefully employed within CDA to track the build-up of reader positioning. Using a story from *The Sun* newspaper website as illustration, they show how, due to a cumulative groove of semantic patterning, the reader is dynamically positioned to interpret a seemingly neutral statement at the end of the story in a negative way. The authors show how potential analyst 'over-interpretation' can be checked through the use of a concordancer. They also demonstrate how a specialised corpus can go some way to grounding the APPRAISAL analysis in terms of the context of the target readership and the meanings they are routinely exposed to. This they argue facilitates an explanatory critique of the way in which a text is likely to be understood by its target readership in relation to the socio-political-economic context.

Chapter 8 by Tom Bartlett highlights a recent contrastive perspective to CDA called Positive Discourse Analysis (PDA). PDA celebrates discourse which is effective for some purpose, e.g. because it inspires or uplifts, because it has led to peace and reconciliation. Like CDA, PDA engages with real-world problems. CDA tends to identify problems (with texts and discourse practices) in the first instance before offering potential solutions, i.e. it begins with the negative first. Bartlett makes the argument that PDA is a more effective method than CDA for engaging with real-world problems because from the start of a PDA investigation it seizes on discourse that *works* – positive discourse – and through detailed analysis explains why this is the case. To demonstrate PDA, Bartlett uses data from an ethnographic study he conducted in Guyana, South America, with an Amerindian community called the Makushi. The two bits of data come from explanations of a type of forestry management (Sustainable Utilisation Areas – SUAs) to the Amerindian community by 1) a local Makushi authority figure; 2) an international development worker. Drawing on SFL also, Bartlett shows why the discourse of the Makushi community leader was more effective in persuading the community about the value of SUAs.

In Chapter 9, by Mary Hanrahan, the problem focus is challenging the dominant discourse in teacher–student interactions in science classrooms which, she holds, limits acquisition of scientific literacy. For Hanrahan, CDA can help to 'emancipate' science education because it can help to make visible the less explicit facets of classroom discourse which impact upon the kinds of relationships, affective responses, and identities that she believes are likely to enhance or limit the development of scientific literacy. Her research 'addresses the issue of documenting the use of hybrid discourses for emancipatory purposes'. This is because, for Hanrahan, hybridisation can increase the accessibility of science education. She demonstrates this through comparative analysis of a negative exemplar and an effective exemplar of teaching science; the latter teacher achieved a hybrid identity: friendly community member, (gently) controlling teacher and classroom manager, motivating communicator (including amusing storyteller), learning facilitator, and goal-oriented task manager. To some degree Hanrahan's work can be characterised as interventionist PDA. This is because she not only investigates successful practice in science education, but also communicates to teachers examples of what she views as their effective discourse.

Chapter 10 by Henry Widdowson concludes this Part by offering a useful critical perspective on SFL and SFL-based CDA. The distinctions he makes between 'semantic' and 'pragmatic', and 'text' and 'discourse', reflect his perspective that meaning in text is not the same as what texts mean to users in context. In principle, SFL theorists and practitioners in SFL and CDA would agree with this. Rigorous SFL and CDA would map problems in texts and be careful not to make assumptions about the effect of texts on readers; in other words, rigorous SFL analysis and CDA which do not involve ethnographic or other types of investigation of reader behaviour would only talk about how a text *positions* readers not how they would understand a text. For Widdowson, however, SFL and CDA have, in practice, overstepped this mark and committed what he terms the *functional fallacy*: the assumption that semantic functions in a text as isolated by the linguist are equivalent to those which are understood by a reader or listeners in actual discourse. For him, (critical) dis-course analysts should take account of people's understandings of text and context, rather than just their own, and indeed an ethnographer would endorse such a perspective, as illustrated in Part 3 of this volume. However, since Widdowson is not an ethnographer, his approach to context might be termed theoretical rather than empirical.

Chapter 6

Norman Fairclough and Ruth Wodak

Critical Discourse Analysis in action

Our aim in this chapter is to give an example of CDA. We shall work with a version of CDA based upon eight principles of theory or method, and we shall show how each affects the practice of CDA through an analysis – necessarily partial – of the following extract from a radio interview with Margaret Thatcher, former Prime Minister of Britain.[1] Some of the principles represent common ground for all approaches within CDA, while others are more controversial.

```
 1    MC:  Prime Minister you were at Oxford in the nineteen
            forties and after the war Britain would embark on a
            period of relative prosperity for all the like of which it
            had hardly known but today there are three and a
 5          quarter million unemployed and e:m
            Britain's economic performance by one measurement
            has fallen to the rank of that of Italy now can you
            imagine yourself back at the University today what
            must seem to be the chances in Britain and the
10          prospects for all now
      MT:  they are very different worlds you're talking about
            because the first thing that struck me very forcibly as
            you were speaking of those days was that now we do
            enjoy a standard of living which was undreamed of
15          then and I can remember Rab Butler saying after we
```

Extract from Fairclough, N. and Wodak, R. (1997) 'Critical Discourse Analysis', in van Dijk, T. (ed.) *Discourse as Social Interaction*, London: Sage, pp. 268–84.

returned to power in about 1951–52 that if we played
our cards right the standard of living within twenty
five years would be twice as high as it was then and
em he was just about right and it was remarkable

20   because it was something that we had never thought
of now I don't think now one would necessarily think
wholly in material terms indeed I think it's wrong to
think in material terms because really the kind of
country you want is made up by the strength of its

25   people and I think we're returning to my vision of
Britain as a younger person and I was always brought
up with the idea look Britain is a country whose
people think for themselves act for themselves can act
on their own initiative they don't have to be told

30   don't like to be pushed around are self-reliant and
then over and above that they're always responsible
for their families and something else it was a kind of
em I think it was Barrie who said do as you would be
done by e: you act to others as you'd like them to act

35   towards you and so you do something for the
community now I think if you were looking at
another country you would say what makes a country
strong it is its people do they run their industries well
are their human relations good e: do they respect law

40   and order are their families strong all of those kind of
things
        ⌈and you know it's just way beyond economics
MC: ⌊but you know people still   people still ask
        though e: where is she going now General de Gaulle

45   had a vision of France e: a certain idea of France as he
put it e: you have fought three major battles in this
country the Falkland Islands e:m against the miners
and local councils and against public expenditure and
people I think would like to hear what this vision you

50   have of Britain is it must be a powerful one what is it
that inspires your action
MT: I wonder if I perhaps I can answer best by saying how
I see what government should do and if government
really believes in people what people should do I

55   believe that government should be very strong to do
those things which only government can do it has to
be strong to have defence because the kind of Britain I
see would always defend its freedom and always be a
reliable ally so you've got to be strong to your own

60   people and other countries have got to know that you
stand by your word then you turn to internal security
and yes you HAVE got to be strong on law and order

and do the things that only governments can do but
there it's part government and part people because
65   you CAN'T have law and order observed unless it's
in partnership with people then you have to be strong
to uphold the value of the currency and only
governments can do that by sound finance and then
you have to create the framework for a good
70   education system and social security and at that point
you have to say over to people people are inventive
creative and so you expect PEOPLE to create thriving
industries thriving services yes you expect people
each and every one from whatever their background
75   to have a chance to rise to whatever level their own
abilities can take them yes you expect people of all
sorts of background and almost whatever their
income level to be able to have a chance of owning
some property tremendously important the
80   ownership of property of a house gives you some
independence gives you a stake in the future you're
concerned about your children

MC: but could ⌈ you sum this vision up
MT: ⌊ (   ) you said my vision
85   please let me just go on and then that isn't enough
if you're interested in the future yes you will
probably save you'll probably want a little bit of
independent income of your own and so constantly
thinking about the future so it's very much a Britain
90   whose people are independent of government but
aware that the government has to be strong to do
those things which only governments can do

MC: but can you sum it up in a in a in a phrase or two the
aim is to achieve what or to restore what in Britain
95   when clearly risking a lot and winning in a place like
the Falkland Islands is just as important in your
philosophy ⌈ for Britain as as
MT: ⌊ I think
MC: restoring sound money reducing the money supply in
100   the Bank of England
MT: but of course it showed that we were reliable in the
defence of freedom and when part of Britain we: was
invaded of course we went we believed in defence of
freedom we were reliable I think if I could try to sum
105   it up in a phrase and that's always I suppose most
difficult of all I would say really restoring the very
best of the British character to its former
preeminence.
MC: but this has meant something called Thatcherism now

110 is that a description you accept as something quite
    distinct from traditional conservatism in this country
  MT: no it is traditional conservatism
  MC: but it's radical and populist and therefore not
115 conservative
  MT: it is radical because at the time when I took over we
    needed to be radical e: it is populist I wouldn't call it
    populist I would say that many of the things which
    I've said strike a chord in the hearts of ordinary
120 people why because they're British because their
    character IS independent because they DON'T like to
    be shoved around coz they ARE prepared to take
    responsibility because they DO expect to be loyal to
    their friends and loyal allies that's why you call it
125 populist. I say it strikes a chord in the hearts of
    people I know because it struck a chord in my heart
    many many years ago

1 CDA addresses social problems

CDA is the analysis of linguistic and semiotic aspects of social processes and problems. The focus is not upon language or the use of language in and for themselves, but upon the partially linguistic character of social and cultural processes and structures. For example, a CDA of the extract above might be seen as a contribution to the analysis of Thatcherism – or, in more international terms, the new right in politics. As this example suggests, CDA is by its nature interdisciplinary, combining diverse disciplinary perspectives in its own analyses, and being used to complement more standard forms of social and cultural analysis. Such an analysis might be linked to particular problems and struggles of dominated groups under Thatcherite govern-ments, such as those of the miners and other trade unionists. It could help develop a critical awareness of the discursive strategies of Thatcherism which might be one resource in struggles against it.

  Seen in this context, the key claim of CDA is that major social and political processes and movements such as Thatcherism (Fairclough 1993) have a partly linguistic-discursive character. This follows from the fact that social and political changes in contemporary society generally include a substantive element of cultural and ideological change. This is certainly true of Thatcherism, which has been described as being an attempt to construct a new hegemony, a new basis for winning popular consent, as well as being a set of free market economic strategies, and a political project for strengthening and centralizing the state, pushing back the structures and institutions of social democracy, weakening the trade unions, and so forth (Hall and Jacques 1983).

  Thatcherism as an ideological project for building a new hegemony can be seen as an attempt to restructure political discourse by combining diverse existing discourses together in a new way. This is evident in the extract above. There is a characteristic combination of elements of traditional conservative discourse (the focus on law and order, the family, and strong government, for example *do they respect law and order are their families strong*) and elements of a liberal political discourse and economic discourse (the focus on the independence of the individual, for example *because their character IS independent because they DON'T like to be shoved around coz they ARE prepared to take responsibility*; and on the individual entrepreneur as the dynamo of the economy, for example *you expect PEOPLE to create thriving industries thriving services*).

These are mixed with elements from discourses of ordinary life and ordinary experience which give Thatcher's discourse the populist quality referred to by the interviewer – for example, the expressions *stand by your word*, *shoved around*, and *strikes a chord in [people's] hearts*. This novel combination of discourses is associated with distinctive representations of social reality and distinctive constructions of social and political relations and identities (see below). It achieved a dominant position in the field of political discourse, though it is arguable to what extent it became hegemonic in the sense of winning widespread acceptance.

2 Power relations are discursive

CDA highlights the substantively linguistic and discursive nature of social relations of power in contemporary societies. This is partly a matter of how power relations are exercised and negotiated in discourse. One issue that receives a great deal of attention is power relations between the media and politics – whether in broad terms mediatized political discourse is the domination of the media over politicians, or the exploitation of the media by politicians. Close analysis of power relations in political interviews in the media can cast some light on this issue (Bell and van Leeuwen 1994). On the face of it, interviewers exercise a lot of power over politicians in interviews: interviewers generally control the way in which interviews begin and end, the topics which are dealt with and the angles from which they are tackled, the time given to politicians to answer questions, and so forth. In the case of the Thatcher interview, Michael Charlton's questions do set and attempt to police an agenda (see for instance lines 83, 93–4). However, politicians do not by any means always comply with interviewers' attempts to control interviews, and there is often a struggle for control. Charlton for instance in line 83 tries to bring Thatcher back to the question he asked in lines 49–51, but she interrupts his attempt at policing her talk, and carries on with what is effectively a short political speech. The fact that Thatcher makes speeches in her answers to Charlton's questions – or perhaps better, interprets Charlton's questions as opportunities to make speeches rather than requiring answers – points to another dimension of power relations in discourse. Thatcher tries to exercise what we might call rhetorical power, the power which comes from a facility in the rhetoric of political persuasion, a form of 'cultural capital' which according to Bourdieu (1991) is the prerogative of professional politicians in contemporary societies. This power – in so far as it is effective – is primarily power over the radio audience, but it is also germane to power relations between Thatcher and Charlton in that it circumvents and marginalizes Charlton's power as interviewer. Thatcher's rhetorical power is realized for instance in the large-scale linguistic devices which organize her contributions, such as the triple parallel structure of lines 56–67 (*it has to be strong to have defence, 56–7; you HAVE got to be strong on law and order, 62; you have to be strong to uphold the value of the currency, 66–7).*

In addition to the question of power in discourse, there is the question of power over discourse (Fairclough 1989). This is partly a matter of access. As Prime Minister, Mrs Thatcher could use the media largely on her own terms. Less powerful politicians have access that is more limited and more on the media's terms, while most people have no access whatever. But power over discourse is also a matter of the capacity to control and change the ground rules of discursive practices, and the structure of the order of discourse. We have already referred above to the Thatcherite project for a reconstructed hegemony in the field of political discourse, involving novel combinations of existing discourses. The extract above also illustrates, as we have just indicated, a reconstruction of genre: the genres of political speech and media interview are articulated in a way which makes this interview a powerful political platform for the distinctive Thatcherite style of authoritative and 'tough' but populist political rhetoric.

These examples suggest that discursive aspects of power relations are not fixed and monolithic. Much work in CDA has been characterized by a focus upon the discursive reproduction of power relations. We also need a focus on discursive aspects of power struggle and of the transformation of power relations. It is fruitful to look at both 'power in discourse' and 'power over discourse' in these dynamic terms: both the exercise of power in the 'here and now' of specific discursive events, and the longer-term shaping of discursive practices and orders of discourse, are generally negotiated and contested processes. Thatcherism can for instance be partly seen as an ongoing hegemonic struggle in discourse and over discourse, with a variety of antagonists – 'wets' in the Conservative Party, the other political parties, the trade unions, the professions, and so forth.

3 Discourse constitutes society and culture

We can only make sense of the salience of discourse in contemporary social processes and power relations by recognizing that discourse constitutes society and culture, as well as being constituted by them. Their relationship, that is, is a dialectical one. This entails that every instance of language use makes its own small contribution to reproducing and/or transforming society and culture, including power relations. That is the power of discourse; that is why it is worth struggling over.

It is useful to distinguish three broad domains of social life that may be discursively constituted, referred to as representations, relations and identities for short: representations of the world, social relations between people, and people's social and personal identities (Fairclough 1992a). In terms of representations, for instance, lines 11–21 of the example incorporate a narrative which gives a very different representation of history to the one in the interviewer's question: the latter's contrast between prosperous past and depressed present is restructured as a past Conservative government creating present prosperity.

The extract constitutes social relations between Thatcher as a political leader and the political public contradictorily, as in part relations of solidarity and in part relations of authority. Thatcher's use of the indefinite pronoun *you*, which is a popular colloquial speech form (in contrast to *one*), implicitly claims that she is just an ordinary person, like her voters (this is the populist element in her discourse). So too does some of her vocabulary: notice for instance how she avoids the interviewer's term *populist* and the interviewer's technical use of *radical* as a specialist political term in lines 113–20, perhaps because their intellectualism would compromise her claims to solidarity. Thatcher's deployment of political rhetoric referred to above is by contrast authoritative. So too is her use of inclusive *we*: she claims to speak for the people. Similar are the passages (including 27–36 and 119–23) in which she characterizes the British, claiming the authority to articulate their self-perceptions on their behalf.

These passages are also interesting in terms of the constitution of identities: a major feature of this discourse is how it constitutes 'the people' as a political community (note Thatcher's explicit foregrounding of the project of engineering collective identity – *restoring the very best of the British character to its former preeminence*), and the listing of characteristics in these examples is a striking discourse strategy. Notice that these lists condense together, without explicit connections between them, the diverse discourses which we have suggested (principle 1) are articulated together in Thatcherite political discourse: conservative and liberal political discourses, liberal economic discourse, discourses of ordinary life. Since the connections between these discourses are left implicit, it is left to audience members to find ways of coherently articulating them together.

Notice also the vague and shifting meanings of the pronoun *we* (lines 13–25, 101–4) in Thatcher's talk. *We* is sometimes what is traditionally called 'inclusive' (it includes the audience and the general population, for example *we do enjoy a standard of living which was undreamed of then*, 13–14), and sometimes 'exclusive' (for example, *after we returned to power*, 15–16, where *we* refers just to the Conservative Party). In other cases, it could be taken as either (for example, *if we played our cards right*, 16–17; *we went we believed in defence of freedom we were reliable*, 103–4). Even if we take the first of these examples as exclusive, it is still unclear who the *we* identifies: is it the Conservative Party, or the government? Also, calling *we* 'inclusive' is rather misleading, for while *we* in for instance *we do enjoy a standard of living which was undreamed of then* does identify the whole community, it constructs the community in a way which excludes those who have not achieved prosperity. Similarly, *we went we believed in defence of freedom we were reliable*, on an 'inclusive' reading, may leave those who opposed the Falklands adventure feeling excluded from the general community. The pronoun *you* is used in a similarly strategic and manipulative way on lines 59–88. We are not suggesting that Thatcher or her aides are consciously planning to use *we* and *you* in these ways, though reflexive awareness of language is increasing among politicians. Rather, there are broader intended strategic objectives for political discourse (such as building a popular base for political positions, mobilizing people behind policy decisions) which are realized in ways of using language that are likely themselves to be unintended.

Finally, the discourse also constitutes an identity for Thatcher herself as a woman political leader who has political authority without ceasing to be feminine. Notice for example the modality features of lines 52–92. On the one hand, there are a great many strong obligational modalities (note the modal verbs *should*, *have to*, *have got to*) and epistemic ('probability') modalities (note the categorical present tense verbs of for instance lines 80–2), which powerfully claim political authority. On the other hand, this section opens with a very tentative and hedged expression

(*I wonder if I perhaps I can answer best by saying how I see . . .*) which might stereotypically be construed – in conjunction with her delivery at this point, and her dress and appearance – as 'feminine'.

A useful working assumption is that any part of any language text, spoken or written, is simultaneously constituting representations, relations, and identities. This assumption harmonizes with a multifunctional theory of language and text such as one finds for instance in systemic linguistic theory (Halliday 1994; Halliday and Hasan 1985). According to this theory, even the individual clauses (simple sentences) of a text simultaneously function 'ideationally' in representing reality, and 'interpersonally' in constructing social relations and identities, as well as 'textually' in making the parts of a text into a coherent whole.

4 Discourse does ideological work

Ideologies are particular ways of representing and constructing society which reproduce unequal relations of power, relations of domination and exploitation. The theory of ideology developed as part of the Marxist account of class relations (Larrain 1979), but it is now generally extended to include relations of domination based upon gender and ethnicity. Ideologies are often (though not necessarily) false or ungrounded constructions of society (for example, gender ideologies which represent women as less emotionally stable than men). To determine whether a particular (type of) discursive event does ideological work, it is not enough to analyse texts; one also needs to consider how texts are interpreted and received and what social effects they have.

In our example, the political and economic strategies of Thatcherism are an explicit topic, and are clearly formulated, notably in lines 52–92, including the central idea of strong government intervention to create conditions in which markets can operate freely. But Thatcher's formulation is actually built around a contrast between government and people which we would see as ideological: it covers over the fact that the 'people' who dominate the creation of 'thriving industries' and so forth are mainly the transnational corporations, and it can help to legitimize existing relations of economic and political domination. It is a common feature of Thatcherite populist discourse. The opposition between government and people is quite explicit here, but ideologies are typically more implicit. They attach for instance to key words which evoke but leave implicit sets of ideological assumptions – such as *freedom*, *law and order* or *sound finance*. Notice also *thriving industries thriving services*. This is another instance of the list structure discussed above, though it is a short list with just two items. *Thriving industries* is a common collocation, but *thriving services* is an innovation of an ideologically potent sort: to achieve a coherent meaning for the list one needs to assume that services can be evaluated on the same basis as industries, a truly Thatcherite assumption which the listener however is left to infer. Note that not all common-sense assumptions in discourse are ideological, given our view of ideology.

Ideology is not just a matter of representations of social reality, for constructions of identity which are linked to power are (as Althusser emphasized) key ideological processes too. It is useful to think of ideology as a process which articulates together particular representations of reality, and particular constructions of identity, especially of the collective identities of groups and communities. In this case, the ideological work that is going on is an attempt to articulate Thatcherite representations of and strategies for the economy and politics with a particular construction of 'the people' as a political community and base for Thatcherism. Thatcher is simultaneously discursively constructing a political programme and a constituency for that programme (Bourdieu 1991).

5 Discourse is historical

Discourse is not produced without context and cannot be understood without taking the context into consideration (Duranti and Goodwin 1992; Wodak *et al.* 1990, 1994). This relates, on a metatheoretical level, to Wittgenstein's (1967) notion of 'language game' and 'forms of life': utterances are only meaningful if we consider their use in a specific situation, if we understand the underlying conventions and rules, if we recognize the embedding in a certain culture and ideology, and most importantly, if we know what the discourse relates to in the past. Discourses are always connected to other discourses which were produced earlier, as well as those which are produced synchronically and subsequently. In this respect, we include intertextuality as well as sociocultural knowledge within our concept of context.

Thus, Thatcher's speech relates to what she and her government have said earlier, to other speeches and proclamations, to certain laws which have been decided upon, to reporting in the media, as well as to certain actions which were undertaken.

This becomes very clear if we consider allusions which occur in the text and which presuppose certain worlds of knowledge, and particular intertextual experience, on the part of the listeners. For example, to be able to understand and analyse Thatcher's responses profoundly and in depth, we would have to know what the situation in Britain in the *nineteen forties* (1–2) was like, who Rab Butler (15) or Barrie (33) were, what kind of *vision* de Gaulle had (44–5), why the war in the Falkland Islands was important and what kind of symbolic meaning it connotes (58), etc. It becomes even more difficult when Thatcher alludes to *traditional conservatism* (111) and to what is meant by this term within the Thatcherite tendency in contrast to other meanings.

In the study of antisemitic discourse during the Waldheim affair in Austria (1986) a method was developed which allows the inclusion of layers of historical knowledge (Wodak *et al.* 1990): the discourse-historical approach. Thus were analysed documents on the Wehrmacht, Waldheim's own speeches as well as those of his opponents, newspaper reports on Waldheim in Austria and abroad, and finally also *vox populi*, conversations on the street by anonymous participants. The discourse history of each unit of discourse had to be uncovered. This naturally again implies interdisciplinary analysis; historians have to be included in such an undertaking.

6 The link between text and society is mediated

CDA is very much about making connections between social and cultural structures and processes on the one hand, and properties of text on the other. But these connections are rather complex, and are best seen as indirect or 'mediated' rather than direct. One view of this mediated relationship is that the link between text and society is mediated by 'orders of discourse' (see earlier). In the Thatcher example, this approach would aim to show that changes in British policies, in the relationship between politics and media, and in British culture at a more general level (some of which we have pointed to above) are partly realized in changes in the political order of discourse, and in how texts draw upon and articulate together discourses and genres which had traditionally been kept apart. Such new articulations of discourses and genres are in turn realized in features of language, making an indirect, mediated link between sociocultural processes and linguistic properties of texts.

We have already indicated some of this articulatory work in the Thatcher interview: it hybridizes discourses which are traditionally kept apart in the political order of discourse (conservative and liberal discourses), and in its populist features hybridizes the political order of discourse with orders of discourse of ordinary life. We have also suggested that it hybridizes the genre of media interview and the genre of political speaking, drawing together the media and political orders of discourse. However, the mixing of genres needs to be more carefully formulated. The Charlton–Thatcher interview was one of a series of in-depth interviews with prominent figures in public life. Its conventions are those of a 'celebrity interview'. Questions probe the personality and outlook of the interviewee, and answers are expected to be frank and revelatory. Audience members are constructed as overhearers listening in on a potentially quite intense interaction between interviewer and interviewee. The programme should at once be educative and entertaining. However, while Charlton is working according to these ground rules, Thatcher is not. She treats the encounter as a political interview. As politicians commonly do, she therefore uses the interview as an occasion for political speech making, constructing the audience rather than the interviewer as addressee, not answering the questions, and avoiding the liberal intellectual discourse of the questions in favour of a populist discourse. The interaction thus has rather a complex character generically: there is a tension between the participants in terms of which media genre is oriented to (celebrity interview versus political interview), and Thatcher's recourse to political interview entails a further tension between media practices and the rhetorical practices of political discourse.

There are other views of mediation of the link between text and society. The emphasis in Smith (1990) for example is upon the practices of social actors in producing links between society and text in the enactment of local relations, drawing together aspects of ethnomethodological and Marxist theories. Van Dijk on the other hand stresses the sociocognitive mediation of the text-society link (van Dijk 1985, 1989, 1993b; Wodak 1992; Mitten and Wodak 1993) and sets out to specify the cognitive resources social actors draw upon in their practice, and the relationship between individual meanings or interpretations and group representations (in the case of racist discourse, for instance). On the one hand these different views of mediation indicate contrasting priorities of different theories, but on the other hand they might be regarded as complementary, as pointing to the need in the long run for a complex and multi-sided theory of text-society mediation which gives due weight to orders of discourse, practices of social actors, and sociocognitive processes.

7 Discourse Analysis is interpretative and explanatory

Discourse can be interpreted in very different ways, due to the audience and the amount of context information which is included. In a study of the comprehension and comprehensibility of news broadcasts, for example, Lutz and Wodak (1987) illustrate typical but different interpretations of the same text, depending on emotional, formal and cognitive schemata of the reader/listener (*Soziopsychologische Theorie des Textverstehens* (SPTV), sociopsychological theory of text comprehension). Class-, gender-, age-, belief- and attitude-specific readings of the texts occurred which demonstrate that understanding takes place not through a *tabula rasa*, but against the background of emotions, attitudes and knowledge. The same is even more true for complex texts like the Thatcher interview where we deal with historical and synchronic intertextuality, the hybridization of genres and the opaqueness of certain elements and units. Several important issues have to be raised at this point. What are the limits of the discourse unit under investigation: what are the limits of the sign (Kress 1993)? How much contextual knowledge do we need for an interpretation? Are the critical readings provided by CDA privileged, better, or just more justifiable? For example, the meaning of *you have to say over to people people are inventive creative and so you expect PEOPLE to create thriving industries thriving services yes you expect* (lines 72–3) is certainly opaque. Who is meant by *people*: all British subjects, government included or excluded? Human beings *per se*, or people in the sense of citizens, of the German *Volk*? People who vote Conservative, who are ideologically committed to Thatcherism, or everybody? The group is not clearly defined, which allows readers to include or exclude themselves according to their own ideologies and beliefs. If we continue in the text, it becomes clearer that these *people* have to be able to influence the growth of industries and services in a positive way (*thriving*). But only powerful people are able to do this – elites, managers and politicians. If that is the case, the use of *people* is certainly misleading; it suggests participation where there is none. It mystifies the influence ordinary men and women might have on decisions of the government, an influence which they actually do not have and never would have. This piece of text exemplifies a contradiction which only a CDA might deconstruct and in doing so show the different implications of different readings for social action. Knowledge of Thatcherite argumentation structures and politics (using a discourse-historical methodology) would make it much easier to disentangle manifest and latent meanings and to find out more about the political rhetorics which are used in this interview. Critical reading thus implies a systematic methodology and a thorough investigation of the context. This might narrow down the whole range of possible readings. The heterogeneity and vagueness of the text condenses contradictions which only become apparent through careful analysis. The text is thus deconstructed and embedded in its social conditions, is linked to ideologies and power relationships. This marks the point where critical readings differ from reading by an uncritical audience: they differ in their systematic approach to inherent meanings, they rely on scientific procedures, and they naturally and necessarily require self-reflection of the researchers themselves. In this point, they differ clearly from pure hermeneutics (in this respect see the 'objective hermeneutics' of Ulrich Oevermann and his group: Oevermann *et al.* 1979). We might say they are explanatory in intent, not just interpretative. We also have to state that interpretations and explanations are never finished and authoritative; they are dynamic and open, open to new contexts and new information.

8 Discourse is a form of social action

We stated at the beginning of our chapter that the principle aim of CDA was to uncover opaqueness and power relationships. CDA is a socially committed scientific paradigm, and some scholars are also active in various political groups. In contrast to many scholars, critical linguists make explicit interests which otherwise often remain covered.

The Thatcher example we have analysed arguably has such applicability in political struggles. But there exist also other examples of important applications of CDA. Wodak and De Cillia (1989) published the first official school materials dealing with post-war anti-Semitism in Austria. These materials are now used in schools and accompany an exhibition about anti-Semitism in the Second Austrian Republic. Both the exhibition and the book are used by teachers who want to discuss the different ranges and variations of anti-Semitic discourse in their classrooms. Similarly, van Dijk (1993a) has analysed Dutch schoolbooks in terms of their potential racist implications. This led to the production of new school materials. Similar educational applications have taken place in the UK under the heading of 'critical language awareness' (Fairclough 1992b), and the term 'critical literacy' is also widely used especially in Australia. CDA is also used for expert opinions in court. Gruber and Wodak (1992) wrote an expert opinion on a column in the biggest Austrian tabloid which denied the Holocaust (this can be punished with up to seven years in prison). They were asked for their analysis by the Jewish community. The expert opinion showed – through the analysis of many other columns in this paper and by the same author – that the one racist column was not accidental, but was consistent with the usual practice of the newspaper. Unfortunately, the case was lost due to the tremendous power of this tabloid and its financiers, but the expert opinion was published and widely read and cited, and influenced public opinion.

Non-discriminatory language use is widely promoted in different domains. One important area is sexist language use. Guidelines for non-sexist language use have been produced in many countries (Wodak et al. 1987). Such guidelines serve to make women visible in language and, thus also socially, in institutions. Different discourse with and about women can slowly lead to changes in consciousness. Finally, CDA has had much success in changing discourse and power patterns in institutions. For example, while analysing doctor–patient communication, it became apparent that on top of their expert knowledge doctors use many other strategies to dominate their clients (Lalouschek et al. 1990; Mishler 1977; West 1990). The critical analysis of such communication patterns led to guidelines for different behaviour patterns, which were and are taught in seminars for doctors. The same is true for other institutions, for bureaucracies, legal institutions and schools (Gunnarsson 1989; Danet 1984; Pfeiffer et al. 1987).

Conclusion

A key issue for critical discourse analysts is how the analyses which they produce in academic institutions relate to critical activity in ordinary life. There is no absolute divide between the two: critical discourse analysts necessarily draw upon everyday critical activities (associated for instance with gender relations, patriarchy and feminism) including analysts' own involvement in and experience of them, and these activities may be informed by academic analysis (as feminism has been). Yet CDA is obviously not just a replication of everyday critique: it can draw upon social theories and theories of language, and methodologies for language analysis, which are not generally available, and has resources for systematic and in-depth investigations which go beyond ordinary experience. We think it is useful to see the relationship between everyday discourse critique and academic CDA in terms of Gramscian perspectives on intellectuals in contemporary life, and the relationship of intellectuals on the one hand to the state and the dominant class, and on the other hand to struggles against domination on the basis of class, gender, race, and so forth. Critical discourse analysts ought in our view to be aiming to function as 'organic intellectuals' in a range of social struggles (not forgetting 'new social movements' such as ecological movements or anti-road-building alliances), but ought at the same time to be aware that their work is constantly at risk of appropriation by the state and capital.

Notes

1   The interview was conducted by Michael Charlton, and was broadcast on BBC Radio 3 on 17 December 1985. For a fuller analysis, see Chapter 7 of Fairclough (1989).

References

Bell, P. and van Leeuwen, T. (1994) *Media Interview*. Sydney: University of New South Wales Press.
Bourdieu, P. (1991) *Language and Symbolic Power*. Cambridge: Polity Press.
Danet, B. (ed.) (1984) 'Legal Discourse'. Special issue of *Text* 4.
Duranti, A. and Goodwin, C. (eds) (1992) *Rethinking Context: Language as an Interactive Phenomenon*. Cambridge: Cambridge University Press.
Fairclough, N. (1989) *Language and Power*. London: Longman.
Fairclough, N. (1992a) *Discourse and Social Change*. Cambridge: Polity Press.
Fairclough, N. (ed.) (1992b) *Critical Language Awareness*. London: Longman.
Fairclough, N. (1993) 'Critical discourse analysis and the marketization of public discourse: the universities'. *Discourse and Society* 4 (2): 133–68.
Gruber, H. and Wodak, R. (1992) *Ein Fall für den Staatsanwalt?* Institut für Sprach-wissenschaft Wien, *Wiener Linguistische Gazette*, Beiheft 11.
Gunnarsson, B.-L. (1989) 'Text comprehensibility and the writing process'. *Written Communication* 6 (1): 86–107.
Hall, S. and Jacques, M. (1983) *The Politics of Thatcherism*. London: Lawrence and Wishart.
Halliday, M.A.K. (1994) *Introduction to Functional Grammar* (2nd edn). London: Edward Arnold.
Halliday, M.A.K. and Hasan, R. (1985) *Language, Context and Text*. Oxford: Oxford University Press.

Kress, G. (1993) 'Against arbitrariness: the social production of the sign as a foundational issue in critical discourse analysis'. *Discourse and Society* 4 (2): 169–91.

Lalouschek, J., Menz, F. and Wodak, R. (1990) *Alltag in der Ambulanz*. Tübingen: Narr.

Larrain, J. (1979) *The Concept of Ideology*. London: Hutchinson.

Lutz, B. and Wodak, R. (1987) *Information für Informierte*. Vienna: Akademie der Wissenschaften.

Mishler, E. (1977) *The Discourse of Medicine*. Norwood, NJ: Ablex.

Mitten, R. and Wodak, R. (1993) 'On the discourse of racism and prejudice'. *Folia Linguistica* XXVII (3–4): 192–215.

Oevermann, V., Allert, T., Konau, E. and Krambeck, J. (1979) 'Die Methologie einer "objectven Hermeneutik"', in H.G. Soeffner (ed.) *Interpretative Verfahren in den Sozial- und Textwissenschaften* (pp. 352–434). Frankfurt am Main: Metzler.

Pfeiffer, O.E., Strouhal, E. and Wodak, R. (1987) *Rechtaufsprache*. Vienna: Orac.

Smith, D. (1990) *Texts, Facts and Femininity*. London: Routledge.

van Dijk, T. (1985) *Prejudice in Discourse*. Amsterdam: Benjamins.

van Dijk, T. (1989) 'Structures of discourse and structures of power', in J.A. Anderson (ed.) *Communication Yearbook 12* (pp. 18–59). Newbury Park, CA: Sage.

van Dijk, T. (1993a) *Discourse and Elite Racism*. London: Sage.

van Dijk, T. (1993b) 'Principles of critical discourse analysis'. *Discourse and Society*, 4 (2): 249–83.

West, C. (1990) 'Not just "doctor's orders"; directive–response sequences in patients' visits to women and men physicians'. *Discourse and Society* 1 (1): 85–112.

Wittgenstein, L. (1967) *Philosophische Untersuchungen*. Frankfurt am Main: Suhrkamp.

Wodak, R. (1992) 'Strategies in text production and text comprehension: a new perspective', in Dieter Stein (ed.) *Cooperating with Written Texts: The pragmatics and comprehension of written texts*. Berlin, New York: Mouton de Gruyter.

Wodak, R. and De Cillia, R. (1989) 'Sprache und Antisemitismus'. *Hitteilungen des Instituts für Wissenschaft und Kunst*, 3.

Wodak, R., Menz, F., Mitten, R. and Stern, F. (1994) *Die Sprachen der 'Vergangenheiten': Gedenken in österreichischen und deutschen Medien*. Frankfurt am Main: Suhrkamp.

Wodak, R., Moosmüller, S., Doleschal, U. and Feistritzer, G. (1987) *Das Sprachverhalten von Frau und Mann*. Vienna: Ministry for Social Affairs.

Wodak, R., Pelikan, J., Nowak, P., Gruber, H., De Cillia, R. and Mitten, R. (1990) '*Wir sind alle unschuldige Täter': Diskurshistorische Studien zum Nachkriegsantisemitismus* Frankfurt am Main: Suhrkamp.

Chapter 7

Caroline Coffin and Kieran O'Halloran

Finding the global groove

Theorising and analysing dynamic reader positioning using APPRAISAL, corpus, and a concordancer

Introduction

An important goal of Critical Discourse Analysis (CDA) is to reveal the way in which the language of a text positions readers to view and evaluate social and political reality in particular ways (e.g., Fairclough, 1992; Mills, 1995). By showing how influential texts such as those in newspapers may influence and shape the valuational viewpoints of their communities of readers, the micro-to-macro analytical framework of CDA (e.g., Fairclough, 2001) provides a means of social critique. Significantly, CDA reader positioning analysis has not focused on dynamic reader positioning – that is, how positioning is built up as the reader progresses through a text. It is important, however, to consider the cumulative build-up of evaluative meaning since an earlier section of a text may affect how subsequent sections are interpreted. As a simple illustration, let us take a short extract from a news story in *The Sun* newspaper, a UK tabloid. In the story, the Deputy Prime Minister of the UK, John Prescott, is reported to have made a rude hand-gesture:

> The gesture is the latest in a series of gaffes by Mr Prescott, dubbed Two Jags for his love of the cars. He has THUMPED a protester during an election campaign, caused a STORM by using two cars for a 250-yard drive, DOZED off at a summit and got a SOAKING by Chumbawamba at the Brits.
>
> (Kavanagh & Lea, 2003)

Edited version of Coffin, C. and O'Halloran, K.A. (2005) 'Finding the global groove: theorising and analysing dynamic reader positioning using APPRAISAL, corpus, and a concordancer', *Critical Discourse Studies* 2 (2): 143–63.

Signalled by the word 'gaffes', many readers would understand from the first sentence above that Mr. Prescott is responsible for the actions that follow and this indeed seems to be the case as indicated by the sequence of clauses in which Prescott is responsible for 'thumping', 'causing a storm', and 'dozing off'. We could argue that this sequence of similarly structured clauses creates a kind of vertical 'groove' of meaning which reinforces the message that Prescott is responsible for the various gaffes reported in the story. However, if we consider the final clause – 'and [he] got a soaking by the pop band Chumbawamba at the Brits – we see that Mr. Prescott, rather than being responsible for the 'soaking' (caused, in fact, by a member of the pop group pouring a bucket of water over him at a British music awards ceremony), was the recipient of the water. This last incident then is not a 'gaffe'. However, the construction of the text groove would seem to position the reader dynamically to think that John Prescott was responsible for the soaking he received.

The above is merely an illustration of how readers may be dynamically positioned as a result of textual patterning. Clearly, though, we have not performed anything like a systematic analysis; indeed we were only dealing with an extract from a longer news report. It is to the recent development of a framework within systemic functional linguistics referred to as APPRAISAL (see Martin, 1997, 2000; White, 2003a, 2003b) that we will turn in order to borrow tools to perform a systematic analysis of dynamic reader positioning.[1] In this chapter, we use a complete news story to illustrate how the APPRAISAL framework can be used systematically to trace the build-up through a text of an evaluative groove and to show how such a groove positions readers to evaluate seemingly neutral sentences in a text.

We use the word 'groove' in order to capture the way in which interpersonal meaning through a text can dynamically channel readers to take up an overall evaluative stance towards the content of subsequent text.

As a result of our analysis we propose that APPRAISAL is a useful tool for critical discourse analysts identifying how dynamic reader positioning is built up. Such a claim raises, however, a key issue in CDA: to what extent can analysts make claims about the positioning power of a text for other readers? Many practitioners in CDA argue that all analysis is value-laden (see Gouveia, 2003). We are sympathetic to this argument. If we wish to judge how a text might be positioning readers other than ourselves, we need to put in place mechanisms which help to reduce as much as possible the intrusion of our own values and idiosyncratic judgements of text meaning which may not be those of other readers. We will explore this issue by showing how the computer technology of a concordancer can substantiate APPRAISAL analysis by helping to reduce an analyst's subjective intrusion.

There is another important methodological point to consider. If we wish to gain an understanding of how a text positions its target readership, a readership that analysts may not be part of, we will ultimately need to connect the linguistic analysis to the context of the target readership. Below, we will show how a specialised corpus can help establish this link in grounding the APPRAISAL text analysis from a more discursive, intertextual perspective and in doing so bolstering it. We also show how, in doing this, explanatory critique of the wider socio-political context in which a text is likely to be read is facilitated.

The data

The object of our linguistic analysis is a news story published in *The Sun* (May 27, 2003), a UK tabloid newspaper which has a very large circulation of over 3.5 million.[2] This large circulation means *The Sun* has the potential to exert a large influence in Britain, particularly among the working-class readership it targets.[3] The news report relates to the signing of a new European Union (EU) constitution which is concerned with, among other things, making progress in the areas of freedom, security, and justice, and in the fields of common foreign and security policy. Brussels, mentioned in the text, is where the European Commission is based, this being the driving force within the EU's institutional system in that it proposes legislation, policies, and programmes of action and is responsible for implementing the decisions of the European Parliament and the Council. Eastern Europe is also mentioned in the article; a significant issue which faced the EU when the text was written was its imminent expansion to include several countries from eastern Europe such as Poland, Latvia, and Lithuania.[4] Finally, the euro or 'single currency' of the EU is also referred to, having been introduced in 2002 in 12 of the then 15 countries of the European Union (including Germany, France, and Italy – countries mentioned in the article).

Consider the last sentence of the report: 'Mr Blair will be expected to sign up to the constitution blueprint by the end of June.' On its own, we felt that such a statement would carry little weight for many readers. Coming at the end of the report, however, we thought it had a particular resonance, which we encourage you to reflect on when you come to it shortly. Here now is the whole text data:

Two million jobs in peril
By GEORGE PASCOE-WATSON
Deputy Political Editor

TWO million jobs will be lost if Tony Blair signs the new EU treaty, it was feared last night.

A revised draft of the proposed constitution revealed that Britain would be forced to surrender control of its economy to Brussels.

And other key elements of our way of life would be affected even more drastically than first thought.

The draft proved Brussels also aimed to snatch power over UK employment, foreign affairs, defence and welfare.

And it meant Britain would have to dish out generous benefits to millions of migrants from eastern Europe.

They would be allowed to flock here after ten new nations join the EU next year.

The scale of the masterplan for a United States of Europe triggered outrage last night.

Critics said booming Britain would be crippled by the sort of economic edicts that have wrecked Germany.

Tory MP David Heathcoat-Amory said: 'We could be facing another two million British workers on the dole.'

'The EU will be driving our employment policies in the same direction as Germany. They are struggling with mass unemployment and their dole queue is rising.'

Mr Heathcoat-Amory sits on the convention thrashing out the constitution but his attempts to limit its powers have been swept aside.

He backed The Sun's call for Britain to be allowed a referendum on joining the treaty. Mr Blair has refused to stage one – although other EU states will get a vote.

A crucial phrase in yesterday's blueprint stated: 'The Union shall work for a Europe of sustainable development based on balanced economic growth with a social market economy.'

Experts leaped on the final three words and warned they would be a death sentence to our freewheeling economy.

Germany has laboured for years under this system which forces firms and individuals to pay high taxes which stifle growth and enterprise.

Dr Madsen Pirie, president of the Adam Smith Institute – a free market think-tank – said the constitution would be disastrous for UK employment.

He said: 'There is no doubt that if we were to sign up to the proposals it would result in large numbers of people being unemployed.'

'The reason we are not in the bad position that most of our European partners are in is because we kept our independence from the single currency '

'This constitution would make us lose an important part of that independence. We absolutely must have a referendum.'

Patrick Minford, professor of economics at Cardiff University, said: 'This could easily put another two million on the unemployment register.'

'We will bring back mass unemployment just as they have got in Germany, France and Italy.'

Mr Blair will be expected to sign up to the constitution blueprint by the end of June.

(our bold)

We feel sure that for many readers, the final sentence, when read after the preceding text, is likely to trigger strong disapproval rather than be read as an impartial, factual statement. But how does the statement lose its neutrality? Impressionistically, we could say that the story is an overtly biased piece of news reporting designed to position its target readers to take a strongly anti-Tony Blair (UK Prime Minister) and anti-EU line, and that this statement is netted into such an overall evaluative perspective. But these are just impressions about the text. We need, then, ways of corroborating, falsifying, or just limiting these impressions by systematically showing how such a perspective is built up through the text and how it may influence the reading of the final statement. This is the aim of the next section.

An APPRAISAL analysis of dynamic reader positioning

In this section we show how the tools of APPRAISAL serve as a means of tracing the build-up of evaluative meaning and hence a means of providing a systematic linguistic explanation of the positioning power of the final statement of *The Sun* news report. In other words we are interested in using APPRAISAL analysis to corroborate, falsify, or limit our intuitions concerning reader positioning.

The APPRAISAL framework

In essence, APPRAISAL is a framework for the resources open to language users for giving value to social experience. These resources are set out in Figure 7.1 (see Martin, 1997, 2000; White, 2003a, 2003b for a full account of the framework). Analysts using APPRAISAL argue that it is the cumulative, dynamic dimension of evaluative meaning that positions readers; we have already introduced what we mean by the notion of dynamic build-up of meaning with reference to the John Prescott news story extract.

APPRAISAL analysis proposes that patterns of evaluation in parts of a text serve to build up a particular evaluative position over the course of a text (Coffin, 2002, 2003; Macken-Horarik, 2003a, 2003b; Martin & Rose, 2003). This approach has parallels with Lemke's proposition that 'evaluations propagate or ramify through a

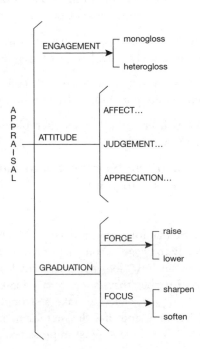

Figure 7.1
An outline of APPRAISAL resources
in English

text' (Lemke, 1998). In Lemke's approach, however, the focus to date has been on how evaluative stances towards one structural element may transfer to another element within adjacent stretches of text or on how evaluation may flow through cohesive reference chains. In our analysis, we are particularly interested in the territory of 'longer range cohesive propagations' (Lemke, 1998, p. 53) operating across whole texts, which Lemke flags as significant but does not explore in detail. And, unlike Lemke, we have a much greater focus on the target reader of a text when showing how patterns of evaluative meaning combine with intertextually generated evaluative resonances to create a consistent value-orientation stance in the course of a text.

The kind of dynamic analysis we produce below is also a response to ongoing criticism of approaches to text analysis which focus on selected pieces of text as proof of a text's ideological slant and which read off meaning 'without regard to textual modification' (Widdowson, 2000, p. 19; see also O'Halloran, 2003 for a cognitive perspective on these dangers).

The three APPRAISAL systems of most relevance to this chapter are those of AFFECT, JUDGEMENT, and GRADUATION. Figure 7.1 shows these systems in the context of the overall APPRAISAL framework. AFFECT comprises a set of language resources for appraising experience in affectual terms, for indicating the positive or negative emotional effect of an event, as in: 'TWO million jobs will be lost if Tony Blair signs the new EU treaty, it was *feared* [negative AFFECT] last night.'

JUDGEMENT, on the other hand, encompasses meanings which serve to appraise human behaviour by reference to a set of norms about how people should and should not behave. For example: 'Blair's refusal to stage a referendum was regarded as an indication of his *stubborn* [negative JUDGEMENT] personality' (N.B. this sentence was created for illustrative purposes).

GRADUATION comprises a set of resources for grading – 'turning the volume up or down' – as in: 'The scale of the masterplan for a United States of Europe triggered *outrage* last night' (GRADUATION – compare with the less charged item *anger*).

APPRAISAL has not only been designed to account for the way in which patterns of evaluative meaning accumulate through a text but the way in which such meanings are expressed both directly and indirectly. The theory acknowledges that a writer may explicitly signal in the text a direct JUDGEMENT such as the example of Blair's stubbornness above. Alternatively, the text may create the conditions for the reader to make a particular JUDGEMENT; in such cases the writer has left the JUDGEMENT as indirect in the text. As an example of an indirect JUDGEMENT in the text, consider the following sentence: 'TWO million jobs will be lost if Tony Blair signs the new EU treaty, it was feared last night.'

There is no direct JUDGEMENT on Blair's personality here such as we saw with the 'stubbornness' example. However this sentence, we would argue, functions as an indirect JUDGEMENT since it is likely to prompt many readers to judge Blair's action as morally irresponsible (given the cause–effect relation between Blair signing the treaty and 2 million people being made unemployed). Indirect JUDGEMENTS, it has emerged in recent research (e.g., Coffin, 2002), are often accompanied by GRADUATION.

Finding the negative semantic groove

Below is *The Sun* report analysed from the perspective of JUDGEMENT, GRADUATION, and AFFECT. Note that, in the analysis, single underlining indicates less morally charged JUDGEMENTS concerning, for example, people's competence and resolve, whereas double underlining indicates more morally charged JUDGEMENTS concerning ethics and truth (see Martin, 2000 for further detail on different types of JUDGEMENT). Sentences are numbered for ease of reference.

Single underlining = JUDGEMENT (less morally charged)

Double underlining = JUDGEMENT (more morally charged)

Italics = Indirect JUDGEMENT

Bold = GRADUATION

Dashed underlining = AFFECT

+ve = positive

−ve = negative

1. **Two million jobs in peril**
2. **TWO million jobs** will be lost *if Tony Blair signs the new EU treaty* (−ve JUDGEMENT of Blair), it was feared last night.
3. A revised draft of the proposed constitution revealed that Britain *would be* ***forced** to surrender control of its economy to Brussels* (−ve JUDGEMENT of Brussels).
4. *And other key elements of our way of life would be affected* ***even more drastically*** (−ve JUDGEMENT of Brussels) than first thought.
5. The draft proved *Brussels also aimed to* ***snatch** power over UK employment, foreign affairs, defence and welfare* (−ve JUDGEMENT of Brussels).
6. And it meant *Britain would have to dish out* ***generous** benefits to* ***millions of** migrants from eastern Europe* (−ve JUDGEMENT of EU, as opposed to +ve JUDGEMENT of Britain's generosity).
7. *They would be allowed to* ***flock** here after ten new nations join the EU next year* (−ve JUDGEMENT of EU).
8. The scale of the masterplan for a United States of Europe triggered **outrage** last night (−ve JUDGEMENT of EU).
9. Critics said **booming** Britain (+ve JUDGEMENT of Britain) would be *crippled by the sort of economic edicts that have* ***wrecked** Germany* (−ve JUDGEMENT of economic edicts and by implication the EU).
10. Tory MP David Heathcoat-Amory said: 'We could be facing another two million British workers on the dole.'
11. *'The EU will be* ***driving** our employment policies in the same direction as Germany'* (−ve JUDGEMENT of the EU).
12. *'They are* ***struggling** with* ***mass** unemployment and their dole queue is rising'* (−ve JUDGEMENT of Germany).
13. *Mr Heathcoat-Amory sits on the convention* ***thrashing** out the constitution but his attempts to limit its powers* (+ve JUDGEMENT of Mr. H.-A.) *have been* ***swept** aside* (−ve JUDGEMENT of EU).
14. He backed The Sun's call for Britain to be allowed a referendum on joining the treaty.
15. *Mr Blair has* ***refused** to stage one* (−ve JUDGEMENT of Blair)—*although other EU states will get a vote.*

16.   A crucial phrase in yesterday's blueprint stated: 'The Union shall work for a Europe of sustainable development based on balanced economic growth with a social market economy.'

17.   Experts **leaped** on the final three words and warned _they would be a **death sentence**_ (–ve JUDGEMENT of EU constitution) to _our freewheeling economy_ (+ve JUDGEMENT of Britain).

18.   Germany has laboured for years under _this system which **forces** firms and individuals to pay **high** taxes which **stifle** growth and enterprise_ (–ve JUDGEMENT of EU).

19.   Dr Madsen Pirie, president of the Adam Smith Institute—a free market think-tank—said the constitution would be **disastrous** for UK employment (–ve JUDGEMENT of EU constitution).

20.   He said: 'There is no doubt that _if we were to sign up to the proposals it would result in **large** numbers of people being unemployed_ (–ve JUDGEMENT of EU constitution).'

21.   'The reason we are not in the bad position (+ve JUDGEMENT of Britain) that most of our European partners are in (–ve JUDGEMENT of European partners) is because _we kept our independence from the single currency_ (+ve JUDGEMENT). _This constitution would make us lose an important part of that independence_ (–ve JUDGEMENT of EU constitution).'

22.   'We **absolutely must** have a referendum.'

23.   Patrick Minford, professor of economics at Cardiff University, said: _'This could **easily** put another two million on the unemployment register'_ (–ve JUDGEMENT of EU constitution).

24.   _'We will bring back **mass** unemployment_ (–ve JUDGEMENT of EU constitution) just as _they have got in Germany, France and Italy'_ (–ve JUDGEMENT of EU partners).

25.   _Mr Blair will be expected to sign up to the constitution blueprint by the end of June_ (–ve JUDGEMENT of Blair).

From a synoptic perspective, Table 7.1 displays the patterns of JUDGEMENT in _The Sun_ news report in terms of the targets of the journalist's appraisal and whether these appraisals are made directly or indirectly.

It shows that the _EU/Brussels/those behind the constitution_ is the group most frequently judged. It also shows that many of the JUDGEMENTS present in _The Sun_ news story are indirectly rather than directly inscribed, thus indicating a certain subtlety in reader positioning. Furthermore, we can see that all groups and individuals fall into one or other of the two camps – 'positive' or 'negative'. JUDGEMENTS, then, are 'black and white' and do not allow for groups to be assessed as a more complex mix of both positive and negative dimensions.

The APPRAISAL analysis of the news report also reveals that GRADUATION and/or values of AFFECT often accompany indirect JUDGEMENT in the text, the former supporting previous research as mentioned earlier (Coffin, 2002). Indeed, stripped of GRADUATION, it is likely that readers would be less inclined to pass JUDGEMENT on a particular sentence. Compare, for example: 'Critics said booming Britain would be **crippled** by the sort of economic edicts that have **wrecked** Germany,' with 'Critics said Britain would be affected by the sort of economic edicts that have not changed Germany for the better.'

Table 7.1 Targets of JUDGEMENT

	direct +ve JUDGEMENT	indirect +ve JUDGEMENT	direct −ve JUDGEMENT	indirect −ve JUDGEMENT
Tony Blair	0	0	0	3
EU/Brussels/those behind the constitution	0	0	1	15
Britain	2	1	0	0
Germany	0	0	0	1
Mr. H.-A	0	1	0	0
EU partners	0	0	1	1

From the APPRAISAL analysis, we can see that a cumulative groove of evaluative semantic meaning is built up through the text. Thus, for example, with each repeated association of *Brussels/EU* with destruction to the UK economy and employment (e.g., *snatch power*, *crippled*, *wrecked*, *death sentence*) the reader is primed and positioned to perceive negatively any ensuing proposition concerning *Brussels/the EU*. In particular, repeated use of GRADUATION in association with the potential negative effects of the constitution on the UK economy serves to intensify this position. In this way, clauses which on their own may appear evaluatively neutral or possibly ambiguous are less so from a globally dynamic point of view.

For example, in isolation, the following clause might appear to be a positive JUDGEMENT of Britain's generosity to migrants. However, the preceding co-text, with negative JUDGEMENTS of the EU and Brussels in relation to the UK economy, positions readers to interpret this as a negative JUDGEMENT of EU policy, particularly given that there is an 'economic issue' here too in providing benefits for migrants: 'And it meant *Britain would have to dish out generous benefits to millions of migrants from eastern Europe*' (−ve JUDGEMENT of EU policy). Similarly, the sentence '*The EU will be driving our employment policies in the same direction as Germany*' is seemingly neutral on its own. However, the build-up of negative JUDGEMENTS of the EU, in relation to the effect on the UK economy/employment, positions readers to see the statement as indicating further disapproval of the EU.

That is why we have assigned −ve JUDGEMENT to the above sentences; −ve JUDGEMENT has been dynamically assigned. And it is this dynamic aspect of evaluative meaning that, we would argue, positions readers to assign a negative charge to the seemingly neutral final statement in the story: '*Mr Blair will be expected to sign up to the constitution blueprint by the end of June*' (−ve JUDGEMENT).

Analysing this sentence, then, as a morally charged JUDGEMENT when it might otherwise appear as an interpersonally neutral statement (e.g., there is no intensifying presence of GRADUATION) is an outcome of cumulative negative JUDGEMENTS concerning Blair's actions (e.g., refusing to stage a referendum) combined with the constant build-up of negativity, especially through GRADUATION, surrounding *Brussels/the EU* and the potential negative economic effects of the treaty on Britain.

To sum up: we have shown that APPRAISAL is a useful set of tools for systematically revealing a global semantic groove of cumulative evaluation through a text and showing how readers generally can be dynamically positioned to evaluate as negative sentences which would be seemingly neutral out of context. We now move on to consider some potential problems with the analysis and ways of responding to these problems. These problems relate to our subjectivity as analysts and to what extent our reader positioning analysis really is about how the text positions readers generally. The first problem here relates to the partiality of text analysis.

The problem of analyst subjectivity and the partiality of text analysis

All text analysis is likely to be executed in relation to a goal. And so, in one sense, all text analysis is likely to be partial. Our goal here has been to describe the global negative semantic groove of the text and how this is likely to impact upon the seemingly neutral last sentence. With this interpersonal concern we have focused on APPRAISAL patterns and thus excluded other potential areas of grammatical and lexical analysis. But there is another sense of partiality which is more troubling for text analysis and thus potentially troubling for our APPRAISAL analysis. One criticism that has been levelled at CDA is that practitioners select parts of a text which corroborate their own interpretation while potentially missing features which do not (Widdowson, 1995). They then misleadingly go on to pass off their own analysis as the interpretation which the unsuspecting reader is likely to make.

We acknowledge the prospect of our own partiality in our APPRAISAL analysis. As readers of this chapter you may feel we have glossed over local parts of the text and left some sentences analytically untouched which you may have assigned evaluative meaning to. Equally, you may disagree with parts of our analysis. But these differences would be local ones to be argued over. In line with our goal, our analysis has stretched across the whole of the text and in doing so we have shown the global groove of evaluative semantic meaning. So, whether all the potential indirect judgements have triggered in us a particular response or not, and therefore whether there are 15 or 17 indirect judgements in the text, etc., this would not affect the fact that there is, at least in APPRAISAL terms, a dominant global groove of negative evaluation throughout the text which we have empirically accounted for.

Let us come back to the phrase, 'at least in APPRAISAL terms'. Despite making progress by taking into account how the dominant groove of evaluative meaning affects potentially neutral or ambiguous sentences, APPRAISAL is ultimately a text descriptive apparatus, the use of which begs the following question. To what extent is the global semantic groove that we have found a reflex of how APPRAISAL categories are activated by us as analysts through our own idiosyncratic judgements of text meaning? After all, we are interested in how the APPRAISAL analysis is likely to position readers generally, not just us as analysts. We need, then, to find some way of corroborating the analysis which gives us some distance on how we have activated the descriptive apparatus. We are thus in tune with the critical discourse analysts Chouliaraki and Fairclough when they say:

> [T]o gain the necessary distance from initial understandings, one has to be aware of the distinctiveness of one's own language of description (the theoretical

framework and the construction and analysis of the research object) and be reflexive in managing their interplay.

(1999, p. 68)

In the next section, we consider ways in which the technology of a concordancer can play an important role in 'checking' APPRAISAL and thus in effect can help to reduce the possibility that we are over-interpreting the text from the point of view of a general reader through over-activation of APPRAISAL categories. We say 'reducing' rather than 'removing' since total value-free analysis is unlikely if indeed it is possible at all.

Checking potential over-interpretation with the concordancer

A concordancer is a piece of software which is used to investigate patterns of meaning in large bodies of texts known as corpora. Typically this applies to searches which explore over one million word banks of undifferentiated texts. However, concordancers can also be useful in the examination of patterns within a single text, pointing to regularities that might otherwise elude the conscious attention of the casual reader. The kinds of pattern that concordancers reveal are what are known as lexico-grammatical patterns, patterns of interrelating lexis (vocabulary) and grammar. So far, we have used APPRAISAL to reveal in *The Sun* text a global semantic groove of negative evaluative meaning. If we use a concordancer and find a corresponding global lexico-grammatical groove of negative meaning, this would support our APPRAISAL analysis and thus help to show we had not over-interpreted the text on behalf of readers generally. Furthermore, this would be strong evidence since a concordancer generates these patterns objectively – the lexico-grammatical patterns that are revealed are not 'tainted' by our intrusion as analysts.

To begin with, we used the concordancer to construct a word frequency list (see Figure 7.2). We were then in a position to see whether the high-frequency words cluster with one another to form some regularity of lexico-grammatical patterning in the text.

We can see in the word frequency list of Figure 7.2 that *the* is the most common word with 25 instances, *of* is the next common with 15 instances, and so on. We chose several of the relatively high-frequency words and, searching for them using concordancer software, we looked to see whether they clustered with one another. This was something of a trial and error process. As Figure 7.3 reveals, we found a strong clustering between two relatively high frequency words: *would* (9 instances) and *be* (11 instances) as well as between *will* (5 instances) and *be*. Figure 7.3 also shows that the clustering takes place in a set of negative predictions, such as: 'would be affected even more drastically…'

This clustering is significant given that the last sentence of the text contains *will be* and because our APPRAISAL analysis argued that the text cumulatively positions the reader to read the last sentence negatively.

In our trial and error exploration, we also found an additional lexico-grammatical pattern with another relatively high frequency word, *to* (15 instances). In Figure 7.4

Count	Pct	Word	Count	Pct	Word	Count	Pct	Word
25	5.3879%	the	3	0.6466%	this	2	0.4310%	up
15	3.2328%	of	3	0.6466%	unemployment	2	0.4310%	which
15	3.2328%	to	2	0.4310%	allowed	2	0.4310%	with
11	2.3707%	be	2	0.4310%	another	1	0.2155%	absolutely
10	2.1552%	a	2	0.4310%	as	1	0.2155%	adam
9	1.9397%	would	2	0.4310%	blueprint	1	0.2155%	affairs
8	1.7241%	and	2	0.4310%	brussels	1	0.2155%	affected
7	1.5086%	in	2	0.4310%	could	1	0.2155%	after
6	1.2931%	on	2	0.4310%	dole	1	0.2155%	aimed
6	1.2931%	we	2	0.4310%	draft	1	0.2155%	also
5	1.0776%	constitution	2	0.4310%	economic	1	0.2155%	although
5	1.0776%	for	2	0.4310%	from	1	0.2155%	an
5	1.0776%	have	2	0.4310%	growth	1	0.2155%	aside
5	1.0776%	our	2	0.4310%	has	1	0.2155%	at
5	1.0776%	said	2	0.4310%	he	1	0.2155%	attempts
5	1.0776%	that	2	0.4310%	heathcoat-amory	1	0.2155%	back
5	1.0776%	will	2	0.4310%	if	1	0.2155%	backed
4	0.8621%	britain	2	0.4310%	independence	1	0.2155%	bad
4	0.8621%	eu	2	0.4310%	its	1	0.2155%	balanced
4	0.8621%	germany	2	0.4310%	jobs	1	0.2155%	based
4	0.8621%	million	2	0.4310%	last	1	0.2155%	because
4	0.8621%	they	2	0.4310%	market	1	0.2155%	been
4	0.8621%	two	2	0.4310%	mass	1	0.2155%	being
3	0.6466%	-	2	0.4310%	new	1	0.2155%	benefits
3	0.6466%	are	2	0.4310%	night	1	0.2155%	booming
3	0.6466%	blair	2	0.4310%	other	1	0.2155%	bring
3	0.6466%	by	2	0.4310%	out	1	0.2155%	british
3	0.6466%	economy	2	0.4310%	referendum	1	0.2155%	but
3	0.6466%	employment	2	0.4310%	sign	1	0.2155%	call
3	0.6466%	europe	2	0.4310%	states	1	0.2155%	cardiff
3	0.6466%	is	2	0.4310%	treaty	1	0.2155%	control
3	0.6466%	it	2	0.4310%	uk	1	0.2155%	convention
3	0.6466%	mr	2	0.4310%	un	1	0.2155%	crippled

Figure 7.2 Word frequency list for *The Sun* text

proposed constitution revealed that Britain would be forced to surrender control of its econom
ls. And other key elements of our way of life would be affected even more drastically than first t
s, defence and welfare. And it meant Britain would have to dish out generous benefits to million:
ions of migrants from eastern Europe. They would be allowed to flock here after ten new nation
·age last night. Critics said booming Britain would be crippled by the sort of economic edicts th
ed on the final three words and warned they would be a death sentence to our freewheeling ecor
·ee market think-tank - said the constitution would be disastrous for UK employment. He said: '
that if we were to sign up to the proposals it would result in large numbers of people being uner
from the single currency. "This constitution would make us lose an important part of that indep
)N Deputy Political Editor TWO million jobs will be lost if Tony Blair signs the new EU treaty,
million British workers on the dole. "The EU will be driving our employment policies in the san
efused to stage one - although other EU states will get a vote. A crucial phrase in yesterday's blu
) million on the unemployment register. "We will bring back mass unemployment just as they h
got in Germany, France and Italy." Mr Blair will be expected to sign up to the constitution blue

Figure 7.3 Clustering between *would* and *will* and *be*

on the next page we can see that both *to* in an infinitive and *to* in prepositional phrases have fairly negative co-texts. *To* is also significant for our earlier APPRAISAL analysis since the last sentence of the text contains an infinitive 'to sign up' and a prepositional phrase 'to the constitution'.

Since *constitution* is another relatively high frequency word and is also in the last sentence of the text, we used the concordancer to generate concordance lines for this word as well. The concordance lines (see Figure 7.5) show that there is a negative lexico-grammatical pattern for the first four instances of constitution.

Taking all the concordancer evidence for *will* (and the related *would*) + *be*, *to* infinitives, *to* in prepositional phrases, and *constitution*, we can see that there is a global groove of negative evaluative lexico-grammatical patterning which relates to

titution revealed that Britain would be forced to surrender control of its economy to Brussels. /
hought. The draft proved Brussels also aimed to snatch power over UK employment, foreign af
and welfare. And it meant Britain would have to dish out generous benefits to millions of migra
from eastern Europe. They would be allowed to flock here after ten new nations join the EU ne
.hrashing out the constitution but his attempts to limit its powers have been swept aside. He bac
pt aside. He backed The Sun's call for Britain to be allowed a referendum on joining the treaty.
ım on joining the treaty. Mr Blair has refused to stage one - although other EU states will get a
this system which forces firms and individuals to pay high taxes which stifle growth and enterpr
ıt. He said: "There is no doubt that if we were to sign up to the proposals it would result in larg
France and Italy." Mr Blair will be expected to sign up to the constitution blueprint by the en(
l be forced to surrender control of its economy to Brussels. And other key elements of our way of
ritain would have to dish out generous benefits to millions of migrants from eastern Europe. They
·ds and warned they would be a death sentence to our freewheeling economy. Germany has labou
l: "There is no doubt that if we were to sign up to the proposals it would result in large numbers (
nd Italy." Mr Blair will be expected to sign up to the constitution blueprint by the end of June. ..

Figure 7.4 To (infinitive) and *to* (prepositional phrase)

last night. A revised draft of the proposed constitution revealed that Britain would be forced to su
ry sits on the convention thrashing out the constitution but his attempts to limit its powers have be
;titute - a free market think-tank - said the constitution would be disastrous for UK employment. H
;pendence from the single currency. "This constitution would make us lose an important part of th
Mr Blair will be expected to sign up to the constitution blueprint by the end of June. ...

Figure 7.5 Constitution *and negative patterning*

the seemingly neutral lexico-grammatical pattern of the last sentence. Crucially, because lexico-grammatical patterns are objectively generated by the concordancer, its use has helped us to appreciate that our APPRAISAL analysis was not an over-interpretation from the point of view of a general reader. In other words, there really is a global negative groove in the text as revealed by the APPRAISAL analysis. An important corollary is that since there is corroboration of a groove in the text which dynamically positions the general reader, then we are finding support that the dynamic accruing of negative meaning is likely also to be a cognitive reality for readers generally. (This is not to say that the reader has to accept this positioning all the same.) However, the APPRAISAL analysis so far has been concerned with a general reader and has thus not been grounded in the context of the target readership.

Grounding the APPRAISAL analysis in the political-economic context of the target readership

A specialised newspaper corpus gives us as analysts insights into what regular readers of a particular newspaper are routinely exposed to. It thus gives us insight, albeit partial, into the kinds of meanings that are likely to be made by the target readership during dynamic text positioning. In order to ground the APPRAISAL dynamic positioning analysis of text in the context of what the target readership is routinely exposed to, we looked at the connotations of lexical items in *The Sun* text which form part of its key semantic field: *Brussels/EU/Europe*. Given that *Germany* is a relatively high-frequency word in this text and could be said to form part of the same semantic field, we also investigated usage of *Germany*. These are not only key lexical items in terms of the topic of the text but also because of their combined relatively high frequency in the text (see Figure 7.2).

In view of our sample news report, the most appropriate corpus to consult was the *sunnow* corpus, a sub-corpus of the 450 million word Bank of English corpus, which is made up of *The Sun* and its Sunday version, *The News of the World*. The current *sunnow* corpus has editions of *The Sun* and *News of the World* from the period 1999–2003 and has a total of around 45 million words. Our use of this corpus was based on the hypothesis that, although within a specific news report a word or phrase may not be used in an overtly negative (or positive) way, there may be many other instances in *The Sun* where such a phrase is regularly used in negative (or positive) contexts. If so, it could be the case that regular *Sun* readers absorb such negative values over many different readings of the newspaper and hence project negativity onto its use in a particular news report.

Because of the frequency of occurrence of *Brussels / EU / Europe* in the corpus, we restricted our search to a 10% random sampling of the total number of instances. The results showed that contrary to expectation the terms *EU* and *Germany* frequently appeared in neutral or positive contexts with only a small percentage occurring in negative contexts. The next expression in the key semantic field we decided to carry out a search on was *United States of Europe*. This phrase did not immediately hold any particular connotations for us as non-regular readers of *The Sun* newspaper. Figure 7.6 shows a set of concordance lines for *United States of Europe* in the *sunnow* corpus.

The lines in Figure 7.6 show that many of the local lexico-grammatical environments for *United States of Europe* indicate negative evaluation, e.g., *hopeless dream of*, *bleak plan for*, and *fanatics who believe*. For places where the lexico-grammatical environment does not yield a clear perspective on how expressions are being evaluated, the co-text can be expanded. In the Bank of English, for example, co-texts consisting of five screen lines can be activated, as shown in the following expanded co-text for the first line:

> [F]or the same wages paid for one Austrian worker, an employer can get eight from the Czech Republic. The elite in Brussels have been busy for years building towards their ambition of a United States of Europe, stretching from Shetland to the borders of Russia. They have demolished national independence in critical areas, and paid not the slightest attention to genuine fears and problems.

In the above, it is clear that *United States of Europe* is construed with fairly negative attitude and expanded co-texts for the other lines reveal a similar pattern. All 33 instances that were generated by the concordancer were negative. *United States of Europe* then carries what is known in corpus linguistics as a negative semantic prosody (Louw, 1993). This suggests also that regular readers of *The Sun* will recognise the phrase *United States of Europe* as having a negative semantic prosody. This potentially predisposed them to evaluate this expression negatively when they came across it in *The Sun* report.

```
_ towards their ambition of a United States of Europe, stretching from Shetland
    could pave the way for a United States of Europe. British people have made
    leader's bleak plan for a United States of Europe came as a hammer blow to
  the road towards a Federal United States of Europe. Hague has never tried to
         forming into a giant United States of Europe -with the same tax and
        attacks to push for a United States of Europe. <p> The former Italian
      were evidence we need a United States of Europe.4 <p> COMPLETE WOBBLERS
   The empire-builders want a United States of Europe. Thank goodness you have
   thirds say there will be a United States of Europe within the next 20 years.
   for a hopeless dream of a United States of Europe. He is certain to pay the
        was the first step to a United States of Europe - which would cost
   or a state in a newly-formed United States of Europe? These are the central
    Just as many are against a United States of Europe under a federal
  pressure to become part of a United States of Europe. Martin Phillips gives 20
    for EU leaders' dreams of a United States of Europe. Now analysts want to
           the creation of a United States of Europe. The battle is now on to
  SANTER leads the drive for a United States of Europe, and says: 'We must
  elected government running a United States of Europe. Or we can leave the EU
    hurl Britain into a growing united states of Europe run under the same
        to set the pace for a United States of Europe. A triumphant Mr Blair
    fanatics who believed in a United States of Europe." And he warned pro-EU
   the EU is the creation of a United States of Europe. Countries can either be
   stride along the road to a United States of Europe. It demands the same tax
```

Figure 7.6 Concordance lines for *United States of Europe* from the *sunnow* sub-corpus of the Bank of English®. Reproduced with kind permission of HarperCollins Publishers Ltd

Finally, though we used the *sunnow* corpus to reveal a negative semantic prosody for *United States of Europe*, we cannot yet know for sure that this semantic prosody is more likely to be associated with *The Sun* than with other newspapers. As a control we investigated *United States of Europe* in a 32 million-word corpus of news texts in the Bank of English from another newspaper – *The Guardian*. We found no negative instances of *United States of Europe*. So, while a negative semantic prosody for *United States of Europe* may not be solely specific to *The Sun*, nevertheless our comparison here shows us that we might well otherwise have under-interpreted it from the perspective of the target readership.

Since corpus evidence shows that regular readers of *The Sun* are routinely exposed to a negative semantic prosody for *United States of Europe*, we can now start to connect the APPRAISAL analysis (–ve JUDGEMENT of EU via GRADUATION) to potential meanings generated by target readers:

> 8. The scale of the masterplan for a *United States of Europe* triggered **outrage** last night (–ve JUDGEMENT of EU via GRADUATION).

> Outline: negative semantic prosody for a target audience.

Aside from *United States of Europe* carrying a negative semantic prosody, we also found in a search of the *sunnow* corpus that *Brussels* frequently occurs in negative contexts, many of which relate to the euro currency and claims about the negative effects on economic and employment circumstances were the UK to adopt it. This is also reflected in *The Sun* text (*surrender control of its economy to Brussels, snatch power over UK employment*). Out of the 104 lines that we sampled, we found 53 where *Brussels* occurred in negative co-texts (51% of the lines). We also checked this result against *The Guardian* sub-corpus. Out of the 198 lines sampled we only found 8 (4% of the lines) where there were negative co-texts and some of these were because of quotations from other sources. The results of this search showed that *Brussels* very rarely occurs in negative co-texts in *The Guardian*.

Again, through use of the specialised corpus, we are able to ground the APPRAISAL analysis in the context of the target reader:

3. A revised draft of the proposed constitution revealed that Britain <u>would be **forced** to surrender control of its economy to Brussels</u> (–ve JUDGEMENT of Brussels).

4. And <u>other key elements of our way of life would be affected</u> **even more drastically** (–ve JUDGEMENT of Brussels) than first thought.

5. The draft proved <u>*Brussels also aimed to* **snatch** *power over UK employment, foreign affairs, defence and welfare*</u> (–ve JUDGEMENT of Brussels).

With this knowledge of how *Brussels* is treated routinely in *The Sun*, we have additional insight into the position of *Brussels* in the text in early sentences, i.e., where it is likely to have most impact. In this sense we can see how the –ve JUDGEMENTS of Brussels in relation to potential negative effects on the UK economy are even more charged just by use of the metonym, Brussels, for the European Commission.

The negative semantic prosodies we have found for *United States of Europe* and *Brussels* (especially its negative link with the economy) relate to the last sentence of the text; *constitution* is an *EU* constitution after all. Thus, from the point of view of the target readership they not only interact with the –ve JUDGEMENTS and –ve GRADUATION of individual sentences but also with the global semantic and lexico-grammatical text groove. Indeed, the clustering of negative items to create a mutually supporting web of negativity is a phenomenon that has already been identified in corpus research, with Louw (1993, p. 173) arguing 'that in many cases semantic prosodies "hunt in packs" and potentiate and bolster one another' (see also Channell, 2000). Finally, there may still be words or expressions that we have under-interpreted as carrying negative semantic prosodies for target readers which would impact upon *constitution* in the last sentence. But if there are more, their discovery will only serve to support our overall argument rather than detract from it and thus further ground our APPRAISAL analysis in the context of the target reader.

We now indicate how this context-grounded APPRAISAL analysis facilitates a critical discourse perspective on the text.

APPRAISAL-informed explanatory critique

Chouliaraki and Fairclough (1999) and explanatory critique

In using APPRAISAL to describe the text and then go some way to grounding this analysis in terms of the context of the target readership, we have in effect been working with the description and interpretation stages of CDA as defined in Fairclough (2001). The other stage of Fairclough's model, explanation, is where critique of the relationship between text and context occurs. Chouliaraki and Fairclough on explanation:

> We see CDA as a form of what Bhaskar (1986) calls 'explanatory critique' [which] takes the general form of showing (a) a problem, which may be either cognitive, for example, a misrepresentation, or an unmet need ... (b) what obstacles there are to it being tackled; in some cases (c) what the function (including ideological function) of the misrepresentation or unmet need is in sustaining existing social arrangements; and (d) possible ways of removing the obstacles.
>
> (1999, p. 33)

Given that Chouliaraki and Fairclough are explicit that critique can relate to the 'cognitive problem of misrepresentation' or 'unmet need', it is odd to read later in their book that explanatory critique is only tenuously related to a target reader's understandings of a text, if at all:

> We are aware that many analyses carried out within CDA have been partial ... and have not included analysis of understandings. However, CDA does not itself advocate a particular understanding of a text, through it may advocate a particular explanation.
>
> (Chouliaraki & Fairclough, 1999, p. 67)

Our argument is different. To ground explanatory critique truly in context, rather than examining the text as a 'static object', explanatory cognitive critique should not ignore how meanings are likely to be dynamically and intertextually accrued in the reading of a text by its target readers. This is not to say that with our analysis we have reached an actual understanding by an actual target reader. This would, of course, be impossible without interviewing such a reader. Nevertheless, we are 'advocating' a particular dominant, dynamic positioning of the text, based on APPRAISAL analysis, corroborated by a concordancer and empirically grounded in the context of the target readership via use of a specialised corpus. This gives us evidence to posit a likely, dominant, dynamic understanding. And because we do this, our explanatory critique can be more cognitive than an explanation that does not take account of likely, dominant, dynamic understandings.

Cognitive problem of representation in The Sun article

With the above in mind, let us perform an explanatory cognitive critique in relation to the 'cognitive problem of representation' as referred to by Chouliaraki and Fairclough (1999, p. 33). Absent from the text is the representation of a positive or neutral opposing expert voice, a voice which might set out potentially positive economic outcomes for the UK from signing the new EU constitution; the two experts indicated are in fact exponents of right-wing economics. Their credibility is connected with their status (as president and professor) and as Lemke (1998, p. 52) points out, 'the evaluation of the Sayer as reliable' propagates to increase the evaluation in the projected proposition ('projective evaluation'). An explanatory critique not grounded in likely, dynamic, dominant understanding might well suggest (in order to 'remove the obstacle') that the text be more balanced by providing a neutral or positive expert voice. An appropriate place for such a voice would presumably be at the end of the text, alongside the anti-EU constitution voices. But given the dynamic groove of negative meanings, it is unlikely that such a positive voice would register so strongly with the target audience. Indeed, even if the positive voice occurred near the beginning of the article, it would still be competing with Brussels, strategically located for impact (deliberately or not) in the initial part of the text, and its cueing of a negative semantic prosody with regard to negative effects on the UK economy.

A major cognitive problem, then, with this text is not so much lack of representation of other voices – it is to do with the dynamic positioning of the semantic groove which enables intertwining of –VE JUDGEMENTS, GRADUATION, and negative semantic prosodies with regard to effects on the UK economy. It is these phenomena taken together which mean habitual target readers stand a good chance of producing a dynamic understanding of the text which is knitted into an extant anti-European-economic-integration ideology, one regularly promoted in *The Sun* as our corpus investigation indicates. As a result of this, an alternative voice in the text stands a good chance of being obscured in reading by the target reader if not overridden. Our explanatory critique thus shows the text's representational problem, albeit in a more cognitive way.

The Sun *article's unmet need*

The EU's roots are in socio-political reconciliation (in the aftermath of World War II and particularly as a result of conflict between two of the most significant powers of Europe, France and Germany).[5] Forms of socio-political unity in the EU continue to be stressed and are indeed reflected in the constitution draft *The Sun* article refers to. Nevertheless, in the news report, it is almost exclusively the economic dimension of the constitution and the hypothesised negative impact of economic integration which is evaluated. This economic framing of the EU, as our corpus evidence suggests, has been built up over a period of time and doubtless has been inculcated through additional forms of mediation (see Graham, 2002, for discussion of the production and distribution processes by which evaluative patterns may be globally inculcated). *The Sun* is sceptical of forms of European economic integration since these are often characterised by higher levels of job protection and (perceived) bureaucracy. Given that *The Sun* has been in the ownership of the global media mogul, Rupert Murdoch, for around 30 years, this is perhaps not surprising.[6]

Thus, in addition, our explanatory cognitive critique highlights the following: rather than 'meet a need', by expanding *Sun* readers' understanding of a highly complex socio-political phenomenon (as represented by the EU constitution), it is clear that the reductive and simplified nature of the article is likely to reinforce an economic and thus narrow understanding of how the EU operates. Indeed, this narrowness is reinforced by the writer promoting the view that being British involves a shared, homogenous economic identity, reinforced through the use of collective (and coercive) pronoun use: '*our* freewheeling economy'; '*our* employment policies'; '*we* kept *our* independence from the single currency'.

Conclusion

This chapter has demonstrated how APPRAISAL analysis can be used in CDA to show systematically how readers can be dynamically positioned to view seemingly neutral sentences in a negative way. By extension, APPRAISAL analysis could be used to show how readers are dynamically positioned to read seemingly neutral sentences in a positive way. We have shown, then, that linguistic analysis can help to illuminate how a writer's (conscious or unconscious) use of lexico-grammatical and semantic patterning may act as a groove to direct the reader to interpret subsequent text in a particular way. Martin (1996) has referred to this linguistic persuasive process as naturalising a reader position.

We have also made the point that critical discourse analysts are faced with a difficult task when trying to establish how a text positions readers, particularly when analysts are not members of a target readership. Whilst recognising that not all texts will have well-established grooves of semantic or lexico-grammatical patterning, in the case of *The Sun* news article we were able to check the subjective element of APPRAISAL analysis through the use of concordancing techniques. We then showed how specialised corpora of news texts provide insight into the kinds of evaluative meanings that target readers are routinely exposed to, which may be meanings missed by non-insider readers/analysts. As a result we were able to go some way to grounding the APPRAISAL analysis in the political-economic context of *The Sun* text (while recognising that the academic ideal would involve empirical research with actual target readers and how they interact with *The Sun* text). Doing so has facilitated explanatory cognitive critique of the text in relation to context. Crucially though, this explanatory cognitive critique has been in relation to how the text is likely to be read in context. Finally, as a result of our APPRAISAL analysis and our use of corpus-based empirical evidence, we argue the following: reader positioning analysis of texts in CDA needs to be dynamic reader positioning analysis which in turn can lead to a proper explanatory cognitive critique because the latter is based on likely dominant dynamic understandings.

Notes

1   Small capitals are used to distinguish APPRAISAL systems as semantic systems.
2   This is the figure for January 2003. See: http://media.guardian.co.uk/presspublishing/tables/0,7680,893996,00.html
3   Just over half of *The Sun*'s readers are in working class occupations, and only about 10% are in the professions or in management (Whiteley, 2000).
4   See http://europa.eu
5   In the period 1870–1945, France and Germany fought each other three times, with large numbers of fatalities. Following World War II, a number of European leaders promoted the idea that lasting peace was best established through forms of economic and political unity. It was this conviction which led the French Foreign Minister, Robert Schuman, to propose the substantial economic integration of the coal and steel industries of Belgium, West Germany, Luxembourg, France, Italy, and the Netherlands. This took place in 1951. As France and Germany were at the birth of economic integration, this idea is more entrenched on the whole in these countries

than in the UK. In any case, the UK has traditionally had strong political and economic ties with non-European, Anglo-sphere countries such as the USA. The UK did not join a political and economic form of European integration until 1973.

6   Rupert Murdoch, as an advocate of free-market economics and deregulation, played an important role in supporting and shoring up the success in the 1980s of the British Prime Minister Margaret Thatcher. Thatcher's brand of free-market economics ('Thatcherism') engendered profound changes in British socio-economic life, leading to a free-market, enterprise-driven, short-term contract economic culture which is currently more pronounced than in many other countries of the EU.

References

Bhaskar, R. (1986). *Scientific realism and human emancipation*. London: Verso.

Channell, J. (2000). Corpus-based analysis of evaluative lexis. In S. Hunston & G. Thompson (Eds.), *Evaluation in text: Authorial stance and the construction of discourse* (pp. 38–55). Oxford: Oxford University Press.

Chouliaraki, L., & Fairclough, N. (1999). *Discourse in late modernity: Rethinking critical discourse analysis*. Edinburgh: Edinburgh University Press.

Coffin, C. (2002). The voices of history: Theorising the interpersonal semantics of historical discourses. *Text, 22*, 503–528.

Coffin, C. (2003). Reconstruing the past: Settlement or invasion? In J. R. Martin & R. Wodak (Eds.), *Critical approaches to the discourse of history* (pp. 21–246). Amsterdam: John Benjamins.

Fairclough, N. (1992). *Discourse and social change*. Oxford: Polity.

Fairclough, N. (2001). *Language and power* (2nd ed.). Harlow, UK: Longman.

Gouveia, C. (2003). Critical discourse analysis and the development of the new science. In G. Weiss & R. Wodak (Eds.), *Critical discourse analysis: Theory and interdisciplinarity* (pp. 47–62). Basingstoke, UK: Palgrave.

Graham, P. (2002). Predication and propagation: A method for analysing evaluative meanings in technology policy. *Text, 22*, 227–268.

Kavanagh, T., & Lea, M. (2003). The same two you, John. *The Sun*. Retrieved 6 June, 2003, from http://www.thesun.co.uk

Lemke, J. L. (1998). Resources for attitudinal meaning. *Functions of Language, 5*, 33–56.

Louw, B. (1993). Irony in the text or insincerity in the writer? In M. Baker, G. Francis, & E. Tognini-Bonelli (Eds.), *Text and technology: In honour of John M. Sinclair* (pp. 157–176). Amsterdam: John Benjamins.

Macken-Horarik, M. (2003a). APPRAISAL and the special instructiveness of narrative. *Text, Special Issue, Negotiating Heteroglossia: Social Perspectives on Evaluation, 23*, 285–312.

Macken-Horarik, M. (2003b). Envoi: Intractable issues in appraisal analysis? *Text, Special Issue, Negotiating Heteroglossia: Social Perspectives on Evaluation, 23*, 313–319.

Martin, J. R. (1996). Evaluating disruption: Symbolising theme in junior secondary narrative. In R. Hasan & G. Williams (Eds.), *Literacy in society* (pp. 124–171). London: Longman.

Martin, J. R. (1997). Analysing genre: Functional parameters. In F. Christie & J. R. Martin (Eds.), *Genres and institutions: Social processes in the workplace and school* (pp. 3–39). London: Pinter.

Martin, J. R. (2000). Beyond exchange: APPRAISAL systems in English. In S. Hunston & G. Thompson (Eds.), *Evaluation in text* (pp.142–175). Oxford: Oxford University Press.

Martin, J. R., & Rose, D. (2003). *Working with discourse*. London: Continuum.

Mills, S. (1995). *Feminist stylistics*. London: Routledge.

O'Halloran, K. A. (2003). *Critical discourse analysis and language cognition*. Edinburgh: Edinburgh University Press.

White, P. R. R. (2003a). Appraisal: The language of evaluation and stance. In C. Verschueren, J. J. Östman, J. Blommaert, & C. Bulcaen (Eds.), *The handbook of pragmatics* (pp. 1–27). Amsterdam: John Benjamins.

White, P. R. R. (2003b). Beyond modality and hedging: A dialogic view of the language of intersubjective stance. *Text, Special Issue, Negotiating Heteroglossia: Social Perspectives on Evaluation*, 23, 259–284.

Whiteley, P. (2000, April 11). Paper politics. *The Guardian*. Retrieved December 2, 2004, from http://www.guardian.co.uk/Archive/Article/0,4273,3984707,00.html.

Widdowson, H. G. (1995). Discourse analysis: A critical view. *Language and Literature*, 4, 157–172.

Widdowson, H. G. (2000). On the limitations of linguistics applied. *Applied Linguistics*, 21, 3–25.

Chapter 8

Tom Bartlett

Towards intervention in Positive Discourse Analysis

1 Introduction

In this chapter, I outline a relatively recent movement in discourse analysis, a movement that has shifted the emphasis from highlighting injustices to identifying and promoting alternatives. This approach is firmly based on existing work that critically illuminates how language can be used by powerful interest groups to maintain their privileged role in society; but it also goes beyond this to identify discourse which has been effective in promoting equality and enhancing cooperation within specific contexts. The most recent development is for discourse analysts to apply this knowledge and to contribute directly to struggles for equality and justice. It is important to see this approach as growing out of existing methods of discourse analysis and I outline the important features of these related methods as well as some of their limitations. In particular, I will go through some examples of how well-known approaches, such as Critical Discourse Analysis (CDA), are able to identify ideologically problematic language. This would include texts that reproduce racist or sexist stereotypes, for example, or dialogues in which one speaker is able to dominate as a result of their powerful social position. The CDA approach attempts to engage with real-world problems by bringing to light obstacles to social justice, by highlighting where discourse *goes wrong*. However, I will suggest that this emphasis on the negative is based on an understanding of 'power' that does not reflect the many different ways that people can be powerful and so fails to recognise potential challenges to the status quo. In contrast to this is Positive Discourse Analysis (PDA), a relatively new approach that celebrates precisely such alternatives. I argue that

PDA is an essential part of engaging with real-world problems because it highlights where discourse *works*. However, celebrating something that works is not the same as understanding why it works, so I go on to suggest that PDA can be strengthened through a more *ethnographic* approach. This would mean, firstly, that the analyses of effective texts are framed within broader description of the customs and routines of the people who produce them, read them and hear them; and, secondly, that it is the responses of these same people which show whether a particular text is effective or not. In this way we can try to understand what it is about particular contexts that make particular discourses work, for good or bad. Once analysts understand these processes, they will be in a better position to *contribute solutions* rather than focusing on problems.

In the second half of the chapter I will illustrate this approach to PDA using data from fieldwork in Guyana, South America. The case study examples bring out the point that what makes language powerful depends on the context in which it is used and includes a brief account of the concept of *socialisation* – how we learn to become members of a particular social group. My argument is that unless we consider how different groups operate on a daily basis we cannot fully explain why one text illustrates a social problem while another text contributes to a solution. While this chapter includes illustrative analysis from a specific case study, it calls for a greater use of ethnographical description generally in making sense of the way language works differently for different social groups and in promoting ways of speaking that make positive and effective use of these differences.

2 Problem identification: The rise of Critical Linguistics

In the 1970s and 1980s the study of texts took a decidedly political turn in the UK, with the rise of what came to be known as Critical Linguistics (Kress and Hodge 1979; Fowler *et al*. 1979). The principal concern of this approach was to reveal how texts can conceal or distort important aspects of the events they purport to represent through the grammatical structures used and the vocabulary chosen just as much as through their general content. A central task of the critical linguist was therefore the 'unpackaging' of biases and points of view that were concealed, deliberately or unwittingly, within influential and widely published texts such as newspaper articles or schoolbooks. One area that continues to receive much coverage in the literature, for example, is the question of *agency*, how the grammar allocates *responsibility* for significant or controversial processes, as in the following example of a much discussed contrast (O'Halloran, 2003: 18):

1   *Police shot dead 10 people today as violence again flared in Jerusalem.*
2   *Ten people were shot dead today as violence once again flared in Jerusalem.*

The point of interest to critical analysis is that the two texts *construe* the same event differently: in 1 we are clearly told who did the shooting, who is responsible for the deaths, whereas in 2 the shootings are simply presented as something that happened to these ten people without any reference to responsible parties.

Another focus of interest for Critical Linguistics is to analyse who has *control* over communicative events: who does most of the speaking and shows most authority when they do. For example, in traditional classroom talk, in doctors' surgeries and in the courtroom, we very often see one-sided patterns in which one participant controls the flow of information with the second participant simply providing appropriate responses as requested or authorised. The following extract (in Fairclough 2001: 123) from an interview between a policeman (P) and a witness (W) demonstrates this one-sidedness:

Text 1:
P: Did you get a look at the one in the car?
W: I saw his face, yeah.
P: What sort of age was he?
W: About 45. He was wearing a . . .
P: And how tall?
W: Six foot one?
P: Six foot one. Hair?
W: Dark and curly.

Generally, we are so used to who does what in these situations that we take these roles for granted, without considering the implications of the different roles or questioning whether there are alternatives. This is what Fairclough (2001) calls the 'power behind language': where control over talk is a feature of the particular social institution in which the talk takes place, with its own well-established speaking roles, rights and responsibilities. However, even when certain speakers have powerful institutional roles they need to maintain this position in *real time*, as the talk progresses, through their use of different features of language. Fairclough calls this ability to maintain a social position through talk the 'power in language'. Typical instances would be showing a certain level of authority by asking plainly for someone to do something, as in example 3, as opposed to asking indirectly and politely, as in example 4:

3   *Close the door.*
4   *Would you mind closing the door, please?*

Another example of authority in language would be in making strong claims about the truth of a statement, as in example 5, as opposed to stating something less categorically, as in example 6:

5   *That was definitely a mistake.*
6   *I think that possibly might not have been the best approach.*

Examples 3 to 6 demonstrate that the way people speak to each other is connected with their relative social position and so we can see that Critical Linguistics shows a concern with the role of texts in social life, rather than say a purely linguistic or literary interest. These examples have also suggested that the way we interact has become *naturalised*, we take it for granted, even though there are many aspects of the way we act on a day-to-day basis that would appear odd to people from other communities.

The insights that these early Critical Linguistics studies provide are still very relevant and, although the perspective in this chapter is quite different, the basic tools remain very similar. For, as we shall see later on, a consideration of what counts as natural language behaviour for different groups not only helps to show where there are imbalances of power within these groups but is also an important element in understanding where these different groups are unable fully to understand each other and why. This applies not only to examples of social status and control over speaking, but also to the different ways we construe everyday goings on in our talk about people and events, the different emphases we place on different aspects, and the things we take for granted and leave out. A further aspect of Critical Linguistics that is very important for the approach adopted here is the concern to take the findings of our work back to the people involved and to contribute to improving social interaction in various contexts.

3 Understanding problems: Discourse and socialisation

The understanding that language could be a significant factor in maintaining one group's control over others, and that such processes were taken for granted, led to efforts to take discourse analysis out of the lecture halls and into the wider public sphere (Fairclough 1992). This movement was concerned with taking critical linguistic theory and developing accessible and practical methods of linguistic analysis as consciousness-raising tools within a range of social groups such as trades unions and women's groups. At the heart of such approaches to discourse analysis is a radical political agenda which aims to open up public participation in the organisation of society through developing a critical understanding of how text and talk can be linked to relations of power and control. An important feature of this approach is that, while each text is unique, individual texts do not work in isolation. Instead, texts are seen as examples of the wider *discourses* that pervade society and, just as importantly, they are also seen as one of the most effective ways of reproducing these discourses.

At this point I should clarify what we mean by 'discourse' in this context as, unfortunately, this term is used differently at different times, even by the same author. Generally speaking there are two connected uses of the word in critical language studies. On the one hand, when we talk about analysing discourse (an uncountable noun), we mean that we are looking at real language as it is spoken in context, rather than texts that are simply written down and considered in isolation. On the other hand, when we talk about the discourses (often a plural noun) that are dominant in one society, for example, we are referring to the shared representations of the world that circulate through the media, the school system and even everyday talk. These oft-repeated discourses create and maintain common understandings of the world, shared ideas that we do not need to work out afresh every time we have a conversation. While such discourses can be viewed positively as the necessary glue that holds the social fabric together, enabling members of the community to understand each other at various levels, the critical approach to language would argue that if these shared discourses are repeated on a daily basis, accepted as 'common sense' without any conscious reflection, then they consistently confirm the status quo as 'the natural order of things', and so consolidate the control of dominant social groups to the exclusion of weaker and more marginalised sectors of society. When control is effectively managed in this way, through the manufacture of consensus rather than the use of physical force, we have a situation described by the Italian socialist theoretician Antonio Gramsci as *hegemony*, and you will at times hear reference to hegemonic discourses. The idea, then, is that the dominant discourses (ways of seeing the world) are maintained invisibly through the everyday discourse (talk in context) of the population, and what most critical approaches to language hope to achieve is to bring into the open the injustices within the social order that are often masked or 'naturalised' in this way.

4 Addressing problems: From Critical to Positive Discourse Analysis

The move away from the analysis of individual decontextualised texts to look at the sociocultural factors that lie behind the production of particular types of texts is a defining feature of Critical Discourse Analysis (CDA), an approach that draws on both socially oriented linguistic theories especially Systemic Functional Linguistics (SFL; e.g. Halliday and Matthiessen 2004), and on sociological theories that are interested in language behaviour. Though CDA is a rather broad umbrella, including many aspects of Critical Linguistics, the central approach is to identify language patterns consistently associated with texts from the same general area, such as political speeches, advertising, or doctor-patient interviews, and to demonstrate how these patterns can be systematically related to wider areas of public and political life in terms of the picture of reality they present and the methods of control they maintain (N.B. Fairclough 1992). When texts serving a similar purpose show regularities in the language they use and the way they are structured we refer to *genres*, a term that can cover everyday interactions such as going to the shops as well as broader areas such as marketing, politics and education. Central to this project is an analysis of how the features of particular genres have, during specific historical and political periods, gained in prominence *within* other genres. For example, the adoption within education discourse of linguistic features generally associated with marketing discourse is said to demonstrate how education has come to be seen as a 'commodity'. The use of linguistic features from one genre within another is known as *intertextuality* and the text is often described as a *hybrid*.

However, critical approaches to discourse have attracted criticisms of their own. For example, much CDA theory and analysis is based upon the assumption that power is uniquely located within the dominant sectors of society and that this power is channelled through discourses that maintain a distorted view of society and social relations favouring the existing *dominant bloc* economically and strengthening its hold politically. In this way CDA tends to view intertextuality as essentially a negative process that enables already dominant sectors of society to extend their control into new areas of society. CDA has also been criticised for its assumption that behind every 'false ideology' promoted by the dominant sectors of society there is a true and liberating version of reality. One result of these emphases has been that much work has focused on the negative, such as highlighting the propagation of sexist and racist stereotypes in the press or cataloguing the detrimental effects of marketisation on education, while much less attention has been paid to addressing such problems and seeking practical solutions. However, this is not to say that CDA never crosses the line from unearthing problems to addressing them, a reemphasis that is signalled clearly in Chouliaraki and Fairclough's (1999:60) methodological framework for CDA, simplified as:

1   Identify a problem.
2   Identify obstacles to tackling the problem.
3   Identify the function of the problem.
4   Identify possible ways past the obstacle.
5   Reflection on the analysis.

This broad approach is apparent in the work of Ruth Wodak (see Fairclough and Wodak, this volume), who uses the methods of CDA to highlight problematic areas of communication in areas such as doctor-patient interaction and to make suggestions for improvements, many of which medical professionals successfully adopted. However, even in this work the emphasis would appear to be on solving problems by removing the negative rather than through positively promoting radical alternatives. In contrast, Positive Discourse Analysis (PDA) aims to celebrate and promote alternative voices. In the first article to suggest the term PDA, Jim Martin (2004: 84) stresses that attempts to alter discourse practices must be underpinned by a knowledge of how discourse works in the social here and now, for good as well as harm:

> The lack of positive discourse analysis (PDA?) cripples our understanding of how change happens, for the better, across a range of sites – how feminists re-make gender relations in our world, how indigenous people overcome their colonial heritage, how migrants renovate their new environs and so on. And this hampers design and perhaps even discourages it since analysts would rather tell us how the struggle was undone than how freedom was won.

Martin goes on to propose a 'yin and yang' approach in which 'deconstructive and constructive activity are both required' (p. 83). Following this lead, Sally Humphrey's research project on the representation of social issues in adolescents' blogs emphasises the constructive goals of PDA (Humphrey 2006: 144):

> although the semiotic [i.e. meaning-making] resources deployed by these young people are different from those valued in their school-based literacy pursuits, they are nonetheless powerful in the particular context in which they are produced. I will argue, however, that it is necessary to explore resources associated with different contexts of social activism in order to better support young engaged citizens in realising their broad social and political goals.

PDA then is an attempt to enable marginalised groups to identify and solve their own problems, developing their own distinctive voices rather than relying on the *advocacy* of intermediaries from traditionally powerful groups. However, while this approach clearly recognises that there are various ways of being powerful through language and that these depend on the social context, there still seems to be a reliance on the trained linguist to provide the evaluation of the different texts and their effectiveness. The approach to PDA advocated in this chapter is that a proper evaluation of how texts are taken up should be based on responses from the intended audience and explained within a broader description of the behaviour and conventions of the groups involved (an ethnography, in other words). As argued in the introduction, an extended PDA approach of identifying what discourses *work* within a specific context and *why* has greater potential for positive applications than an approach that sets out to locate what is ideologically problematic.

5 Living in the solution: The need for common ground

PDA can be used practically to address real-world problems, such as how minority groups might develop their discourses within the struggle for equal access to jobs or the negotiation of land rights. These are areas where they will naturally meet with opposition as their demands challenge the power of those who are served very well by the existing discourses and are able to control and maintain them. This means that simply championing marginalised discourses and the social values that underlie them while attacking dominant values is likely to be ineffective in itself. Let me put this idea into a real-life example. A friend of mine was working for the World Bank at the time of the annual street protests against global financial institutions. This caused her great soul-searching as, to tell the truth, she would have been happier on the streets with the protesters as she has severe misgivings about the role of these organisations. But the point is this: without people such as my friend *inside* the World Bank, who is going to pay any attention to the protesters? No-one, as there is simply a disconnect between two worldviews, no area of common understanding or common will. For dialogue you need more than simply ideas, no matter how worthy; you also need potential listeners and, crucially, the right way of saying things to engage these listeners. We will come back to the idea of ideas, listeners and ways of presenting later, as these provide the link from critical analysis of discourse to SFL as a tool for marking up and analysing texts.

If we accept the idea that we need to find areas of common understanding and common will, then the CDA notion of false ideologies which must be unmasked is unhelpful. It is more constructive to think of an 'ideology' as the way a community connects what they do (their social practice) and how they communicate (their discourse) in an attempt to make sense of their social life, to give it coherence. On the positive side, this serves to unite and make sense of different practices and discourses within the same community; on the negative side, it serves to make the practices of other communities appear illogical and inferior. But here CDA's notion of intertextuality comes in useful if we see it not simply as a means of the dominant bloc extending their view of society into an ever greater range of social activities, but also as a means for alternative voices to get themselves heard in mainstream discourses. Taking the themes of this section then, the approach to PDA presented here is based on the ideas that:

1   problems between different groups do not arise because there is one right viewpoint opposed to many false ideologies; instead, ideologies are all seen as having developed as a means of unifying the communities which live by them;

2   linguistic analysis of texts and genres can be used to reveal the ideas, personal relationships and ways of getting things done effectively within specific groups;

3   linguistic analysis of different, even ideologically opposed groups will reveal areas of shared understanding and common ways of getting things done effectively;

4   where the beliefs and practices of different groups overlap, language practices that make sense within this shared framework can be encouraged and developed as a means of increasing this common ground.

6 Language and powers

The following invented examples, all dealing with the dangers of smoking, bring out the points made above that different people have to use language in different ways if they want to persuade others of their points of view or control their behaviour:

7   *My dad smoked 40 a day and he was dead by the time he was 52.*
8   *Smoking is harmful to you and those around you.*
9   *You should really consider giving up smoking.*

Which one do you think is more effective? Why? Is this just more effective for you or do you think that different groups of people would react to the three texts in different ways? My own feeling is that 7 might work if it was a concerned friend speaking, while 8 would appear on a cigarette packet as the voice of experts from the government, and 9 would be the advice of a doctor (though some doctors might be considerably less polite). Imagine the effect if either example 7 or 9 was printed on cigarette packets instead of example 8.

Let's now compare two longer texts taken from real life. These two examples come from fieldwork in Guyana looking at discourse between the local, mainly Makushi Amerindian community and international development organisations, in particular the Iwokrama International Programme for Rainforest Conservation and Development. The following extracts come from attempts by one member from each of these groups to explain an aspect of forest management called Sustainable Utilisation Areas, or SUAs. See if you can work out which extract is produced by a development worker and which by a local Makushi authority figure. Think of the language features that signal this to you and also consider which text would have more positive effect on you if you were a member of the local community being told how to manage your livelihoods. (Note: (xxx) means I wasn't able to make out what the speaker said, while examples such as (the government) represent my best guess.)

Text 2:

The processes are dealt with under (xxx), and they have come up with a system where they meet . . . they have created a team, and on that team you have the four NRDDB representatives, and there are two representatives from (the government), from the Guyana Forestry Commission, which is a government agency, Guyana Environmental Protection Agency has representatives there and it's always within their (x), the idea was what they thought they could do was bring together communities, these government representatives, Iwokrama, to sit down and think about what would be the best way to plan the area, to plan the businesses that they would develop in the area, the management of the land in terms of SUA. The thinking behind it is that these people would meet quarterly, that's (xxxx) couple of months in between, and what they would do is sit down and talk about how the process is going and they could share what are their concerns and what they think should happen. So from the community perspective the idea was that the NRDDB representatives would be able to bring to the meeting what they think are important for their villages. Because, remember, the SUA is really Iwokrama developing businesses in the preserve. And those businesses are going to be operating, it's — one possible business is logging; a second is ecotourism; a third is harvesting things like nibbi and cassava, for selling, we call it non-timber forest products.

Text 3

Now the meeting we attended with this group of all the representatives of various organisations: We sat down there to discuss relatively commonplace intuitions, but we discussed the Sustainable Utilisation Area, in that the Wilderness Preserve is another area, that is where the zoning is important. Had they not that place zoned to identify the Sustainable Utilisation Area, here is where you all knowledge — all of us knowledge comes into play. Because we are the people who are familiar with that forest, we are people closest to the forest, more than anybody else who live outside, because it's a way of life that's part of it, and we are the ones to give an advice. And we should state it in that vein. Because whenever you're down, whoever comes from there will return, we remain here. And whatever is built or constructed, whatever it is, we will remain. Of course some of it (has been lost). But then we're working to defend (xx) all of us, (xx) worry. Now, the Sustainable Utilisation Area means the area which you can use natural resources (be) there. In the sustainable use you keep it . . . not going down. But if possible you keep it increasing so that those things, whatever it may be, whether it be (x), medicinal plants, frogs, centipedes, snakes, fishes, baboon, or what-you-call-it, there's nothing in there and you must not be (xxxxxx), so that our generation have just a few years to keep it. You take out, but then you must stop, to have that recycling going on, so that the interaction of the resources going on (xxxxxx), reforestation, planting seedlings should grow up, you could find a special medicinal plant. Because if you find — obviously if you find a very valuable medicinal plant, which can cure some diseases, you would have it in (xx). Which means if you go and take all that natural resource you have there, you're going to be (depleting established connexion) . . . (stand) the line, so that you can observe . . . changes. How can you change it? How do you farm? What path do you take a year after, take a year, five year, or ten year or fifteen year period? So, we get to understand the forest better and those things will be left in their natural state. Because there are other important issues which we, because we live among them, we live inside, it's a way of life, we take it for granted. We (xxx). Many of us do not have sense of why, we (don't??) know how valuable those things are to us, and we just discard it, like many of us who (pushing) fire in the savannah — you know

how many innocent birds' lives you destroying (probably, even though you set xxx)? If
a snake (xxxxxxx xxxxxx). So, don't blame the snakes where you can't go (x) in the
savannah, it's not good, it's a very bad habit, like poisoning, all these things are
detrimental. But we never study it in depth, we don't know how disastrous it is. So
these are things which we have now asked to participate in, our knowledge about it,
to find certain things.

Keep thinking about these texts as you read this section, in which we will explore
some of the reasons why people are affected differently by different types of texts.
These ideas are based on an understanding of language not as a means simply of
expressing ideas but as the way we interact with our friends and neighbours and
become part of the same group as them, working together with a shared understanding
of how our social group works together to get things done. This 'apprenticeship'
begins from the moment we are born and continues through adolescence and into
adulthood:

> The learning of and through language takes place through conversation whose
> overt goal is simply to get on with the business of everyday life. Children learn
> language and become socialised into the culture at home by others who may
> have minimal conscious knowledge about either language or the social system.
> The effectiveness of everyday talk as a means of initial apprenticeship into the
> culture indeed lies in the very implicitness of what is taught and learned –
> the 'commonsense' knowledge that can henceforward be taken for granted
> as the basis for living.
>
> (Painter 1998: 63)

In these terms language is seen as a means of behaving together and socialisation
represents a process of learning the rules of the game so that we can play too.
Halliday (1978) refers to the process of socialisation as a process of 'learning how
to mean'. As children grow up they become increasingly socialised and come to
share with their social group a complex understanding of the world that is based on
what they hear around them all the time, the common narratives of the group, with
all their assumptions about who does what and why, what it means to be one way
or the other, and what's the right way to behave at different times. Fairclough
(2001: 9, 118ff.) uses the term *members' resources* to refer to the common experience
we draw on to make sense of each other, while Wetherell and Potter (1988: 172,
in Burr 1995: 116) use *interpretative repertoires* to mean more or less the same thing:

> the building blocks speakers use for constructing versions of actions, cognitive
> processes and other phenomena. Any particular repertoire is constituted out
> of a restricted range of terms used in specific stylistic and grammatical fashion.

These interpretative repertoires include shared conceptions of various topics,
but also the appropriate ways of talking to different members of the community
and of matching rhetorical style to the purpose at hand. These three factors of topic,
social relations and stylistic conventions relate to what Systemic Functional Linguistics

refers to as the *ideational*, *interpersonal* and *textual metafunction* respectively. Each metafunction refers to one major area of meaning in language and these areas of meaning can, in turn, be related to different aspects of our social life.

We can see a little of how this works in the examples about the dangers of smoking, above. What these show is that different texts are suitable for the same purpose in different contexts and with different relationships between the speaker and their audience. However, between societies, the way that language and context link up might be very different because of the different interpretative repertoires (or members' resources) that different groups bring with them, subconsciously, as a result of their socialisation. For example, if a British politician were to use the language of religious texts to make a political point it would almost certainly sound ridiculous and gather very little support from the public:

10   *Verily, I say unto you, that the righteous man regardeth inflation as the workings of the vile serpent.*

However, modifying the language just a bit and moving to a different sociocultural context we might find that the language of religion and the language of politics do indeed mix:

Text 4. Ayatollah Ruhollah Khomeini 5 November 1979 (Quoted in http://en.wikiquote.org/wiki/Ruhollah_Khomeini):

America is the Great Satan, the wounded snake.

Text 5. Remarks from President George Bush to the Asia Society, 22 February 2006. (*Chicago Sun-Times* online http://blogs.suntimes.com/sweet/2006/02/bush.html):

Some people have said the 21st century will be the Asian century. I believe the 21st century will be freedom's century. And together, free Asians and free Americans will seize the opportunities this new century offers and lay the foundation of peace and prosperity for generations to come.

May God bless India and Pakistan. May God continue to bless the United States.

We talked above of Fairclough's concepts of the *power behind language* and the *power in language* as if they were fixed features of language and society, but these examples and the following analysis of the Guyanese texts will suggest that different speakers carry more weight in specific contexts, and that the language they use to convey their authority depends on the nature of their relationship with their audience, the topic being discussed and the style of language expected – SFL's three metafunctions. Let's now look at the two texts in detail, using SFL's three metafunctions to link aspects of language to the social context in order to see the extent to which the different speakers managed to create an effective discourse that brought together the two very different communities they represent.

The ideational metafunction – talking about things and events

The ideational metafunction relates to the way we talk about people, things and events and is generally *realised* through the language features of clauses, nouns, verbs and adjectives. Just looking at the two texts we can see that, although both speakers are talking about the Sustainable Utilisation Areas, they vary considerably in how they describe these in terms of the things and events that make them up (Participants and Processes in SFL terms). In Text 2 the SUAs are described in terms of processes, plans and management, where government agencies think about and develop ideas. The community is introduced into the equation a little later and local skills and products are individually mentioned, but there is the very explicit message 'remember, the SUA is really Iwokrama developing businesses in the preserve'. In Text 3, on the other hand, while the speaker starts off with reference to a meeting, a little like Text 2, he soon moves on to talk in detail about local knowledge of the area, referring to the forest, the community way of life, farming and natural resources. He talks of dangers the community face, such as fires in the savannahs and, rather than just talking of wildlife in general, he list plants and animals that would be familiar to his audience: 'medicinal plants, frogs, centipedes, snakes, fishes, baboon, or what-you-call-it' – ending very informally! This speaker also refers to the interaction between Iwokrama and the local community, but from a rather different perspective, emphasising the importance of the local contribution: 'So these are things which we have now asked to participate in, our knowledge about it, to find certain things.'

The interpersonal metafunction – expressing solidarity and commitment

The interpersonal metafunction corresponds to the way different speakers relate to each other. Over short texts such as these it is not always possible to find the full array of features that bring out interpersonal meaning (don't be fooled by the artificially rich examples in a lot of textbooks!), but there are still a number of examples that demonstrate the different interpersonal work done by the two texts, looking in particular at: 1) the use of pronouns, such as WE or YOU, to create solidarity or distance; 2) the use of modals, such as CAN, MUST and SHOULD, to express strength of feeling towards an idea; 3) the use of evaluative language to express an opinion on something or some event (see Martin and White 2005 for the fullest introduction to this area of language use).

Text 2 consistently uses the pronoun THEY to refer to those who make the decisions and plan the meetings, including the conservation organisation Iwokrama, who have organised the present meeting along with the communities. This creates a feeling of distance not only from those outside the meeting making the decisions, but also between Iwokrama and the local communities. Text 3 is very different, and also much more complex. In this extract the speaker switches between WE and YOU to refer to the local community and between WE and THEY to refer to Iwokrama, with whom he is associated. This is not random; what the speaker does is to refer to the community as WE when he is emphasising shared values and traditions, but as YOU when he wants to talk about poor wildlife management. This is because he has a role in both communities. As a local elder he can claim solidarity with the community in terms of their history on the land, yet he can also distance himself from the community's poor practices as a result of his connections with the scientists of Iwokrama. In the same way he will at times emphasise his connections with Iwokrama, referring to them as WE, and at other times distance himself, referring to them as THEY.

The two texts also contrast in terms of the modal meanings they use. In Text 2, we find WOULD and COULD referring to possible events in the future – entirely consistent with the detached scientific approach of the speaker. In Text 3, in contrast, we find uses of SHOULD and MUST as the speaker takes on the role of instructing the community as to how they are to behave. The same contrast appears with evaluative language, with the first text using neutral and detached language such as 'one possible business', but with the second evaluating existing practices as 'not good' or 'very bad', 'detrimental' and even 'disastrous', so emphasising the shared importance that these ideas have for the speaker and his audience.

The textual metafunction – speaking style and the grounding of knowledge

Very simply put, the textual metafunction of language is concerned with how ideas are connected to our experience and to each other. The linguistic features I will focus on here are the use of tense for verbs and the degree to which prominent noun groups refer to specific people and things or to distant and abstract ideas. In this way we can compare Texts 2 and 3 in terms of whether the speakers ground their description in the here and now of concrete realities or whether they refer to abstract classes in hypothetical time. There are, of course, many other combinations of things and events that fall between these two extremes, but there is no room to go into the distinctions here (see Cloran 2000). Running through the two texts quickly we can say that Text 2 deals with the past meetings of organisations that are not at the present meeting and puts forward their hypothetical plans for the local community. The general picture then is of remoteness, with the only local referent, the communities, embedded in a network of participants and events removed from the present context. In contrast, Text 3 *reconstrues* the abstract purposes and workings and of the SUA in terms of the everyday practice of the community members who are present at the meeting.

7 Conclusion

Well, I've gradually given away which text was produced by the development worker and which by the local authority figure, and I imagine that you had already reached this conclusion for yourself. You were probably able to do this as each speaker spoke in a way that was appropriate to their status in their own community and their role at the present meeting. Now, this creates an interesting situation in that the first speaker, Sarah, was an outsider whose status at the meeting was not only different from the local speaker's, but also different from the everyday status prestige she would normally enjoy. In contrast, the second speaker, Uncle Henry, was operating on his home patch, with all the rights and authority that entailed.

So, while Uncle Henry's discourse was indeed the more effective in persuading the local community of the virtues of SUAs (and this was commented on at the meeting and in interviews with me afterwards), his particular way of speaking was not an option for Sarah as the ideational, interpersonal and textual features employed were all dependent upon a particular relationship between speaker, audience and the topics being discussed, a result of the relationship between language and ideology as a way of making sense of the world.

However, while Sarah's text may not have been sufficient to get the idea of the SUA process across to the local audience, it surely had its part to play. Given that Uncle Henry's contribution came hard on the heels of Sarah's speech and served to clarify it for the local community audience, it seems likely that the prestige Sarah brought to the event as a social scientist with an international organisation was transferred to Uncle Henry as he 'interpreted' what she had said. This is reflected linguistically in his use of YOU, WE and THEY to switch solidarity between the two groups, his explanation of abstract ideas in terms of local practices, and his evaluation of past habits in terms of new thinking. Uncle Henry's use of language therefore serves to create a new type of genre that combines features of the traditional discourses of the community with the format of institutional meetings and represents in action what this approach to PDA seeks to develop: the discovery and development of common ways of meaning and acting between groups that at first sight appear to have radically divergent worldviews. These examples, then, show us positive aspects of discourse in action; but what use was made of this, and how can we apply these findings to other situations?

Those working for Iwokrama soon recognised the power and authenticity of voices such as Uncle Henry's, and he and others from the local communities took part in board meetings as well as international meetings on sustainable development, putting across the views of those most directly affected. Here it was Uncle Henry's prestige as a local elder that was transferred to Iwokrama scientists as they adapted what he said and put it into ways of speaking more generally expected at such conferences. In this way the roles were reversed from local meetings, and we can see a two-way process in which each group's ways of acting and seeing the world encroach into the taken-for-granted world of the other. In another development Iwokrama helped the local communities to visit indigenous groups in other parts of America and to establish internet contact with them. This provides interesting parallels with Humphrey's work, as new voices will have to develop that simultaneously match local Makushi ways of speaking with the technology of the internet and also create spaces for mixing the discourses of different indigenous groups from around the world. In each of these areas a specialist knowledge of how discourse can work positively, combined with an understanding of the local context, can be brought in to help in designing these discourses. In the case of the World Bank similar positive intervention might mean working to forge alliances between protestors and agents for change within the Bank itself. Ideationally, there might be an emphasis on shared concerns on global issues rather than on differences in approach; interpersonally and textually, protestors might focus on communicating the intensity of their feelings through the dulling mechanisms of institutional talk as well as through the thrill of slogans and placards. Conversely, World Bank workers might learn to explain their abstract ideas in everyday non-technical language. There is little doubt that such exercises would also prove beneficial to the groups themselves as they are forced into rethinking their deeply held views in new and 'un-naturalised ways'. However, it is not the purpose of this chapter to suggest how such discourses might develop. Quite the opposite, in fact: the message is that each context is complex and unique, as are the problems that come with them. The positive belief is that the voices that can solve these problems are also already out there, waiting to be brought into action.

References

Burr, V. (1995) *An Introduction to Social Constructionism*. London and New York: Routledge.

Chouliaraki, L. and Fairclough, N. (1999) *Discourse in Late Modernity: Rethinking critical discourse analysis*. Edinburgh: Edinburgh University Press.

Cloran, C. (2000) 'Sociosemantic variation: different wordings, different meanings', in L. Unsworth (ed.) *Researching Language in Schools and Communities: Functional linguistic perspectives*. London and Washington: Cassell.

Fairclough, N. (2001) (2nd edn) *Language and Power*. Harlow: Longman.

Fairclough, N. (1992) (ed.) *Critical Language Awareness*. London and New York: Longman.

Fowler, R., Hodge, B., Kress, G. and Trew, T. (1979) *Language and Control*. London: Routledge and Kegan Paul.

Halliday, M.A.K. (1978) *Language as Social Semiotic: The social interpretation of language and meaning*. London: Edward Arnold.

Halliday, M.A.K. and Matthiessen, C.M.I.M. (2004) (3rd edn) *An Introduction to Functional Grammar*. London: Hodder Arnold.

Humphrey, S. (2006) '"Getting the Reader On Side": Exploring adolescent online political discourse'. *E-Learning* 3 (2).

Kress, G. and Hodge, B. (1979) *Language as Ideology*. London: Routledge and Kegan Paul.

Martin, J.R. (2004) 'Positive discourse analysis: power, solidarity and change'. *Revista Canaria de Estudios Ingleses* 49.

Martin, J.R. and White, P.R.R. (2005) *The Language of Evaluation: Appraisal in English*. Basingstoke: Palgrave Macmillan.

O'Halloran, K.A. (2003) *Critical Discourse Analysis and Language Cognition*. Edinburgh: Edinburgh University Press.

Painter, C. (1998) *Learning through Language in Early Childhood*. London: Cassell.

Wetherell, M. and Potter, J. (1988) 'Discourse analysis and the identification of interpretative repertoires', in C. Antaki (ed.) *Analysing Everyday Explanation (A Casebook of Methods)*. London: Sage.

Chapter 9

Mary U. Hanrahan

Highlighting hybridity
A Critical Discourse Analysis of teacher talk in science classrooms

Introduction

This chapter uses textual analysis of science classroom discourse to re-examine the failure of science education to achieve its avowed goal of producing scientifically literate citizens (cf. Goodrum *et al*. 2001), which could only be achieved by enacting a science curriculum that is accessible to all students. To do this, I employ the epistemological perspective and tools of Critical Discourse Analysis (CDA) (Fairclough 1989, 2003; Luke 2002). Arguing that the nature of the typical discourse of the secondary science classroom may be a significant factor in failure to engage students, I compare two instances. My focus is on the extent to which the two teacher participants have been able to creatively adapt the hegemonic discourse to make science accessible and relevant to the needs of a greater proportion of their students.

The research context

Investigating successful practice

In contrast to much research in science education which simply finds fault with teachers, I am doing this on the whole by identifying and investigating positive educational instances. More specifically, I am investigating the discourse practices

Edited version of Hanrahan, M. (2006) 'Highlighting hybridity: a Critical Discourse Analysis of teacher talk in science classrooms', *Science Education* 90 (1): 8–43.

of teachers who have been nominated as having classes where students are generally believed to be positively engaged in science, during the years in which science is most likely to be a compulsory school subject and regularly taught. For this analysis, I recorded one or at most two lessons, conducted by each of the teachers. (In the larger study of which this is part, twenty-nine teachers participated.) I also interviewed each teacher observed to learn more about the particular local, institutional, and social contexts backgrounding the lesson observed. My criterion for initial nomination was that teachers should be confident about saying "Yes" to three questions:

> Do practically all your students look forward to their science class?
> Do they have a positive attitude towards science?
> Are they engaging with science?

It is important to note that I was interested in both emotional *and* intellectual engagement. I did not want teachers who simply made science classes fun without helping students overcome barriers preventing them from understanding science and being successful academically. In general I found teachers hesitant to volunteer even when they fulfilled my criteria. However, I set out to convince them that what they were doing *was* indeed exceptional and that it was important to value and celebrate it and show others how such engagement was achieved.

The curriculum context

Before introducing my analysis of a sample of the practices of two junior secondary science teachers, I need to explain something of the context of my choice of texts. Because I wanted to illuminate new possibilities in terms of a teacher enacting curriculum emphases that make science accessible to most students, I had to find a way to demonstrate in some detail how such pedagogy might differ from more restricted ways of teaching science. An obvious solution is to supply a comparison between two classrooms that are highly contrasted in these aspects. Hence, even though my broader project has been about collecting positive exemplars of science-teaching practice, I have decided to include a negative example in my analysis. The latter appears to be almost a prototypical example of a teacher using all the features of the stylistic norms as Lemke (1990) described them, but is nevertheless not too far removed from what I have found to be fairly typical of the less exemplary secondary science classrooms in Australia.

After first describing the methods of CDA, I will compare and contrast extracts from the texts of two classroom lessons (one extract from each teacher). My goal is to illustrate both how school science is likely to affect students when it is taught, firstly, in the generalized abstract way that is traditionally considered acceptable, and secondly, in a way that has been adapted to make science more accessible to a particular class. The two extracts represent the first few minutes (approximately four and a half minutes) of each lesson observed, and the context for each is briefly summarized before each extract to provide a context for the CDA I will then perform.

linguistic , micro
social — macro

Methodology and methods

Methodology: Critical Discourse Analysis

Critical Discourse Analysis is *critical* in that it focuses on how power is maintained through accepted social practices that implicitly tend to favor the interests of those currently in power and hinder those of their competitors. It can also show how hegemonic power can be challenged by participants using creative practices.

Now more commonly known by its acronym, CDA, this methodology came into being largely through the work of Fairclough (e.g. 1989). It is a sociolinguistic research tool that facilitates a simultaneous focus on the linguistic features of a specific text (such as vocabulary, grammar, semantics, and graphological or phonological features) and on the social structures and practices underlying the text. In contrast to both linguistic analysis, where texts are analyzed at the *micro* level only, and social analyses, where the *macro* level is the focus of attention, CDA is concerned with analysis at both these levels, via analysis at an intermediate level: that of social practices and structures, in terms of the genres, discourses and styles accessed. Hence, it includes both linguistic analysis and "interdiscursive analysis" (Fairclough 2003: 3). Because of aspects it shares with a Systemic Functional Linguistics (SFL) approach to language (Halliday 1994; Lemke 1990; Martin 1992), CDA can help to make visible the less explicit facets of classroom discourse.

Since it has roots in social theory as well (Fairclough 1989, 2003; Luke 2002), CDA can also be used to critique texts in terms of the ideologies they promote. Consequently, CDA has often been used to critique policy documents and other public texts. However, as Luke (2002) in a recent view of the history of CDA pointed out, it has less often been used to show how power operates in face-to-face contexts or how hegemonic discourses can be challenged. He proffered a challenge to CDA researchers "to begin to develop a strong positive thesis about discourse and the productive uses of power. . . . [to] begin to capture an affirmative character of culture where discourse is used aesthetically, productively and for emancipatory purposes" (p. 106). He took this a step further and challenged CDA researchers to use their critique for positive action. "If CDA is avowedly normative and explicitly political," he wrote, "then it must have the courage to say what is to be done with texts and discourse" (p. 107). He suggested that the purview of CDA could include documentation of "emergent discourses of hybrid identity . . . counter to dominant pedagogic discourses" (p. 107).

This is particularly relevant to my current work of identifying pedagogies that empower students to engage positively with school science (cf. "productive pedagogies," Lingard *et al.* 2000). More specifically, it addresses my interest in identifying the tacit as well as explicit features of teacher talk (and accompanying nonverbal communication) that impact upon the kinds of relationships, affective responses, and identities that I believe are likely to enhance or limit the development of scientific literacy for all (Hanrahan 1999). Consequently, as well as addressing the issue of broadening science pedagogy to enable positive outcomes for all students, this chapter is a response to two of the challenges posed by Luke (2002). It uses CDA to analyze texts derived from face-to-face interactions, and it addresses the issue of documenting the use of hybrid discourses for emancipatory purposes.

I will now present the two extracts in context and show how, using CDA, I went about identifying the ways in which discourse practices apparent in the text were likely to limit or enhance access to science for students, and hence how these texts exemplify particular ideologies about science. The next section can be seen largely as analysis at the level of the event (the *description* stage), and the following one as analysis at the level of social structures and social practices (the *explanation* stage). Both stages, however, necessarily involve *interpretation*, which is seen as the intermediate level of a three-level CDA analysis process (Fairclough 1989).

The *description* stage of CDA involves highlighting lexical items (vocabulary, pronouns, words that suggest a particular conception of how the classroom operates, and words implying metaphorical meanings), grammatical features, assumptions being made, and absences. It should be noted that this is not intended to be an exhaustive description but rather focuses on aspects relevant to the issue of access.

A comparison of teacher discourse practices

Describing the discourse practices in two junior secondary science classrooms

Exemplar 1: Energy changes lesson with a Year 8 science class. Mr. D was science Head of Department/Chair (HoD) in a nondenominational independent school in a rural area near the state capital. Although academic subjects in general were mentioned in the promotional literature and the current newsletter available in the school office when I visited, in these documents science appeared to me to have rather a low profile compared to such activities as competitive sports, performing arts, and public speaking.

The class in question was midway through a physics unit on energy changes and later in this lesson the students were directed to perform a practical "experiment" ("recipe prac." might be a more appropriate term) using laboratory equipment. Mr, D was a tall man who towered over the students. He always remained standing, and generally spoke in a loud voice meant for all students in the classroom. During the class I attended, the students seemed to have little choice in anything that happened. The experiment to be carried out, the groups they were in, and the format for tabulating the data, were all given to them. They seemed quite accepting, and although they showed little enthusiasm, were generally very compliant. In fact the class ran like clockwork. The procedures for collecting the materials and instruments, copying the data-table from the blackboard, moving to the laboratory benches in given groups, dividing up tasks among group members, and for cleaning up and returning the materials to the appropriate trolleys, all seemed well learnt and to require no discussion.

What follows is the text resulting from the transcription of the first four and a half minutes of the lesson.

Mr. D[1] [Outside classroom where he is settling students down (approx. 15 s)] Year 8 [Indistinct]. Right, move in quietly please. [Students move in with some talk, and two whispered "sh"s, and eventually stand silently behind their desks (approx. 45 s)]

Mr. D   Good afternoon, Year 8s.

Ss   Good afternoon, Mr. [D]

Mr. D   Sit down, please. [Noises of chairs scraping, some talking] We've got a visitor this afternoon. [Recites in an expressionless voice] This is Dr Hanrahan who is from the Queensland University of Technology. She has been a science teacher for a number of years and has just come out to see how we do things at Forestcrest for this afternoon. As you carry on and do your experiments she'll be just walking around the room. Last night's homework, please↑, was questions, 10, 11, 12 & thirt-een↑. [Whistling of electric kettle goes unremarked. Then noises and talk recommences as students get books out] So if you can get your homework out please. [One and a half minutes pass as he walks around inspecting books with brief comments. Those that can be made out are "Thank you," "Have I seen yours?" "You've done yours?" Then with raised voice:] Right [indistinct] please. [Noisy talk continues] Ah, excuse me↑. [As noise stops, reads in a monotone] Questions what are some of the energy changes which are being described in each of the following: "The wind blew hard and turned the windmill as he pumped the water from underground to the top." Yes, John?

S   The wind's kinetic.

Mr. D   Kinetic energy, yes. It is turning into_____? So the wind is kinetic, turning the windmill – what's it doing to the water?

S   Pumping.

Mr. D   Lifting it from↑?

Ss   The ground.

Mr. D   Lifting the ground to the top. So that means it's creating?

S1   Potential.

S2   Potential energy.

Mr. D   Gravitational potential energy. [Continues reading rapidly in deadpan voice as though to get HW out of the way] "At the flick of a switch the washing machine started turning and (turning/churning) the [indistinct] clothes." What did (the switch do/we switch to)?

Ss   Power.

Mr. D   Which is what form of energy?

S   Electric.

Mr. D   Electrical. And it's making the machine?

Ss   Kinetic.

Mr. D   Which is kinetic. [Maintaining a deadpan voice] "C1. 2–1–0 and the rocket belts fire and smoke the ground shook and with a deafening roar the rocket left the launch↑-pad." What's the energy in the rocket?

S1   Fuel.

S2   Electric.

Mr. D   Which is? That's not one of your turn.

S   Chemical

Mr. D   Chemical. And it's turning into?

S   Kinetic.

Mr. D   Kinetic.

S   Isn't it gravitational?

Mr. D   And as it takes off from the ground it's turning into gravitational potential
energy.

In relation to his way of representing the world and indicating what could be
taken for granted, the first features of the text that struck me were the way pronouns
were being used, assumptions were being made, as well as some notable absences,
and some discourse-specific words. For example, the impersonal use of pronouns
such as "you" and "we" suggest the set roles expected of all participants in this
classroom. Uses of "the" may indicate what can be taken for granted as given (such
as the discrete range of words that can be used to describe "the" different types
of energy in science). Other assumptions are contained in "how we do things at
Forestcrest" which assumes a singular perspective that applies to everyone, and in
"as you carry on and do your experiments," which assumes unquestioning student
compliance with his plans. Notable absences in the extract include absence of talk
that would facilitate transitions in the lesson or would help build relationships with
students, and the absence of any appreciation of narrative or dramatic intent in the
homework questions. Terms with particular connotations include "move in quietly,"
"homework," "questions," which depict the classroom as a workplace where tasks
are to be completed (cf. Roth 1992 – more on this below).

Lexical density, a measure of the proportion of content words to the total count
of words used (Eggins 1994), is high both in the exchanges that take place as the
homework is being publicly "corrected" and later in the instructions for the bench
(practical) work. It is lower, however, for both the teacher narrative about the
researcher at the beginning of the class and in the story-like sentences he takes
directly from the textbook. While correcting the homework, the pacing of the talk
was hurried, with minimal repetition and minimal elaboration. Yet the practical
activity itself was relatively unhurried with students apparently having more than
enough time to copy down the table, take the minute-apart temperature readings,
and tabulate the results. The excerpt reveals little metatalk that might be seen to
detract from the science talk, not even at the level of classroom management. There
was no checking that students were ready to move on to the next stage of the lesson,
or checking for understanding of concepts or of the purpose of the particular
experiment.

A transitivity analysis[2] shows that, once the researcher has been introduced and
the homework books viewed, people (including even the teacher and students) are
rarely referred to again. After disposing as efficiently as possible of the introduction
to the visiting researcher, the nature of the participants referred to by the teacher
changes. Although one student, John, is referred to by name, personal pronouns
such as I, me, you, he, or she are virtually absent. There was one reference to an
impersonal "he" as an agent in one of the homework questions but even this is
omitted from the subsequent discussion about wind, windmills, and water. Also
absent are words referring to mental or verbal processes. There is no reference to
thinking, understanding, discussing, and so on (no-one is asked or states what they
think or why, or what they understand, mean or are learning). Even in the one
exception, quoted directly from the textbook, the verbal process "are being described"
is in the agentless passive voice. On the other hand, material processes (e.g. blew,
turned, pumped, belts, etc.) abound, as do identifying relational processes that

classify (i.e. [this] is [that]), which account almost entirely for the remainder of the processes used by Mr. D. "That means" is impersonal and is another example of identification and classification. Circumstances are sometimes referred to (e.g., "from the ground to the top," "at the flick of a switch") to cue students into the type of energy involved, and sometimes ignored ("with a deafening roar").

Mr. D shows no sign of particular commitment to what he is saying. In a verbal equivalent to his lack of tonal expressivity, he seems to avoid using language belonging to what Martin (1997) calls the "appraisal" system (attitudinal words communicating affect, judgement, or appreciation; words that attempt to engage; or words expressing force or focus). These behaviors could be seen to increase his status, as more powerful persons do not need to show deference, explain themselves, or make themselves vulnerable to challenge (Eggins 1994). More significantly, it could also imply that science, the process of learning science, and his method of teaching science are all purely objective processes, and as such are not to be questioned. On the other hand, he does soften his commands at the beginning of the class, with the use of "please" and sometimes responds with "Thank you" when a student shows him his homework, like a polite person who respects his students.

Exemplar 2: Introductory aerodynamics lesson with a Year 10 science class. The second teacher, Mrs. L, was both a science and mathematics HoD/Chair, and had a few years previously been a sports and physical education HoD. She was teaching in a girls' secondary Catholic school in a large regional city in Queensland. In her mid-forties, hyperactive by her own description, labeled a "livewire" by another science HoD in the area, she was of short stature, and was almost indistinguishable from her students when she mingled with them for group work, both in terms of voice, and visibility, though in the instruction segment her voice was louder and she used considerably more emphasis. The Year 10 class was described as a middle level class.[3] The school had an unusually high rate of enrolment in senior physics and chemistry, and commendable results in both subjects.

Parallel to my treatment of the first lesson segment, the first four and a half minutes of Mrs. L's lesson, in this case slightly abridged in that the researcher's introduction has been omitted as being largely irrelevant to my purpose here of analyzing teacher talk.

[*Indistinct talking and noises in the background as teacher and students come into the classroom.*] Tomorrow. [*Indistinct but sounds like one student talking with another near the microphone*] . . . What do I have to do?

Mrs. L   [*Enthusiastically, to a student who shows her something*] O↑-oh! Very well done! [*Giving activity handout to researcher*] You can introduce yourself and that's the task. [Researcher] Oh, OK. Thanks.

Ss   [*As talking continues for approximately 45 s, snatches of voices near the tape recorder emerge, mainly spoken by one (student) voice with some of the responses possibly provided by the teacher*] Do we have that [Indistinct] thing today or tomorrow? [*Indistinct*] well, we're moving house and I couldn't find it this morning [indistinct] late tomorrow? Is it? . . . What do I have to do? . . . late tomorrow afternoon . . . I have to go to art . . . have to go to your ordinary class. When is it? Tomorrow? In the morning? [*Continuing noise, including some raucous laughter.*]

Mrs. L   [Indistinct] I know, **you're** with Miss R's group, and Mr. L's and Mrs. C's are together but I can't remember [indistinct]. [*Raises voice*] Ah, girls, excuse me, are we all here now, do you think?

S1   Yes.

S2   [Indistinct] in 102 or 304.

Mrs. L   A-a-ah, yes. It's one, two. Alright. Thanks. Sh-h. [Indistinct] Can I ask you to remove your hats, then [indistinct]?

Ss   [Students are now silent]

Mrs. L   That's tempting, isn't it, Tessa, to play with that?

Ss   [*Giggles.*]

Mrs. L   U-um.

Ss   Giggles petering out.

S   [Indistinct]

Mrs. L   [*Quietly, as though to the one student*] Thank you. [*Raises voices to announce*] Ah, I have a **guest** who would like to introduce herself to you↑ and tell you a little bit about why she's here with me↑ and then we'll start the lesson.

[*Researcher introduces herself and explains that she is there to research science education and will be observing, recording, and taking photos of the teacher but generally not the students who are not the focus of her research. This takes about 50 s.*]

Mrs. L   Right, so it's to do with looking at me. Alright?

S   [Indistinct but sounds like a question]?

Mrs. L   Ah, no, I volunteered, didn't I?

MH   Yeah.

Mrs. L   I volunteered.

S |Indistinct|

Mrs. L   Are you ready? Yes girls, alright? Who's ever **flown** a **paper** plane?

Ss   [*Inaudible, but it is likely that students have raised their hands*]

Mrs. L   Excellent! How many different types have you made?

Ss   [*Several voices including "One"*].

Mrs. L   Have you made only one? Right, because how many different types of paper planes are there?

Ss   [*Several voices speaking at once including "a lot" "a million"*]

Mrs. L   Only one?

Ss   A lot.

Mrs. L   Are you ready? [*Adopting a more formal tone*] Mrs. L has never studied paper planes in her life↑ until –

S   [Indistinct]

Mrs. L   [*Aside in lower voice*] – we'll just check that she's got on the floor [*several paper planes have been set out on the low platform on which she is standing at the front of the classroom*] – that's the other one, isn't it? – until [*raising her voice again and speaking clearly and deliberately*] – a true story girls [*Slight giggle*] –

Ss   [*Polite giggle from at least one student in response*]

Mrs. L   – until, the other night – I will share with you a bit of my **personal** life – the other night I decided I wanted to look at paper planes a bit because we're studying **physics**. This is really interesting and my computer's in my bedroom.

So the other night (*continues with "smile" in her voice*) — this is true — my husband and **I**↑ were **throwing** paper planes in the bedroom for about an hour and a half.

Ss   [*Giggles*]

Mrs. L   We downloaded all these directions off the Internet. And I said to him "Please help me" — because I'm female and he's male, and I **presumed** that **I** wasn't any good at making paper planes and **he** was. Then he had to spend an hour and a half helping me make the paper planes. [*Adopting a more serious tone*] So have a look. (*Indicates the paper plane models she has displayed on the platform.*) These are the a, like these are the **three** that I found to make. I do actually have copies of lots of other ones, and I'm led to believe there's heaps more, and heaps of Internet sites — on paper planes. So, you're going to make three today for me [*Indistinct as she drops her voice*] experiment and we'll go through that. [*Raises voice*] But anyway, this is my first one. Alright?

S   [*Coughs*]

Mrs. L   Now, the other interesting thing — I find these paper planes — [*adopts an amused tone*] **never perform** the way you **want** them to **perform**!

This extract seems to provide evidence of a quite different way of representing the world of school science, and the roles and identities of the participants. A transitivity analysis reveals that Mrs. L made extensive use of mental and verbal processes (e.g., "remember," "think," "like," "introduce," "tell," "studied," "presumed," "find") that would indicate that what is going on in minds is seen as a significant part of the lesson ("Are you ready?" would also fit here). They imply that teaching and learning are to some extent interpersonal processes and to some extent individual processes depending on one's frame of mind. The participants in most clauses are people (or pronouns standing in for them), and they are generally represented as being actors rather than acted upon. For example, Mrs. L represented students as active agents (makers of paper planes) like her, and later directly related this activity to physics. On the other hand, the students were the objects of the (very polite) "Can I ask . . . ?" but are then made the subjects of "to remove your hats," and "do you think?"

Making paper planes in itself might be something that any science teacher of the topic might refer to, but there is novelty in giving a whole class period to it. (In other cases, experience in making them might be assumed, seen as unimportant, or even seen as a threat to future control by the teacher.) Along with her choice of activity, Mrs. L used (generally non-Latinate) inexact, colloquial language ("a little bit," "all these directions," "like these are," "heaps more," "have a look") and to accept its use by her students in a way that a more typical scientist or science educator might not do in a science-related context. She also mixed talk about physics with talk about her (and the students') personal experiences, and mentioned the word "physics" in the context of a personal tale.

The "bedroom" story could be seen as quite transgressive in the context of teaching a serious subject like physics, not only because it was personal, but also because it was a narrative of an actual event, and was introduced humorously as a third-person narrative with overtones of "girl-talk." At the same time, this story subtly demonstrated both that the activity could be a fun social activity that you could share with a male, and one that she had chosen to do in her own personal time. Her use of pronouns (I, me, you, and she) was also more personal (she even seems to make a point of including them where they could be omitted, for example, when she uses "to you" and "with me" in the introduction to the visitor) thus transgressing the stylistic norm of depersonalization (cf. Lemke 1990). She also chose to talk in terms of actual concrete events and did not shy away from humor or hinting at possible drama, thus transgressing another of the stylistic norms Lemke listed.

Her talk was much less dense lexically, especially in this extract with its narrative, but given that she did talk more extensively, with the talk developing along a designed track, she did (in the five minutes following those represented in the extract above) eventually introduce (or, rather, prompted the students to introduce) the relevant technical terms, expressed as abstract nominalizations, however taking care to stress them and repeat the words so that all students had a chance to hear and think about them explicitly.

With regard to interpersonal teacher–student ways of relating, the first features that struck me included the fact that, in Mrs. L's class, students could apparently initiate interactions, questions, and comments without fear of repercussions for taking control from the teacher (including a potentially challenging question about the teacher's role in the researcher's project that was indistinct on the audiotape but that merited a teacher response, including checking out her reply with the researcher). In general preclass chat suggests that students were affirmed (praised, named, answered) without having to be top science students, that science was not treated as overriding and excluding everything else, and that the teacher could express ignorance or doubt and model the taking of risks in trying out new and unfamiliar behavior (which also included volunteering for research). Metatalk was used to manage the class and check that students were ready to proceed ("Are you ready? . . . Alright?"), as well as providing a commentary on her own behavior ("We'll just check that she's got . . . ," "I will share with you a bit of my personal life"). She used many questions, thus involving students. They were questions that recognized difference and assumed a range of student responses (e.g., "Who's ever . . . how many different types"). At the same time they were closed questions, which allowed her to keep tight control of interactions in this segment of the lesson. As well as being evident in the student practice of initiating dialogue with the teacher both at the beginning and later in the class, true dialogue (cf. Lemke 1990) was also evident in the type of questions (real questions) the teacher asked of the students ("Who's ever flown a paper plane?") and the way she enthusiastically welcomed responses by the students ("Excellent!"). Students were permitted private cross-discussion (cf. Lemke 1990) later in the class but this did not occur while Mrs. L was addressing the class as a whole.

Mrs. L was also quite explicit in her expression of appraisal, including affect and personal judgements, and did so clearly and forcefully. She committed herself to a range of value expressions ("excellent," "true," "really interesting") and seemed to mean it even in the instances when she is also to some extent speaking "tongue in cheek." She was very affirming when someone had achieved something she believed was important ("O-oh! Very well done!"), very enthusiastic when students joined in the discussion and answered her questions, and empathetic even when indirectly reproving a student for playing with something prohibited (at least for the moment) ("Oh, it's tempting, Tessa, isn't it to play with that?"). Her tone and pace ranged widely, for example including clearly accentuated questions and statements, lower toned asides, fast-paced chat, and more formal, if ironical, story telling.

She used a variety of speech actions (questions, orders, and statements) and modal forms (including "Can I ask . . . ," "who would like . . . ," and "I'm led to believe") that modify her truth claims and invite or allow negotiation on them by her listeners. As such they also represent a choice that showed deference and reduced the status she had by virtue of the power differences inherent in their teacher and student roles (cf. Eggins 1994; Martin 1997), a power difference evident in the fact that the teacher, was, after all, doing most of the talking at this stage. Such deferential use of modalization can also reflect relative lack of recent frequent contact (Eggins 1994) and, as such, could be seen as evidence that Mrs. L was not presuming too much on her prior relationship with the class, but was renegotiating to gain their trust and respect. She took risks and made herself vulnerable by showing definite and strong commitment to her evaluations, and by owning her own experiences, decisions, and presumptions, both in the language she used ("This is really interesting," "Mrs. L has never studied paper planes," "I decided I wanted," "I find") and in her use of tonal emphasis.

With regard to personal style, Mrs. L resembles Mr. D in that in some ways her use of language was quite formal and more like written text, while in other ways it was more like spoken text. However, her choice of which features of each mode she used are in contrast with those of Mr. D. She used very little ellipsis, generally speaking in complete sentences, and clearly repeating key words (paper plane(s) is repeated in full nine times in this extract as well as being referred to in other ways by herself and her students), and being explicit in her use of cohesive ties. Her storytelling was rather formal, even to the extent of creating herself as a character ("Mrs. L") in the story, and adding an explanatory, authorial commentary ("This is a true story . . . I will share with you . . . because we're studying physics . . . This is really interesting . . . because I'm male and he's female").

On the other hand, she also used many features of more informal spoken language, including colloquial terms, a lower use of nominalization or grammatical metaphor (e.g. "It's to do with looking at me" (cf. a possible alternative, "research on my teaching"); "Mrs. L has never studied [making and flying] paper planes" (cf. "studied aerodynamics"); and "never perform the way you want them to perform" (cf. "don't perform properly")). However, some of her questions could also be seen as implied commands ("Can I ask you to remove your hats . . . ?") and hence may be grammatical metaphors. She used more intricate sentence structures (e.g. "We downloaded . . . because . . . and . . . and I said to him . . . and I presumed that I wasn't . . . and . . .") than would be normal in written English, and also used direct speech ("And I said to him, 'Please help me'"). She also made use of all the resources at her disposal in relation to intonation, pacing, and volume, within every sentence. Keywords were stressed and repeated carefully until she was sure that all students had heard them.

In summary, Mrs. L's talk invited personal input from students, she allowed a student to question her and took the time to give her a serious answer, and she talked in a more conversational way and used a range of intonation to make the lesson more interesting. Yet she also spoke formally and at times quite slowly and carefully, making sure that all students could hear and understand the keywords and would know what was going on, and how the different parts of the introduction led to the following part. She distinctly explained what she was doing and why. Hence it could be said that she treated her students with deference and was concerned about their needs being met (with psychological concerns being seen as also relevant to having their educational needs met). In doing so she relinquished some of her power and control but probably gained some respect and trust in return. Hence, this extract could be seen as representing a more engaging and democratic way of enacting the curriculum than that evident in Example 1.

Ideological perspectives affecting equitable access

The following discussion will extend the interpretation into an explanation of the main differences found between the discourse practices of the two teachers in terms of the problem identified in the introductory part of this chapter, inequitable access to science education, and in the light of what the teachers told me in interviews. I posit the notion that the two different sets of discourse practices represent two fundamentally different ideological positions.

Ways of representing school science

Science was represented in different ways by the two teachers. This was indicated by the different ways they talked about science, by the ways they kept or shared control, and by the way the learning environment was represented as a place of work or as a learning community.

   Classroom science. In the Exemplar 1 extract, both explicitly and implicitly, school science is represented as being almost entirely about things and about classifying material processes in scientific terms, and as having little to do with students' lives and interests or people more generally. In the Exemplar 2 extract, science is made directly relevant to everyday happenings and social experiences and can be approached initially using nonspecialized language.

   Both classrooms exemplified what their teachers believed the goals of science to be, as expressed in their interviews with me. Mr. D indicated that he saw laboratory activities as being very important to teach process skills that future scientists would need. He described himself as being opposed to using new curricula that presented science in the context of applied situations or included sections on language. Apparently in ignorance of the huge literature on misconceptions, he asserted that if students were taught the basic scientific concepts and principles, they would be able to apply scientific principles to their everyday lives. Mrs. L, on the other hand, asserted that students needed to be taught how to make connections between science knowledge and its applications, and to be encouraged to take responsibility for their own science-related decisions. She said she had adopted the national goals for science and wanted to make sure that students were developing skills (thinking and communicating along with investigating), attitudes and values, as well as building up their knowledge in the discipline-related strands.

The learning environment: Workplace versus "learning community" orientation. Roth (1992, citing Marshall 1990) described different approaches to teaching science by comparing a work-oriented classroom with a "learning community" oriented classroom. Mr. D's class typifies a work-oriented classroom, with completing tasks (preferably all students doing so at the same time), being obedient, observing strict hierarchical roles, and having right answers all taking priority over personal understanding. Mrs. L's class, on the other hand, typifies a learning community ethos. Personal understanding is a high priority, and taking risks and making personal decisions (and mistakes) within a supportive community environment are seen as normal, with different people taking different lengths of time to learn things, depending on factors such as prior experience (which in turn may depend on sociocultural factors such as gender). Roth (1992) commented that a "learning community" supported a notion of learning as both personal and social development and science as something with which all students could identify. The "learning community" curriculum addresses additional purposes for school science such as exploring the nature of science and its relevance to students' personal and social needs.

Overall, in terms of representing science, which I interpret as *access limiting*, Mr. D's talk generally portrays school science as being for future scientists only and as showing little concern for anyone who does not have familiarity with its ways or is not prepared to accept them without question. In the second case, which I interpret as *access enhancing*, Mrs. L's talk generally portrays school science as a natural extension of everyday happenings, and hence open to anyone, regardless of their prior learning and attitudes towards science. This teacher is implicitly communicating that she will allow students to learn in a way that, while somewhat challenging and risky, will take their interests, concerns, and reservations into consideration and provide a supportive learning environment for making mistakes.

Teacher roles. The two teachers expressed very differing understandings of science literacy in the interviews, and this would explain the very different roles they could be seen to be enacting in their talk. Mr. D presented himself as a technical expert, both as presenter of knowledge and as an evaluator of student homework. The laboratory was generally used as an extra way of demonstrating scientific truth and technical expertise rather than as a place of real investigation where students could be active scientists with real questions. He also presented as a manager with firm control over procedures in the room so that the class could proceed efficiently according to his agenda; this is likely to have been reinforced by his role as science HoD. This is consistent with his seeing science literacy in terms of being able to use correct scientific terms and explanations (i.e. reciting principles correctly), understand scientific arguments, and have good laboratory skills. As such he bears out Fensham's (1998) findings about those who see themselves as guardians of science.

Mrs. L, on the other hand, rather than setting herself up as an expert on everything to do with science, presented herself as a model for her (female) students' own learning, particularly as she explicitly brought up gender as an issue. She also had a focus on developing technical competencies. However, the discussion preceding the practical activity (and the assessment task sheet accompanying it) made it clear that understanding the principles of a physics topic was also an important goal of the exercise and that she saw herself as responsible for helping students make links between the two. She seemed to envisage her role as being to facilitate a complex, multistage process of learning, beginning with getting her students to engage with a topic and then getting them to want to engage in a practical activity that would help them develop the concepts she had envisaged. Consistent with her understanding of science literacy as including communication skills, and positive attitudes and values, as well as discipline knowledge, she presented with a hybrid identity, with different facets becoming visible as the lesson developed, from friendly community member, (gently) controlling teacher and classroom manager, motivating communicator (including amusing storyteller), learning facilitator, and goal-oriented task manager.

The tenor of her talk (as read in her tendency towards negotiation, her expressiveness of affect, judgement, and appreciation, and her level of comfort with emphasis, both in the words she used and in her intonation), conveyed a belief in the normality of expressing a point of view or intentionality, which meant that her talk in this science lesson was not sharply demarcated from everyday living, in contrast to that of Mr. D, in whose talk intentionality was hidden, with almost any sign of appraisal being absent. The latter suggests that Mr. D took it for granted that school science, at least in this instance, was already highly valued by his students, thus implicitly disaffirming anyone who had reservations about it. Mrs. L seemed to be more realistic about the place of physics in most of her students' lives and to accept it as normal, such that she then made it her business to set about changing apprehensions or negative attitudes.

Conclusion

In this chapter, I have used Critical Discourse Analysis (CDA) to compare the discourse practices of two teachers and highlight the messages being conveyed about what school science is, who it is for, how teaching and learning should happen in classrooms, how teachers should communicate with students, and what teacher and student roles should be. In this way, CDA has assisted me in raising awareness of aspects of teacher discourse practices that are likely to enhance or limit students' access to school science, particularly for disadvantaged students, and the relative power or powerlessness of students in relation to science teachers more generally. My analysis suggests that science teachers can engage and energize students by enacting an appropriate hybrid discourse. Such a discourse would employ scientific terminology and argument when necessary, but would also appropriate features of other pedagogical discourses better geared to teaching and learning, to respond to the needs of the full range of science students.

References

Eggins, S. (1994) *An Introduction to Systemic Functional Linguistics*. Londer: Pinter.
Fairclough, N. (1989) *Language and Power*. London: Longman.
Fairclough, N. (2003) *Analysing Discourse: Textual analysis for social research*. London: Routledge.
Fensham, P.J. (1998) 'The politics of legitimating and marginalising companion meanings', in D. Roberts and L. Ostman (eds) *The Many Meanings of Science Curriculum* (pp. 178–92). New York: Teachers College Press.

Goodrum, D., Hackling, M. and Rennie, L. (2001) *The Status and Quality of Teaching and Learning of Science in Australian Schools*. Canberra: Department of Education, Training and Youth Affairs.

Halliday, M.A.K. (1994) *An Introduction to Functional Grammar* (2nd edn). London: Edward Arnold.

Hanrahan, M. (1999) 'Conceptual change and changes of heart: a reflexive study of research in science literacy in the classroom.' Unpublished Ph.D. thesis, Queensland University of Technology, Brisbane.

Lemke, J.L. (1990) *Talking Science: Language, learning, and values*. Norwood, NJ: Ablex.

Lingard, B., Mills, M. and Hayes, D. (2000) 'Teachers, school reform and social justice: challenging research and practice'. *Australian Educational Researcher* 27 (3): 99–115.

Luke, A. (2002) 'Beyond science and ideology critique: developments in critical discourse analysis'. *Annual Review of Applied Linguistics* 22: 96–110.

Martin, J.R. (1992) *English Text: System and structure*. Philadelphia, PA: John Benjamins.

Martin, J.R. (1997) 'Analysing genre: functional parameters', in F. Christie and J.R. Martin (eds) *Genre and Institutions: Social processes in the workplace and school* (pp. 3–19). Washington, DC: Cassell.

Roth, K.J. (1992) *The Role of Writing in Creating a Science Learning Community* (Elementary Subjects Center Series No. 56). East Lansing, MI: Michigan State University, The Centre for the Learning and Teaching of Elementary Subjects. (ERIC Reproduction Service No. ED 352 259.)

Notes

1   The following applies to both extracts:
   •   all proper nouns have been changed to preserve the anonymity of participants;
   •   bold type represents emphasis;
   •   "↑" refers to a raised inflexion in places where a question mark would not be appropriate;
   •   [indistinct] refers to words that could not be deciphered at all; text within parentheses indicate our best guess (mine and a transcriber's) at an indistinct utterance; such text separated by "/" indicates two possible hearings; text between square brackets indicates that the word has been replaced to preserve someone's confidentiality or anonymity;
   •   "S" refers to any student, "S1" and "S2" are used when two different students speak immediately after one another, and "Ss" refers to several students (almost in unison or with one or more voices echoing the first);
   •   while greatest when more than one student responded to a question from the teacher, overlap between speakers was so minimal that it has generally been disregarded.

2   This is a term from Systemic Functional Linguistics, which refers to the parsing of clauses to show the relative positions of participants, processes, circumstances and connectors (cf. Martin 1992, citing Halliday 1973).

3   Students seen as at increased risk of failing science had been filtered into another class, and another Year 10 class was described as more advanced. Nevertheless this class had a spread of levels and some would go on to do Year 11 Chemistry.

Chapter 10

Henry Widdowson

Text, grammar and Critical Discourse Analysis

1 Introduction

In this chapter I present a critique of Systemic Functional Grammar and a critique of an example of how it is used in Critical Discourse Analysis. In doing so, I draw on two key distinctions which have been important in my work: semantic meaning versus pragmatic meaning and text versus discourse. **Semantic** meanings are those which are encoded in the language itself and recorded in dictionaries and grammars; to know a language is to know what these are. But, in using a language we do not put this knowledge on display but act upon it as appropriate to our communicative intentions. In other words, we make semantic meaning serve a **pragmatic** purpose for particular contexts. Consider the following as an example: a husband and wife are sitting at home and the window of the living room is open; the husband says 'it's cold in here'. The wife understands the semantic meaning of 'cold', i.e. a relatively low temperature. She will also understand the intended pragmatic meaning – the husband wants her to shut the window. The wife won't subject 'It's cold in here' to formal analysis (e.g. 'It' is a subject pronoun, 'here' is an adverb). Instead, she will take note of 'It's cold in here' to the extent that she recognizes its purpose, as something not to analyse but to act upon. In other words, she will treat 'It's cold in here' as **text**, in exactly the same way as she would when coming across a written notice such as 'Keep off the grass'. People produce texts to get a message across, to express ideas and beliefs, to explain something, to get other people to do certain things or to think in a certain way, and so on. So, there is a

Extracts from Widdowson, H. G. (2004) *Text, Context, Pretext: Critical issues in discourse analysis*, Oxford: Blackwell.

complex of communicative purposes which underlies the text and motivates its production in the first place, as well as affecting how the text is interpreted. This I refer to as **discourse**. So, the husband's intended meaning that the wife shut the window is not in the text itself but in the discourse. The wife's pragmatic inference that the husband means her to go to the window to shut it is not in the text but in the discourse, and so on. On my perspective, text only exists in conjunction with context as the reflex of discourse; text is then a trace of discourse and so not equivalent to it.

2 Systemic Functional Grammar

Systemic Functional Grammar (henceforth S/F Grammar) has the express purpose of analysing language into systems of options which constitute the 'meaning potential' for the creation of text. As Halliday puts it: 'The aim has been to construct a grammar for the purposes of text analysis: one that would make it possible to say sensible and useful things about any texts, spoken or written, in modern English' (Halliday 1994: xv). Although English is specifically mentioned here, the same would presumably apply to any language. Perhaps the first thing to be clear about is that the aim of the grammar so formulated is to account for text as a linguistic unit in its own right, to explain it as such and not simply to use it to exemplify the occurrence of other structural units, like clauses or phrases. The purpose, it would appear, is not therefore to show how different grammatical features simply show up in stretches of language, but how they operate to form larger units of meaning. As Halliday says: 'The grammar, then, is at once both a grammar of the system and a grammar of the text' (Halliday 1994: xxii).

One might reasonably infer from this statement that text analysis is taken as a straightforward matter of applying the categories of the grammar. But only, it would appear, up to a point. Halliday explains that analysis works on two levels:

> One is a contribution to the *understanding* of the text: the linguistic analysis enables one to show how, and why, the text means what it does. In the process, there are likely to be revealed multiple meanings, alternatives, ambiguities, metaphors and so on. This is the lower of the two levels; it is one that should always be attainable provided the analysis is such as to relate the text to general features of the language – provided it is based on the grammar in other words.

At this level, then, application of grammatical categories reveals the properties of the text, not only, we should notice, how it is constructed, but what it means. That is to say, the meaning is internally in the text, and understanding derives directly from analysis. Analysis, it would seem, does not just *contribute* to, but actually *constitutes* understanding. Certainly there is no mention here of where any other contribution might come from. But this is the lower level of analysis. There is a higher one:

> The higher level of achievement is a contribution to the *evaluation* of the text: the linguistic analysis may enable one to say why the text is, or is not, an

effective text for its own purposes – in what respects it succeeds and in what respects it fails, or is less successful. This goal is much harder to attain. It requires an interpretation not only of the text itself but also of its context (context of situation, context of culture), and of the systematic relationship between context and text.

(Halliday 1994: xv)

At this level, the text is interpreted externally in relation to context. We are concerned here not with what texts mean but what users mean by texts in the realization of their communicative purposes. At this level, presumably, the multiple meanings, ambiguities and so on which emerge from the first level get resolved by reference to contextual factors.

Halliday talks about the processing of text at two levels. The first level is concerned not only with the *identification* of textual features, but also with an understanding of their meaning, and therefore some degree of *interpretation* as well. So it would appear that for Halliday the meaning of a text is compounded of the meanings of its constituent sentences, so that understanding it is a cumulative matter. A text, it seems, is taken to be simply a sum of its sentential parts, so understanding it is straightforwardly a function of a grammatical analysis which reveals the multiple meanings, alternatives, ambiguities, metaphors encoded in the separate sentences it is composed of.

Halliday's first level of analysis seems not to address the question of how sentences are related to form larger linguistic units, and so long as it does not do that, it is hard to see how the grammar that is applied is actually a grammar of text as such as distinct from the sentences in a text. Furthermore, the meaning that is taken into account at this level of 'understanding' has to do not with the pragmatic matter of 'what the author was about when he produced the text', but with what is semantically encoded in the sentences of the text itself. The pragmatic meaning of a text only comes into consideration at the second level of 'evaluation' when attention is shifted from the text itself to its relationship with context.[1]

The model that we are presented with here is based on the assumption that there is meaning contained within a text, an understanding of which will result directly from a linguistic analysis of its constituent sentences. Thus text is isolated as a linguistic object for analysis (and understanding), but in consequence, of course, it is dissociated from the contextual conditions which make it a text in the first place. For, as I have argued, text only exists in conjunction with context, as the reflex of discourse, and understanding in the usual sense would normally imply not the identification and subsequent elimination of alternatives, ambiguities and so on, but a more direct homing in on relevant meaning. The two levels of analysis that Halliday proposes would not appear to correspond with the normal process of assigning meaning to texts. In normal circumstances of use, people do not process utterances (spoken or written) as separate sentences, one by one, and then consider how the text so analysed might relate externally to contextual factors. We do not first come to an understanding of the semantics of a text, and then evaluate what its possible pragmatic import might be. We do not read possible meanings *off* from a text; we read plausible meanings *into* a text, prompted by the purpose and conditioned by the context. In other words (in my words) you derive a discourse from it and it is that which realizes the text as text. What is happening in Halliday's formulation, I suggest, is that analysis is confused with interpretation. This confusion, as we shall see in section 3, has far-reaching consequences.

I want to argue against Halliday that the linguistic analysis of text is not necessary for understanding. Indeed, if anything, it deflects attention from an inference of meaning and interferes with interpretation, so that the first level of analysis in Halliday's scheme has a way of obstructing the processing at the second level. Consider the case of multiple meanings and ambiguities. These occur in texts with a fair degree of frequency. But in many cases, though they can be revealed by semantic analysis, they are not pragmatically activated because the signification is overridden by contextual factors. So it is that we might conceive of a man in the London underground setting about understanding the text DOGS MUST BE CARRIED by semantic analysis and being confused by two possible meanings:

1   *It is necessary to carry dogs* (by analogy with TICKETS MUST BE SHOWN).
2   *If you have a dog, it is necessary to carry it.*

It seems more likely, however, that the man, like thousands of other passengers, would simply identify the text as a notice, relate it to context and notice nothing ambiguous about the language at all. The same applies to the following utterance that occurred some time ago in the text of a news broadcast about stormy weather on the British coast:

Five people were lost in a rowing boat.

This too is semantically ambiguous:

1   Five people in a rowing boat were lost.
2   Five (very small) people were lost in (side) a rowing boat.

Normal listeners, concerned with interpretation, do not notice ambiguities of this kind. Linguists do. This is because their attention is attuned to semantic analysis, and in the process they abstract sentence from utterance and thereby detextualize the text.

So if we take these expression as *textual*, that is to say as used in a communicative context of some kind, and not as exemplifying the semantic resources of the system, the ambiguity will, likely as not, pass unnoticed. Noticing it, indeed, is likely to interfere with communicative efficiency. So making ambiguity noticeable by analysing semantic features out of text would actually be *dys*functional as far as interpreting the text is concerned. Indeed, one might argue that the more detailed the linguistic analysis, the further one is likely to get from the significance of the text. And this follows because only some of the semantic meaning encoded in linguistic form is activated as contextually appropriate on a particular occasion.

I have been arguing that when language is put to use, the resulting text acts upon context, and in this pragmatic process the encoded semantic potential is only partially realized. This is why evaluation cannot be a function of understanding in

Halliday's sense. But there is a further difficulty: the semantic analysis is bound to be partial on its own terms as well. This is because the potential that the grammar seeks to capture is misrepresented by the very process of accounting for it. The grammar, in other words, can never be an account of what people can mean. A model, of its very nature, classifies and categorizes, makes divisions and distinctions which separate aspects of language out from each other. But these aspects co-occur in texts in complex relationships which cannot be grammatically accounted for.

It is taken as axiomatic in S/F linguistics that a model of description should reflect the essential social nature of language. Human language did not just take the form it did by random mutation, but evolved in the process of adaptation to human need, and a linguistic model should reflect this fact. So it is that S/F Grammar is functionally iconic in that its design is meant to represent the essential human purposes which language has evolved to serve. Thus we arrive at the tripartite structure of the model. This is how the general design principle is expressed:

> All languages are organized around two main kinds of meaning, the 'ideational' or reflective, and the 'interpersonal' or active. These components, called 'metafunctions' in the terminology of the current theory, are the manifestations in the linguistic system of the two very general purposes which underlie all uses of language: (i) to understand the environment (ideational), and (ii) to act on the others in it (interpersonal). Combined with these is a third metafunctional component, the 'textual', which breathes relevance into the other two.
>
> (Halliday 1994: xiii)

We might formulate the ideational and interpersonal functions in terms of the relationship between the trinity of positions which are linguistically encoded in the personal pronoun system. Thus the ideational function can be understood as the relationship between ego, first-person self, to third-person reality out there, and the interpersonal function as the relationship between first-person self and second-person other. (Diagrammatically illustrated in Figure 10.1.) Since this trinity does indeed seem fundamental to human perception, we can acknowledge that there is good reason for basing the design of a model of language on the two functions which express their essential relationship.

There is, however, a difficulty about the third of the metafunctions which Halliday identifies. It is different in kind from the others in that it is not related to any external social or communicative need. It simply serves an enabling purpose: it is a kind of functional catalyst which combines with the other functions only in order to 'breathe relevance into them'. This implies that these other functions are

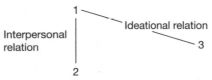

Figure 10.1 1st, 2nd, 3rd person and the ideational/interpersonal functions

inert and are only made relevant (presumably to the communicative process) when acted upon by the textual. But how this comes about is far from clear. If the textual function is to combine with the others and make them relevant, then one would expect that the grammar would reveal how the various options associated with the other functions are realized through the options associated with the textual. We would expect to find some clear indication of functional interrelations and inter-dependencies. But what the grammar does is to show how the three metafunctions are encoded in three separate systemic components: theme, mood and transitivity. They are categorized as three distinct kinds of meaning, and options from each constitute separate strands, three lines of meaning which come together in the clause. There they coexist but they do not act upon each other. So each clause can be characterized as message or exchange or representation in respect to the theme, mood and transitivity systems respectively.

In the grammar, the systems are kept apart. In actual use, however, they are not. When the semantic resources are actualized pragmatically as text, they act upon each other in various ways. Consider theme and rheme, for example, as constituents of the clause as message. In actual use they do indeed combine with other meanings: indeed their *only* function is to realize other functions. The organization of information in the clause is motivated by some ideational or interpersonal purpose. Thus, theme and rheme may be associated with topic and comment, in which case the first person adopts a position in relation to the third-person world, interprets reality, if you will, in reference to self. In this sense, assignment of topic and comment is an ideational matter. Alternatively, theme and rheme may be associated with given and new. In this case the information is being organized to key in with what is assumed to be known by the second person, so the thematic arrangement now discharges an interpersonal function. We can show this diagrammatically in Figure 10.2.

What Figure 10.2 represents, in a modest way, is one case of interrelationship across the systems of the grammar. It may be that there are other and more specific inter-systemic dependencies that could be identified and made explicit in the grammar. It might be possible, for example, to establish that particular theme options co-occurred regularly with particular options in the transitivity and mood systems so that they are bound implicationally together. The more such inter-systemic dependencies could be accounted for, the closer the grammar of the system would approximate to the grammar of text in that it would obviously increase semantic constraints on pragmatic meaning, and narrow down interpretative possibilities. But the quest for such relational dependencies seems to be precluded by the divisions

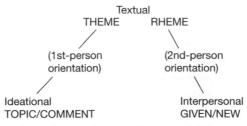

Figure 10.2 Some interrelationships in Systemic Functional Grammar

built into the design of a S/F Grammar whereby each of the three system types is singled out for separate treatment: the emphasis is on intra-systemic distinctions rather than inter-systemic connections. But even if S/F Grammar were to become a more integrated model along these lines, it would still not account for all possible textual realizations. It could not determine which combination of theme, transitivity and mood features was operative on a particular textual occasion.

So whether a particular thematic arrangement is to be understood as having ideational or interpersonal significance is a matter of interpretation beyond analysis. The textual function in the grammar does not, in fact, reveal how the text functions. Consider the case of the passive as a thematic device for message organization. When it occurs pragmatically in text it is bound to take on ideational or interpersonal significance. It is indeed frequently cited by critical discourse analysts as an example of specific representation, of how a particular first-person perspective is projected on reality.

In Lee (1992) we are presented with an analysis of two texts; extracts from two newspapers which deal with the same event. The texts differ in their organization of the clause as message, that is to say in the way the information is thematically organized. One of them uses the active, and the other the passive. The *Guardian* newspaper has the headline:

Police (*theme*) shoot 11 dead in Salisbury riot

The text then continues:

Riot police (*theme*) shot and killed 11 African demonstrators . . .

The Times text has the headline:

Rioting blacks (*theme*) shot dead by police as ANC leaders meet

followed by:

Eleven Africans (*theme*) were shot dead . . .

Lee comments: 'It is noticeable that the *Guardian* uses active structures in both the headline and in the text . . . whereas *The Times* uses passives. The effect of the passive is to further attenuate the agentivity of the police, particularly in the case of the truncated passive with agent deletion' (Lee 1992: 100).

It is a matter of fact that these texts manifest active and passive structures. The question is: what meanings do they realize? Lee asserts that the selection of the passive necessarily implies a first-person position on the event, presents the topic in a certain light. This may be the effect of the passive on him, but it has no warrant in the grammar. For he takes the passive here not as a message-forming option from theme systems, but as if it were an option from the transitivity systems of the grammar: he reads the passive, as opposed to the active, as signalling a different representation of the event. But the specific ideational meaning which Lee assigns to the passive is actually a function of his interpretation of this structure as it occurs in this particular text, an interpretation which is itself related, of course, to a context of socio-political beliefs and values. If the passive is textualized differently, it becomes more difficult to assign such a meaning to it. Suppose, for example, we were to give the event described in these newspaper texts the following wording:

> Police opened fire on African demonstrators in Salisbury today as ANC leaders were meeting. Eleven Africans were shot dead.

It would surely be somewhat perverse in this case to interpret the passive ideationally as representing the event as happening without agentivity, since the agentivity is explicitly described in the preceding clause. It would seem more reasonable to suggest that this is not a case of reference evasion, but reference avoidance, motivated by communicative economy. The agent is deleted because it is redundant. The writer, we might suggest, is co-operatively taking account of what the reader already knows and fashions the message accordingly on given/new considerations. The passive with deleted agent in this case can be understood not ideationally as representing the event in a certain way, but as having the interpersonal function of facilitating the exchange.

Lee talks as if the passive structure always signifies a particular kind of representation, a signification that is carried over from grammar into text. But as we have seen, the significance of the structure depends on how it relates to others in a text. Even if one could show systematically (and systemically) that agentivity is a function of the convergence of theme and transitivity options in the grammar, it does not follow that this semantic feature is focused on in a particular instance of text, or even pragmatically activated at all. It would seem then that active/passive message forms can, as parts of *text*, function in different ideational and interpersonal ways. But these cannot be captured by the grammar.

In this section, I have been exploring the relationship between text and grammar by questioning the S/F claim that it can account both for the systems of the code and for their textual use within the same model of description. I have argued that this claim is sustained by a confusion in the concept of function. S/F Grammar is functional in the sense that the systems of semantic encodings that it identifies are derived diachronically from how language has developed as social semiotic as a formal reflex of the functions it is required to serve. It does not follow at all, however, that the functioning of language pragmatically as discourse is simply a function of these systems. The fact that S/F Grammar is modelled *on* use does not make it a model *of* use. So I think it is misleading to claim that it is 'at once both a grammar of the system and a grammar of the text'. It cannot be an account of text as the pragmatic use of language, the product of a discourse process.

What it can, and does, provide is an extremely detailed set of descriptive devices which can be used in specifying the linguistic features of texts, and it may be that this description of semantic signification might serve as a pointer to where pragmatic significance is to be found. But just what these directions are, and how closely interpretation follows them, are precisely the kinds of question that discourse analysis needs to grapple with. There must obviously be a crucial relationship between semantic and pragmatic meaning, between the potential and its realization, between abstract systems that are informed by function and the functions that are actualized in their use. But we cannot look for relationships between phenomena without first making a distinction between them.

3 Systemic Functional Grammar in Critical Discourse Analysis

I turn now to a consideration of a particular approach to discourse analysis that has become prominent and influential over recent years and which has appropriated the term critical as a designation of its distinctive character. The approach is critical in the sense that it is quite explicitly directed at revealing how language is used for the exercise of socio-political control. As van Dijk puts it:

> Critical Discourse Analysis (CDA) is a type of discourse analytical research that primarily studies the way social power abuse, dominance, and inequality are enacted, reproduced, and resisted by text and talk in the social and political context. With such dissident research, critical discourse analysts take explicit position, and thus want to understand, expose, and ultimately resist social inequality.
>
> (van Dijk 2001: 352)

This critical perspective is of crucial importance in that it engages scholarly enquiry with matters of immediate and pressing concern in the non-scholarly world. What CDA has done, greatly to its credit, is to make discourse analysis relevant by relating it to a moral cause and an ideological purpose. In this respect, I regard its work as highly significant. It happens, furthermore, that the socio-political position its proponents take up is one which I share. So I should stress that in what follows I take no issue with the critical perspective of CDA as such. My concern is with its effects on the kind of discourse analysis that is carried out, and how such analysis relates to the issues I have discussed.

How then is discourse analysis done in CDA? Although, as Luke points out, 'the stances, positions, and techniques of CDA vary' (Luke 2002: 98), one can identify certain features of common principle and practice which characterize the approach that has been most prominent to date. This approach has its origins in the work of Roger Fowler and his colleagues (for a succinct review, see Fowler 1996) and was subsequently developed by others, notably Norman Fairclough, its most impressive and influential practitioner. In this approach to CDA, the linguistic model that is generally invoked as particularly appropriate to the purpose is that of Halliday's S/F Grammar. As an account of language as social semiotic which, as we have seen in section 2, claims to deal with text, it would appear on the face of it to be well suited to an analysis of discourse as social action. It turns out, however, that the application of an S/F model in CDA work is far from straightforward.

Thus, in expounding his own 'social theory of discourse', Fairclough (1992) finds it necessary to modify the model. Discourse, he explains, is itself 'constitutive' or 'constructive' of social structure (and not simply constrained by it), and one needs to distinguish between three kinds of 'constructive effect': one concerns the construction of social self or identity, another the construction of social relationships

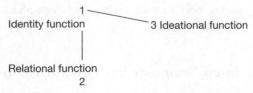

Figure 10.3 1st, 2nd, 3rd person and the ideational and identity/relational functions

between people, and a third the construction of 'systems of knowledge and belief'. These effects, he says, 'correspond respectively to three functions of language and dimensions of meaning which coexist and interact in all discourses' (Fairclough 1992: 64). They do not, however, correspond with the three functions of language that are proposed in S/F Grammar. The third, the ideational, is common to both. The first two, however, the identity and relational functions, are incorporated by Halliday into a single interpersonal function. What Fairclough is proposing, then, is that we can distinguish between how discourse serves reflexively to create a first-person position or self, and how it serves as the means for establishing relations with the second-person other. We might illustrate this by reference to Figure 10.1 (see Figure 10.3).

There is a good deal of theoretical appeal in this specification of discourse functions by reference to the trinity of first-, second- and third-person positions: the representation of first-person self, the relation with second-person other, the representation of third-person reality. The question arises, however, as to how this threefold distinction can be made operational in actual analysis. And this brings us to the third function in the S/F scheme of things, namely the textual. Where does this figure in Fairclough's social theory of discourse?

'Halliday also distinguishes a "textual" function', says Fairclough, 'which can be usefully added to my list' (1992: 65). The somewhat offhand nature of this comment would seem to suggest that the textual function does not have the same status in the discourse theory being propounded as the central constitutive functions mentioned earlier. It is a useful addition. Just where its usefulness resides, however, or how it relates to these other functions, is left unclear.

Fairclough's discourse theory, then, would seem to depart from an S/F model by proposing three main functions, two of which are subdivisions of the inter-personal, and by demoting the textual function to the level of useful appendage. His apparent uncertainty as to what to do with this function is consistent with the view I expressed in section 2 that it does indeed have a different status from the ideational and interpersonal in that, unlike these, it is not expressive of any external social function but is an enabling device for their realization in text. The ideational and interpersonal (including the identity and relational) are, as Fairclough suggests, *discourse* functions. The textual is (true to its name) not a discourse function at all but a textual one. As such, it is not just a useful addition to discourse theory but the indispensable means whereby the theory can be exemplified by analysis. We return to the key issue of how the analysis of textual features leads to discourse interpretations.[2]

Fairclough himself outlines what he calls 'a framework for analysing texts', but without any explicit reference to the textual function as defined in S/F linguistics:

> Text analysis can be organized under four main headings: 'vocabulary', 'grammar', 'cohesion', and 'text structure'. These can be thought of as ascending in scale: vocabulary deals mainly with individual words, grammar deals with words combined into clauses and sentences, cohesion deals with how clauses and sentences are linked together, and text structure deals with large-scale organizational properties of texts. In addition, I distinguish a further three main headings which will be used in analysis of discursive practices rather than text analysis, though they certainly involve formal features of texts: the 'force' of utterances, i.e. what sorts of speech acts (promises, requests, threats, etc.) they constitute; the 'coherence' of texts; and the 'intertextuality' of texts.
>
> (Fairclough 1992: 75)

This view of text analysis would appear to correspond quite closely to that proposed by Halliday, as discussed in section 2. The first four headings here have to do with text-internal properties, the analysis of which, according to Halliday, yields 'understanding'. The additional three headings have to do with text-external factors and constitute a second and higher level of what Halliday calls 'evaluation'. It is at this latter level that the text is interpreted as a discourse realization, or, as Fairclough puts it, as a discursive practice. But as was pointed out in section 2, the difficulty here is that if texts are to be taken as texts, and therefore as necessarily carrying discourse implications, they cannot be analysed as linguistic objects in isolation. It is not that the first-level analysis is carried out as an input to the second level for subsequent evaluation: this second level of interpretation regulates what textual features are attended to. Fairclough's three discursive factors are not additional to his four levels of text analysis, but are bound to be implicated in them. They do indeed 'involve formal features of texts'. The crucial issue is the nature of this involvement. Given a text, you can, of course, analyse it exhaustively into its constituent parts, and note how its morphemes, words, clauses and sentences combine. But this, as was argued in section 2, will tell you nothing about its essential nature as a text.

Fairclough presents his framework of analysis as the means whereby one arrives at the constitutive discourse functions of the identity, relational and ideational kind that he has earlier specified. What the actual procedures are for drawing on this framework to infer social significance of this kind are not made explicit. We find no demonstration of how one might work through the headings that are proposed in any systematic way, ascending (or descending) the scale from 'individual words', for example, to 'the large-scale organizational properties of texts', or at what point issues concerning 'force' or 'coherence' in the second series of headings come into play. The headings constitute not so much a framework, in fact, as a check list of different factors that one might bear in mind, and put to use as and when it seems expedient to do so.

This is borne out by the example Fairclough provides of his own use of the framework in an analysis of the newspaper headline:

Gorbachev Rolls Back the Red Army

'My comments here', he says, 'will be restricted to certain aspects of the clause.' It seems reasonable to ask why, when seven headings for analysis have been outlined, only one should be singled out for special attention. It is true, of course, that this particular text cannot of itself be used to illustrate aspects such as cohesion and text structure, but then why not choose another text which would lend itself to a more comprehensive treatment? But let us consider Fairclough's comments on the clause:

> In terms of ideational meaning, the clause is transitive: it signifies a process of a particular individual acting physically (note the metaphor) upon an entity. We might well see here a different ideological investment from other ways of signifying the same event, for example 'The Soviet Union Reduces its Armed Forces', or 'The Soviet Army Gives up 5 Divisions'. In terms of interpersonal meaning, the clause is declarative (as opposed to interrogative, or imperative), and contains a present tense form of the verb which is categorically authoritative. The writer-reader relationship here is that between someone telling what is the case in no uncertain terms, and someone being told; these are the two subject positions set up in the clause.
>
> (Fairclough 1992: 76)

The metaphor we are asked to note is a feature of the vocabulary used in this text, but since the analysis does not concern itself with this part of the framework, there is no indication as to why it is noteworthy, or how this particular lexical choice might relate to the syntax of the clause. We are presented with 'other ways of signifying the same event' but as a matter of fact neither of them is different in clause structure from the original headline: they too are transitive, and so, on Fairclough's own account, must be assigned the same ideational meaning. The fact is that the difference in signification has to do with the vocabulary. The event is represented differently by lexical means: the choice of *The Soviet Union* rather than *Gorbachev*, of *The Soviet Army* rather than *The Red Army*, of the verbs *reduces* and *gives up* rather than *rolls back*, and so on. We should note too that sameness of the event cannot be inferred from textual evidence but only by relating the text to external contextual factors. Only then can you infer that what rolling back the Red Army actually amounts to is reducing it in size, or even, more specifically, to giving up five divisions. Whatever 'ideological investment' you might wish to see in the choice of one expression rather than another has, then, to do with the choice of vocabulary, and a knowledge of context, neither of which is taken into account in this analysis. Even if one does take these other factors into account, there still needs to be some argument as to why they might lead us to see this 'ideological investment' that Fairclough refers to.

And here we come to a further difficulty. The framework of analysis is designed as a means of revealing discourse functions. One of these is ideational: the use of language to represent knowledge and belief. But Fairclough, following Halliday, here talks of ideational meaning as already formally encoded in the transitivity of the clause. If this is so, then a particular representation of knowledge and belief is achieved automatically by grammatical choice, and is unaffected by any other factors, in which case, all the other headings in the framework that is proposed would appear, in effect, to be irrelevant. The same point applies to what Fairclough says of the interpersonal meaning of this headline:

In terms of interpersonal meaning, the clause is declarative (as opposed to interrogative, or imperative), and contains a present tense form of the verb which is categorically authoritative. The writer-reader relationships here is that between someone telling what is the case in no uncertain terms, and someone being told; these are the two subject positions set up in the clause.

Again, the interpersonal function that is formally encoded in the grammar is equated with the interpersonal use of language: in other words, how the language is used to construct social identity and social relationships is directly inferable from linguistic forms. But declarative, interrogative and imperative are linguistic categories. They are things that are said, as distinct from assertions, orders, questions, which are things that are done, and which bring all kinds of social factor into consideration. But if an interpersonal function is necessarily discharged by a selection from the mood system of the grammar, then there is no distinction between saying and doing, and consequently no relationship between them to investigate.

But it is not only the clause type that directly signals interpersonal significance in this analysis. Thus the occurrence of the present tense form of the verb in this text (*rolls*) is said to be 'categorically authoritative' and, as it occurs in this clause, to create relational positions of assertiveness and submission between first and second persons. Of course this tense might be used pragmatically in this way, but then one needs to explain how it does so by reference to other factors that appear under other headings in the Fairclough framework. Nobody, I imagine, would seriously argue that categorical authoritativeness is actually semantically encoded in the present tense in English. And yet this is what seems to be implied in assigning such an interpersonal meaning to it in this analysis.

Fairclough says no more about the interpersonal meaning of this headline. Rather surprisingly, he makes no explicit reference to the distinction that figures so prominently in his theory between identity and relational effects. Instead, he follows the standard S/F line and next turns his attention to the textual function:

> Thirdly, there is a textual aspect: 'Gorbachev' is topic or theme of the clause, as the first part of a clause usually is: the article is about him and his doings. On the other hand, if the clause were made into a passive, that would make 'the Red Army' the theme: 'The Red Army is Rolled Back (by Gorbachev)'. Another possibility offered by the passive is the deletion of the (bracketed) agent, because the agent is unknown, already known, judged irrelevant, or perhaps in order to leave agency and hence responsibility vague.

As we have already seen (in section 2) the formal property of thematic position can signal either topic or given, and so has interpersonal implications. So it does not necessarily follow that 'Gorbachev' as theme makes Gorbachev the topic of the headline, even less that it indicates that the article that follows is about him and his doings. But here Fairclough does acknowledge that you cannot read off discourse significance directly from a mode of signifying. The use of a passive construction might indeed be intended and interpreted in different ways, depending on how it figures in relation to other factors in his framework.

What, then, are we to make of this analysis, presented as an illustration of how a framework for analysing texts can be used in the service of a social theory of discourse? In the first place, very little of the framework is actually drawn upon, and there is little if any indication of how the features that are focused on ('certain aspects of the clause') relate to others under other headings in the framework. In restricting his attention to the clause, Fairclough can only make comments on what is clause-like about the headline. But this necessarily misrepresents the nature of the headline as such: the fact that it is always part of a larger text, and that its discursive function is to attract immediate attention. Hence the use of capitals, and hence, one might suggest, the use of the metaphorical *Rolls Back* and of the phrase *Red Army* which links alliteratively with it, and is more evocative than the alternative *Soviet Army*. So it is too that we cannot infer from its thematic structure as a clause what is to be topicalized in the text that follows, for the attention-seeking function of headlines makes them unreliable indicators of what the articles they are attached to are actually about.

The point is not that Fairclough's self-imposed restriction to the clause only provides a partial analysis, which could in principle be continued and complemented by taking other aspects of his framework into account. The point is that it misrepresents the very nature of the text by reducing it to a clause. What it exemplifies is what we might refer to as the *functional fallacy*. This is the assumption that semantic signification is directly projected as pragmatic significance in language use, that people make meaning by the simple expedient of activating the socially motivated linguistic encodings described in S/F linguistics.

Interestingly (and paradoxically) enough, Fairclough himself, in a passage immediately preceding the outline of his framework of analysis, points out the importance of distinguishing between meaning that is semantically encoded, and that which is pragmatically realized:

> Another important distinction in relation to meaning is between the meaning potential of a text, and its interpretation. Texts are made up of forms which past discursive practice, condensed into conventions, has endowed with a meaning potential. The meaning potential of a form is generally hetero-geneous, a complex of diverse, overlapping and sometimes contradictory meanings, . . . so that texts are usually highly ambivalent and open to multiple interpretations. Interpreters usually reduce this potential ambivalence by opting for a particular meaning, or a small set of alternative meanings. Providing we bear in mind this dependence of meaning on interpretation, we can use 'meaning' both for the potential of forms, and for the meanings ascribed in interpretation.
>
> (Fairclough 1992: 75)

What is curious is that having made this distinction so clearly, and having stressed its importance, Fairclough should then proceed to pay no heed to it. For it is precisely because encoded meaning always gives rise to various pragmatic interpretations that one cannot talk about a particular choice from the transitivity systems of the grammar expressing a particular ideational function in use, or why one cannot talk about a mood or a tense signifying of itself a particular position or perspective. Fairclough's approach to discourse analysis, at least as exemplified here, is, I would suggest, open to criticism precisely because he fails to act on the distinction which he makes so clearly in this passage, and does not bear in mind this dependence of meaning on interpretation. And it seems perverse to court conceptual confusion by not making terminologically explicit a distinction which is so crucial to the development of a coherent theory of discourse.

As said earlier, CDA generally takes its descriptive bearings from S/F Grammar, and the functional fallacy that informs the analysis we have just been considering can be traced back to its influence. This is not to say that S/F Grammar could not serve as a basis for discourse analysis. The kinds of pragmatic meaning that are *ascribed* to particular uses of language must be related to the semantic meanings which are *inscribed* in the grammar. The externalized functions are realizations, under various contextual and other conditions, of the internalized functions that constitute meaning potential. The question is how this potential gets realized under these different conditions. One might approach this question by the thorough and systematic application of the S/F model to the analysis of texts, seeking to show how semantically inscribed meanings get realized – extended, modified, nullified even – in pragmatic ascriptions. In this way, one might hope to demonstrate the relationship between the internal semantic and the external pragmatic functioning of language, and put discourse analysis (the relationship between what is said and what is done) on a more secure and rigorous footing.

Notes

1   Halliday does not talk about his two levels of text interpretation in terms of semantics and pragmatics. There is every indication that, as with the terms *text* and *discourse*, they are taken as terminological variants which have no conceptual significance in his scheme of things. The term *pragmatics*, indeed, rarely, if ever, occurs in his writing: it makes no appearance, for example, in the index of Halliday (1994). *Semantics*, on the other hand, does, and this term is used to cover all aspects of meaning. Thus he refers to 'the semantic system of the language', 'the semantic interpretation of a text' (xx) and 'discourse semantics' (15). There is no recognition of the distinction I drew at the start of the chapter between (semantic) meaning that is encoded in the language and (pragmatic) meaning that is realized in language use. Halliday talks about realization, but in a very different sense:

> The relation between the semantics and the grammar is one of realization: the wording 'realizes', or encodes, the meaning. (Halliday 1994: xx)

For Halliday, encoded and realized meanings are, it would appear, the same (semantic) thing.

2   It should be noted that Fairclough rejects the view of discourse as 'the analysis of text structure above the sentence' (Fairclough 1995: 7) and has made a distinction in principle between the two concepts, not, it would seem, greatly different from that I proposed at the start of this chapter:

> A text is a product rather than a process – a product of the process of text production. But I shall use the term *discourse* to refer to the whole process of social interaction of which a text is just a part. This process includes in addition to the text the process of production, of which the text is a product, and the process of interpretation, for which the text is a resource. (Fairclough 1989: 24)

In practice, however, the distinction is more honoured in the breath than the observance, as will be evident from the examples of analysis in this chapter. And it does not seem to figure as having any key theoretical status in later work: there is no explicit mention of it, for example, in Chouliaraki and Fairclough (1999).

References

Chouliaraki, L. and Fairclough, N. (1999) *Discourse in Late Modernity: Rethinking critical discourse analysis*. Edinburgh: Edinburgh University Press.

Fairclough, N. (1989) *Language and Power*. London: Longman.

Fairclough, N. (1992) *Discourse and Social Change*. Cambridge: Polity Press.

Fairclough, N. (1995) *Critical Discourse Analysis: The critical study of language*. London: Longman.

Fowler, R. (1996) 'On critical linguistics', in C.R. Caldas-Coulthard and M. Coulthard (eds) *Texts and Practices: Readings in critical discourse analysis*. London: Routledge.

Halliday, M.A.K. (1994) *An Introduction to Functional Grammar* (2nd edn). London: Edward Arnold.

Lee, D. (1992) *Competing Discourses*. London: Longman.

Luke, A. (2002) 'Beyond science and ideology critique: developments in critical discourse analysis'. *Annual Review of Applied Linguistics* 22: 96–110.

van Dijk, T.A. (2001) 'Critical discourse analysis', in D. Tannen, D. Schiffrin and H. Hamilton (eds) *The Handbook of Discourse Analysis*. Oxford: Blackwell.

PART THREE

Ethnography

Caroline Coffin, Theresa Lillis, Kieran O'Halloran

Introduction to Part Three

Part Three of the reader aims to illustrate the way in which ethnography contributes to identifying real-world language problems as well as offering specific ways of engaging with these same problems. The first chapter offers a theoretical perspective on the role of ethnography for coming to understand what's involved and at stake in the real worlds of language users. This is followed by two chapters focusing specifically on ethnography as a practical tool for engaging in literacy development and policy making, and two chapters focusing on ethnography for generating contextualised understandings of spoken interaction.

The first chapter in Part Three directly engages with a key theme running throughout this book, that is the relationship between text and context. Jan Blommaert writes as a critical discourse analyst who sees ethnography as central to his goal of engaging in a 'critical science of language' and for whom there can be no division between text and context: 'context is not something we can just "add" to text – it is text, it defines its meanings and conditions of use'. This anthropological perspective on language is central to his critique of CDA and in particular the tendency within CDA to engage in *a priori* understandings about context(ualisation): that is, to rely on the researcher-analyst's assumptions about relevant aspects of context (institutions, power relations, etc.) through which texts are then read. Drawing on his research with African asylum seekers and their experiences in the asylum application procedures in Belgium, Blommaert illustrates the importance of focusing on what he refers to as 'forgotten contexts' in CDA; most obviously, the highly differentiated (and globally stratified) range of communicative resources that people have access to, but also 'text trajectories', that is the shifting of texts between and across contexts (for example, the production and distribution processes of official documents as they move from one department – in one part of the world – to another). Blommaert's chapter illustrates the theoretical underpinning of ethnography as well as its practical relevance to professionals in positions of power who need to make informed judgements about the status of a range of texts and documentation.

In Chapter 12, Brian Street echoes Blommaert's view of ethnography as an epistemology rather than a set of methodological tools. At the heart of this epistemology is a questioning of the relationship between 'self/other and of what counts as cultural knowledge', the key challenge being, 'how to characterize "other" ways of thought without slipping into negative or deficit accounts of their practices'. In relation to adult literacy, the focus of his chapter, his ethnographic perspective engages explicitly with the problem of identifying what counts as literacy in a range of national/cultural contexts. This enables both researchers and educators to shift the lens away from dominant perspectives and definitions of 'literacy', which, Street argues, often fail to meet learners' needs and interests, towards a recognition of the kinds of literacy practices in which adults engage and want to engage. While signalling the importance of holding on to the specific epistemological roots to ethnography, Street argues that there are different ways (and purposes) of 'doing ethnography' and illustrates how adult literacy trainers and educators in different national contexts – including Pakistan, India, Afghanistan – can use 'ethnographic style' research as a form of intervention in their own pedagogic practice. Such projects are being used as a way of enabling trainers and educators to learn about adults' existing knowledge and skills and to explicitly build on these in literacy teaching and learning.

The third chapter in Part Three continues with the theme of adult literacy, focusing on a specific historical period in South Africa. Cathy Kell critically re-examines the ethnographic-interventionist projects she was involved in for a period of more than ten years. Illustrating the same criticisms made by Street about national and international literacy campaigns, she seeks to address the real-world language problem of literacy development, specifically: how and why do well-meaning literacy campaigns fail? In the specific context of South Africa, she states, 'even while the proposals were being developed, figures indicated that adult literacy take-up in existing facilities was very low, teachers battled to keep up the numbers of learners and drop out rates were very high – the "masses" in need of literacy were not pressing their claims'. Drawing on a range of data, Kell offers an ethnographic account for the failure of literacy campaigns to engage adults in literacy learning as well as a meta-commentary about her shifting engagement with ethnography as an epistemology. In reflecting on her position and commitment as both ethnographer and educator, her chapter reflects the importance of bringing ethnographic understandings to the attention of policy makers and educators, as well as the inherent tensions in attempting to do so.

Chapter 14 by Ben Rampton shifts the focus away from literacy and adult education towards spoken interaction and the specific ways in which identity is *enacted* – brought into being – by young people in urban classrooms. Rampton argues that identity research is important because it 'addresses some of the most troubling phenomena of our times: communal violence, xenophobia and exclusion and discrimination on the basis of gender, ethnicity, sexuality, disability and religion'. The particular contribution that Rampton brings to this large field of inquiry is that of 'linguistic ethnography', which, in his specific concern with spoken interaction, involves combining notions and analytic tools from interactional sociolinguistics and ethnography. Rampton makes a strong case for the kind of rigorous 'nose down' in data work in which he engages as a linguistic ethnographer and is cautious about the specific ways in which any 'findings' might be put straightforwardly to practical use (for pedagogy or policy) as 'there is no complete or definitive interpretation either for analysts or participants'. Arguing in 'defence of complexity' he views his contribution, as an academic, to real-world language problems as generating an 'end-product that is mindful of the scholarly virtues of care, coherence, accuracy, accountability, scepticism and cumulative comparison'.

In the final chapter in this part of the book, Stef Slembrouck writes from an explicitly ethnographic perspective to strongly critique the ways in which SFL and CDA engage with context. While recognising the stated goal of SFL and CDA to study language in context and their commitment to critical programmes of intervention in order to benefit language users – he argues that these very language users are mostly absent in SFL and CDA accounts. Pointing to both SFL and CDA's concentration on language as *texts* and taking the example of public leaflets (from social services) he asks – 'If our aim is to understand the role of leaflets in contemporary social processes, how much of that role can in fact be gleaned from just the text itself? And, how much is to be inferred from what real users do with it, in some cases, irrespective of what the text might say?' Echoing calls across all chapters in this part to value the insider perspectives of language users, he advocates ethnography as an 'epistemology of contact'. Most obviously, 'contact' signals the centrality of the relationship between researcher and researched but also between researcher and practitioner. Slembrouck's specific focus is on the significance of social class in interviews and he illustrates the relevance of ethnography both as process and findings to child protection practices.

Chapter 11

Jan Blommaert

Text and context

Introduction: Context is/as critique

There is a vast and significant literature on context (see, for example, Auer and Di Luzio 1992; Duranti and Goodwin 1992; Auer 1995), and the most general way of summarising it is to say that it addresses the way in which linguistic forms – 'text' – become part of, get integrated in, or become constitutive of larger activities in the social world (see also Scollon 2001). To some extent, this is self-evident: language is always produced by someone to someone else, at a particular time and place, with a purpose and so forth. But, given the history of linguistics as the study of an object defined as necessarily non-contextual and autonomous, attention to the context-sensitive dimensions of language was something that required substantial argument. We are beyond such arguments now, fortunately, and we can turn to a whole complex of approaches to text–context relations. We can now accept without having to go into detailed discussion that the way in which language fits into context is what creates meaning, what makes it (mis)understandable to others.

Context comes in various shapes and operates at various levels, from the infinitely small to the infinitely big. The infinitely small would be the fact that every sentence produced by people occurs in a unique environment of preceding and subsequent sentences, and consequently derives part of its meaning from these other sentences. The infinitely small can also pertain to one single sound becoming a very meaningful thing – 'yes' pronounced with a falling intonation is declarative and affirmative;

Extracts from Blommaert, J. (2005) 'Text and context', Chapter 3, *Discourse: A critical introduction*. Cambridge: CUP, pp. 39–67.

spoken with a rising intonation it becomes a question or an expression of amazement or disbelief. The infinitely big would be the level of universals of human communication and of human societies – the fact that humanity is divided into women and men, young and old people, and so on. Context is *potentially* everything and contextualisation is *potentially* infinite. But, remarkably, in actual practice it appears to be to some extent predictable. People seem to have rather clear (though not necessarily accurate) ideas about how they have to make language fit into activities and how they have to create meaning out of this blending.

In this chapter, I shall address some of the main challenges posed by context for a critical analysis of discourse, reviewing the ways in which context has been used so far in mainstream CDA. After that, I shall survey a number of 'forgotten' contexts of discourse and illustrate their potential usefulness as critical tools. But before embarking on that discussion, I shall offer some general guidelines for addressing context as conceived here.

Context: Some general guidelines

Interpretation and contextualisation

Perhaps the most basic principle we have to use is that we cannot do without context, that we absolutely need it in any kind of analysis. This sounds self-evident, but it is not, it has considerable implications. In order to clarify this, I need to start from John Gumperz's (1982, 1992) seminal concept of 'contextualisation'. Contextualisation 'comprises all activities by participants which make relevant, maintain, revise, cancel . . . any aspect of context which, in turn, is responsible for the interpretation of an utterance in its particular locus of occurrence' (Auer 1992: 4).

Gumperz developed the notion of contextualisation to account for the ways in which people 'make sense' in interactions and, taking on board both broad ethnographic concerns as well as narrower conversation-analytic ones, he observed that people pick up quite a few 'unsaid' meanings in such interaction. These are indexical meanings: the connections between language form and social and cultural patterns. People detect these indexical meanings because speakers provide verbal and nonverbal, behavioural 'cues' that suggest a fit between utterances and contextual spaces in which they become meaningful:

> I argue that conversational interpretation is cued by empirically detectable signs, contextualization cues, and that the recognition of what these signs are, how they relate to grammatical signs, how they draw on socio-cultural knowledge and how they affect understanding, is essential for creating and sustaining conversational involvement and therefore to communication as such.
> (Gumperz 1992: 42)

The pivot of this process is the utterance itself: 'it is the linguistic form itself which serves to signal the shift in the interaction' (1992: 43). And the target of contextualisation consists of complexes of presupposable knowledge in which utterances are made coherent (contextualised).

Such forms of framing are linguistic and cognitive, to be sure, but also eminently social and cultural. They have a perduring, conventional, normative character: 'we can speak of *systems of contextualization conventions* in terms of which individual cues are related' (Gumperz 1992: 51, italics added).

Of course, contextualisation is not unproblematic, and all kinds of things can go dramatically wrong. Gumperz and his associates devoted enormous efforts to demonstrating the perils of contextualisation in everyday interactions, especially in situations where power asymmetries prevailed and/or sociopolitically sensitive categories such as race, gender, or ethnicity were involved (Gumperz 1986; Gumperz and Cook-Gumperz 1982; Jupp *et al.* 1982; Gumperz and Roberts 1991). 'Misplacing' utterances in contexts – intentionally or not – results in misunderstandings, conflicts, or breakdowns of communication. Let me give an innocent (though embarrassing) autobiographic example.

Some time ago, I went to a conference together with a young female research associate of mine. We had just checked into our hotel and upon entering my hotel room, I had discovered that it had a very nice balcony overlooking part of the city. Half an hour later, we met in the hotel lobby and went off to have dinner. As we walked out of the hotel, I asked her 'do you have such a nice balcony too?' The term for 'balcony' in our native language Dutch, *balkon*, is among other things a rude, deeply sexist male term used to refer to female breasts – the rough equivalent of what in American English is known as 'a rack'. While asking this question, I had failed to spot a woman who was walking in the opposite direction to us, wearing a deeply cut summer top exposing parts of her breasts. Unfortunately, my young female research associate had noticed this woman – she had picked up a contextualisation cue – and the term 'balcony' suddenly acquired a very suggestive, sexually offensive, meaning, which called for extensive explanation and damage repair afterwards. My words had been placed in (or made to 'point to', to index) a context which had altered their meaning, triggering a shift from a descriptive, neutral meaning for 'balcony' to an implicit, male sexist slang meaning. In this contextualisation process, our identities had shifted as well from a friendly, professional, and organisational–hierarchical sphere to a sexualised, masculine, power-laden sphere. My female associate had been pictured as an object of lust, and I had become an abusive male chauvinist. All of a sudden, we found ourselves in a threatening, embarrassing, sexualised situation. Thus, meanings of words as well as the identities of those who exchanged them, and indeed the whole situation, had been affected by a mismatch between text and context.

The point to all of this is: what we often call 'interpretation' or 'understanding' (as in 'I *understand* what you are saying') is the result of contextualisation processes in which text (utterances, statements, oral as well as written) are indexically 'made to fit' a particular (set of) context(s) by participants in the interaction. We understand something because that something makes sense in a particular context.

Our first guideline is therefore: if we want to explain the way in which people make sense socially, in real environments, we need to understand the contexts in which such sense-making practices develop.

Contextualisation is dialogical

The second principle is an elaboration of something that should already have become clear from the example given above. Context and contextualisation are dialogical phenomena. It is not the speaker alone who offers context to statements and generates context, but the other parties in the communication process do so as well. And often what counts or what is most consequential is the contextualisation performed by the one who receives and decodes the message – the *uptake*. In Gumperz's words, 'signs have meaning only by virtue of being taken to stand for an object *by some interpreter*' (Gumperz 2003: 113, italics added). In the example above, it was my colleague who spotted the possible contextual fit between my use of the term 'balcony' and the *décolleté* of the woman walking in our direction. My words received an unexpected uptake, taking them into directions of meaning and social effect I had (honestly) not intended.

Most discourse analysts would subscribe to the dialogic nature of communication, and would very often refer to the classic formulations by, for example, Bakhtin (1981, 1986); Voloshinov (1973); or Kristeva (1986, 1989) that meaning is always a meeting of (at least) two minds and consciousnesses, creating results that cannot be reduced to either one of them. People have contextualisation universes: complexes of linguistic, cognitive, social, cultural, institutional, etc. skills and knowledge which they use for contextualising statements, and interaction involves the meeting of such universes. Bakhtin captures this process under the term 'responsive understanding': meaning is 'contextual':

> integrated meaning that relates to value – to truth, beauty and so forth – and requires a *responsive* understanding, one that includes evaluation.
>
> (Bakhtin 1986: 125, italics in original)

This responsive meaning is active and transformative, it is not just a 'reception' of meaning, but a process in which meaning is changed in the sequence of interaction and made dialogical, i.e. a product of two (or more) minds.

In spite of this consensus on the importance of the dialogic nature of meaning, there are three general problems which can be encountered over and over again in published work and which lead to a reduction of the scope of dialogicity. I shall mention them briefly here (they are discussed and illustrated at greater length elsewhere, see Bloomart 2005).

a   *Dialogue does not presuppose co-operativity*. It is very often assumed in much discourse analysis that the dialogic nature of communication involves exchange of meanings between co-operative, willing, and bona fide partners, who offer large spaces for negotiating meanings (see, for example, Grice 1975 for a classic discussion). This is, of course, unjustified: dialogue is the meeting of different contextualisation universes, and very often this meeting is a clash and a conflict rather than a friendly encounter (Sarangi and Slembrouck 1992). Co-operativity is a *variable* in dialogue, not a rule.

b   *Dialogue does not presuppose sharedness*. Similarly, it is very often assumed that participants in communication share lots of common ground – language or language variety, referential and indexical meanings attributed to words, utterances or speech events, and so on. Again, this is a mistake: the meeting of contextualisation universes is not necessarily a meeting of *similar* contextualisation universes. On the contrary, it may be more productive to take the non-sharedness of contextualisation universes as our point of departure.

c   *Dialogue does not presuppose symmetry in contextualising power.* The assumption of
negotiability of meaning, derived from Gricean pragmatics, suggests symmetry
in contextualising power, the fact that all the participants in communication
have equal access and control over contextualisation universes. We should not
forget, however, that precisely this degree of access and control is a feature
of power and inequality, and that power and authority in societies depend,
among other things, on *exclusive* access to particular contextual spaces (Briggs
1997a; see also Barthes 1957). Lawyers, doctors, judges, politicians, academics,
etc. can all be characterised as professional and social-status groups by their
exclusive access to specific, powerful, contextualising spaces – the law,
medicine, intelligence reports, scientific canons – and the fact is that non-
members of these groups have no (or less) access to such spaces. (Think also
of gender, ethnicity, and class as critical features in this respect.) Consequently,
very often the process of contextualisation is not negotiable but unilateral,
with somebody *imposing* a particular contextualisation on somebody else's
words.

Thus, I believe we need to be more careful in the ways in which we actually
use the dialogic principle in analysis. My suggestion is to exploit it fully, turning it
into a general awareness that what we call 'meaning' in communication is something
which is, on the one hand, produced by a speaker/writer, but still has to be granted
by someone else. This can be done co-operatively and on the basis of sharedness
and equality, but it need not, it can also be done by force, unilaterally, as an act of
power and an expression of inequality. The concept of voice[1] is all about that: it is
about the capacity to cause an uptake close enough to one's desired contextualisation.
What people do with words – to paraphrase Austin (1962) – is to produce *conditions
for uptake*, conditions for voice, but as soon as these conditions are produced, uptake
is a fully social process, full of power and inequality. Consequently, context is not
something we can just 'add' to text – it *is* text, it defines its meanings and conditions
of use.

Context is local as well as translocal

A third guideline is that we should not restrict the notion of context to what happens
in specific communicative events. As we have seen above, Gumperz already insisted
on the systemic character of contextualisation conventions. But there is another simple
reason: a lot of what we perform in the way of meaning-attributing practices is the
post-hoc recontextualisation of earlier bits of text that were produced, of course, in
a different contextualisation process, at a different time, by different people, and for
different purposes. This is clearest in the field of literacy: whenever we read a book,
we recontextualise what we read and add or change meanings. The book is re-set in
a new contextualising universe and becomes a new book – but we do drag along with
us the baggage of the history of contextualisation/interpretation of the text. There
is no reason to restrict this observation to literate text, for similar processes occur
in all fields of communication, and several useful concepts have been developed to
address these phenomena. Erving Goffman's concept of *frames* (Goffman 1974) comes
closest to the concept of contextualisation used here. Goffman, like Gumperz,

assumed that people construct interpretive universes in which utterances are set and offered for interpretation, and Goffman added to this the idea of multiple frames operating at the same time – different potential sets of interpretive universes, between which the interlocutors can choose or shift *footing*. In the space of one conversation, for instance, something that was a 'serious' utterance can be re-framed as a joke by a change in footing.

Two other concepts deserve some more detailed comments. The first, and well-known, concept is that of *intertextuality*, a concept often ascribed to Bakhtin (and usefully developed by, for example, Kristeva 1986; Thibault 1989; and Fairclough 1992; Slembrouck 2002 provides an overview). In its simplest form, intertextuality refers to the fact that whenever we speak we produce the words of others, we constantly cite and re-cite expressions, and recycle meanings that are already available. Thus every utterance has a history of (ab)use, interpretation, and evaluation, and this history sticks to the utterance. It accounts for the fact that the term 'balcony', in the example given above, suddenly acquired the offensive and sexist meaning it had in the particular context: this attribution of meaning is an effect of the tradition-of-use of terms such as 'balcony' by male groups in a particular society to derogatively describe female breasts. Intertextuality grounds discourse analysis firmly into histories of use – histories that are social, cultural, and political, and which allow the synchronic use of particular expressions to acquire powerful social, cultural, and political effects. It invites us to look beyond the boundaries of particular communicative events and see where the expressions used there actually come from, what their sources are, whom they speak for, and how they relate to traditions of use. To illustrate the latter: terms traditionally having extremely negative connotations such as 'nigger' and 'bitch' can acquire positive, even self-celebrating, meanings central to identity pride when used by individuals or groups negatively described by the terms, because of their peculiar inverted relationship with the (negative) tradition of use of the terms. Intertextuality accounts for a lot of what we understand by the 'normative' or the 'standard' in language use, and Gumperz (2003: 117) rightly emphasises the value of intertextuality in uncovering the indexical ties between signs and interpretations.

The second concept is *entextualisation* (Bauman and Briggs 1990; Silverstein and Urban 1996). It has considerably less currency than intertextuality, but adds important qualifications and turns intertextuality into an empirical research programme. Entextualisation refers to the process by means of which discourses are successively or simultaneously decontextualised and metadiscursively recontextualised, so that they become a new discourse associated to a new context. Entextualisation is part of what Silverstein and Urban call the 'natural history of discourse'. 'Original' pieces of discourse – socially, culturally, and historically situated unique events – are lifted out of their original context and transmitted, by quoting or echoing them, by writing them down, by inserting them into another discourse, by using them as 'examples' (or as 'data' for scientific analysis). This decontextualisation and recontextualisation adds a new metadiscursive context to the text; instead of its original context-of-production, the text is accompanied by a metadiscursive complex suggesting all kinds of things *about* the text (most prominently, the suggestion that the discourse is indeed a *text*).

Entextualisation builds further on notions of the reflexive nature of language usage (for the latter, see Lucy 1993). Every utterance not only says something *in* itself (i.e. about the world, about an extralinguistic referent of some kind), but it also says something *about* itself, and hence, every 'pragmatics' (every way of handling language) goes hand in hand with a 'metapragmatics' (comments about, and references to, the way of handling language). At the same time and through this reflexive dimension, it amends overly linear or static views of context, adding an important praxis-related dimension to text-context relationships. In the eyes of Bauman and Briggs (1990: 69):

> Contextualization involves an active process of negotiation in which participants reflexively examine the discourse as it is emerging, embedding assessments of its structure and significance in the speech itself.

In other words, while talking, participants themselves mark those parts of speech that are 'text' and those that are 'instructions about how that discourse is to be approached as a text, through replication or with some form of response' (Urban 1996: 33) (e.g. by means of self-corrections, hedges, hesitations, interjections, false starts, explicit qualifications such as 'what I really mean is . . .', 'I don't want to say that . . .').

If we take intertextuality and entextualisation together, we have instruments that allow us to set unique communicative events within larger historical frames, both those of the text itself and of the interpretations given by the text. This provides us with bridges between the micro-local events and the macro-patterns of which they are part (either by insertion in these patterns or by departing from them), and it allows us to understand individual discourse events as eminently social, cultural, and political.

[. . .]

Context in CDA

One of the most important methodological problems in discourse analysis in general is the *framing* of discourse in particular *selections of contexts*, the relevance of which is established by the researcher but is not made into an object of investigation. Part of this problem appears to be unavoidable: one always uses all sorts of presuppositions and assumptions, real-world and commonsense knowledge in analysis (see Verschueren 2001; Blommaert 1997). But this problem is especially pressing in the case of CDA, where the social situatedness of discourse data is crucial, and where context is often taken to include broad systemic and institutional observations. Not just discourse is analysed, but *political* discourse, *bureaucratic* discourse, *doctor–patient* discourse. In CDA, discourse is accompanied by a narrative on power and institutions, large portions of which are just copied from rank-and-file sources or inspired by received wisdom. Charles Briggs observes that:

> the question of what is 'ordinary' or 'everyday' involves more than simply which data we select but crucially depends on how we frame and analyze them. By severing indexical links to broader social, political and historical parameters we can give even the most historically compelling discourses the look and feel of the mundane.

(Briggs 1997b: 454)

I would add: and vice versa. Even the most mundane talk can be transformed in an instance of vulgar power abuse if framed properly. It all comes down to establishing the indexical links referred to by Briggs, identifying them, and specifying their precise structure and function. In this respect, a lot of *a priori* contextualisation goes on in work qualified as CDA, which I find objectionable. Thus, in much CDA work, *a priori* statements on power relations are being used as perspectives on discourse (e.g. 'power is bad', 'politicians are manipulators', 'media are ideology-reproducing machines'), and social-theoretical concepts and categories are being used in off-hand and seemingly self-evident ways (e.g. 'power', 'institutions', also 'the leading groups in society', 'business', and so on). This leads to highly simplified models of social structures and patterns of action – politicians *always* and *intentionally* manipulate their constituencies; doctors are *by definition* and always the powerful party in doctor–patient relations, etc. – which are then projected onto discourse samples. Power relations are often predefined and then confirmed by features of discourse (sometimes in very questionable ways – see Verschueren 2001).

Of particular interest here is the use of what could be called *primafacie ethnographies*: dense descriptions of contexts and institutions used as framing devices in analyses. Let us turn to a concrete example: Ruth Wodak's (1997) classic paper 'Critical discourse analysis and the study of doctor–patient interaction'. In the beginning of her paper she brings to our attention that:

> In modern societies [socially important] domains are embodied in institutions which are structured in terms of social power relationships and characterised by specific divisions of labour . . . Within institutions, elites (typically consisting of white males) occupy the dominant positions and therefore possess power. They determine what Bourdieu . . . calls the 'symbolic market' . . ., i.e. the value and prestige of symbolic capital (or certain communicative behaviour) This can be seen most readily in the technical registers used by all professional groups . . . but it also manifests itself less obviously in the form of preferred styles and certain communicative strategies
>
> (Wodak 1997: 174)

And some pages further, she introduces her research in the hospital in the following way:

> For an understanding of the context, it is important to realise that the outpatients' ward has very low status and prestige in relation to the rest of the hospital. It is a type of outpost and . . . serves as a training ground for young doctors, which results in inexperienced insiders working where experienced ones are arguably most necessary. Hierarchy, knowledge, experience and gender are interlinked in a strange and unique way in the outpatients' ward.
>
> (Wodak 1997: 179)

We are not informed about where such crucial ethnographic information comes from. Neither do we see any questioning here of whether 'contextual' features such as the low prestige of the outpatients' ward may precisely *be discursively produced, as a result of systemic interactional patterns* within the hospital. In other words, the possibility that the general status-rank of the locus of fieldwork may be related to the object of fieldwork – discourse patterns – is not addressed (while this reality-creating dimension of discourse is openly professed as part of the CDA agenda). This is the 'context' for the rest of the analysis, and this context is offered as an unquestionable, untheorised set of 'facts' contradicting part of the methodology of discourse analysis. The source of such contextual accounts is often obliquely referred to as on-site observation and interviewing (again, untheorised and without any explicitised procedures). Their function, however, is crucial: they are central contextualising features that facilitate claims about an 'insiders' perspective' on the communication patterns studied in CDA (Wodak 1997: 178). The ethnographic basis of these claims is placed outside the scope of CDA, and one will rarely encounter discussions of fieldwork procedures and approaches in CDA writings. Analysis starts as soon as the data 'are there'.

In the sort of CDA examined here, it is through such *a priori* contextualisations that talk is socially situated and that distinctions are established between instances of communication that are potential topics for CDA and others that are not. The distinction usually has to do with the presence and salience of power relations. The problem is that such power relations are often already established before the actual analysis of discourse can start, by means of – all in all often very 'uncritical' – contextual narratives.

[. . .]

Forgotten contexts

CDA focuses strongly upon simple relationships between individual instances of text/discourse and context(s). The question is generally that of '(a) context for (a) (particular) text'. I hope to have shown that the connection between discourse and social structure leaves much to be desired. I want briefly to present some other contexts – or better, present some phenomena of discourse and suggest that they might be seen as 'contexts' to 'texts'. In all the cases, the contexts I shall offer will give us additional – accumulatively refining – inroads into social structure. In other words, their contextualising function will consist in *merging* discourse and social structure, thus offering better prospects for critical analysis. In all the cases, the contexts are not features of single texts but of larger economies of communication and textualisation. They are not adequately dealt with in CDA; they are often 'forgotten' contexts.

To substantiate this claim, I shall use a particular type of data: data reflecting globalisation processes. I shall illustrate my arguments with material drawn from research on African asylum seekers' narratives in the asylum application procedure in Belgium (Blommaert 2001a, 2001b; Maryns and Blommaert 2001). These data, collected through long narrative interviews in 1998 at the height of a political crisis on asylum seekers in Belgium, are prime targets for 'traditional' critical analysis. The people who perform them belong to a marginalised group in Belgian society whose rights and opportunities in life are fragile, and who are the object of repression and administrative control. They are faced with huge institutional pressure to tell stories in specific ways – the outcome of the asylum procedure is almost completely based on (perceptions of) the cogency and coherence of the stories they tell. But the telling and interpretation of their stories involves complex contextualisation work – more complex than can be captured by the context conceptions discussed in the previous section, because we are dealing with communication events that can only be understood against the background of globalisation, or, more precisely, of structural inequalities within the world system. Such features of communication do not occur when one studies material from (the perspective of) one's own society; yet, in the present world such data become more and more frequent. They have one big advantage: they compel us to accept that the world is not an abstract thing somewhere 'out there' but that it is right at our doorstep.

Resources as contexts

The first forgotten context I wish to discuss is the complex of linguistic means and communicative skills usually identified as resources. And, right from the start, that means that we are addressing macro-contexts, contexts that have to do with the structure of the world system and that create situations over which individuals have hardly any control. Speakers can/cannot speak varieties of languages, they can/cannot write and read, and they can/cannot mobilise specific resources for performing specific actions in society. And all these differences – different degrees of proficiency ranging from 'not at all' to 'full mastery' of codes, language varieties, and styles – are socially consequential. Resources are hierarchised in terms of functional adequacy, and those who have different resources often find that they have unequal resources, because access to some rights and benefits in society is constrained by access to specific communicative (e.g. narrative) resources (cf. Hymes 1996).

Asylum seekers in Belgium are confronted with a complex set of administrative procedures, involving and presupposing access to various genres (e.g. legal texts, welfare regulations), various languages (Dutch, French, English), language varieties and channels (written, spoken, visual, electronic). Apart from what they need for the asylum procedure, they also need to be able to lead a life in a Belgian village or town. The approximately fifty asylum seekers we interviewed all used English, French, and Dutch for conducting their daily business. Many of them did, however, display considerable difficulties in expressing themselves in these languages. Restricting ourselves to spoken discourse here, the degrees of proficiency ranged from very poor to sophisticated, and these differences obviously affect the structure and content of narratives. Shifting and mixing of codes, varieties, and styles was a crucial ingredient of the stories as well (see Maryns and Blommaert 2001). Let us take a look at example (1), a brief fragment from a narrative by an Angolese man told in French.*

Fragment (1)

> oui/l'autre président . . . (xxxxxx)/ on l'a empoisonné/ c'est le président Mobutu/ qui a mis le poison retardé/ il est parti au russe / l'URSS/ pour traiter/ il a retourné/ il est mort/ mais on a abandonné son corps hein/ oui/ {{*Question: c'était un président de MPLA?*}} c'était le même mouvement MPLA/ dans le temps / année septante-cinq/ quand il est mort on dit/ comme on

---

* = rapid successions of turns or syllables in self-corrections; / = for intonationally marked phrase or sentence ends; dots indicate pauses.

=il est marxisme/ on a pris on a choisi =on= on a fait faux testament/ cette testament c'était au temps du russe qui a fait ça/ comme toi tu =le= le président il est mort/ il a décidé Eduardo qui va me remplacer/ sans vote/ parce que il est toujours du même parti/ Eduardo il est d'origine angolais/ mais il est des Cap Verdiens/ parce que ce sont des anciens prisonniers/ et Portugais il a mis à l'île hein/ nous sommes à l'océan/ et on a mis une prison là-bas/ parce qu'il est venu pour commander l'indépendance/ c'était une petite ville=une petite=une petite village/ on a mis au pouvoir/ maintenant le président/ c'est on dit/ it dit que non/ tous les gens/ qui parlent Lingala/ les gens du Nord/ ce sont des gens plus malins/ plus intelligents/ par rapport au gens du Sud/ en Angola nous sommes quatre couleurs/ comme le Bré=le Brésil.

Translation

yes/the other president . . . (xxxxxx)/they have poisoned him/ it's president Mobutu/ who put the delayed poison/ he has left to Russian/ the USSR/ to treat/ he gave back/ he died/ but they have left his corpse, right/ yes/ {{*Question: it was a president of the MPLA?*}}/ it was the same movement MPLA/ in those days/ year seventy-five/ when he died they say/ like they=he is Marxism/ they took they chose=they=they have made false testament/ those testament it was in the time of Russian that has made it/ since you you=the=the president is dead/ he decided Eduardo who is going to replace me/ without vote/ because he is always of the same party/ Eduardo he is of Angolan origin/ but he is of the Cape Verdians/ because they are former prisoners/ and Portuguese has put on the island, right/ we are at the ocean/ and they have put a prison over there/ because he had come to command the independence/ it was a small town=a small=a small village/ they have put to power/ now the president/ that is what they say/ he said that no/ all the people/ who speak Lingala/ the people from the north/ they are more clever people/ more intelligent/ in relation to the people from the south/ in Angola we are four colours/ like Bra=Brazil

The Angolese man is at pains to explain the wider political context in which his escape from Angola should be set. In doing so, he is forced to provide detailed information about the political regime in Angola, including digressions into the Portuguese colonial practices (sending MPLA fighters into exile on the Cabo Verde islands), and into linguistic and ethnic divisions in the country. The story is highly complex and detailed, and apparently all these details count for the narrator. Such detailed and complex digressions on the home country feature in almost all the narratives we recorded, to the extent that they can generically be identified as 'home narratives' (Blommaert 2001b). Home narratives fulfil often crucial contextualising functions in the larger stories: without them, a precise understanding of the causes and motives for the escape cannot be reached. Narrators often explicitly flagged the importance of these dense contextual accounts for an understanding of who they were and why they came to Belgium. The point is that this complex and important package of information has to be transmitted by means of a very 'broken' variety of French, informally acquired during sojourns in Congo and during his stay in Belgium (and bearing traces of this migration itinerary). The French used by the Angolese man is, like the English and Dutch of many others, a product of refugee life and it mirrors the marginality in which they find themselves wherever they go.

The shape of narratives cannot be separated from their content: stories such as this one are shaped to a large extent by the resources people have for telling them, *what* can be told depends on *how* one can tell it. Complex stories become even more complex when they are told in uncomfortable varieties of languages. The way in which the temporal sequentiality of events is organised in fragment (1), for instance, is highly problematic (e.g. where do we have to situate the 'parce qu'il est venu pour commander l'indépendance' in the passage on Cabo Verde?); the same goes for crucial qualifications given by means of less than adequate lexical choices (e.g. 'il est *marxisme*' instead of 'il est *marxiste*'); deixis and reference are another domain of problems (see the 'il' in 'parce qu'il est venu pour commander l'indépendance'). The struggle with the medium of narration also has an effect on the rhythm and the prosody, causing disruptions in the flow of narration and the loss of an important range of contextualisation cues. Told to Belgian interlocutors who are either native speakers (in the case of Dutch and French) or non-native speakers commanding a sometimes equally problematic variety of English, the potential for being misunderstood is obviously very high. And, in the punitive atmosphere of application interviews, 'rambling' stories are quickly turned into 'bad' stories, qualified as 'unreliable' or full of 'unclear elements' and 'contradictions'. Parts of the stories that are difficult to understand during the interaction are often *not* understood at all. The resources controlled by the narrators and their interlocutors are part and parcel of the interpretations given to their stories, and given the central role of the stories in the asylum procedure matters of resources may influence the outcome of their asylum application.

Resources and the way in which they feature as elements of social structure are often 'invisible' contexts in discourse analysis. Illiterates will not show up in analyses of written discourse; their perceptions of 'news' and 'politics' do not feature in analyses of newspaper reporting. There is no conversation analysis possible when people don't converse because they do not share resources. Such analyses are not about, nor *for* them. The errors in discourse of people who lack access to 'high' standardised varieties of a language are often edited and corrected, and thus disappear as indexes of social structure and inequality-asidentity for those people. Their utterances are usually transcribed in standard orthographies of languages, so that social stigmas in accents and 'small' discourse features are being effaced and a homogenisation of such language users with 'average' features of the speech community is accomplished (Ochs 1999). However, the importance of resources lies in the deep relation between language and a general economy of symbols and status in societies. The point is that one does not just 'have' or 'know' a language. Such seemingly innocuous phrases hide a complex and highly sensitive political–economic dynamics of acquisition and differential distribution. Words, accents, intonation contours, styles all come with a history of use and abuse (Bakhtin's intertextuality); they also come with a history of assessment and evaluation. This is where language leads us directly to the heart of social structure: an investigation into language becomes an investigation into the systems and patterns of allocation of power symbols and instruments, and thus an investigation into basic patterns of privilege and disenfranchisement in societies (see Bourdieu 1991; Gumperz 1982; Heller 1994). Looking at issues of resources makes sure that any instance of language use would be deeply and fundamentally socially contextualised; connections between talk and social structure would be *intrinsic*.

At the same time, the context-shaping role of resources extends beyond the occurrence of single texts or instances of discourse. They are not strictly features of texts, but of societies and social structures, and in the final instance, of worldwide relations between parts of the globe. Hence, the chances that they would emerge from doctrinaire (linguistic) discourse analysis are very slim – often, they belong to the realm of the 'normal' and of the 'usual', they *condition* interactions in society, and they make sure that some interactions will simply never occur. Hymes accurately notes:

> There is a fundamental difference . . . between what is not said because there is no occasion to say it, and what is not said because one has not and does not find a way to say it.
>
> (Hymes 1974: 72)

In a critical study of language, the absence of certain discourse events and the particular shape of others *because of matters of resource allocation* should be a major preoccupation. Why cannot everyone speak or write in certain ways? Why is some discourse the privilege of some people because it is based on exclusive usages of rare resources? For an understanding of what language does in society, I believe these are fundamental questions.

Text trajectories

A second 'forgotten' context has already been briefly mentioned above when we discussed the importance of translocal contexts. One of the features of, for instance, institutional communication processes is the shifting of discourse across contexts: talk finds its way into notes, summaries, case reports, citations, discussions of others. Briggs (1997a) and Silverstein and Urban (1996) have argued that precisely this shifting of texts between contexts – re-entextualisation practices – involves crucial questions of power. To recapitulate briefly what we said above, not every context is accessible to everyone, and re-entextualisation practices depend on who has access to which contextual space. Access here also depends on resources: re-entextualisation often involves a technology of contextualisation, a degree of expertise that is very exclusive and the object of tremendous inequality in any society (e.g. legal re-entextualisations require access to legal expertise, see Philips 1998). The dynamics of entextualisation clearly leads us back into issues of differential access to power resources, and thus again leads us directly to social structure.

In the Belgian asylum procedure, the story of the applicant is the central ingredient, and obviously a number of things happen to these stories. The long interview on their motives for seeking asylum in Belgium is followed by a number of administrative text-making procedures: a case report, quotation of fragments in notes and letters exchanged between the administration and lawyers or welfare workers, official interpretations and summaries in verdicts from the asylum authorities, and so forth. Consider the following fragment from an official letter to the Angolese man whose home narrative we discussed above. In this letter, he was notified of the rejection of his asylum application. The rejection is motivated by means of interpretive summaries of parts of the story of the man (Dutch original, my translation):

Fragment (2)

> The concerned was interrogated on November 23, 1993 at the Commissariat-General [for Refugees and Stateless Persons], in the presence of [name], his attorney.
>
> He claimed to be a 'political informant' of the MPLA. On October 18, 1992 however, he passed on information to UNITA. At the UNITA office, however, he met with Major [name], who works for the MPLA. Two days later, Major [name] had the concerned arrested. Fearing that the concerned would give the Major away at the trial, [name of the Major] helped the concerned to escape. The concerned fled to [locality] where a priest arranged for his departure from Angola. The concerned came, together with his wife [name and register number] and three children, through Zaïre and by plane, to Belgium. They arrived on May 19, 1993.
>
> It has to be noted that the concerned remains very vague at certain points. Thus he is unable to provide details about the precise content of his job as 'political informant'. Furthermore the account of his escape lacks credibility. Thus it is unlikely that the concerned could steal military clothes and weapons without being noticed and that he could subsequently climb over the prison wall.
>
> It is also unlikely that the concerned and his wife could pass the passport control at Zaventem [i.e. Brussels airport] bearing a passport lacking their names and their pictures.
>
> Furthermore, the itinerary of the concerned is impossible to verify due to a lack of travel documents (the concerned sent back the passports).
>
> The statements of the concerned contain contradictions when compared to his wife's account. Thus he declares that the passports which they received from the priest [name] were already completely in order at the time they left Angola. His wife claims that they still had to apply for a visa in Zaïre.

Two comments are in order. First, the asylum application is not constructed in one act of communication; it is constructed through a sequence of re-entextualisations, involving far-reaching reinterpretations of the story, summarising and rewording practices, and the reframing of a story in a legal and procedural framework containing criteria for 'truth' and 'plausibility' (Blommaert 2001b). This sequence is fixed: the text trajectory is a uniform administrative procedure. The 'procedurally consequent' context, to adopt CA² terminology, involves a series of individual events as well as the relations between these events: the fact that talk is translated, written, summarised, and put into a legal/procedural framework, in sum, that every step in the systematically and uniformly performed process involves not replication but far-reaching transformations of the 'original' story. Yet, throughout this series of transformations, the story is still said to be that of the asylum applicant (cf. phrases such as 'the statements of the concerned'). So, what is 'the story of the applicant'? The story is the whole text trajectory.

Second, in light of the remarks on resources made above, the salience of text trajectories becomes even greater. Every step in the trajectory involves inequalities in resources. The story told either in a native language and translated (usually into French or English) by an interpreter, or in the sort of varieties of French, English, or Dutch illustrated in fragment (1), is put into a standard, written variety of Dutch or French. It is filtered in the way discussed above: parts that were hard to understand while the story was being told are either deleted from the story or misinterpreted. The administrator has selected those parts of the story that appear to be of consequence for the outcome of the asylum application, using criteria of coherence and consistency that are directly fed into legally consequential assessments of truth and reliability. The story is measured against legal criteria and evaluated as either 'truthful' or 'unreliable'. Inequalities in linguistic-communicative resources in the asylum procedure accrue as the story is processed along the text trajectory.

Attention to this type of shifting of discourse across contexts involves issues of control and power in each of the phases of recontextualisation. In CDA, some attention to such phenomena is given by Fairclough (1992), though the focus is on textual flows rather than on the shifting between contextualising universes and resources that determine recontextualisation work. My approach is derived from ethnography – an awareness that text is contextualised in each phase of its existence, and that every act of discourse production, reproduction, and circulation or consumption involves shifts in contexts (Silverstein and Urban 1996; Philips 1998). In studying discourse and social structure, such shifting of discourse across contexts containing important power features appears to be a crucial critical enterprise, if for nothing else because in the context of globalisation processes one can only expect enormous intensifications of such shifts.

Data histories

A third 'forgotten context' is directly related to the foregoing: the history of discourse data. As said above, analysis is entextualisation – it is, in other words, also part of a text trajectory. Hence, some sensitivity to what professionals do with discourse samples as soon as they call them data can be useful. I have noted above that, especially in CDA, the ethnographic origin and situatedness of data are hardly treated. In ethnography, however, the history of data is acknowledged as an important element in their interpretation. It is recognised that the way in which data have been gathered, recorded, and treated by the analyst influence what these data tell us (e.g. Bauman 1995; Silverstein 1996; Haviland 1996; Urban 1996). The time, place, and occasion at which data are being gathered have an effect on the data: they are what they are because they occurred in that shape in that context. The question 'Why do we investigate *this now*?' is an important question, for it points towards the social situatedness of our own research.

This is important, for it is often either overlooked as a factor in research and interpretation or treated as a self-evident matter and given little prominence. I intend to foreground it, for it is again a case of often invisible context determining what can happen, how and at what time. Some things can only be said at certain moments, under certain conditions. Likewise, and very often as a correlate of this, some things can only be researched at certain moments and under certain conditions. I mentioned at the beginning of this section that our data were collected in 1998. A few weeks prior to the start of our fieldwork, an important political crisis erupted over matters of asylum in Belgium. The cause of the crisis was the violent death of a Nigerian female asylum seeker in the hands of police officers. As a reaction to this incident, there was a spontaneous outburst of sympathy for the predicament of asylum seekers among large sections of the Belgian population; asylum seekers organised themselves and demonstrated in large numbers for the first time in history. They occupied churches and schools and were eager to tell their stories. Suddenly, and for a brief period of just a couple of months, we found ourselves in unique, unprecedented, research conditions. Prior to this incident it was very difficult actually to locate asylum seekers, most of them being clandestine and preferring not to disclose the locations where they lived. And after a few months the protest movement lost momentum and the asylum seekers went underground again. During this brief period, we recorded the stories of people who wanted to tell the stories of their miserable lives back home, on the road, and in Belgium. People told their stories eagerly and repeatedly to anyone who cared to listen. One important feature of this period was *contact*: the public outcry after the death of the Nigerian girl created a forum for debate between Belgians and asylum seekers – a forum in which stories about asylum and asylum seekers' lives could be circulated. Consequently, the stories changed and many of the stories in our corpus display features of what Hymes (1998) calls 'fully-formed narratives': narratives that display growing tightness in narrative structure due to repeated instances of narrating, 'rehearsals' so to speak. Thus, the concrete context of the fieldwork had an impact on our data on at least two levels: (1) the fact that people could be interviewed at all and were willing to disclose their identities and 'cases' to us; (2) the particular structural characteristics of some of the stories, bearing traces of repeated narrating.

The narratives only exist as research objects because their sheer genesis is a matter of context: the stories were only available during that period and because of the political upheaval which foregrounded the issue of asylum in public debate. It was a crisis phenomenon, an affect of one of these moments when chaos and acceleration seem to take over and force all kinds of 'hidden transcripts' to the surface (Scott 1990). After this brief period, the stories disappeared together with the people who told them. So they can only be researched as instances of inequality because they were recorded at a moment in which such inequality had become visible and salient and had become accessible for research.

The fact that certain discourse forms only become visible and accessible at particular times and under particular conditions is in itself an important phenomenon, which tells us a lot about our societies and ourselves, and which necessarily situates particular discourses in the wider sociopolitical environment in which they occur. The stories have a particular 'load' which relates to (and indexes) their place in a particular social, political, and historical moment. Removing this load from the narratives could involve the risk of obscuring the reasons for their production as well as the fact that they are tied to identifiable people and to particular, uniquely meaningful, circumstances that occasioned them.

Conclusion

Conceptions of context can be critical to the extent that, rather than as direct referential contributions to text-meaning, they are seen as *conditions* for discourse production and for looking at discourse, both from lay and professional perspectives. We should be looking at how the linguistic generates the economic, social, political, as well as how the economic, social, and political generate the linguistic. The problems I have identified with the treatment of context in CDA all had to do with the centrality of text. Despite claims voiced about the mutually constitutive relationship of discourse and society, the ultimate ambition remains explaining discourse, not explaining society through the privileged window of discourse. My own suggestions were informed by the opposite strategy: using discourse as a social object, the linguistic characteristics of which are conditioned and determined by circumstances that are far beyond the grasp of the speaker or user, but are social, political, cultural, and historical. It is remarkable that whenever we say that text is 'situated' in discourse-analytical terms, we seem to refer to forms of strict locality: the unique, one-time, and micro-situatedness of text. From this individual situatedness, larger structures, patterns, or 'rules' can then be deduced, but these generalisations do not involve higher-level situatedness: discourse seems to lose context as soon as it is raised above the single-text level. This different degree of situatedness – large, general, supra-individual, typical, structural, and higher than the single society – should have a place in any form of critical study of discourse.

To the extent that critical approaches to discourse should be concerned with power, they cannot be concerned exclusively with predefined power – power of which text is only illustrative or symptomatic, as in CDA. It must also be concerned with invisible, hegemonic, structural, and normalised power sedimented *in* language and not only *through* language. As we all know, language itself is an *object* of inequality and hegemony; revealing the power effects of language cannot overlook this dimension of how language and speech themselves have been 'molested', to use Hymes' (1996) term. That simple phenomenon in itself – people talking and writing, using language for specific functions – is not an unquestionable given, and analysis should not start, so to speak, as soon as people open their mouths. It should have started long before that.

Notes

1   For discussion of 'voice', see Blommaert 2005, Chapter 4.
2   CA = Conversation Analysis. For discussion of context in CA, see Blommaert 2005, Chapter 3.

References

Auer, P. (1992) 'Introduction: John Gumperz' approach to contextualization', in Peter Auer and Aldo DiLuzio (eds) *The Contextualization of Language* (pp. 1–37). Amsterdam: John Benjamins.

Auer, P. (1995) 'Context and contextualization', in J. Verschueren, J.O. Östman and J. Blommaert (eds) *Handbook of Pragmatics* (pp. 1–19). Amsterdam: John Benjamins.

Auer, P. and Di Luzio, A. (eds) (1992) *The Contextualization of Language*. Amsterdam: John Benjamins.

Austin, J.L. (1962) *How to Do Things with Words*. Oxford: Oxford University Press.

Bakhtin, M.M. (1981) *The Dialogic Imagination*. Austin, TX: University of Texas Press.

Bakhtin, M.M. (1986) *Speech Genres and Other Late Essays*. Austin, TX: University of Texas Press.

Barthes, R. (1957) *Mythologies*. Paris: Le Seuil.

Bauman, R. (1995) 'Representing Native American oral narrative: the textual practices of Henry Rowe Schoolcraft'. *Pragmatics* 5 (2): 167–83.

Bauman, R. and Briggs, C. (1990) 'Poetics and performance as critical perspectives on language and social life'. *Annual Review of Anthropology* 19: 59–88.

Blommaert, J. (1997) *Workshopping: Notes on professional vision in discourse analysis*. Antwerp Papers in Linguistics 91 Antwerp: UIA-GER.

Blommaert, J. (2001a) 'Context is/as critique'. *Critique of Anthropology* 21 (1): 13–32. (Special issue on *Discourse and Critique*, ed. J. Blommaert, J. Collins, M. Heller, B. Rampton, S. Slembrouck, and J. Verschueren.)

Blommaert, J. (2001b) 'Investigating narrative inequality: African asylum seekers' stories in Belgium'. *Discourse and Society* 12 (4): 413–49.

Blommaert, J. (2005) 'Text and context', in *Discourse. A critical introduction* (pp. 39–67). Cambridge: Cambridge University Press.

Bourdieu, P. (1991) *Language and Symbolic Power*. Cambridge: Polity.

Briggs, C. (1997a) 'Notes on a "confession": on the construction of gender, sexuality, and violence in an infanticide case. *Pragmatics* 7 (4): 519–46.

Briggs, C. (1997b) 'Introduction: from the ideal, the ordinary, and the orderly to conflict and violence in pragmatic research'. *Pragmatics* 7 (4): 451–9.

Duranti, A. and Goodwin, C. (eds) (1992) *Rethinking Context*. Cambridge: Cambridge University Press.

Fairclough, N. (1992) 'Discourse and text: linguistic and intertextual analysis within discourse analysis'. *Discourse and Society* 3: 193–217.

Goffman, E. (1974) *Frame Analysis: An essay on the organization of experience*. New York: Harper & Row

Grice, H.P. (1975) 'The logic of conversation', in M. Cole and J. Morgan (eds) *Syntax and Semantics Vol. 3: Speech Acts* (pp. 64–75). New York: Academic Press.

Gumperz, J. (1982) *Discourse Strategies*. Cambridge: Cambridge University Press.

Gumperz, J. (1986) 'Interactional sociolinguistics in the study of schooling', in J. Cook-Gumperz (ed.) *The Social Construction of Literacy* (pp.45–68). Cambridge: Cambridge University Press.

Gumperz, J. (1992) 'Contextualization revisited', in P. Auer and A. DiLuzio (eds) *The Contextualization of Language* (pp. 39–53). Amsterdam: John Benjamins.

Gumperz, J. (2003) 'Response essay', in S. Eerdmans, C. Prevignano and P. Thibault (eds) *Language and Interaction: Discussions with John Gumperz* (pp. 105–26). Amsterdam: John Benjamins.

Gumperz, J. and Cook-Gumperz, J. (eds) (1982) *Language and Social Identity*. Cambridge: Cambridge University Press.

Gumperz, J. and Roberts, C. (1991) 'Understanding in intercultural encounters', in J. Blommaert and J. Verschueren (eds) *The Pragmatics of Intercultural and International Communication* (pp. 51–90). Amsterdam: John Benjamins.

Haviland, J. (1996) 'Text from talk in Tzotzil', in M. Silverstein and G. Urban (eds) *Natural Histories of Discourse* (pp. 45–78). Chicago, IL: University of Chicago Press.

Heller, M. (1994) *Crosswords: Language, education and ethnicity in French Ontario*. Berlin: Mouton de Gruyter.

Hymes, D. (1974) *Foundations in Sociolinguistics: An ethnographic approach*. Philadelphia, PA: University of Pennsylvania Press.

Hymes, D. (1996) *Ethnography, Linguistics, Narrative Inequality: Towards an understanding of voice*. London: Taylor and Francis.

Hymes, D. (1998) 'When is oral narrative poetry? Generative form and its pragmatic conditions'. *Pragmatics* 8: 475–500.

Jupp, T.C., Roberts, C. and Cook-Gumperz, J. (1982) 'Language and disadvantage: the hidden process', in J. Gumperz and J. Cook-Gumperz (eds) *Language and Social Identity* (pp. 233–56). Cambridge: Cambridge University Press.

Kristeva, J. (1986) *The Kristeva Reader* (ed. T. Moi). Oxford: Blackwell.

Kristeva, J. (1989) *Language, The Unknown. An initiation to linguistics*. New York: Columbia University Press.

Lucy, J. (ed.) (1993) *Reflexive Language: Reported speech and metapragmatics*. Cambridge: Cambridge University Press.

Maryns, K. and Blommaert, J. (2001) 'Stylistic and thematic shifting as a narrative resource: assessing asylum seekers' repertoires'. *Multilingua* 20: 61–84.

Ochs, E. (1999 [1979]) 'Transcription as theory', in A. Jaworski and N. Coupland (eds) *The Discourse Reader* (pp. 167–82). London: Routledge.

Philips, S. (1998) *Ideology in the Language of Judges: How judges practice law, politics and courtroom control*. New York: Oxford University Press.

Sarangi, S. and Slembrouck, S. (1992) 'Non-cooperation in communication: a reassessment of Gricean pragmatics'. *Journal of Pragmatics* 17: 117–54.

Scollon, R. (2001) *Mediated Discourse: The nexus of practice*. London: Routledge.

Scott, J. (1990) *Domination and the Arts of Resistance: Hidden transcripts*. New Haven, CT: Yale University Press.

Silverstein, M. (1996) 'The secret life of texts', in M. Silverstein and G. Urban (eds) *Natural Histories of Discourse* (pp. 81–105). Chicago, IL: University of Chicago Press.

Silverstein, M. and Urban, G. (1996) 'The natural history of discourse', in M. Silverstein and G. Urban (eds) *Natural Histories of Discourse* (pp. 1–17). Chicago, IL: University of Chicago Press.

Slembrouck, S. (2002) 'Intertextuality', in J. Verschueren, J. Östman, J. Blommaert and C. Bulcaen (eds) *Handbook of Pragmatics 2002* (pp. 1–25). Amsterdam: John Benjamins.

Thibault, P. (1989) 'Semantic variation, social heteroglossia, intertextuality: thematic and axiological meaning in spoken discourse. *Critical Studies* 1: 181–209.

Urban, G. (1996) 'Entextualization, replication, and power', in M. Silverstein and G. Urban (eds) *Natural Histories of Discourse* (pp. 21–44). Chicago, IL: University of Chicago Press.

Verschueren, J. (2001) 'Predicaments of criticism'. *Critique of Anthropology* 21: 59–81.

Voloshinov, V.N. (1973) *Marxism and the Philosophy of Language*. Cambridge, MA: Harvard University Press.

Wodak, R. (1997) 'Critical discourse analysis and the study of doctor–patient interaction', in B.-L. Gunnarsson, P. Linell and B. Nordberg (eds) *The Construction of Professional Discourse* (pp. 173–200). London: Longman.

Chapter 12

Brian Street

Adopting an ethnographic perspective in research and pedagogy

Introduction

The turtle and the fish

There was once a turtle who lived in a lake with a group of fish. One day the turtle went for a walk on dry land. He was away from the lake for a few weeks. When he returned he met some of the fish. The fish asked him, "Mister turtle, hello! How are you? We have not seen you for a few weeks. Where have you been?" The turtle said, "I was up on the land, I have been spending some time on dry land." The fish were a little puzzled and they said, "Up on dry land? What are you talking about? What is this dry land? Is it wet?" The turtle said "No, it is not," "Is it cool and refreshing?" "No it is not," "Does it have waves and ripples?" "No, it does not have waves and ripples." "Can you swim in it?" "No you can't." So the fish said, "it is not wet, it is not cool, there are no waves, you can't swim in it. So this dry land of yours must be completely non-existent, just an imaginary thing, nothing real at all." The turtle said that "Well maybe so" and he left the fish and went for another walk on dry land.

(Buddhist tale, http://www.beyondthenet.net/dhamma/
nibbanaTurtle.htm. Accessed 12/11/08)

In another version the fish said "Don't tell us what it isn't, tell us what it is." "I can't" said the turtle, "I don't have any language to describe it."

I begin with this vignette because I want to locate ethnography firmly in the mindset addressed here, namely the ways in which we conceptualize our own and "others'" culture and meaning making, rather than as a technical set of skills to simply add to the array of procedures available for researching literacy. The issues faced by the turtle in his to-ing and fro-ing between the sea and land raise exactly the epistemological and conceptual issues that ethnography deals with – how to characterize "other" ways of thought and being without slipping into negative or deficit accounts of the kind the fish here appeared to encourage; "what do they **not** have that we have?" Early travelers from Europe to Africa and Asia adopted a similar frame, noting whether the peoples they encountered had or did not have "politics," "religion," "morality," even "language." Current policy in the literacy field still maintains this tradition, characterizing large numbers of people around the world as "illiterate" mainly, I would argue and as we shall see from the examples in the second part of this chapter, because of their inability to "see" the actual literacy practices in which people are engaged. The lenses available for seeing local literacies are sometimes as myopic as were those available in past times for seeing people's cognitive and conceptual ways of thought. It is precisely here that ethnography has a contribution to make, not only to academic disciplinary work but also more broadly to policy and pedagogy.

In this chapter I will firstly spell out more fully what the term "ethnography" has come to mean, not just for anthropologists who laid original claim to the practice but more recently to members of other disciplines, specifically here, education. I will then indicate ways in which ethnographic perspectives have been applied in educational policy contexts, specifically with respect to adult literacy programmes. One of my examples – "Hidden Literacies" – illustrates especially the ethnographic issue that ethnocentric lenses can blind us to the meanings and uses of literacy by local people which might be different from those of policy makers and educators from outside the local environment. The second example provides an indication of how these ideas might be put into practice in the training of adult literacy teachers.

The meanings of ethnography

Clifford Geertz, one of the leading anthropologists in the USA, recognized the dilemma of starting from one's own preconceptions and tried to develop a longer and fairer historical perspective, that did not simply berate ethnocentrism nor fall into mindless relativism. Shweder recalls:

> In his essay "Anti-Anti-Relativism" Geertz quotes a famous passage in Montaigne
> – "Each man calls barbarism whatever is not his own practice . . . for we have
> no other criterion of reason than the example and idea of the opinions and
> customs of the country we live in" – and then adds, in his own voice: That
> notion, whatever its problems, and however more delicately expressed, is not
> likely to go entirely away unless anthropology does.
>
> (Shweder 1984: 13)

My own preferred way of referring to the to-ing and fro-ing that these conceptual pressures entail, is to cite Todorov's (1988) analysis of the relationship between proximity and distance. Anthropologists privilege their ability to act as a "fish out of water," (or the turtle, to pursue our initial story) taking a distant view of local practices. Yet they also give highest credit to immersion in local practices and coming to think like the locals, or "natives." Todorov suggests that the issue is not seeing the either/or (distance or proximity) but recognizing the full axis. Fieldworkers distance themselves from their home culture as they come into proximity with an unfamiliar social group. They then become more immersed before distancing themselves from their field site as they return home, drawing near again to their own culture. Many return to their field site, thus repeating the cycle of proximity and distance which becomes a reflex for all such engagement with difference and similarity. The "ethnographic imagination" (see Comaroff and Comaroff, 1992) is founded on this cycle and can be applied in micro situations of engagement and comparison, as well as larger ones, including those where researchers enter and leave sites of learning over a period of time (see discussion in Heath and Street 2008).

The broader context in which all of these move in the ethnographic field can be articulated as "ethnography as epistemology" (Blommaert 2005a, 2005b). Blommaert calls upon Bourdieu, who is usually referred to as a sociologist but in fact conducted ethnographic fieldwork in his own native environments in France and also in Algeria among Kabyle people. Blommaert focuses on Bourdieu's conceptual framing of ethnography:

> **For Bourdieu, ethnography is an epistemological issue.** In its traditional, codified form it evokes frightening questions of power and unilateral interpretation; but when brought down to the level of practice (in Bourdieu's sense) driven by *habitus*, it becomes a site for constructing subjective knowledge and questions about knowledge. These questions have validity for theory, for they involve questions of contextualized understanding versus universal or transcontextual patterns and models. **It is by accepting ethnography as the epistemological point of departure for theoretical questions that Bourdieu can come up with theory.** It is a mature position; he accepts ethnography in its fullest sense, including the inevitable quagmires of subjectivity, bias and doing-as-if in the field, and in that sense prefigures what later came to be known as Critical Ethnography.
>
> (Blommaert 2005b, my emphasis)

Blommaert, then, sees Bourdieu's work as an "ethnographic invitation," a call to empirically explore in micro-ethnography the structures suggested in his work, an appeal to continue thinking theoretically while we work ethnographically. He quotes Bourdieu as saying, "I believe it is possible to enter into the singularity of an object without renouncing the ambitions of drawing out universal propositions" (Bourdieu 1986: xi). Ethnography is the epistemological tool to arrive at theory.

Thus far I have cited anthropologists in trying to establish the epistemological framing of ethnography given its centrality to anthropology as a discipline; that is, as not just a technique or method but as a framing of self/other and of what counts as cultural knowledge. However, ethnography has been taken up by many disciplines and in different ways, which challenge any proprietorial rights claimed by anthropologists as to the meaning of "ethnography." Rather than seeking to impose one meaning, Green and Bloome developed a typology consisting of three principal categories: *doing ethnography*, *adopting an ethnographic perspective* and *using ethnographic tools*:

> *doing ethnography* involves the framing, conceptualizing, interpreting, writing and reporting associated with a broad, in-depth, and long-term study of a social or cultural group, meeting the criteria for doing ethnography as framed within a discipline or field . . . By adopting an *ethnographic perspective*, we mean that it is possible to take a more focused approach (i.e. do less than a comprehensive ethnography) to study particular aspects of everyday life and cultural practices of a social group. Central to an ethnographic perspective is the use of theories of culture and inquiry practices derived from anthropology or sociology to guide the research. The final distinction, *using ethnographic tools*, refers to the use of methods and techniques usually associated with fieldwork. These methods may or may not be guided by cultural theories or questions about the social life of group members.
>
> (Green and Bloome 1997: 183)

This broadening out of the "ownership" stakes around ethnography is central to the LETTER project described below in which we attempted to work with educators on developing 'ethnographic perspectives' on educational practice, without wanting to train participants to be anthropologists – that is to "do a (full) ethnography" in Green and Bloome's terms above.

One important notion that links *ethnography as epistemology* to the specific work of *doing ethnography* is that of "case studies." Dyson and Genishi offer a useful overview of the nature of case studies within the context of education:

> In their case studies, qualitative researchers are interested in the meaning people make of their lives in very particular contexts. They "combine close analysis of fine details of behavior and meaning in everyday social interaction with analysis of the wider societal context – the field of broader social influences" – within which their everyday interactions take place (Erickson, 1986, p. 120). Whether they are studying children learning to read, or to write, or to talk in a first language or second, researchers assume that learners and their teachers make sense of talk and text within physical settings and through social activities that are informed by the world beyond the visible one. Everyday teaching and learning are complex social happenings, and understanding them as such is the grand purpose of qualitative case studies.
>
> (Dyson and Genishi 2005: 9)

What specific case studies can tell us about a particular (and larger) phenomenon – and how they do this – is discussed by Mitchell:

> A good case study . . . enables the analyst to establish theoretically valid connections between events and phenomena which previously were ineluctable. From this point of view, the search for a "typical" case for analytical exposition is likely to be less fruitful than a telling case.
>
> (Mitchell 1984: 239)

We shall see in the second part of this chapter how the notion of case studies as "telling" can be helpful both in defining the object of study but also, more contentiously, in challenging approaches by many policy makers to literacy.

Lenses, labels and literacy

In this section I will relate the theoretical debates above – and in particular the account of what constitutes an ethnographic perspective – to policy and practice in international development work in literacy and numeracy. To refer back to the opening quotation of this chapter, international policy with respect to literacy can be seen to precisely fall into the "not" discourse that the fish in the Turtle and the Fish story above were stuck within; policy makers and educators from "literate" societies, see others' practices as lacking "literacy"; like the fish from their water, they ask "do they have x" – water, waves, literacy – and when their lenses prevent them from seeing what the local people actually do have, they invoke the "not" – "illiteracy." But perhaps local people do have significant uses of reading and/or writing that are not exactly like those the travelers bring with them. Perhaps, as ethnographers have demonstrated around the world, the literacy practices of other cultures are simply different from those defined by some educators and statisticians. In order to know whether this is the case, we need other lenses than those worn by dominant (usually but not always) Western commentators: we need to "untie the (k)not." The turtle began to do this when he realized that there was a problem and went off to look again. He began to consider what other experiences people on land might be having, to use his imagination and, eventually, to develop a language of description for describing this to people back home. In the last twenty years ethnographers have traveled to many parts of the world, or looked closely within their own communities, to look for different literacies and have built multiple rich descriptions (for examples, see Aikman 1999; Besnier 1995; Barton and Hamilton 1998; Collins 1998; Heath 1983; Hornberger 1998; Kalman 1999; Robinson-Pant 2004; Street 1993; Wagner 1993). The *language of description* has been refined to cater for this rich data set emerging from New Literacy Studies (Box 1).

Here I would like just to point up the implications of adopting an *ideological* rather than an autonomous *model* (see Box 1) of literacy for how we conceptualize literacy in international contexts. An ideological approach to cultural meanings recognizes the central importance of the power to name and define (Parkin 1984). If we can prescribe the label that is attached to a given phenomenon then we have considerable power over how the events and practices associated with it are seen and what policy implications are drawn. Similar arguments can be made with regard to definitions of literacy. Those who hold an "autonomous" model of literacy, for instance, might claim that it is not a cultural perspective they are adopting but rather a "natural," "known" or even "objective" account. When they compare their own literacy practices with those of, for instance, Indian villagers or working class youths in the US, they can claim that they are not being ethnocentric, they are not simply being fish demanding that everything looks like it does from their own wet environment, but rather that this is how it is – the others are in "deficit," they lack

Box 1

New Literacy Studies – key examples of the "language of description"

The "new" in New Literacy Studies (NLS) signals an approach to literacy that differs from a conventional view of reading and writing as an individual or cognitive activity, and emphasizes instead that literacy is a fundamentally social phenomenon, with reading and writing embedded in social relationships and institutional practices.

Literacy events are activities where literacy has a role, such as writing letters, reading newspapers, responding to emails and are made up of key elements including participants, settings, artifacts and activities.

Literacy practices refers both to a collection of observable single literacy events and at a more abstract level, to the meanings and values attached to literacy within particular social and cultural contexts (after Swann *et al.* 2004; see Barton and Hamilton 1998: 8; Hamilton 2000).

Autonomous model of literacy – the view that literacy in itself has consequences irrespective, or autonomous, of context.

Ideological model of literacy – the view that literacy not only varies with social context and with cultural norms and discourses regarding for instance, identity, gender and belief, but that its uses and meanings are always embedded in relations of power. Literacy in this sense always involves contests over meanings, definitions and boundaries and struggles for control of the literacy agenda (after Street 1984, 1993).

literacy – or "proper literacy," or "functional" literacy or other labels that qualify the term but retain its narrow focus on one way of doing things. This autonomous view – that literacy in itself, autonomously, will have effects, creating inequality for those who "lack" it and advantages for those who gain it – is, of course, itself deeply ideological: one of the most powerful mechanisms available to ideology is to disguise itself (Street 1993). People are rightly suspicious if someone claims we should define a phenomenon, or act towards it in policy terms, because it conforms to their own cherished customs and beliefs. But if they can claim that it is nothing to do with their own preconceptions but is instead a natural, objective account, then others can be encouraged to act upon it, to provide funds to develop this view, to agree policy. With respect to literacy this means that the power to define and name what counts as literacy and illiteracy also leads to the power to determine policy, to fund and develop literacy programmes in international contexts, to prescribe ways of teaching, development of educational materials, texts books and assessment (see Campbell 2007). So, from this perspective what counts as "literacy" depends crucially on who has the power to define "it."

Applying an ethnographic perspective in education and policy contexts

To illustrate and discuss specific ways in which ethnography can be applied to real-world literacy problems in both education and in practice, I will describe two projects in which I and colleagues have been involved: 1) the "Hidden Literacies" project by Rafat Nabi, whose account of everyday, ordinary people in her own country, Pakistan, shows how uses and meanings of literacy were not always recognized by those in the policy field; 2) the LETTER project, Learning Empowerment Through Training in Ethnographic Research, in which myself and colleagues introduced an ethnographic perspective to the training of adult literacy and numeracy teachers to help them build pedagogy and curriculum more attuned to local cultural meanings and uses of literacy and numeracy. In both cases an ethnographic perspective enables us to "see" the actual literacy practices in which people engage, offering insights that are often missed in the more formal definitions and perceptions of literacy used by agencies and those who would "measure" literacy (see Campbell 2007) and which provides an alternative basis for developing learning that builds on what learners already know.

Project 1: Hidden literacies

One way to address the problems in practice of the alternative views of literacy I have been outlining is to focus on contexts where literacy is indeed being defined for other people. Recent work by Rafat Nabi, an adult literacy practitioner and organizer in Pakistan, provides vivid concrete examples of the imposition of definitions and the responses to such power. Nabi has worked in Adult Literacy Programmes in Pakistan for a number of years and she recently went back there in order to evaluate some of the community literacy provision she had been involved with. However, she found herself adopting more of an ethnographic perspective than in her previous role as organizer and programme planner and so began to listen more to what "ordinary" people on the ground had to say about literacy and about their own uses of reading and writing and how these contrasted to what was presented in the official programmes. Nabi (forthcoming) describes a number of case studies in which local people in Pakistan demonstrated that they could read and write yet accepted outsiders' definitions of themselves as "illiterate":

> several of the case study respondents assert strongly that they are "illiterate," perhaps because they have never been to school or adult literacy class. "*I am not educated and cannot read and write,*" says Amen the vegetable seller, and he repeats it: "*I am not educated and cannot read and write but that does not mean that I am a fool and have no wisdom.*" Zia the plumber is stronger in his self-identification: "*I told you, I have never been to school, so how can I read and write?*" was his answer to the researcher's question, "Can you read and write?" He was even more assertive when challenged by the researcher: "You can write very well, why did you say you are *Jahil* [illiterate]?" "I do not have any certificate or paper to show that I am literate, which means I am illiterate. People who are educated like you call me illiterate. Educated people's decision

about me perhaps is right, I am illiterate." I said, "Illiterates cannot read and write but you can, so you are literate." He said, "Bibi, I feel good. I sure on God when you say I am literate."

* * *

Razia the domestic servant too asserts that she is uneducated: when asked to show something she had written, she replied, "*You are highly educated and I have not even attended a school, you will laugh at me.*" And Amen repeats himself, as so often: "*I did not see the inside of a school. So people regard me as illiterate.*" Their lack of literacy skills is perceived as a stigma and a disadvantage. – And yet they all write and read many things. Razia read the schedule in the kitchen on which the family members had indicated their breakfast preferences and the spice container labels; she wrote a brief message about a phone call and a shopping list of ingredients for a meal, and she kept a notebook of the items taken by the cleaner. But if the researcher had asked her what she was doing on each occasion, she would not have said "reading" or "writing" but simply "preparing breakfast," "answering the telephone" or "dealing with the cleaner." The literacy practices were so deeply embedded that they had become invisible. Karima the beggar wrote her own name and dates. The bangle seller and Zia the plumber both offered to provide receipts (in Zia's case, in two languages) while asserting that they were "illiterate." As Zia said, "*When [people] ask me, I give them a receipt, and I write down all the names of the parts which I purchased, their cost and my labour charges.*" Amen the vegetable seller had taught himself a considerable amount of reading and writing in his own way. Sakina the dyer attached a label to each of the cloths she made. Within the occupations these people did, there were many embedded literacies and numeracies of which they were hardly conscious.

(Nabi forthcoming)

Learning about the experiences of Amen, Zia and Karima, and of Rozina, a dyer who learned the literacy practices necessary for her trade from colleagues not from a formal class, leads Nabi to reflect on the ways in which literacy programmes, including her own, have been defined and implemented:

How can a literacy course be developed keeping the local knowledge and practices in mind? Can one type of literacy be effective for the entire nation? How can literacy courses preserve indigenous knowledge and transfer this knowledge to the next generation? Is a literacy centre necessary or are there other alternative ways of learning, as Rozina learned from her colleagues?

Are policy makers whole heartedly learning the lessons from Rozina, that literacy can go beyond centres and beyond primers and attendance registers? A profound question to ponder. Where does this example of social literacy fit into the broader literacy scenario?

(Nabi forthcoming)

But the programmes she has seen take the more usual view, they tie the deficit "not" and prescribe their learners as "illiterate." When Zia a plumber attempts to

attend an adult literacy class in order to learn the literacy necessary to obtain a
driving license, he came up against the same lack of understanding of the literacy
skills such learners already possess:

> In my area, an NGO opened an adult literacy centre. I thought it is only a
> matter of three months; I will get a certificate and learn more. So I obtained
> admission to attend this literacy centre. They started teaching me ABC. I told
> them that I can write a few words, just teach me some words related to driving.
> However, the teacher refused and said, "We will teach according to our
> programme, not according to your programme." I found this useless. What
> they are teaching, I already knew. I went there to learn more, not what I
> already knew, and to get a certificate which will be helpful for me. So I left
> the centre.

Nabi reflects on the implications of such stories for our understanding of literacy
and development of programmes:

> Zia had posed serious questions for me. Why did the literacy centre not respect
> his knowledge? With his knowledge and skills, Zia could be a great resource
> to assist the teacher. Why is he calling himself illiterate?

The power to name someone as "illiterate," as "not" having skills that the definer
considers crucial, means that the programmes developed on this basis fail to listen
or to see what learners bring. The teachers' problem is precisely one of definition
but probably it was not they who named and defined the state of literacy. They –
like Zia, Amin, Rozina and countless others – have been subjected to the kinds of
definitions that those in power pass down – the accounts provided for instance by
economists such as Sen (2002) and Nussbaum (2006) (see also Maddox 2008) or
by educators such as those cited in UNESCO's Global Monitoring Report on literacy
(see http://portal.unesco.org/education/) or who developed the UK National
Literacy Strategy (Stannard and Huxford 2007) and the USA 'No Child Left Behind'
programme (US Department of Education, http://www.ed.gov/policy/elsec/leg/
esea02/index.html).

An ethnographic approach can pose alternative sources of definition and naming
against each other in stark relief, as these examples and many others in the literature
testify; but they cannot necessarily challenge the power to name that comes with
the respective positions these parties occupy. If we wish to pursue questions of
inequality out there in the world of economics and of literacy, then, we will also
need to pursue firstly the questions of inequality in the world of policy making and
academic definition.

Project 2: LETTER

I will now provide an example of ways in which educators have indeed adopted this
broader perspective, applying ethnographic insights to the development of
programmes for teaching adult literacy facilitators. The LETTER Project, 'Learning
Empowerment through Training in Ethnographic Research', involves workshops in

India and Ethiopia, involving participants from these countries as well as from Bangladesh, Pakistan and Afghanistan. The Project started in 2001 after an approach from Nirantar, a women's organization in Delhi, made to myself and to Alan Rogers, an adult educator and researcher (UK). Here, I focus mainly on the programme in India: see Nirantar http://www.uppinghamseminars.com/page3.htm for details of other projects.

The background to the request was that Nirantar, engaged in developing alternative adult learning programmes with a group of *dalit* women in southern Uttar Pradesh, India, had discovered that the women held alternative ways of looking at the world of which Nirantar knew little and of which the teachers were sometimes disparaging while the women themselves were to a large extent unconscious of their distinctiveness. For example, the women said they believed that rivers were animate objects rather than inanimate, as Western scientific categories held. Not knowing what views were held, but aware that there were often sensitivities in how such views were perceived across different groups of people whom the learners encountered, the Nirantar staff felt that careful study needed to be made of the literacy and numeracy practices of the communities with which they were working and that ethnographic approaches would form a foundation for such research and a basis for more respectful relations across the participants. The approaches that we drew upon were those of the New Literacy Studies and of ethnographic perspectives outlined above, as well as approaches to adult learning which emphasize the importance of "starting from where learners are" while at the same time recognizing that finding out where learners are is a challenging task (see Rogers 2002, 2004). As Rogers points out:

> adults have built up through experience very extensive amounts of "tacit knowledge" and hidden skills – knowledge and skills which form the basis of the practices they engage in and the discourses they use. But this is largely unconscious – the participant-respondents will often not know what epistemologies they hold, what "funds of knowledge" (Moll *et al*. 1992) and banks of skills they have built up through this informal experiential learning.
> (Rogers and Street forthcoming)

The aim of LETTER, then, was to train some adult education practitioners – programme planners and trainers in ethnographic style research (Green and Bloome 1997) – taking as a focus the literacy and numeracy practices of the learners and the communities from which they came. Adopting an ethnographic-style approach would help practitioners gain insights into these practices which would challenge many of the sweeping assumptions on which so many existing adult education programmes are built. It would provide nuances to the generalizations often made about adult illiteracy and innumeracy.

The design of the overall programme was for three workshops in each context allowing space in between for learners to return to their own home environments and to apply the ideas there. For instance, after the first workshop in Delhi, the participants returned to their home countries – Bangladesh, Pakistan, Afghanistan and various regions of India – and tried out some of the methods and ideas they had encountered in the Delhi workshop.

Box 2

Starting from where learners are – The Collect–Reflect–Build on approach for adult educators and trainers

1   Collect, observe and describe local practices;
2   Discuss practices in class in a critical way – including issues of equality and justice, gender and power;
3   Build new ways of knowing and doing – include the more formal and standardized ways of the classroom alongside the local and more informal practices.

The first workshop progressed through sessions devoted to discussion in plenary and small groups, including presentations on ethnographic perspectives and readings given out and discussed (including Uta Papen's (2005) book *Adult Literacy as Social Practice*), and through a small-scale practice session of fieldwork. At the India workshop, the participants were sent into Delhi for an afternoon to see what they could find out about the literacy and numeracy practices in their area; they presented and debated their findings (see Box 2). The latter part of the week was spent designing a somewhat bigger research project to be conducted individually or in very small groups between the first and second workshop.

Figure 12.1 "Happy Divali"; woman writing on house wall in Mehroni, Uttar Pradesh, India (Photograph: Brian Street 1993)

These larger research projects (mostly into local numeracy practices) were undertaken in the participants' home countries in the period between the first and second workshops. They then returned to the second workshop and spent a good deal of time finalising the reports on these topics. Then a start was made on working out how to use the findings of these local projects in developing ways of helping adults to learn new literacies and numeracies, which was the topic of a third workshop (see http://www.uppinghamseminars.com/page3.htm for details of this stage). In the Ethiopia workshops there was similarly a small-scale field exercise in both the first and second workshops, and larger scale research projects were compiled by the participants between the first and second workshops and revised further between the second and third workshops.

It was in the third workshop in Ethiopia that the LETTER project made significant advances in educational terms, especially in how to adapt the research findings for adult teaching and learning programmes. Malini Ghose, who is one of the directors of the Nirantar Project and had been present in the workshops in Delhi, came to the third workshop in Ethiopia and outlined how her group had identified certain literacy and numeracy activities in the area they were working in as suitable for building new learning programmes on (http://www.nirantar.net/). One such was "calendars." They found that many homes and offices in the area had calendars; they collected these up. They debated these with the learners, including issues such as

Figure 12.2 "Before entering the house, take off your gossip bonnet" – one of a number of sayings seen on the walls of houses in Ethiopia (Photograph: Negussie Hailu, Ethiopia, with kind permission)

the difference between local ways of measuring time (a lunar system) against the formal printed measures (a solar system); how these calendars were used, for example how far for recording past events and how far for planning future activities; gender differences in the approach to calendars; the languages and scripts in which these calendars were presented, and the balance between numbers and words; the cost of the calendars; the difference between religious and secular calendars. During these discussions, new ways of looking at time were found, new numeracy and literacy activities were devised, and new learning took place. Formal "schooled" practices were introduced alongside the local practices. All of these were collected, debated fully and critically in the class, and formed the basis for the learning of more formal literacy and numeracy practices. Here is really "starting where they are," using teaching-learning materials which come from the local communities in which the learners live. Here is learning which is not just exportable from the class-room into the community but which comes into the classroom from the community, is mediated there by educational practices, and returns to inform and enhance everyday activities.

In this way the third workshop in Ethiopia took the LETTER project forward by addressing ways in which the ethnographic dimension of the first two workshops could be adapted and taken up for educational purposes (see Box 3). This stage is still very much in process and workshops in other parts of the world, such as Mexico and Uganda, are being planned in order to develop the approach further.

Box 3

Identifying local literacy and numeracy practices

- different ways of counting (for example, the use of sticks or beans, and different ways of using finger counting, etc);

- different informal ways of measuring, including uses of containers (cf Saraswathi n.d.) (some purely individual, others common to all the traders in one local market but different from other markets) and the code switching of the traders between these and the more formal standardised ways of weighing and measuring;

- different ways of calculating income and expenditure (the difference between unwritten household accounts which start with income and determine the expenditure, and the accounting system of small businesses which starts with how much is spent which in turn determines what income is needed);

- proverbs, sayings and songs/poems found in the local communities, sometimes painted on the walls of buildings, acting as a community "glue" and especially building inter-generational relationships (grand-parents teaching children traditional sayings and children teaching grandparents new songs).

Conclusion

Those involved in projects such as LETTER and "Hidden Literacies" argue that by drawing upon ethnographic perspectives they can add insights that enable educators to draw upon participants' own prior knowledge and thereby enhance their engagement with the programme and their potential for learning. But does it work? In terms of how we might begin to evaluate such activities and for deciding the value and funding of such programmes, I think it is important to shift away from notions of assessment *of* learning to assessment *for* learning. This is a key frame of reference in work by Black and William picked up by Campbell (2007) who argues for the need to get beyond definitions of competence, performance, output indicators, etc and instead engage in practice-based assessments that take into account the learners' cultural and personal histories. Assessment for learning optimizes students' learning and "privileges the needs of students and educators". The kinds of programmes described in this chapter drawing upon ethnographic perspectives do indeed, I would argue, provide a basis for such an approach, taking account of the "learner's cultural and personal histories" and open up the possibility of transforming local literacy practices into formalized learning opportunities.

References

Aikman, S. (1999) *Intercultural Education and Literacy: An ethnographic study of indigenous knowledge and learning in the Peruvian Amazon*. Amsterdam: Benjamins.

Barton, D. and Hamilton, M. (1998) *Local Literacies: Reading and writing in one community*. London: Routledge.

Besnier, N (1995) *Literacy, Emotion and Authority: Reading and writing on a Polynesian atoll*. Cambridge: Cambridge University Press.

Blommaert, J. (2005a) *Discourse. A critical introduction*. Cambridge: Cambridge University Press.

Blommaert, J. (2005b) 'Bourdieu the ethnographer'. *The Translator* 11 (2): 219–36.

Bourdieu, P. (1986) *Distinction: A social critique of the judgment of taste*. London: Routledge.

Campbell, P. (2007) (ed.) *Measures of Success Assessment and Accountability in Adult Basic Education*. Edmonton, Alberta: Grass Roots Press.

Collins, J. (1998) *Understanding Tolowa Histories: Western hegemonies and Native American response*. New York: Routledge.

Comaroff, J.L. and Comaroff, J. (1992) *Ethnography and the Historical Imagination*. Boulder, CO: Westview Press.

Dyson, A. and Genishi, C. (2005) *The Case: Approaches to language and literacy research*. Columbia: National Conference on Research in Language and Literacy, Teachers College Columbia.

Erickson, F. (1986) 'Qualitative methods in research on teaching', in M.C. Wittrock (ed.) *Handbook of Research on Teaching*, (pp. 119–61). New York: Basic Books.

Green, J. and Bloome, D. (1997) 'Ethnography and ethnographers of and in education: a situated perspective', in J. Flood, S. Heath and D. Lapp (eds) *A Handbook of Research on Teaching Literacy Through the Communicative and Visual Arts* (pp. 181–202). New York: Simon and Shuster Macmillan.

Hamilton, M. (2000) 'Expanding the NLS. Using photographs to explore literacy as social practice', in D. Barton and M. Hamilton (eds) *Situated Literacies: Reading and writing in context* (pp. 16–34). London: Routledge.

Heath, S.B. (1983) *Ways with Words*. Cambridge: Cambridge University Press.

Heath, S.B. and Street, B. (2008) *On Ethnography: Approaches to language and literacy research*. Columbia: National Conference on Research in Language and Literacy, Teachers College Columbia.

Hornberger, N (ed.) (1998) *Language Planning from the Bottom Up: Indigenous literacies in the Americas*. Berlin: Mouton de Gruyter.

Kalman, J. (1999) *Writing on the Plaza: Mediated literacy practices among scribes and clients in Mexico City*. Cresskill, NJ: Hampton Press.

Maddox, B. (2008) 'What good is literacy? Insights and implications of the capabilities approach'. *Journal of Human Development* 9 (2): 185–206.

Mitchell, J. (1984) 'Typicality and the Case Study', in R.F. Ellen (ed.) *Ethnographic Research: A guide to conduct* (pp. 238–41). New York: Academic Press.

Moll, L., Amanti, C., Neff, D. and Gonzalez, N. (1992) 'Funds of knowledge for teaching: using a qualitative approach to connect homes and classrooms'. *Theory into Practice* 3 (1): 132–41.

Nabi, R. (forthcoming) 'Hidden Literacies'. Case studies of literacy and numeracy practices in Pakistan.

Nirantar (2007) 'Exploring the everyday: ethnographic approaches to literacy and numeracy'. http://uppinghamseminars.com/page2.htm. Delhi: Nirantar.

Nussbaum, M. (2006) *Frontiers of Justice: Disability, nationality, species membership*. Harvard, MA: Belknap.

Papen, U. (2005) *Adult Literacy as Social Practice*. London: Routledge.

Parkin, D. (1984) 'Political language'. *Annual Review of Anthropology* 13: 345–65.

Robinson-Pant, A. (ed.) (2004) *Women, Literacy and Development: Alternative perspectives*. London: Routledge.

Rogers, A. (2002) *Teaching Adults*. Buckingham: Open University Press.

Rogers, A. (2004) *Non-formal Education: Flexible schooling or participatory education?*. Dordrecht: Kluwer, and Hong Kong: Hong Kong University Press.

Rogers, A. and Street, B. (forthcoming) 'Practitioners as researchers: adult literacy facilitators in developing societies and the Letter Project'. Studies in the Education of Adults.

Saraswathi, S. (n.d.) 'Practices in enumeration by counting and computation of sets of objects in rural Tamil Nadu'. Unpublished manuscript, available from n.subramanian@arkemagroup.com.

Sen, A.K. (2002) *Rationality and Freedom*. Cambridge, MA: Harvard University Press.

Shweder, R. (1984) 'The Resolute irresolution of Clifford Geertz'. *Common Knowledge* 13: 191–205.

Stannard, J. and Huxford, L. (2007) *The Literacy Game: The story of the national literacy strategy*. London: Routledge.

Street, B. (1984) *Literacy in Theory and Practice*. Cambridge: Cambridge University Press.

Street, B. (ed.) (1993) *Cross-cultural Approaches to Literacy*. Cambridge: Cambridge University Press.

Swann, J., Deumert, A., Lillis, T. and Mesthrie, R. (2004) *A Dictionary of Sociolinguistics*. Edinburgh: Edinburgh University Press.

Todorov, T. (1988) 'Knowledge in social anthropology: distancing and universality'. *Anthropology Today* 4: 2–5.

US Dept of Education 'No Child Left Behind' http://www.ed.gov/policy/elsec/leg/esea02/index.html.

Wagner, D. (1993) *Literacy, Culture and Development: Becoming literate in Morocco*. Cambridge: Cambridge University Press.

Chapter 13

Catherine Kell

Ethnographic studies and adult literacy policy in South Africa

Introduction

> The fact that good ethnography entails trust and confidence, that it requires some narrative accounting, and that it is an extension of a universal form of personal knowledge, make me think that ethnography is peculiarly appropriate to a democratic society . . . As envisioned here, ethnography has the potentiality for helping to overcome division of society into those who know and those who are known.
>
> (Hymes 1996: 14)

In this chapter I focus on the value of ethnography in the study of literacy with reference to my own research into adult literacy in South Africa from the early 1990s. This was a time of tremendous change in South Africa, as the country moved towards overthrowing the legacy of apartheid and building democratic governance. My research was orientated towards problems of literacy and basic education among adults, a huge proportion of whom had had minimal or disrupted schooling during the decades of apartheid. The chapter shows the potential as well as the constraints of connecting ethnographic research with policy making, at the same time as it points to the importance of a long view of ethnographic research, in which the connections and overlaps between research projects might be viewed as more important than the findings of specific projects.

My first study was an ethnography of literacy practices in a shanty-town called Masiphumelele near Cape Town, undertaken just before South Africa's first democratic election in 1994. This study linked to a much broader research project in South Africa called the Social Uses of Literacy (SoUL). My next project, done in the mid-1990s, was an evaluation of a new national diploma in Adult Basic Education and Training (ABET) for adult literacy teachers, and this linked to a further study on letter-writing. The third project, which started in 1998, was a study of a participatory development project in which people classified in development discourse as "the poorest of the poor" were building their own houses using a government subsidy for first time home-owners.

Period	Project/s	Focus
1. 1993–1996	Masiphumelele and the SoUL	Particular groups in single bounded sites
2. 1996 and 1997	ABET evaluation and letter-writing study	Topic-oriented studies Comparisons and contrasts
3. 1998–2003	Khayalethu	Hypothesis testing Moving beyond the single site

Ethnography is traditionally viewed as involving the lone anthropologist entering into and undertaking fieldwork in a 'strange' culture, in an unfamiliar but bounded location for a lengthy period, returning 'home' and rendering these experiences into monographs for – often – educated Western audiences. While the dialectic of 'strangeness/familiarity' continues to figure as a central premise of contemporary ethnography (see Street, this volume), every other aspect of this description has since been challenged and changed. Ethnographers work collaboratively or in partnership with their research subjects. The single, bounded site no longer necessarily establishes the framing of the inquiry. The 'multi-sited imaginary' (Marcus 1995; Burawoy et al. 2000) challenges boundedness and promotes methodological freedom (Candea 2007). Ethnographic 'time modes' (Jeffrey and Troman 2004) and the lengths of time for ethnographic research are highly variable, as are the genres through which it is reported (Van Maanen 1998). These shifts correspond with the uptake of ethnography in a much wider range of fields than just anthropology.

What is shared across ethnographic approaches is the overall epistemological orientation: the idea that the ethnographer seeks to engage with the subjects' experiences first-hand and that ethnographic data is *produced* dialogically in the field, as well as dialectically in an engagement with existing theoretical frameworks and wider research. In later sections of this chapter I show how these different types of inquiry, each implying different takes on boundaries and moments, worked out in relation to my own ethnographic studies on adult literacy.

Adult literacy: problems and policies in South Africa

My research in the early 1990s took as its starting point the suddenly taken-for-granted assumptions about adults who had not had schooling, their need for 'new skills and competencies' and the best ways in which this should be done. Framed within a discourse about the urgency of policy formulation as the new government started to take shape, these assumptions had crystallised into a discourse about 'needs' and 'deficits', captured in the following:

> It is estimated that about 15 million Black adults (over one third of the population) are illiterate . . . The lack of access to basic education, including literacy and numeracy, has consigned millions of our people to silence and marginalisation from effective and meaningful participation in social and economic development.
>
> (CEPD 1994: 1; ANC 1994: 87)

At the same time there were debates about what factors would contribute to economic success as South Africa 'modernised', making the transition from apartheid to democracy and becoming integrated into the global economy. An emerging discourse about economic development, human resources and productivity intersected with the discourse about needs and deficits (seen as the legacy of apartheid) forming a strong base for policy decisions in the field of adult education and training. Policy proposals outlined an approach for mass-scale provision of adult literacy, having formal equivalence with schooling for children, and as the entry point to a national system which integrated education and training. This proposal would be based on standards, accreditation and a core curriculum, all set within a proposed National Qualifications Framework. 'Competency-based education and training' (CBET), later renamed as 'outcomes based education and training' (OBE) provided the rationale for this approach and was seen as the path whereby South Africa could address the key social problems of redress and development.

These proposals made the assumption that, once the new government and its systems were in place, the 15 million 'illiterate' adults[1] would be expectantly waiting outside the classrooms ready to take up their opportunities to access education they had been denied. Here was an emerging discourse of literacy as human capital, rapidly becoming naturalised among 'stakeholders' in the literacy field on all sides of the political spectrum. This discourse carried a modernist version of educational reform quite at odds really with what had been happening in South Africa over the previous decade, when millions of people had taken part in forms of mass struggle developing abilities to survive, resist and negotiate. At the same time, it also diverged substantially from the emancipatory discourses that circulated, particularly among non-governmental organisations in the adult literacy field, throughout the 1970s and 1980s, and which had granted work in this field tremendous moral authority. However, even while the proposals were being developed, figures indicated that adult literacy take-up in existing facilities was very low, teachers battled to keep up the numbers of learners and drop out rates were very high – the 'masses' in need of literacy were not pressing their claims.

It was in pursuing clarity around this largely disregarded conundrum that the research question for the first project in Masiphumelele and for the others undertaken as part of the later SoUL project became an inversion of the familiar policy question – from 'what can we (where the "we" are the adult literacy planners and providers) do about illiteracy?' to the open-ended ethnographic question: 'what are they (unschooled adults) doing in relation to print literacy?'

In the following sections, I present an overview of the focus of this first project as well as the later projects – and how each one led on to the next one – focusing on the kinds of data collected, the form of the final reporting and subsequent publications. I also focus on the work of engaging with policy that happened in the interstices between each project.

Masiphumelele and the social uses of literacy: a comprehensive picture

1993 and 1994 in Masiphumelele: literacy practices in an informal settlement

This was an ethnography of literacy practices in a shanty-town called Masiphumelele. This settlement of around 3,000 people was formalised and recognised in 1990 after years of struggle by its 'black' residents to win the right to live in what was then a 'white group area'. For around seven months I visited Masiphumelele up to five times a week, spending between three and five hours a day there. I attended literacy classes of the recently established night school for adults, as well as meetings of various organisations involved with development. I came to spend time with people at home, church services and local gatherings, and, quite often, simply hung around. I focused in on one woman in particular, Winnie Tsotso, a powerful and popular community leader, with roles in the local creche committee, ANC (African National Congress) branch, Catholic Welfare and Development Branch and who participated in numerous activities and meetings. Winnie, who was fluent in the three local languages and had knowledge of a further three languages, was also a literacy learner in the adult literacy night school, classified as a 'beginner', where I watched her night after night slowly spelling out her name and reading short sentences in isiXhosa such as '*Ndingu Winnie Tsotso*' (I am Winnie Tsotso), '*ndihlala eKapa*' (I live in Cape Town). Winnie had never spent a day in school, and saw herself as totally 'illiterate'.

I tracked Winnie through the various institutions and organisations to which she belonged. I recorded whatever literacy events occurred, who participated in each event, what language was spoken or written, what domain they fell into (for example, the household domain, the development domain, the domain of religion) and what discourses were evident. The descriptions showed that Winnie, far from being 'consigned to silence and marginalisation' by her 'illiteracy', had played an important role politically and was living a productive and satisfying life. But the picture became more complex when Winnie's everyday literacy practices were mapped against the practices of the adult literacy night school and the development agencies.

The domain of development was in a state of tremendous flux as Masiphumelele was becoming incorporated into local government structures, and there was intense engagement with municipal bureaucrats, NGO representatives and local do-gooders from the surrounding 'white' suburbs. Most of these activities were textually mediated, and there was seldom translation from English into the other local languages of isiXhosa or Afrikaans. In contrast with the other domains that I identified, the domain of development was saturated with printed texts. I watched Winnie starting to struggle to participate in this domain, and noted that in certain meetings her place was being taken by younger community activists. At the same time I watched her slowly withdrawing from the night school.

In making sense of Winnie's withdrawal, I argued that what was being promoted in the night school was a particular type of literacy akin to 'essay-text' literacy (Scollon and Scollon 1981; Gee 1992). There were three tensions involved in the transmission of this kind of literacy in Masiphumelele. Firstly, this kind of schooled literacy was insulated from the literacy practices that I observed in other domains. Secondly, this insularity promoted pedagogical practices which were unfamiliar to learners, for example, answering questions in full sentences. These practices often involved the *recontextualisation* of everyday materials into 'schooled' texts. Thirdly, in order to acquire epistemological access to these kinds of practices, learners would have to 'recapitulate' (see Heath 1983) the sorts of literacy experiences mainstream children acquire at home in their first few years: this is often done through apprenticeship to a literate person. For adults attending classes on average four hours a week, at the most, this kind of socialisation would be very difficult.

I argued that the people attending the classes were acquiring the identity of 'adult learner' which resulted in the personal acknowledgement, confirmation and internalisation of deficit, in line with the discourse which was informing national policy and provision as argued above. I argued that this resulted in identity conflicts involving disempowerment and subjection. Winnie explained that her children now knew that she couldn't read or write:

> now they know. The one is going to school at Kalk Bay. He laugh now, he say 'mama, are you Sub A' [the first year of formal schooling for children]. Sometimes I'm sitting here and write my things and he say 'Oooh look my mother, she's Sub A. Come, come and look'. I close my . . . if he *roep* (calls) their friends, I just close my door.

This quote was a powerful indication of the way in which the arrival of the night school infantilised Winnie, foregrounding her deficit and backgrounding her strengths as an effective and powerful community leader.

On the basis of detailed transcripts from meetings combined with general observations I developed descriptions of discourses which I saw as circulating in the site, for example, the discourse of entitlement, the discourse of survival, and how these legitimated values and meanings of literacy. These discourses were not specific to Masiphumelele, they were part of a wider set of discourses circulating in South Africa at the time. In this way I located 'the local' within the wider national struggles at that time. In this work I was moving upwards from participant perspectives, gained through the descriptions from field notes to analytical perspectives (Hammersley 2006), developed through situating what I was seeing in relation to broader theoretical frames and other research studies. The approach was therefore 'holistic and comprehensive' (Blommaert 2008: 13). Holistic, in the sense that my descriptions of what was happening in the local context were located in a wider picture (Hammersley 2006: 6); comprehensive, in the sense that they examined the whole setting and did not try to 'reduce the complexity of human conduct to core features' (Blommaert 2008: 13). Furthermore, I found that I was developing methods iteratively and intuitively in response to the object of inquiry. So, for example, I accumulated sufficient descriptions of events to trace what I called 'life histories of agenda items' across a series of meetings of different organisations.

In the final writing of the ethnography I was able to claim that the rapid social stratification that was taking place, as Masiphumelele became incorporated into more formal structures of local government, was mediated through printed texts and the practices surrounding them. This was leading to rapid changes in the form and function of leadership of the grassroots organisations which had played such an important role in the struggle against apartheid. In addition, I showed that there was no chance that the adult literacy classes and curriculum, as they were designed at the time, could provide people like Winnie with what they needed, to deal with the textually-mediated changes they were taking part in. This led me to suggest that diversified forms of adult literacy provision might better address the problem, rather than the formalised 'one-size-fits-all' system being set up within the policy frameworks.

1995 and 1996: the social uses of literacy

This research fed into the SoUL project in South Africa, where twelve researchers each spent up to a year studying the social uses and meanings of literacy among groups of people considered to be the *targets* of the adult literacy policy and provision: people living in shanty-towns, Black townships, housing schemes for 'Coloured' people, among mini-bus taxi drivers, farms, a factory and so on. In the book which resulted from this project (Prinsloo and Breier 1996) these twelve ethnographic studies 'spoke for themselves': there was little attempt to generalise across them or to synthesise findings. To use Hammersley's (2001) image, the text was cumulative in the sense of pieces adding to an overall mosaic.

However, the project had received substantial funding and there were criticisms that it did not address itself directly enough to issues of adult literacy policy and provision. In a sense it was speaking a different language from the language of policy makers. It was providing twelve narratives involving detailed and intricate descriptions of people's lived literacy practices, but policy makers wanted summaries and figures in order to find solutions. I was concerned about these criticisms and intrigued by questions about what seemed to be different languages. Ethnographers, while using forms of generalisation within case studies, tend to be wary of generalising across cases. However, the fact that the twelve studies had been done at the same time, had started off with the same theoretical framework, and that many of the descriptions echoed findings of other ethnographies of literacy around the world indicated that it might be possible to categorise some of the data across the case studies into some general patterns. I therefore trawled through the full reports from the twelve ethnographies and came up with a set of patterns (Kell 1996b) which were later extended and refined in Prinsloo and Kell (1997). They included the following:

*   Diverse orientations towards schooling and learning on the basis of gender, age, family structure and location.
*   A sense of identity and of social competence arising from attributes and experiences other than 'being educated'.

- The valuing of local knowledge or 'common sense', and its use in achieving purposes without written language.
- The acquisition of literacy skills outside of schooling or any other formal instruction.
- The importance of the role played by literacy mediators.
- Scepticism of adult literacy provision arising from experiences of attending classes.
- Perceptions and experiences of vernacular literacies as 'hidden literacies'; and the idea of literacies as gendered.
- Literacy for gatekeeping among groups stratified according to race and class.
- Experiences of literacy as surveillance and control, as people living under apartheid experienced their oppression as regulated through printed texts and regulations.

I presented these patterns at a number of meetings of literacy organisations and policy groupings, attempting to stimulate discussion about differences between the meanings and valuing of literacy as represented in these patterns and the meanings and valuing of literacy that were being constructed by the new policy frameworks. I argued that the patterns above contradicted the policy framework's view of unschooled people as being in a state of cultural deficit, and that they showed that people without extended schooling were not socially marginalised, 'silenced', dependent on others or cognitively restricted. The new framework was based on an ideology of modernisation, in which the movement from 'illiteracy' to literacy was seen in an evolutionary way, with a direct relation to increased productivity and social mobility. Literacy was being conceptualised simply as the entry point to further education and progression up a standards-based ladder. It assumed that learning only took place through progression in the formal mode – an assumption which devalued out-of-classroom learning. The standardisation into levels and stages was based on mainstream definitions of standard or normative behaviour, failing to acknowledge that people are often denied comparable access to a particular literacy because of differential status within a particular context.

Most of the conclusions drawn in the Masiphumelele and SoUL studies were based on ethnographies of people's out-of-classroom literacy practices and were not based on an analysis of what was actually happening in literacy classes. In my next project I therefore turned in this direction.

The ABET evaluation and literacy practices in and out of class

1996 and 1997: the ABET Diploma evaluation

In the mid to late 1990s I was invited to evaluate a new National Diploma in Adult Basic Education and Training. The Diploma was initiated by an adult literacy agency wanting to professionalise and accredit its adult teacher training in line with the new National Qualifications Framework. The evaluation took place at quite a critical juncture, 1996, when the effect of the new policies could just be traced in the pedagogical practices in actual literacy classes. Influenced by the work of Feldman (1995), I decided to adopt an ethnographic perspective and I saw this as an opportunity to bring the work I had done in Masiphumelele and after the SoUL project into a closer engagement with the policy framework.

Over a period of about five months I observed teacher training sessions in the college in Cape Town and in Port Elizabeth, examined curriculum documents and teaching materials, interviewed curriculum developers, tutors and in-service teachers in training and observed their classes with adult literacy learners in shanty-towns and townships across Cape Town. The ethnographic approach to the collection of data in this evaluation provided something of an 'emic' perspective (see Box 1) on the emerging identities and practices of these in-service teachers at a time of tremendous flux. The more interesting work came, however, when I juxtaposed the teacher and classroom-based data with the out-of-classroom data from the earlier Masiphumelele and SoUL studies.

As I entered the different sites in which the Diploma programme operated, the ethnographic sensibility I had gained from the earlier projects led me to feel that I was entering a rarified environment with a specialised language. In many cases I observed what appeared to be a ritualised scripting of lessons, according to plans conceived within the framework of staged unit standards on which the teachers had received instruction in the technical college. Suddenly, the kinds of adults I had come to know in the earlier projects who managed complex tasks in their lives and played powerful roles in their communities and families appeared rather like children sitting behind desks and being told what to do. One example among many: in a class which took place in a small room in a migrant workers' hostel, the teacher outlined what the 'outcomes' for the session were; that the learners could expect to learn about what TB was, the symptoms of TB and to read and write lists of these symptoms. It was clear, however, that the learners knew what TB was and had no difficulties coming up with the symptoms of TB. The teacher listed these and then paid great attention to the learners' writing of their individual lists of symptoms (this was among learners with very low levels of literacy), at the same time as she ignored the fact that a goat had entered the room and disrupted the class. This was followed by a kind of chanting of how the outcomes had been learnt: 'we have learnt what TB is'; 'we have learnt the symptoms of TB'; 'we have learnt how to write a list of symptoms'.

This example provided an illustration of what I called the 'evacuation of content' that was happening in the new system. The learners were already knowledgeable about the content that was raised in the lesson, but none of the more complex content was covered that may have been useful in their lives and that they may not have understood, for example, methods of contagion, the emergence of drug-resistant forms of TB, the complexities of forms of treatment and so on. At the same time as this evacuation of content, there was a filling of the pedagogic vacuum thus created with a set of procedures specified by the outcomes which stated what learners at particular levels needed to be able to do. The writing of the list of symptoms was an example of this. While it may be useful for people to be able to read lists of symptoms, it is not usually necessary for them to be able to write them.

In this case, and although I had earlier been a literacy teacher myself, working in the same types of sites, my experiences of researching literacy outside of classes in the earlier ethnographic projects rendered what I was seeing in the ABET programme 'anthropologically strange' (Bowker and Star 1999). This provided a new twist on the anthropological trope of emics and etics. Usually the etic is viewed as outside (knowledge), an academic perspective based on disciplinary apprenticeship and immersion into research in the area of study (although the relationship between etic and emic is more complex, as briefly indicated in Box 1). While I had that kind of etic perspective as an academic, I also had another kind of 'outsider' knowledge now, from the earlier research which had shown me about unschooled people's knowledge and ways of coping outside of schools and classrooms. My social origins and co-ordinates were so different from the teachers' in term of class, race, language, geographical location and so on (see Bourdieu and Wacquant, 1992). Yet the teachers seemed to have distanced themselves from the learners' lifeworlds (with whom they shared social origins and co-ordinates), even as they believed they needed to teach the learners 'relevant' lesson content. I could also see that these frames and scripts, while rarified and specialised to me, had become rapidly naturalised for many of the programme developers, lecturers and literacy teachers.

Still puzzled by what I saw as the rapid naturalisation of these new frames and scripts about learning, I felt I needed to test out my own understandings further and I did a further study on letter-writing (Kell 2000).

Letter-writing practices inside and outside of classes

The ABET evaluation provided data from discussions with teachers and observations of classes where teachers taught letter-writing. In addition, official curriculum statements specified 'outcomes' for different levels of literacy learning which made

---

Box 1

The relationship between emic and etic in ethnography

Sometimes presented as if these were a dichotomy
Emic – outside/outsider perspectives, descriptions, discourses
Etic – inside/insider perspectives, descriptions, discourses
But emic/etic involves a dialectical relationship
Etic 1 – A frame of reference with which an analyst or observer approaches data

$\updownarrow$

Emic – The discovery of valid relations internal to what is being studied

$\updownarrow$

Etic 2 – A reconsideration of the initial frame of reference in the light of new understandings
Kell (2006)

reference to personal letters. However, social practices around writing letters were described a few times in the Masiphumelele study and the SoUL project. It therefore became possible to look further at what was happening in classrooms with an 'out-of-classroom' gaze.

As with the list in the TB lesson, the focus in letter-writing in the classes was on what were called the basic 'elements' of the letter (which were always personal letters) – like the 'address', the 'greeting', the 'opening sentence', the 'acknowledgement' and so on. These elements were elevated to the point of being fetishised by the teachers, in the sense that they insisted that the learners needed to get these right. The page in Figure 13.1 from a very widely used book of lessons shows these elements.

One observation in particular showed that established patterns of communication were being over-written by the standardised Western forms as can be seen in the letter in Figure 13.1, particularly with regard to the expression of affect. In this lesson (which was with a group of beginner learners – migrant workers in a large plant processing alcohol) the learners resisted using an expression of affect in the final acknowledgement, such as 'your dear husband, Sipho'. It emerged that the learners did not feel comfortable about using such expressions of affect because of the Nguni custom of *hlonipha*, which requires that close relatives express bashfulness and distance. The teacher (despite her own class, race and linguistic origins in the same community) insisted, however, that the learners comply with the specified

D.   Fill in the missing words

Read this letter and fill in the gaps with words from the box.

| write | | love | | driver | |
| | you | | everybody | | job |

P O Box 213
Pietersburg
3200

1 August 1995

Dear Sipho

How are _____ ? I am missing you and the family. I am still waiting for your letter. When are you going to _____ to me?

I am fine, but I am still looking for a _____ here in Pietersburg. My friend Thabo has got a car, and he is teaching me how to drive. I am going to do my driving test next month, and I hope I can get a job as a _____ soon.

Give my love to _____ at home.

With _____ from

Your brother, Ben

Figure 13.1 Page from a widely used literacy lesson (Independent Examinations Board, Mock Language Exam, May 1995, pp. 4 and 5)

form. What were called the 'old ways' (in an interview with a different literacy teacher) were seen as deficient, the new form was naturalised as what was seen by this person as unnegotiably 'the standard'.

I then compared this schooled letter-writing with the letter-writing practices of unschooled migrant workers communicating with their families living up to 1,000 kilometres away (Kell 2000). Although this only involved interviewing the railway workers and studying a small collection of the letters they let me copy (twenty in all), it involved a kind of further testing of the Masiphumelele and SoUL findings.

These findings were confirmed: the interviews and descriptions of practices and actual letters painted a picture of resourceful people who did not seem to see stigma in their individual lack of literacy skills, drawing on complex, inter-locking social networks involving literacy mediation at different levels to accomplish communication between urban and rural areas. Literacy skills were distributed across these networks. Letter-writing played a central role in this communication, even among those who had never been to school, for whom at least four letters passed back and forth between family members per month. Very little of this correspondence entered into the South African Postal Service. The workers explained that they preferred to send their letters with the buses that travelled weekly between Cape Town and their homes in the rural areas, as they saw these as totally reliable and were able to send substantial amounts of money this way. Despite the literacy teachers' insistence that there was compliance with the elements of the letter like the address, date, initial greeting, acknowledgement, and the end greeting, none of the letters shown me by the workers had any such elements, and there was a strong rationale for why those elements were not necessary. For example, the men said that their letters did not need dates as they were sent on the buses that only went every Sunday so the family members on the other side always knew when the letter had been sent. They did not need a detailed address because the bus organiser was told verbally where they needed to be delivered. They did not need an acknowledgement as the reader would know who the letter was from having read the content of the letter.

I argued that the data on letter-writing illustrated that two parallel systems of letter-writing were going on, and they were fairly well insulated from each other. Yet, the pedagogic letter-writing made claims that it 'empowered' learners to deal more effectively with everyday demands in their lives, by recontextualising everyday practices in the adult literacy curriculum. The providers and teachers would have it that learners took a loop out of everyday life within the family and into pedagogical life within education. After that they would go back into everyday life and the family, supposedly as more effective family members – the 'modernist discourse' of educational reform was here at play (Luke 1992: 2). They may have gone back with a changed subjectivity but whether that could be called empowered may be questioned. Rather, what would seem at stake here was the "discursive construction of a distinctive schooled subjectivity" (Green 1993: 196). This needs to be seen in the wider context of social stratification in South Africa.

I argued that in the recontextualisation from one domain of practice to the domain of the class (while drawing on a discourse of 'relevance') everyday practices lost their specificity, their location in particular participation frameworks and their social meaning. This problem was compounded by the curriculum developers and teachers who were doing the recontextualising, as they tried to isolate, simplify and

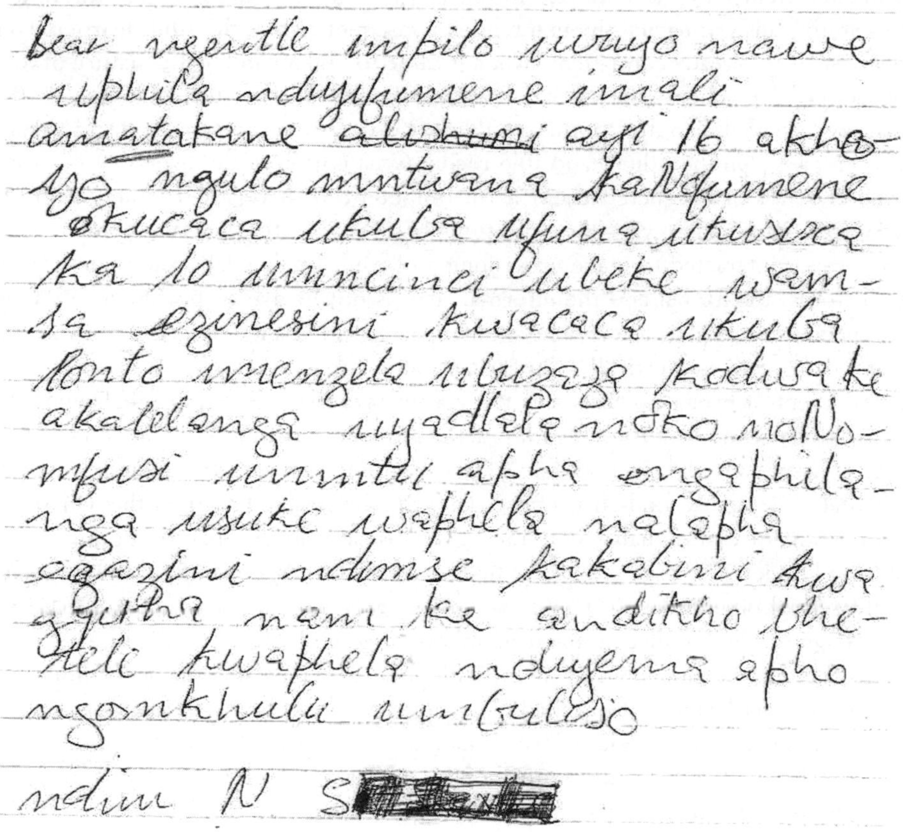

Dear I'm fine hoping you are the
same I've received the money there
are 16 calf Nofumene's child is not
well she took the child to the
nurse but that didn't help it just
cause more seriousness but the
child is awake the child is playing No
mfusi is not feeling
well she lost weight I took her
twice to the doctor I'm not
feeling well also my letter
is coming to an end
greetings to all

I am N S

Figure 13.2 Letter written by migrant worker's wife to her husband

sequence elements of the practice into literacy skills. In South Africa at the time of this study, this was having the unintended consequence that the adult learners were being seen as 'already competent' when it came to understanding the nature of these pegadogised practices (they could not have knowledge of such practices as they had not attended school). But they could not be already competent, and so a vacuum was created. On the other hand, the recontextualisation of the everyday tasks into schooled tasks constructed them as incompetent with regard to their everyday practices (such as knowing the symptoms of TB or writing a letter home). These two trends interacted to make provisioning of adult literacy fall exactly in between two stools, the formal and the informal. It was not formal or professional enough to anchor potential learners who wanted a second chance at learning, and who wanted to progress vertically. But at the same time learners were not becoming more adept at everyday tasks and the classes were simply confirming deficit and doing violence to learners' everyday practices by spuriously pedagogising them. What was at issue was the problematic of the relation between the formal vertically orientated system (second-chance schooling) and the assumed need for the widespread promotion of contextualised literacy at grassroots level (mainly among NGOs and civil society). These findings confirmed what I had argued in the Masiphumelele night-school observations.

Together with colleagues and members of some NGOs I made an attempt to bring this analysis into an engagement with policy. At that time the government had set up a special committee called the Language Task Group (Langtag) to make recommendations about South Africa's Language Policy and had invited experts with particular expertise to make submissions in which they outlined what they saw as the key issues for policy. I wrote a submission for Langtag (Kell 1996a) and I took part in meetings held by the National Literacy Co-operation where I participated in writing a further submission for the Education Department on the government's 'National Adult Basic Education and Training Framework: Interim Guidelines for ABET' (NLC 1996). These submissions cautioned against 'putting all our eggs into the basket of formalised provision' stating that this would not solve or even address the 'literacy problem' in South Africa. I argued that while there are some adults without schooling who both stand to benefit from 'second-chance' learning and were likely to commit themselves, at least initially to such a process, there were significant numbers and groups of people who were less likely to benefit and unlikely to present themselves for such learning. In addition, I argued that if the focus on 'outcomes' was to be accepted, the lack of focus on 'inputs' (such as teacher-training) could hollow out the system and set it up for failure.

In the Langtag submission I argued that a three-pronged approach would lay a stronger basis for literacy development over the longer term, and address some of the problems which the earlier ethnographies of literacy had raised. This approach should include:

1   Diversifying strategies for informal promotion and for supporting, scaffolding and sustaining literacy learning within existing contexts of use, in the informal economy, development projects and civil society. Articulation could occur between these opportunities and the formal system.

2   Overhauling communicative practices and strategies within the state and the formal economy. This would involve a greater commitment to South Africa's policy of multilingualism, expansion of translation services and production of texts in plain English.

3   Strengthening the formal system. This would involve growing the system slowly, resourcing it well, producing strong administrators, researchers and well-trained teachers; while at the same time recognising that it would not provide quick fixes for the 'literacy problem'.

In 1997 my University Department met with the Deputy Minister of Education who invited us to write a submission. In this, Mastin Prinsloo and I (Department of Adult Education and Extra-Mural Studies 1997) argued strongly against a national literacy campaign, reiterating the need for the above three strategies, and suggesting that if a campaign was necessary for the government to demonstrate commitment, then a limited literacy awareness' campaign could complement the above strategies.[2]

Khayalethu

1998–2003 literacy and house-building at Khayalethu

In submissions to policy-making bodies, I had suggested that one prong of an adult literacy strategy could involve embedding literacy promotion in grassroots development work. This issue was then addressed in a later ethnographic project with an intervention component. I wanted to test if it was possible to embed literacy promotion in the context of house-building, at the same time as I wanted to understand the ways in which participation in development was enabled or constrained through the range of literacy practices in which people engaged.

The site was a participatory development initiative (called Khayalethu) in which 240 Xhosa-speaking families identified as the 'poorest of the poor', who were living in backyard shacks, came together in local savings clubs and accessed a government subsidy in order to build brick houses. The activity at Khayalethu occurred within a wider organisational context of a national housing association (HASSOC) with international links, as well as with the support of a service organisation (SO) and a financial service organisation. The clubs, service organisations, and the national association initiated interactions with architects, engineers, City Council officials, the National Housing Board and the Department of Land Affairs. Members at Khayalethu circulated between the building site itself and banks and building supply shops. Ethnographically, it became essential to move beyond the building site in order to understand the different layers involved in such a complex process as well as to clarify the complex and shifting allegiances and schisms among and between these different groups. However, because of the intervention component and perhaps because of my earlier ethnographic experiences, I was committed to staying very close to the site-owners, at the same time as I felt torn between different groups or factions among them. Fieldwork took place over about three and a half years, during which I visited the site three or four times a week, and for short periods of time a fieldworker visited almost daily.

The project proposal had envisaged an initial ethnography followed by an intervention, which would be based on what the ethnography had revealed (following Reder's (1994) typology of ways of 'facilitating literacy development in the context of naturally occurring practices'). In practice these two could not be separated in time and became intertwined. I oscillated between the ethnographer role and a more direct intervention role when I tested out at points, firstly, modifying existing literacy practices, secondly, adding writing to existing cultural practices and thirdly, using writing to innovate new cultural practices. Some of the small interventions tested were as follows:

- Production of a booklet based on oral testimony which outlined the formation of the savings clubs, the groups' struggle for land, and the beginnings of the building process.
- Translation into Xhosa and distribution of a number of different documents produced during the ongoing work of house building, e.g. minutes of meetings with the City Council.
- Documenting of people's experiences of house building which involved writing down people's stories presented to us orally, and combining these with photographs in exercise books.

The small interventions aimed at promoting embedded forms of literacy activity/learning did eventually coalesce around one central issue which was the management and record keeping of the subsidy money to which each family was entitled. Much tension focused on a document called the 'expenditure record sheet'. Over the years my intervention centred on ways of putting control of expenditure back in the hands of individual house builders, and away from a management committee that had been accused of corruption. This process was supported with field workers who could mediate the textual demands of controlling expenditure.

Conclusion: the discipline of ethnography and the 'real-world'

What I have constructed above is a retrospective narrative of different ethnographic projects that I undertook over ten years or so. The three main projects can be seen as a collection of episodes in the narrative, with beginnings and endings of their own, and these were often structured by reporting and funding cycles. This was something I felt my way towards, often intuitively, sometimes by accident or serendipity. Each beginning, however, was both based on and built on the work of the earlier episode. In this way, I came to a view of ethnography as more than the faithful representation of insider perspectives, and rather as a process of theoretical refinement through the careful inter-relating of emic and etic perspectives.

In addition, the work that took place in between the projects, as I engaged with policy debates and wrote submissions to policy committees, for me, brought the domain of ethnography closer to the domain of policy, however, and perhaps more importantly, it gave me an increased awareness of the differences between the two, the specificities of the kinds of languages used in each domain and the need to find ways of translating between these.

What I have learnt in working as an ethnographer is that real-world problems do not exist somewhere separate as 'concrete problems' but they are bound up with sets of 'significations'. The problem of the constraints on academic work in terms of funding for projects and deliverable outputs is as 'real-world' as Winnie Tsotso's problem in Masiphumelele, the teachers' problems as their learners drop out of classes or the government's problems in its need to demonstrate 'delivery'. Viewing real-world problems as 'out there' can lead to a different kind of 'intellectualist bias' (Bourdieu 1990, cited in Wacquant 1992: 39) in which real-world problems can only be worked on (in Hymes's terms, 1996: 14) by 'those who know' and not by 'those who are known'.

South Africa is a country that is still very divided. Ethnography offers a way into understanding such divides. In South Africa it is not an easy way. At the same time as it 'entails trust and confidence' (Hymes 1996: 14), it also involves grappling with issues of identity and risk. At the same time as it involves 'the extension of a universal form of personal knowledge' and 'narrative accounting' (p. 14), it also involves tensions in representing 'the other'. Perhaps most importantly it comes bound up with the idea that the knowledge and experience of ordinary people counts first-hand, not mediated by pre-specified research frameworks and templates. In this sense, perhaps, it may be 'peculiarly appropriate to a democratic society' (p. 14).

Notes

1   There is considerable variation in the figures of 'illiterates' depending on how these are calculated, from 15 million in 1994 to 7.5 million in 1996 (Aitchison and Harley 2006).
2   Since then, however, the government, perhaps under pressure to 'demonstrate delivery', initiated the first 'mass literacy campaign'. When that did not succeed another was started. The third is just in the process of starting, has been allocated substantial funding, is claimed to be 'based on international best practice' and should enable 'the masses who were denied education to become literate 'in six months'. (KhaRiGude 2008).

References

Aitchison, J. and Harley, A. (2006) 'South African illiteracy statistics and the age of the magically growing literacy and ABET learners'. *Journal of Education* 39: 89–112. Retrieved on 10 November 2008 from http://www.ukzn.ac.za/joe/joe_issues.htm.

ANC-African National Congress, Education Department (1994) *A Policy Framework for Education and Training*. Pretoria: Unpublished mimeo.

Blommaert, J. (2008) *Grassroots Literacy: Writing, identity and voice in Central Africa*. New York and London: Routledge.

Bourdieu, P. and Wacquant, L. (1992) *An Invitation to Reflexive Sociology*. Cambridge: Polity.

Bowker, G. and Star, S.L. (1999) *Sorting Things Out: Classification and its consequences*. Cambridge, MA and London: The MIT Press.

Burawoy, M., Blum, J., George, S., Gille, Z., Gowan, T., Haney, L., Klawiter, M. *et al.* (2000) *Global Ethnography: Forces, connections and imagination in a post-modern world.* Berkeley and Los Angeles, CA: University of California at Los Angeles Press.

Candea, M. (2007) 'Arbitrary locations: in defence of the bounded field-site'. *Journal of the Royal Anthropological Institute* 13: 167–84.

CEPD – Centre for Education Policy Development (1994) 'Report of the task team for Adult Basic Education and Training'. University of the Witwatersrand: Unpublished mimeo.

Department of Adult Education and Extra-Mural Studies, University of Cape Town (1997) 'Response to the Deputy Minister of Education'. Unpublished mimeo.

Feldman, A. (1995) 'Ethnographic evaluation and the multicultural dynamics of social literacy in South Africa: a technical assistance report'. Pretoria: Human and Scientific Research Council.

Gee, J.P. (1992) *Social Linguistics and Literacies: Ideology in discourses.* Hampshire: The Falmer Press.

Green, B. (1993) *The Insistence of the Letter: Literacy studies and curriculum theorising.* London: The Falmer Press.

Hammersley. M. (2001) 'On "systematic" reviews of research literatures: a "narrative" response to Evans and Benefield'. *HYPERLINK "http://www.ingentaconnect.com/content/routledg/cber;jsessionid=6b7941rk5jjpc.alice" \o "British Educational Research Journal"* 27 (5): 543–54.

Hammersley, M. (2006) 'Ethnography: problems and prospects'. *Ethnography and Education* 1 (1): 3–14.

Heath, S. (1983) *Ways With Words: Language, life and work in communities and classrooms.* Cambridge: Cambridge University Press.

Hymes, D. (1996) *Ethnography, Linguistics and Narrative Inequality: Towards an understanding of voice.* London: Taylor and Francis

Jeffrey, B. and Troman, G. (2004) 'Time for ethnography'. *British Educational Research Journal* 30 (4): 534–48.

Kell, C. (1996a) 'Submission to Language Task Group on Literacy'. Unpublished mimeo.

Kell, C. (1996b) 'Literacy practices in an informal settlement in the Cape Peninsula', in M. Prinsloo and M. Breier (eds) *'The Social Uses of Literacy'.* Cape Town and Amsterdam: Sached Books and John Benjamin Publishers.

Kell, C. (2000) 'Teaching letters: the recontextualisation of letter-writing practices in adult literacy classes in South Africa', in D. Barton and N. Hall (eds) *Letter Writing as Social Practice.* Amsterdam: John Benjamin Publishers.

Kell, C. (2006) 'Moment by moment: contexts and crossings in the study of literacy in social practice'. Unpublished PhD thesis, the Open University.

KhaRiGude (2008) Official website of the KhaRiGude Literacy Campaign, South Africa. Retrieved on 10 November 2008 from http://www.kharigude.co.za/.

Luke, A. (1992) 'Genres of power: literacy education and the production of capital', in R. Hasan and G. Williams (eds) *Literacy in Society* (pp. 308–38). London: Longman.

Marcus, G. (1995) 'Ethnography in/of the world system: the emergence of multi-sited ethnography'. *Annual Review of Anthropology* 24: 95–117.

National Literacy Co-operation (NLC) (1996) 'Submission on ABET Interim Guidelines to ABET National Stakeholder Forum'. Unpublished mimeo.

Prinsloo, M. and Breier, M. (eds) (1996) *The Social Uses of Literacy.* Cape Town: SACHED Books, and Amsterdam and Philadelphia, PA: Benjamin Publishers.

Prinsloo, M. and Kell, C. (1997) 'Literacy on the ground: a located perspective on literacy policy in South Africa'. *Literacy and Numeracy Studies* 7 (2): 83–101.

Reder, S. (1994) 'Practice-engagement theory: a socio-cultural approach to literacy across languages and cultures', in B. Ferdman and R. Weber (eds) *Literacy across Languages and Cultures.* Albany, NY: SUNY Press.

Scollon, R. and Scollon, S. (1981) *Narrative, Literacy and Face in Interethnic Communication.* Norwood, NJ: Ablex.

Van Maanen, J. (1998) 'Different strokes: qualitative research in the Administrative Science Quarterly from 1956 to 1996', in J. Van Maanen (ed.) *Qualitative Studies of Organisations. The Administration Science Quarterly Series.* Thousand Oaks, CA; London; New Delhi: Sage.

Wacquant, L. (1992) 'Toward a social praxeology: the structure and logic of Bourdieu's sociology', in P. Bourdieu and L. Wacquant *An Invitation to Reflexive Sociology.* Camrbidge: Polity, pp. 1–60.

Chapter 14

Ben Rampton

Linguistic ethnography, interactional sociolinguistics and the study of identities[1]

Introduction

This chapter provides an overview of linguistic ethnography and interactional sociolinguistics, two closely related perspectives on communication, and in order to develop an account of their relevance to 'real-world issues', it discusses their contribution to the study of 'identity'. Both in research and public debate, identity is a major focus of interest. In the UK, the main funding body for social science, the Economic and Social Research Council (ESRC), has been running a large five-year research programme on 'Identities and Social Action', and the programme rationale proposes that:

> [r]esearch on identity provides a window on social change. It can answer questions about what is happening to identities based on familiar social class hierarchies. Are identities based much more now on 'life-style' and consumer choices? It can explore whether traditional political and community commitments are being replaced by a more volatile and dynamic 'identity politics'. The study of identity investigates how different images and narratives 'grab hold' of individuals. It explains why people act from one basis rather than another and why they invest in some affiliations and alliances rather than others. So why research identity, then? Because research on identity addresses some of the most troubling phenomena of our times: communal violence, xenophobia and exclusion and discrimination on the basis of gender, ethnicity, sexuality, disability and religion.
>
> (www.open.ac.uk/socialsciences/identities/pdf/
> programme_aims_themes.pdf, accessed 14/4/08)

Against such a background, it is hard to imagine any research engaging with identity being dry or pointless, and indeed in my own work on everyday communicative practices among young people, I have investigated the tensions between educational and popular cultural identities, the emergence of new ethnic identities, and identity dynamics around social class (Rampton 2005, 2006).[2]

And yet when I am actually nose-down in the empirical analysis of interactional data, 'identity' is not a particularly useful term. Indeed, if it comes in too quickly, there is a risk either of obscuring the dynamic ambiguities in everyday social experience – reducing the social to the fixed forms that Raymond Williams warned against (1977: 129) – or of losing sight of what Foucault called the 'immediate struggles' preoccupying people, overlooking the fact that before drawing on established categories to critique an unpleasant episode as, for example, racist, sexist or ageist, 'people [often] criticise instances of power which are the closest to them, those which exercise their action on individuals. They do not look for the "chief enemy", but for the immediate enemy' (Foucault 1982: 211–12). So the kinds of issue that have greatest currency in public and social science debate don't necessarily jump out at me from the data right away, and instead, it is often only when I step back from the intensive process of trying to work out what's going on in a particular episode that notions like identity become potentially relevant, pointing to a more general set of issues or debates that the episode maybe speaks to. Identity, in other words, tends to feature as a second- or third-order abstraction, a bridge back from data analysis to social science literatures and public debate, just one among a number of potential resources for explaining why the research is important, for answering the ever-pressing questions 'So what? Why bother?'.

What are these investigative procedures and perspectives that speak to identity issues, that often engage with the ideas about identity expressed by informants, but that don't incorporate the term 'identity' into their most basic analytic vocabularies? In what follows, I shall begin with a characterisation of *linguistic ethnography* (LE) and *interactional sociolinguistics* (IS), sketching a set of concepts and frameworks that are certainly capable of accommodating a concern with identity, but that do not depend on it. After that, I shall try to show how these approaches can be used to look at one very significant social identity – social class – though again, during the empirical analysis itself, I shall hold the term 'identity' in abeyance, only bringing it in afterwards in the third section to renew the connection with more general debates and literatures. Finally, in the last section, I shall consider the worry that this kind of analysis is impracticably over-complicated.

So first of all, what are linguistic ethnography and interactional sociolinguistics?

LE and IS: Tenets, scope, resources, goals and interdisciplinary positioning

Linguistic ethnography is something of an umbrella term, and there are a number of different research traditions that participate in the discursive space that LE provides – interactional sociolinguistics and new literacy studies, as well as certain types of Critical Discourse Analysis, neo-Vygotskyan research on language and cognitive development, and interpretive applied linguistics for language teaching (see Rampton

2007a; Rampton *et al.* 2004 for an overview of LE in the UK). But whatever the differences between sub-traditions, linguistic ethnography holds that:

1   The contexts for communication should be investigated rather than assumed. Meaning takes shape within specific social relations, interactional histories and institutional regimes, produced and construed by agents with expectations and repertoires that have to be grasped ethnographically; and

2   Analysis of the internal organisation of verbal (and other kinds of semiotic) data is essential to understanding its significance and position in the world. Meaning is far more than just the 'expression of ideas', and biography, identifications, stance and nuance are extensively signalled in the linguistic and textual fine-grain.

These **methodological tenets** mean that linguistic ethnography can be very wide-ranging in its **empirical scope**, investigating communication within the temporal unfolding of social processes that involve:

•   *persons*: their physical bodies, senses and perceptions; their cultural and semiotic repertoires, and the resources they have at their disposal; their capacities, habitual practices and dispositions; their likes and dislikes, desires, fears, commitments, and personalities; their social status and category memberships;

•   *situated encounters*: the events, genres and types of activity in which people, texts and objects interact together; actions, sequences of actions and the use of semiotic materials (signs, language, texts, media); inferencing, interpretation and the efforts of participants to understand or influence each other; the physical arrangement of the participants and the material setting; origins, outcomes and wider links – how signs, actions and encounters fit with interactional and institutional processes over longer and broader stretches of time and space;

•   *institutions, networks and communities of practice*: varying in durability and scale from e.g. playground peer-groups to clubs to schools, mass media and government policy: how institutions shape, sustain and get reproduced through texts, objects, media, genres and practices etc; how institutions control, manage, produce and distribute persons, resources, discourses/representations/ideologies, spaces, etc.

The assumption is that persons, encounters and institutions are profoundly inter-linked, and a great deal of research is concerned with the nature and dynamics of these linkages – with varying degrees of friction and slippage, repertoires get used and developed in encounters, encounters enact institutions, and institutions produce and regulate persons and their repertoires through the regimentation of encounters. Language has, after all, been extensively studied as a psychological, as an interactional and as a sociological phenomenon, and if these can be linked up judiciously, then there is a point of entry into socialisation (e.g. Ochs and Schieffelin 2001), into literacy (Heath 2001), into artful performance (e.g. Bauman 2001), into practical consciousness shaped in hegemony (Williams 1977; Rampton 2003), etc.[3]

In the branch of linguistic ethnography that I am most closely involved in, interactional sociolinguistics (cf Gumperz 1982; Gumperz 1999; Eerdmans *et al.* 2002; Rampton 2006: Ch. 1.3), these ideas come together in a view of situated communication that pays particular attention to the efforts individuals make to get other people to recognise their feelings, perceptions, interests, etc. Every moment in the unfolding of communicative action is unique and never-to-be-repeated, but this also involves linguistic forms, rhetorical strategies, semiotic materials and institutional genres that have achieved a degree of stability, status and resonance in the world beyond the encounter-on-hand. Individuals only ever have partial control over these forms, materials and strategies, and you can see the partiality of this control in face-to-face interaction, where there are two or more people involved in trying to build a provisional consensus on 'meaning' sequentially from one turn to the next, as well as in the afterlife that signs, texts and utterances have when they get reported or recycled elsewhere. In the words of Ortega Y. Gasset, cited in Becker 1995: 5:

> [t]wo apparently contradictory laws are involved in all uttering. One says 'Every utterance is deficient' – it says less than it wishes to say. The other law, the opposite, declares 'Every utterance is exuberant' – it conveys more than it plans and includes not a few things we would wish left silent.

Working with that basic view of communicative action, interactional sociolinguistics draws on four major sets of **analytic resources**:

a   *linguistics and discourse analysis* provide a provisional view of the communicative affordances of the linguistic resources that participants draw on in communication.

b   *Goffman* and *conversation analysis* provide frameworks and procedures for investigating situated encounters. More specifically, they help us to see: the ongoing, sequential construction of 'local architectures of intersubjectivity' (Heritage 1997); the rituals and moral accountabilities permeating the use of semiotic forms and strategies; and the shifting spatio-temporal distribution of attention and involvement in situations of physical co-presence.

c   *ethnography* provides a sense of the stability, status and resonance that linguistic forms, rhetorical strategies and semiotic materials have in different social networks beyond the encounter-on-hand; an idea of how and where an encounter fits into longer and broader biographies, institutions and histories; and a sense of the cultural and personal perspectives/experiences that participants bring to interactions, and take from them.

d   *other public and academic discourses* provide purpose and relevance for the analysis, as well as a broader picture of the environment where the study is sited. In the importance attached to these external discourses, both IS and LE are aligned with (extended) case study methodology (Burawoy 1998), and instantiate Dell Hymes' motto for ethnography – 'two feet on the ground and one eye on the horizon' (1999: xxxiii, xl). And indeed as I have already noted, it is here that notions of identity tend to show up most explicitly.

When these resources are pulled together in the empirical analysis of recordings of interaction, the **goal** is to produce an account that respects the uniqueness, deficiency and exuberance of the communicative moment, while, at the same time, describing how participants handle specific forms, strategies and materials, considering the ways in which their use feeds into the communication overall, and trying to understand how this feeds off and into local social life more generally. There is no complete or definitive interpretation either for analysts or participants, but you want an end-product that is mindful of the scholarly virtues of care, coherence, accuracy, accountability, scepticism and cumulative comparison, that is sufficiently plausible to stand up to the scrutiny from other analysts, that is open to reformulation in terms that participants can engage with, and that speaks to wider social or intellectual concerns.

Locating all this in wider social science debate – coming to questions of **inter-disciplinary positioning** – there is no doubt that for the *linguistics* side of IS and LE, post-structuralism has been the spur to a major philosophical rethink, shifting the balance from system to agency, from elegance to indeterminacy (see Rampton 2006: Ch.1.2 and 1.3; also Voloshinov 1973; Bourdieu 1977; Giddens 1976; Bauman 1992). More generally, though, neither IS nor LE have been tempted to abandon data and retreat to theory by developments in post-modern thought. On the one hand, the core concepts, tools and procedures we work with come out of long, active and ongoing lines of empirical testing and development, and on the other, social constructionism and the 'discursive turn' have invigorated the *discourse* elements of IS and LE, boosting the idea that there are a great many issues that they can contribute to – including, of course, the debates about 'identity' (see also Fairclough 1992: 1; Coupland 1998: 115–16).

At this point, it is worth looking at what LE/IS can actually do, and for this, I shall refer to some of my own research on the significance of social class for a group of 13 and 14 year olds in a 1990s multi-ethnic comprehensive school in inner London (Rampton 2006: Part III). There is additional background information about this research in Box 1.

Social class in interaction

Rather than setting out to investigate particular ideas about social class itself, I started my investigation with an interest in what was happening when these youngsters either put on exaggerated traditional posh/upper class voices or did Cockney/vernacular London accents, as described in linguistic detail by, for example, Wells 1982: Chs. 4.1 and 4.2. Of course, I had an intuition that class relations and class identities would prove relevant, and drew initial encouragement for the idea of linking these to social interaction from readings of Thompson, Williams, Bourdieu, Burawoy, Skeggs and Reay. But the main work of analysis and interpretation started with the identification and transcription of speech stylisation in radio-microphone recordings of spontaneous interaction, and here is an example, taken from the start of a Science lesson.

Hanif has been away from his table looking around for a book he needs for the writing work they've been set, but now he has arrived back, bringing a copy with

Box 1

Background information on the research reported in this paper

The field-site school: A multi-ethnic comprehensive in inner London in the mid 1990s. About a third of pupils at the school were from refugee and asylum families; over half received free school meals; and almost a third were registered as having special educational needs.

Data collection: The project involved approximately one year of fieldwork, and data collection involved interviews, participant observation, radio-microphone recordings of everyday interaction, and participant retrospection on extracts from the audio-recordings, focusing on four youngsters (two male, two female) in a tutor group of about thirty 14 year olds.

The analysis of social class: My analysis of social class eventually focused on (i) the school's position and ethos; (ii) accounts of social class given in lessons; (iii) the students' ethnic, occupational and linguistic backgrounds, their general dispositions and trajectories within recreational and institutional space; (iv) their views of class, as articulated in interviews, lessons and peer discussion; (v) their routine linguistic performance (assessed through Labovian analysis); and (vi) their mobilisation of posh and Cockney within situated activity.

Analysing stylisation: The analysis of posh and Cockney stylisation centred on *c.*65 transcripts from thirty-seven hours of audio-data, loosely differentiated into: (1) interactions where young people's identities as pupils are at issue; (2) interactions involving an element of conflict between male and female class-mates; (3) sound play interactions; (4) recreational interactions where no-one seeks to exercise institutional control, where there is no obvious conflict over the status of different groups, but where something more than just the sound properties of posh or Cockney seems to be in focus. The data I discuss in this paper falls into category 1.

him, and the hyper-Cockney pronunciation of 'Galaxies' in line 11 provides the starting-point for my analysis:

Extract 1

Hanif (14, male, Bangladeshi descent, wearing the radio-mic), Arun (14, male, Malaysian descent), Simon (14, male, Anglo-descent) are sharing the same table in science.

1   Hanif: *((whistles six notes))*
2   what you doing Arun
3   (.)
4   what you doin Arn
5   (.)
6   (>shup<) leave it Dimbo

7	(2)
8	look what you ma-
9	look what you made me do
10	(4)
11	"Stars and Galax**ies**"
	[stɑ̃ːz n gæləksə̃ĩːːz][4]
12	(1)
13	((quietly reciting page numbers:))
14	one three seven
15	(3)
16	((fast and loud to the teacher:))
17	>SIR can I go check if there's any
18	Essential Sciences left<

In lines 2–4, Hanif asks Arun what he's doing, and after that in line 6, he tries to ward off some kind of territorial incursion. Exactly who's trying what isn't clear from the tape, but Hanif follows it with a reproach in lines 8 and 9. There is no audible apology or retort, the matter drops and Hanif then turns to his worksheet, reading the title aloud and ending the word Galaxies with an exaggerated Cockney dipthong.[5]

To begin with, linguistic phonetics helps to pin down this pronunciation, differentiating it from Hanif's normal accent and lining it up with broad London (I also double-checked on this by playing it back to Hanif himself). The next step is to try to understand what is going on interactionally in line 11, and it is here that Goffman is useful. Hanif seems to be talking to himself when he reads the 'Stars and Galaxies' worksheet title, dedicating himself to the solitary task ahead. But as Goffman says, we're still very alert to the people around us when we talk to ourselves in public, and so in Hanif's self-talk, we are entitled to see an orientation to the over-hearers nearby (1981: 97–8). In fact, in reading out the worksheet title, Hanif is also consolidating a shift of footing, displaying his upcoming involvement in the curriculum task, disengaging from the business with his friends. If we add into this the ethnographic observation that broad Cockney was quite often associated with informal sociability, we can move to an initial interpretation of what is going on here – Hanif may be starting up on schoolwork, but in rounding off the title with hyper-Cockney, he's toning down the signs of his school commitment, showing that he's not a nerd, that he's still in tune.

In fact, dwelling on this a little longer, there is a case for saying that when Hanif uses Cockney to read aloud from a school text, he is contradicting what one would normally expect. Normally, as variationist sociolinguistic research has often shown (Labov 1972; Holmes 2001: 234–42), people's pronunciation tends to get posher when they read aloud or when they turn to school business. But Hanif is doing the opposite, and in fact this becomes more pronounced if we follow the activity unfolding over several minutes. Shortly after Extract 1, Hanif's exclamations suggest that he's really quite interested in the subject matter – "WO:W (2) oh my gard (7) oh my god (1)" – but at the same time, he continues weaving exaggerated accents into the task. The next time he returns to the "stars and galaxies" title, turning from talk to work, he renders it in quasi-Caribbean:

Extract 2

Hanif and Arun have been arguing about how long it takes to reach the moon, and Arun has contested Hanif's claims by showing him that the book he's cited is more out-of-date than Hanif thought, being published in 1993 rather than 1996. Hanif's accent in lines 9, 11 and 13 is quasi-Caribbean (see Wells 1982: 572 *passim* and Sebba 1993: 154) on the TRAP vowel and the non-reduction of unstressed vowels in Caribbean English).

1	Arun:	things can change (in four years)
2	Hanif:	1993 was (.)
3		three years ago
4		(.)
5		>get your facts right<
6		((very fast:)) >oh you ( )<
7	Arun	((turning to John who appears to have said something:)) SHUT UP JOHN
8		(4)
9	Hanif	((with a quasi-Caribbean accent:)) ˈguˈluˈxies ˌmun [galaksiz mʌn]
10		(.)
11		ˈstars ˌmun [stɑːz mʌn]
12		(.)
13		ˈguˈluˈxies ˌmun [galaksiːz mʌn]
14	Arun:	(your sta)
15	Hanif:	shudup

((Hanif now stays silent for 9 seconds, breaks this by briefly noticing a textbook nearby ('someone put an Active Science Book here'), and he then keeps out of conversation for nearly a minute))

And then after a period of attentive silent reading, he begins to turn the worksheet into quiz questions for Simon and Arun. At one stage of the quiz, he uses hyper-Cockney "ok**ay**" ([əʊkʌ̃ĩ]) (cf Wells 1982: 303–4) to get Simon and Arun to attend to the next question:

Extract 3

Later on in the lesson, with the 'quiz' underway

1	Hanif ((writing down an answer:)) Mercury (.)
2	takes (.)
3	the (.)
4	shortest (3)
5	shortest time (1)
6	to trave:l (.)

7	Simon:	all right
8	Hanif:	around (3)
9		thee
10		earth
11		(.)
12		oh-
13		thee sun
14		sorry
15		(2)
16		((very loud, nasalised and Cockney:)) o/kai
		[əõkʌ̃ĩ]
17		(1)
18		number f-
19		free
20		(.)
21		all right
22		let's see if you >don't learn this< one
23		(.)
24		Arun
25	Arun:	yes
26	Hanif:	and no guessin'
27		right
28		(1)
29	Arun:	I DIDN'T GUESS THE FIR[ST ONE
30	Hanif:	[shsh
31		shsh

At moments like these, there seems to be more involved in Cockney stylisation than just toning down the signs of Hanif's own school commitment. Here it is part of an attempt to get his peers to focus on their classwork, and rather than speaking of 'apologetic self-mitigation', it would be more accurate to describe Hanif as making school knowledge more vernacular and accessible, bringing the science worksheet to life with non-standard accents and a popular TV format.

So far, then, our micro-analysis of this situated episode has covered vowel sounds, close attention to the interactional dynamics around one utterance (line 11 in Extract 1), and genre mixing in the development of subsequent activity (Extracts 2 and 3). At this point, it is vital to broaden the focus in at least two ways – on the one hand, it is essential to situate these episodes in longer ethnographic observation of Hanif, his friends and classmates, and on the other, it is important to bring in other episodes where posh and Cockney were stylised.

In the first instance, ethnographic familiarity with Hanif points to a match between the challenge to traditional equations of book learning with poshness glimpsed in Extract 1 and a much more general pattern in his conduct, involving an impressive combination of commitment to learning with a lack of regard for the decorums with which learning is traditionally surrounded. Hanif was identified by teachers as one of the stars of the class, and as very clever at schoolwork – a 'boffin' – by his peers. But he attached a lot of importance to friends, was the ring-leader of his circle, and knew that friendship and success could sometimes conflict – one of his oldest pals, Mansur, was renowned for his ambition to be a judge, but he'd now started to bunk off school quite regularly. This tension between school success and sociability was reflected in Hanif and co's style of participation in class – they were often interested in lessons and attended very closely to teacher-talk, but they nevertheless (a) transgressed the traditional Initiation–Response–Evaluation structure of classroom talk (Edwards and Westgate 1994: Ch. 2) more or less as a matter of routine, and (b) continuously sought to liven things up with the importation of all sorts of extraneous, non-curriculum materials (see Rampton 2006: Ch. 2). Against this background, there is little to surprise us in Hanif's vernacularisation of school knowledge in Extracts 1–3, although in case we're tempted to read him as a radical,[6] it's also worth noting that Hanif's teachers were often very receptive to his transgressive enthusiasms. Out of circa fifteen episodes in which he used an exaggerated posh or Cockney accent in school-related business, eight were either loudly performed on the classroom floor, or directly addressed to teachers themselves. Teachers gave him a lot of discursive space, listened to what he had to say, and largely accepted his stylisations of Cockney, so that overall, Hanif had good cause for thinking of school as a generally hospitable institution, open to his socio-linguistic innovations. Indeed, there is a case for saying that instead of being constructively rebellious, the 'Cockneyification' of the science worksheet was a systemic product of the particular conditions in which Hanif found himself and operated.

Looking sideways, next, to other instances of exaggerated posh-and-Cockney, it was clear that this kind of stylisation was actually rather common, occurring on average about once every 35–45 minutes in my 37 hours of data. In one way or another, about twenty to twenty-five of these performances of hyper-posh-and-Cockney registered processes of stratification and division associated with schooling. As in Extract 1, both posh and Cockney were quite often stylised in the transitions between work and play, and ultra-posh was also used when kids felt patronised by teachers. But in addition, away from the demarcations and ranking involved in schooling, hyper-Cockney and posh were quite extensively used in humour and mockery among kids themselves. In fact, pulling together the connotations evidenced in about twenty of these non-school-oriented episodes, Cockney seemed to be associated with vigour, passion and bodily laxity, while posh got linked to physical weakness, social distance, constraint and sexual inhibition (see Rampton 2006: Ch. 9).

All in all, I looked at well over fifty episodes in detail, and in line with my comments in Section 1 about reckoning with the uniqueness of the communicative moment, I took a lot of time to analyse each of them. For much of this time, I worked to the aesthetic of 'slowness' and 'smallness' that Silverman (1998) associates with conversation analysis, squeezing out the kind of interactional detail illustrated in Extract 1. But as intimated earlier, I was also very interested in how these episodes figured within both biographical and institutional process, and so in the end, like a good deal of linguistic ethnography, the account also covers both individuals and institutions, even though it is situated interaction that occupies the central place.

That is an attempt, then, to illustrate something of the scope of linguistic ethnography. So far, though, there has been no space for the term 'identity' in the analysis, and instead I have been drawing on a mixture of linguistics, discourse analysis and ethnographic detail. But this changes, I think, once we turn to wider debates.

Linking to more general debates about identity

At a meeting of the research programme I mentioned at the outset – the ESRC's 'Identities and Social Action Programme' – we presented an interactional account similar to the analysis in Section 2, and Stuart Hall asked about:

> the relationship between the mobilization or performance of . . . identity at the local, micro, more ethnographic level, and the large thing that brought us into the field at the beginning, namely a [stratified . . .] social world, a world in which material and symbolic resources continue to be deeply unequally distributed. Why are you in this field if you are not concerned about that? It was easier to get to that when the methodology was to take those as given and see how they were working out in that space or that. Once you deconstruct these points of reference – how do you ever get back to the larger field?
>
> (I and SA Ethnicities Workshop at the London School of Economics, 21/6/06)

Much of the answer to this vital question lies in making a connection back to the academic (and public) discourses that I identified earlier in this chapter as the fourth resource for IS/LE, and, staying with social class, there are a number of ways in which the interactional data provides material for case-study engagement with more general debates about identity (cf e.g. Bendle 2002).

Extract 1, for example, can be seen as an instance of reflexive identity negotiation, especially if we use E.P. Thompson (1978) to reinforce the link to social class. In the struggle for resources, Thompson conceptualises social class as an agentive process that involves the 'drawing of lines' to different degrees in different ways at particular times and places, and when kids produced hyper-posh and Cockney in transition between work and play, we can see these stylised performances as fleeting but quite frequently repeated moments of heightened sensitivity to the broader identity implications of different positions within curriculum activity – moments when there's temporarily sharpened reflexivity about social class and the dividing lines between work and sociability (Rampton 2006: 306–7), moments when the class implications of difference become an active concern for participants in interaction.

Elsewhere in the dataset, more psycho-social discussion of identity and class look relevant. There were times, for example, when kids produced contorted mixtures of hyper-posh and exaggerated Cockney during spontaneous performances of the grotesque, and this brings Stallybrass and White's 'classed Imaginary' to mind, where 'ideology and fantasy conjoin' (Stallybrass and White 1996: 25; Rampton 2006: 346–51). Similarly, when some of the boys used deep-voiced ultra-Cockney to caricature one of the powerful but non-conformist girls in the class, there is a lot of relevance in the discussions of fear, desire, sexuality and class provided by, for example, Skeggs or Ortner, who argues that 'class discourse is [often] submerged within, and spoken through, sexual discourse, taking "sex" here in the double English sense of pertaining to both gender and the erotic' (Ortner 1991: 171–2; Skeggs 1997: 99–100; Rampton 2006: 351–60). Following a substantial period from the 1970s to the early 1990s when statistical survey treatments of social class predominated, there has been a resurgence of interest in the psychological significance and costs of class stratification, and the fact that evidence of the complex affective meaning of social class emerges in radio-mic recordings of spontaneous interaction rather than just in, say, psycho-analytically oriented interviews, provides useful supplementary support for the importance of this more recent line of enquiry.

A great deal of the data also contradicted quite major claims about identity transformation in late modernity. Looking across my dataset as a whole and pulling together all of the themes and images evoked in these situated stylisations of posh and Cockney, one can see the over-arching imprint of a set of high/low, mind/body, reason-and-emotion binaries that reach back to the emergence of bourgeois society in the eighteenth and nineteenth centuries (Cohen 1988: 66–7 on England; and Bourdieu 1991: 93 on France). When we consider that this wasn't a traditional white working-class school, that pupils came from all over London, that about a third were from refugee and asylum-seeking families, that less than a quarter in Hanif's class were white, and that Hanif spoke to his parents mostly in Sylheti – in short, when we consider the globalised, multi-ethnic late-modern environment, then these kids' insistent reproduction of a very traditional class imagery contradicts the view that class is losing its salience particularly among contemporary urban youth (e.g. Bradley 1996: 77; Surridge 2007). Maybe more profoundly, if we bring the imagery these kids had at their fingertips together with the interactional situations in which they spontaneously stylised posh and Cockney – and if in addition, we factor in their ordinary London accents as well – then I think we have a graphic empirical picture of what Williams calls the 'saturation of the whole process of living . . . [by] the . . . dominance and subordination of particular classes' (1977: 109; cf Rampton 2003, 2006: 360–79). What the analysis shows, in short, is that these kids' everyday practical consciousness was deeply impregnated with the sensibilities that we traditionally associate with social class in Britain.

So overall, even though 'identity' doesn't figure in its empirical tool-chest, there are a *number of different ways* in which the descriptions produced by IS/LE can speak to the debates about contemporary identity. But what is the practical utility of this kind of analysis?

Defending complexity

Within linguistic ethnography as whole, there is a long and robust tradition of work that combines a substantial contribution to academic knowledge with practical intervention. In the new literacy studies, Shirley Brice Heath's classic work in the Piedmont Carolinas introduced the methods and understandings of research into local schools (1983), and in interactional sociolinguistics, Gumperz, Jupp, Roberts and their associates linked the study of situated interaction with systematic programmes designed to raise social and communicative awareness in multiracial workplaces in Britain (Gumperz *et al.* 1979; Roberts *et al.* 1992; Roberts and Sarangi 1999; also Hymes 1980; Cameron *et al.* 1992). My own analysis in stylised posh-and-Cockney class was partly prompted by the general retreat from class analysis in both academic and public discourse, and in an era when educational policy makers tend to give exclusive emphasis to ethnicity and gender, the testimony here to an insistent class awareness enduring amidst ethnic hyper-diversity is potentially rather consequential. When, for example, (historically) migrant ethnicities are made central to discussions about education, the discourse tends to focus on cultural differences and the social integration of new populations, on the effects of ethnically distinct family structures and parenting, on the need for mother-tongue or English language support, etc. Ethnicity is seen as presenting the nation-state with new challenges, and the assumption is that inequalities are soluble, requiring only an increase in cultural adjustment/hospitality and better-targeted interventions. In contrast, class presents a set of more intractable issues. It is no longer possible to isolate education from central processes in the mainstream production and distribution of cultural and economic capital, and it becomes necessary to consider people's financial resources, their career/job prospects, their stances/positioning within high versus low culture, and their ways of adapting to enduring stratification. Looking back at the data in Section 2, Hanif's family background might be seen as inviting an ethnic analysis of his everyday life at school, but a close look at his language practices suggests the importance of a class interpretation, leading back potentially from a politics of recognition to a politics of redistribution (Fraser 1995; Rampton *et al.* 2008).

As it happens, I haven't personally used my analysis of posh and Cockney stylisation as the basis for intervention in policy or political debate, but there is absolutely no in-principle problem if some of the micro-analytic findings are picked up, shaved of some of their nuanced particularity, and then recontextualized in more public arguments. In terms of the current discussion, there might well be occasions when it was strategically valuable to fast-forward through to 'identity' past the phonetics, the discourse, interaction and ethnographic analysis. In ending, though, I would like to offer a defence of complexity.

Making your point count in politics, and producing a piece of research that makes a difference to academic debate are two different activities, and I think it would be a mistake to underestimate the skill, time and effort it takes to do a decent job in either. In addition, there are a lot of very perceptive cultural commentators able to pick out important issues in social process much faster than empirical researchers can – I'm sure it never occurred to Stuart Hall (e.g. 1988) to wait for the reports to come in from sociolinguistics before he started to talk about 'new ethnicities', and a good thing too! Sometimes, if you have worked in professional or community settings, if your research is animated by frustration with state policy and prevailing institutional discourses, or if your employment itself involves practical activity with health workers, teachers, interpreters, etc., then the methodological proximity of ethnography and action research encourages researchers (a) to read macro-scopic and historical processes only in the most obvious elements of policy, and (b) to attach higher priority to relevance and rapport with people in the field than to theory development and cumulative comparative generalisation. In this context, Hymes' discussion of educational ethnography in the US has much wider relevance:

> [e]thnography, as we know, is in fact an interface between specific inquiry and comparative generalisation. It will serve us well, I think, to make prominent the term 'ethnology', that explicitly invokes comparative generalization, and it will serve schooling in America well. An emphasis on the ethnological

dimension takes one away from immediate problems and from attempts to offer immediate remedies, but it serves constructive change better in the long run. Emphasis on the ethnological dimension links anthropology of education with social history, through the ways in which larger forces for socialisation, institutionalisation, reproduction of an existing order, are expressed and interpreted in specific settings. The longer view seems a surer footing.

(Hymes 1996: 19)

Turning back to my own research, exaggerated performances of posh and Cockney showed up in a number of different ways in my dataset, and it certainly has been both complex and time-consuming trying to analyse, summarise and interpret them all. But this range and complexity is itself significant. The very fact that posh-and-Cockney stylisations showed sensitivity to stratification in a *plurality* of ways and situations is precisely what you'd expect of a social process that reaches deep – if you shied away from accounts that looked long and elaborate, it would be hard to appreciate just how far social class impacts on everyday conduct and experience. By the same token, it should be no cause for regret if, in our attempts to combine broader relevance with as much faithfulness to our findings as we can manage, our summaries end up looking rather baggy, lacking in eye-catching elegance, more interesting for undergraduates than the readers of the Sunday papers. The processes that we inspect are often fairly general, capable of arousing comment and interest in lots of different arenas, but it is surely also important as a moral and political principle that beneath the headlines and beyond the attention to spectacular cases, there is still some documentation of the intricacy, distribution and significance of these processes in ordinary lives.

Notes

1   This paper draws on two research projects funded by the ESRC – 'Urban Classroom Culture and Interaction' (2005–08; RES-148-25–0042) and 'Multilingualism and Heteroglossia In and Out of School' (1997–99; R 000 23 6602). An earlier version of this paper was presented at a British Sociological Association 2007 Conference Symposium Panel entitled *New Ways of Knowing: Bending the Paradigm in Identity Research*, organised by Margie Wetherell. Though its problems are very much my own, I'm grateful to Adam Lefstein and Theresa Lillis for valuable feedback which helped me to clarify the argument in this paper.
2   Issues of practical relevance are explicitly addressed in e.g. Rampton 1996a, 1996b, 2005: Ch.13 and 2007b.
3   A number of the references here are included in A. Duranti (ed.) (2001) *Linguistic Anthropology: A Reader*. Oxford: Blackwell. 'Linguistic anthropology' has much in common with linguistic ethnography, but is much stronger in the US than in Europe. There is a discussion of the relationship between the two in Rampton 2007a.
4   The script in this line (and elsewhere in square brackets) is phonetic, following the International Phonetic Alphabet. There are many good introductions to this area of linguistics, such as e.g. Roach (2000).
5   To clarify the distinctly Cockney aspect of how Hanif says 'galaxies', it's worth noting that the (mid-central) starting point for the dipthong in the last syllable (represented phonetically as [ə]) was highly untypical of Hanif's pronunciation of the vowel in the

*happ*Y group elsewhere, was associated by Hanif with the accent of a cousin who lived in London's East End when the sequence was replayed to him, and is described by Wells as broad Cockney (1982: 319).

6   In fact, there were other occasions when Hanif's exaggerated Cockney looked politically regressive, as when, for example, it was perjoratively targeted, for example, towards non-conformist girls. Indeed, given his status as star student, there's a case for seeing his stylisation in Extract 1 as a piece of Bourdieuian condescension (Bourdieu 1991: 68ff).

References

Bauman, R. (2001) 'Verbal art as performance', in A. Duranti (ed.) *Linguistic Anthropology: A reader* (pp. 165–88). Oxford: Blackwell.

Bauman, Z. (1992) *Intimations of Postmodernity*. London: Routledge.

Becker, A. (1995) *Beyond Translation: Essays towards a modern philology*. Ann Arbor, MI: University of Michigan Press.

Bendle, M. (2002) 'The crisis of identity in high modernity'. *British Journal of Sociology* 53 (1): 1–18.

Bourdieu, P. (1977) *Outline of a Theory of Practice*. Cambridge: Cambridge University Press.

Bourdieu, P. (1991) *Language and Symbolic Power*. Oxford: Polity.

Bradley, H. (1996) *Fractured Identities: Changing patterns of inequality*. Cambridge: Polity Press.

Burawoy, M. (1998) 'The extended case method'. *Sociological Theory* 16 (1): 4–33.

Cameron, D., Fraser, E., Harvey, P., Rampton, B. and Richardson, K. (1992) *Research Language: Issues of power and method*. London: Routledge.

Cohen, P. (1988) 'Perversions of inheritance: studies in the making of multiracist Britain', in P. Cohen and H. Bains (eds) *Multiracist Britain* (pp. 9–118). Basingstoke: Macmillan.

Coupland, N. (1998) 'What is sociolinguistic theory?' *Journal of Sociolinguistics* 2 (1): 110–17.

Duranti, A. (ed.) (2001) *Linguistic Anthropology: A reader*. Oxford: Blackwell.

Edwards, A. and Westgate, D. (1994) *Investigating Classroom Talk* (2nd edn). Lewes: Falmer Press.

Eerdmans, S., Prevignano, C. and Thibault, P. (eds) (2002) *Language and Interaction: Discussions with John J. Gumperz*. Amsterdam: John Benjamins.

Fairclough, N. (1992) *Discourse and Social Change*. Oxford: Polity Press.

Foucault, M. (1982) 'The subject and power', in H. Dreyfus and P. Rabinow (eds) *Michel Foucault: Beyond structuralism and hermaneutics* (pp. 208–26). New York: Harvester Wheatsheaf.

Fraser, N. (1995) 'From redistribution to recognition: dilemmas of justice in a 'post-socialist' age'. *New Left Review* 212: 68–92.

Giddens, A. (1976) *New Rules of Sociological Method*. London: Hutchinson.

Goffman, E. (1981) *Forms of Talk*. Oxford: Blackwell.

Gumperz, J. (1982) *Discourse Strategies*. Cambridge: Cambridge University Press.

Gumperz, J. (1999) 'On interactional sociolinguistic method', in S. Sarangi and C. Roberts (eds) *Talk, Work and Institutional Order* (pp. 453–72). Berlin: Mouton de Gruyter.

Gumperz, J., Jupp, T. and Roberts, C. (1979) *Crosstalk*. Southall, Middx: BBC/National Centre for Industrial Language Training.

Hall, S. (1988) 'New ethnicities', in A. Rattansi and J. Donald (eds) (1992) *'Race', Culture and Difference*. London: Sage/The Open University.

Heath, S.B. (1983) *Ways with Words*. Cambridge: Cambridge University Press.

Heath, S.B. (2001) 'What no bedtime story means: narrative skills at home and school', in A. Duranti (ed.) *Linguistic Anthropology: A reader* (pp. 318–42). Oxford: Blackwell.

Heritage, J. (1997) 'Conversation analysis and institutional talk: analysing data', in D. Silverman (ed.) *Qualitative Research: Theory, method, practice* (pp. 161–82). London: Sage.

Holmes, J. (2001) *An Introduction to Sociolinguistics* (2nd edn). London: Longman.

Hymes, D. (1980) *Language in Education: Ethnolinguistic essays*. Washington, DC: Centre for Applied Linguistics.

Hymes, D. (1996) *Ethnography, Linguistics, Narrative Inequality*. London: Taylor and Francis.

Hymes, D. (1999) 'Introduction to the Ann Arbor Paperbacks edition', in D. Hymes (ed.) *Reinventing Anthropology* (pp. v-xlix). Ann Arbor, MI: Ann Arbor Paperbacks.

Labov, W. (1972) *Sociolinguistic Patterns*. Oxford: Blackwell.

Ochs, E. and Schieffelin, B. (2001) 'Language acquisition and socialization: three developmental stories and their implications', in A. Duranti (ed.) *Linguistic Anthropology: A reader* (pp. 263–301). Oxford: Blackwell.

Ortner, S. (1991) 'Reading America: preliminary notes on class and culture', in R. Fox (ed.) *Recapturing Anthropology: Working in the present* (pp. 164–89). Santa Fe: School of American Research Press.

Rampton, B. (1996a) 'Displacing the native speaker: expertise, inheritance and affiliation', in T. Hedge and N. Whitney (eds) *Power, Pedagogy and Practice* (pp. 17–22). Oxford: Oxford University Press.

Rampton, B. (1996b) 'Language crossing, new ethnicities and school'. *English in Education* 30: 14–26.

Rampton, B. (2003) 'Hegemony, social class and stylisation'. *Pragmatics* 13 (1): 49–84.

Rampton, B. (2005) *Crossing: Language and ethnicity among adolescents* (2nd edn). Manchester: St Jerome Press.

Rampton, B. (2006) *Language in Late Modernity: Interaction in an urban school*. Cambridge: Cambridge University Press.

Rampton, B. (2007a) 'Neo-Hymesian linguistic ethnography in the United Kingdom'. *Journal of Sociolinguistics* 11 (5): 584–607.

Rampton, B. (2007b) 'Everyday anti-racism in ethnolinguistic crossing and stylisation', in special issue of *Noves-sl* on 'Language and Youth', edited by Joan Pujolar and A. Torrijos Lopez. (English and Catalan) *Noves SL* Winter 2007 issue is available at: http://www.gencat.cat/llengua/noves.

Rampton, B., Harris, R., Collins, J. and Blommaert, J. (2008) 'Language, social class and education', in S. May and N. Hornberger (eds) *Encyclopedia of Language and Education* (pp. 71–82), Vol. 1 (2nd edn). New York: Springer.

Rampton, B., Tusting, K., Maybin, J., Barwell, R., Creese, A. and Lytra, V. (2004) *UK Linguistic Ethnography: A discussion paper*: UK Linguistic Ethnography Forum. At http://www.ling-ethnog.org.uk/documents/discussion_paper_jan_05.pdf.

Roach, P. (2000) *English Phonetics and Phonology: A practical course* (3rd edn). Cambridge: Cambridge University Press.

Roberts, C. and Sarangi, S. (1999) 'Hybridity in gatekeeping discourse: issues of practical relevance for the researcher', in Srikant Sarangi and Celia Roberts (eds) *Talk, Work and Institutional Order* (pp. 473–503). Berlin: Mouton.

Roberts, C., Davies, E. and Jupp, T. (1992) *Language and Discrimination*. London: Longman.

Sebba, M. (1993) *London Jamaican: Language systems in interaction*. London: Longman.

Silverman, D. (1998) *Harvey Sacks: Social science and conversation analysis*. Oxford: Polity Press.

Skeggs, B. (1997) *Formations of Class and Gender*. London: Sage.

Stallybrass, P. and White, A. (1996) *The Politics and Poetics of Transgression*. London: Methuen.

Surridge, P. (2007) 'Class belonging: a quantitative exploration of identity and consciousness'. *British Journal of Sociology* 58 (2): 207–26.

Thompson, E.P. (1978) *The Poverty of Theory and Other Essays*. London: Merlin.

Voloshinov, V. (1973) *Marxism and the Philosophy of Language*. New York/London: Seminar Press.

Wells, J. (1982) *Accents of English*. Cambridge: Cambridge University Press.

Williams, R. (1977) *Marxism and Literature*. Oxford: Oxford University Press.

Transcription conventions

Phonetic symbols:

[stɑːz mʌn]   Script like this inside two square brackets draws on the IPA
                   phonetic alphabet (revised to 1979)

Prosody

/   low rise
| high stress
ı   low stress

Conversational features

(.)   pause of less than a second
(1.5)   approximate length of pause in seconds
[overlapping turns
[
~   nasalisation
CAPITALS   loud
>text<   more rapid speech
(   )   speech inaudible
(text)   speech hard to discern, analyst's guess
((text:))   'stage directions'
bold   words and utterances of particular interest to the analysis

Chapter 15

Stef Slembrouck

Discourse, critique and ethnography
Class-oriented coding in accounts of child protection

Introduction

In this chapter I offer a critique of the ways in which Systemic Functional Linguistics (SFL) and Critical Discourse Analysis (CDA) engage with context and argue for the value of ethnography as an 'epistemology of contact'. Drawing on extracts from a larger ethnographic study exploring the significance of social class in child protection practices, my aim is to emphasise the importance of acknowledging the 'data histories' of any specific data source and to illustrate this through one example   interviews with parents. I conclude by briefly considering the relevance of the ethnography both as process and findings, to child protection practices.

Critique and intervention for the long haul

CDA and SFL share a critical programme which is rooted in ideological analysis of inequality and oriented to intervention; they also have a history in common of mutual comment which stresses complementarity and a preferred partnership in the domain of language, discourse and critique. While Chouliaraki and Fairclough (1999: 137) conclude their list of interlocutors for social theoretical dialogue with the observation that 'SFL theorises language in a way which harmonises far more with the perspective of critical social science than other theories of language', Martin and Rose (2002: 263) in a similar vein, observe that 'CDA has regularly visited the

Extracts from Slembrouck, S. (2005) 'Discourse, critique and ethnography: class-oriented coding in accounts of child protection', *Language Sciences* 27: 619–50.

theory [of SFL] in search of tools for analysis where close systematic readings of texts are required'.

CDA and SFL differ substantially in their critical programmes. In as much as for CDA (e.g. Fairclough 1989, 1992), the focus is on enlightenment (cf. the idea of 'critical language awareness') through a critique of practices which sustain inequality and the need to do so in ways which bring social change into view, SFL has tended to stress a need to balance between the constructive and the deconstructive. For Martin and Rose (2002: 264), 'we need to balance critique with Positive Discourse Analysis, so that our interventions must have good news to learn from as well as bad news to overthrow'. Active community creation is a priority for SFL, as is testified by its focus on local 'meaning making' and educational/literacy programmes have been a very specific locus of intervention (e.g. Halliday and Martin 1993; Iedema et al. 1994; Kress et al. 2001; and Schleppegrell 2004). In contrast, CDA, while strongly committed to more egalitarian practices in general terms, has tended to say fairly little about specific strategies of intervention and has tended to be more open-ended about specific domains of research.[1] This difference warrants closer inspection.

CDA's commitment to enabling change by making visible the social determinants of practices in a societal context is primarily oriented to critique and deconstruction. The accompanying emancipatory goals are awareness-raising about the ideological constitution of discourse practices and the naturalisation of power relations in everyday conceptualisations and rationalisations of practice, and, an imperative to so, in a way that brings social change into view. In this view, 'ideology' is broadly equated with representations which present a difference in power as 'common sense' and therefore as 'natural', 'normal', etc. The Marxist materialist underpinnings of such a programme are clear from concepts echoed – e.g. ideology as 'false/distorted consciousness'. Not surprisingly, therefore, CDA's pivotal and privileged moment is that of the social-theoretical interpretation and explanation, and its projected unit of reference is 'societal', broadly speaking, the stage of Late Modern/Advanced capitalist societies.

SFL's commitments are similar, although they betray a different history (with very specific roots in anthropology and the sociology of education). SFL's main commitment is towards equality achieved through the semiotic evolution of cultural formations and social subjectivities afforded by these. 'Where a culture has arrived in its evolution the phylogenetic level of the evolution of discourse formations provides the social context for the linguistic development of the individual [the ontogenetic level of development in social subjectivity], and the point an individual is at in their development provides resources for the instantiation of unfolding texts [the logogenetic level of unfolding texts with naturalised reading positions]' (Martin and Rose 2002: 266–7). In this model, intervention entails a commitment to the deconstruction (and with it, the transformation) of the coding orientations in individual language users. For SFL, the plane of the ideological is the system of the coding orientations which position language users in such a way that options in genre, register and language are made selectively available (with divisions along the lines of class, gender, ethnicity and generation). In this view, social power depends on the range of options available to a particular user, the extent to which these can be used for purposes of control, submission or negotiation, and how these options can(not) be taken up to transform the context which makes them available.

As summed up in Martin (1992: 575ff.), intervention is a matter of exploiting the semiotic tensions which follow from an unequal distribution of meaning potentials within the community. These tensions have to be read against the background of internally-contradictory tendencies within individual cultures (with attendant processes of systemic inertia and evolution).

[. . .]

Linguistic short cuts to context in SFL and CDA

In SFL the starting point for interpreting social discourse is with texts in social contexts: 'Social discourse rarely consists of just single clauses, rather social contexts develop as sequences of meanings comprising texts. Since each text is produced interactively between speakers, and between writers and (potential) readers, we can use it to interpret the interaction it manifests. And since the interaction is an instance of the speakers' culture, we can also use the text to interpret aspects of the culture it manifests' (Martin and Rose 2002: 1). The main point of interest is indeed in channelling an interest in social contexts through an examination of its textual realisations.

When it comes to contextual analysis, the picture across both SFL and CDA is somewhat bleaker. In fact, textualist concerns within CDA have been variously criticised (e.g. Widdowson (1995) and O'Halloran (2004) draw attention to the actual language user's cognition as a major factor which is too often ignored). The textualist concerns of both CDA and SFL also bring out a difference with linguistic anthropological approaches, which are characterised by a much more dynamic conception of text and context, seen as densely intertwined (see Blommaert this volume). However, it is probably more correct to observe that CDA does come with a programmatic commitment to independent contextual analysis, both in the form of 'institutional analysis' and in the form of establishing links of complementarity, reinforcement, opposition, etc. between discourse practice and other forms of practice (e.g. economic practice). Yet, at the same time, CDA does not offer an actual methodology for going about institutional or 'other' contextual analysis.

Within SFL, the picture is much more one-sidedly textual. Here the analysis of social practice is narrowed to textual practice: on a theoretical plane, context is read tryadically through the functions of language. Also in the practical terms of doing research, we do not find any traces of a stated need to engage with context separate from textual analysis, or before one begins to collect textual material, or independently of its immediate bearing on the textual instances which are the primary object of inquiry. In short, context is what can be gleaned from the text (for some, this is where the job of language analysts ends) and one major risk in this is indeed that the social is brought home to exhaustive textual analysis. Thompson's (1996: 10) observation about the clouds of context that come trailing with any naturally occurring stretch of language invites a question in reverse: can texts can be trusted to carry all the necessary hints for what will be relevant context?

Both paradigms insist on systematicity mostly when it comes to the analysis of the text. The ideal of the exhaustive and systematic analysis of the text as a contained materiality which points outwards to a context of origin is a philological inheritance, with ancestry in the reconstructive concerns of students of classical languages (the text is often all they have left and it is on their desk). It is also fed by the scholarly ideal of a hermeneutics of understanding the whole through an analysis of all its constituent parts. And, while within CDA (though much less so in SFL), there is certainly a social-theoretical recognition of the momentary aspects of practice, neither paradigm seems to encourage one towards an analysis of, say, meanings as they are selectively, marginally and fragmentedly attended to by the here-and-now user, or meaning making in situations where the socially relevant textual moment is not one of interpretative decoding, or in instances where that decoding is just one and not necessarily the main engagement with the text. Compare for instance with ethnomethodology (e.g. Watson 1997: 80 on texts as 'active social phenomena') and literacy studies (cf. Barton and Hamilton (2000: 12), who point out that, 'while some reading and writing is carried out as an end in itself, typically literacy is a means to another end'). The following excerpt from a British database of interviews with parents with children in public care poignantly – and painfully – makes the point (see Slembrouck and Hall, 2003). A lone mother with a small infant (she describes herself as 'at the end of her tether') rings social services for help. Social workers visit her the same evening and the next morning the child is removed and entered into voluntary care. Note in particular how the mother's particular interpretation of an institutional leaflet shaped her defeated expectations of how the social services would respond to her telephone call for help.

Excerpt 1*
[IN:]   did you have any idea . what they might be able to do
          did did you have any particular
[MO:]   no I didn't think they would whisk [no] my child off the
          next morning .
[IN:]   no .
          what did you think they might
[MO:]   I thought they might help
          because I've got a booklet over there actually which I've
              put picked up in their place
          which says that they can help you by having someone in
              during the day to . lessen . the burden .
[IN:]   what sort of thing were you thinking of there
[MO:]   erm . to tell you the truth I didn't really know exactly
              what I was thinking .
          I was thinking they might help me in a more in a different
              way than they would .
          no way did I think they would whisk my child off me
[IN:]   no
[MO:]   it says in that book. that they're supposed to send . in
              someone to help beforehand before they take the child
              away from you

---

* The following conventions are used: line breaks = to demarcate meaningful units; [FA] = father [MO] = mother [IN] = interviewer; . = a brief pause; (0.4) = a longer pause; _ = incomplete words; [words in square brackets mark additions which are the researcher's clarifications].

[IN:]   hm .
          so you thought they'd offer some sort of help . during the
          day

The question that I wish to raise here is whether an exhaustive textual analysis of the leaflet can lead us to see the real effects which its insertion into social action had in this particular case. If our aim is to understand the role of leaflets in contemporary social processes, how much of that role can in fact be gleaned from just the text itself? And, how much is to be inferred from what real users do with it, in some cases, irrespective of what the text might say?

In the case of SFL, much effort in textual analysis is also invested in functional-linguistic model building, in particular developing a taxonomy of functional meaning categories, and the systemic options within these, which the poly-system makes available to the user at the levels of genre, register and grammar. Of course, this is an extremely useful and important exercise and it has resulted in a highly detailed and refined set of reading instruments for understanding both local and global textual meaning. Yet, one price paid for this has been a number of abstractions. In their discussion of SFL's analytical response to 'textual hybridity', Chouliaraki and Fairclough (1999: 142) formulate the related remarks that 'the apparatus of SFL [. . .] pushes the analyst to the side of the system' and that it could be more 'fully as possible open to the specificity of events as events'. Yet, the bigger charge may be that of a textual appropriation of the contextual groundedness of specific moments of language use and, with it, a neglect of real language users' orientations in these events as an empirical question in its own right which is difficult to answer if the language user remains only an agency implied 'in the text' and if the language user's voice remains unacknowledged, unaccounted for and absent from the analysis.

Emic beauty and the interpretative beast

SFL's emphasis on a culture's specific 'meaning potential' is *deeply emic*. It is motivated by an inventory of functional distinctions as they are meaningful from an insider's perspective. However, it is a kind of emicity in which language users tend to be seen as complying with structures whose workings they may not be aware of but which are thought of as applying homogeneously across a language community, a cultural space or a specific segment of it. Such an emic perspective does not appear to come with an explicit engagement that it is necessary to examine the metalinguistic orientations of real users empirically, i.e. addressing the question what a practice means to a real, individual user through contact with that user.

CDA's specific disciplinary history is quite different when it comes to this particular aspect of discourse enquiry. Its epistemological credo is 'interpretative' (see e.g. Fairclough 1989: Ch. 6) and, already in its early stages, this was echoed in the claim that the analyst is inescapably also a language user (see especially, Fairclough 1989: 167). The interpretative credo of CDA formed part of an epistemological break with 'descriptive' linguistics as passively committed to objective science and social status quo (the occurrence of divergent interpretations is a major source of conflict over social and ideological outlooks). However, for the analyst to recognise that her/his analytical activity is intrinsically like the language user's on-line interpretative work is one thing. To take such a principle from there to the level of actually examining actual instances of interpretations by real, individualised participants, turns out to be

still quite a few steps removed. Thus far, CDA appears not to have been heading much for this path. Instead, the tendency has been to give a superior edge to social-theoretically informed interpretations which encompass, explain and thus overcome the limitations of the (ideologically-distorted) language user's perspective (Fairclough 1989: 38ff.). Such a one-sided privileging of social theoretically informed explanations comes with a risk of explaining the empirical participant's perspective away. Note that I do not wish to plead against the relevance of social theoretical readings of and reflections on the conditions of contemporary subjectivity. Nor am I pleading in favour of a one-sided preference for insider-interpretations over social-theoretically informed ones. Instead, the suggestion is perhaps that the relevance question of social theory itself must be taken into the field and into the dialogic contact with research subjects.
      [. . .]
      Furthermore, I am arguing that contact with the language user remains in various ways under-valued and under-thematised both within CDA and SFL. Despite a commitment to critique and durable change in the name of a widely acclaimed discursive turn in the social sciences and for the sake of the betterment of the social subject-cum-language user, the main short cut taken by CDA and SFL alike has been to bypass precisely that very language user. And, while the epistemological (and, to a lesser extent, the ethical) implications of a critical contact with researched worlds has received considerable attention (in many cases, underlining the urgency of intervention), the full range of epistemological implications that stem from such a commitment have not been addressed to the full. This is an aspect of critical discourse enquiry for which ethnographic approaches to language study are much more comfortably equipped. [. . .]

Ethnography as a contemporary reflexive epistemology of contact

Ethnography is an epistemology of contact. This means that knowledge is seen as rooted in, and as progressively shaped in the course of, communicative contact with researched worlds sustained over a longer period of time. In the words of Van Maanen (1995: 3), 'ethnography claims and is granted by many if not most of its readers a kind of documentary status on the basis that someone actually goes "out there", draws close to people and events, and then writes about what was learned in situ'. Such an epistemological orientation is often translated methodologically into key techniques such as 'participant observation', 'interviewing' and 'interpretative triangulation',[2] but it is probably more correct to observe how ethnography is in fact amenable to a diversity of formal and informal research instruments and that each of these is seen as revolving around contact (talking for the first time to, sitting in with, conducting formal and informal interviews, administering a questionnaire, hypothesis testing through elicitation, making a video-recording of talk, (temporarily) becoming/being/having been an insider practitioner oneself, etc.). [. . .]
      Ethnography's premium on contact comes with a commitment to and an explicit display of the participant perspective: the participant as a resource of knowledge and as an interpretative perspective that cannot be explained away. Saville-Troike (2003: 97) expresses the ethical imperatives which follow from this in the terms of a limit, i.e. the integrity of the participant perspective entails an action space in which researchers commit themselves to 'contribute to the welfare of the host group in a way they [the host group] recognize and desire'. For the author, this includes

'not "talking" data without returning something of immediate usefulness to the community'. From the point of view of critical approaches, it is important to highlight this dimension, because at one and the same time (i) it states the desirability of acting towards change in the interest of a researched community as lying within the immediate remit of an ethnographic orientation,[3] while (ii) anticipating the complexities and dilemmas that will accompany divergent and conflicting perceptions of what can count as desirable change. For an example of an analysis which reports in detail on such tensions, see Haviland (2003).

[. . .]

Late Modernity has imposed its specific set of themes which now also run through ethnographic debate: global economic and political currents, transformed workplace orders and information technology which tie up formerly 'isolatable' communities with larger worlds, the widespread mediatisation of the 'worlds of others' in the form of journalists' stories, television news, televised documentaries, websites and thematic internet forums, etc. These themes have affected the range of available and relevant data sources, while also prompting the question of social science's specific role in public culture. Multiplicity applies in the sense that in many cases, ethnography can no longer be straightforwardly defined in terms of a single homogeneous culture or subculture; instead, it is increasingly practised within a complex landscape of intersecting practices under diverse conditions of contact (often the conditions involve an amount of time/place-displacement). It is no longer obvious to see ethnography as confined to a single population or a single site, institutional or otherwise. Thus, my own research into accounts of children in public care continually crosses the boundaries of various professional communities (medical, educational, social work, etc.), while intersecting with a client 'population' of parents. Each of these perspectives is intrinsically important to the ethnography: each comes with its own claim and entitlement to integrity. Things get even more complicated once you bring to the research the realisation that accounts of parents with children in public care will also be published in newspapers (in routine news reporting or in special feature articles). Similar accounts have been found as 'exemplums' on internet sites of organised parents groups and, along with the work of professionals, parents' experiences have also been documented in television programmes (in one-off documentaries, during talk shows, or in the carefully-monitored sequences of a human interest documentary-cum-soap).

[. . .]

Social class in an interviewing context of families with children in public care

The study on which this paper is based is an ethnography focusing on child protection in Eastern Flanders. It was initiated in early 2001 with the aim to understand how social class is 'spoken' in versions of child protection and care, and it has thus far concentrated on representations of practice by social workers and family counsellors, televised versions, as well as (what is still) a small number of interviews with parents of children in public care. It has done so, while being engaged dialogically with a body of research on language/class which takes social class to be a relevant category and a major 'variable' for an understanding of the social realities of child protection/

care and the ways in which these social realities are constructed and maintained in institutional interaction and elsewhere. There is a parallel 'British' corpus (largely drawn from districts in Yorkshire), with some comparative findings reported in Slembrouck and Hall (2003).

[. . .]

The institutions of child care/protection maintain tight regulations over the researcher's access to individual parents. Respect for the privacy of parents meant that for my research an institutional representative (who carried an introductory/ explanatory letter written by me) selected and contacted the parents, and that I was given names and addresses only after the parents had agreed to be interviewed (with the explicit proviso that a database with names and telephone numbers cannot be kept). The process of negotiating access was replete with voiced pessimism that few parents would be prepared to be interviewed, and in one of the five district centres the decision was indeed for the special juvenile care committee to opt out from any further involvement in the research because the proposal (as formulated at the time) was felt to be insufficiently clear on the actual benefits which the planned research would bring to the client population. The result of this long and difficult process thus far has been that I have obtained only a small number of interviews with parents, their social workers/counsellors and two directors of child protection committees (all conducted throughout the first half of 2002). Four of the five audio-recorded interviews with parents are with lone mothers, one is with a couple (no. 2). Four of the cases concerned teenagers or adolescents (no. 1 concerns an infant in early primary school). The parents preferred to be interviewed at home (but interview no. 3 was recorded in a tea room in Gent, away from the district, as the parent made a stop-over on the way to work). All names in the transcriptions (parents, their children, institutions, etc.) have been anonymised.

Parents (re)contextualise their case: data analysis and data histories

A broad reading of the accounts, when mapped on a division along occupational lines, yields the following set of salient distinctions as characteristic for the parents' accounts. Table 15.1 highlights significant distinctions in terms of 'who' is articulated as the problem, whether the relationship between the parents enters the account as a contributing factor or cause, how the family crisis is explained, how self-diagnosis relates to institutional voice, and who/what has changed for the better.

Even though the sample reported on in this paper is small, the set of distinctions is striking (and, it is moreover, corroborated by related interviews in the British context). It is important to note that the set of distinctions was not read off entirely or straightforwardly from the 'texture' of just the recorded interviews. In fact, it was arrived at through a combination of, on the one hand, field notes with observations which extend beyond the encounter of the interview and, on the other hand, textual analysis which is sensitive to how the accounts are managed interactionally, how they are established during the interview encounter and how this necessitates a layered reading of the transcribed data. In other words, the interviewed parents are not just recounting events. Nor is the researcher–interviewer just asking questions or offering backchannel signalling attention and/or sympathetic involvement. Both are at the same time doing role identity work which is layered over the roles of interviewer/

Table 15.1 Salient distinctions in parents' accounts

Working-class parent	Middle-class parent
I am the problem – my child is not responsible for this	My child is the problem – I am not responsible for this
The explanation of the 'problem' is oriented to social background/life history of the parent, especially the way the parent was brought up her/himself	The explanation of the 'problem' is oriented to the child's life history, especially problematic peer contact
Gender trouble is listed as a direct cause	Gender trouble is left outside the account
Institutional diagnoses are accepted and endorsed by the parent as their own	Institutional diagnoses are questioned or qualified by the parent(s)
The parent(s) report a change in their self-perception and own behaviour as a result of institutional intervention	The parent(s) report a change in the child's self-perception and behaviour as a result of institutional intervention

interviewee and researcher/researched (for instance, parents speak also as inhabitants of an area, as having an occupational status, as parents, etc. – as to the latter, note that all interviewees have asked *me* if I have children). Table 15.1 is therefore the result of drawing on a range of data.

Seeing parents' accounts as interactionally managed and established in an interview contact

As already hinted at above, interviews do not appear out of the blue. They are social events which need to be planned and staged (also logistically – this involves making telephone calls to agree on a time and place, the setting up of technological equipment, etc.). Interviews also involve a process of legitimation (one must seek permission to interview) and this process extends into the negotiation of a frame of action and interpretation. Very importantly, there is the negotiation of what the interview will be about and also the signalling (and the display of mutual recognition of that signalling) of actual beginnings and endings (cf. Goffman 1974). Vigouroux (2004) draws a distinction between 'la sequence démarrée' – the actual beginning of the interview which often coincides with the switching on of the recorder – and the 'opening sequence' which opens the encounter. The interpretative upshot from this is that an understanding of the recorded and transcribed textual flow, in the more narrow sense, may require one to attune oneself to a particular dynamics of entextualisation and contextualisation (see Bloomaert, this volume) which extends beyond the confines of the recorded segment and invites a considerable amount of interpretative triangulation (Gumperz 2003: 111). How far beyond the borders of, in this particular case, the recorded interview talk, should one move in order to assemble a plausible interpretative take on a particular sequential flow of interpersonal, ideational and textual meanings?

One particularly striking example occurred in the very first interview. This interview belongs in the left column of Table 15.1, but the account's congruence with the third feature (gender friction is invoked as a direct cause) was established only by coincidence and in fact after the minidisk recorder had been switched off and the researcher had been shown the room of the infant in foster care. Unlike the rest of the council flat, the room was completely refurbished and amply equipped with toys and things, in anticipation of the child's return home and shown to me as part of a display of being a parent who takes the trouble to provide what is necessary. As part of the small talk on the way to the door, I asked the mother if this had been the first time she had been interviewed. Her answer was 'no'. She had been previously interviewed by a woman who was doing a project on gender violence. Only at that point did it transpire that the troubled move from Wallonia to Flanders, the difficulties the mother had experienced combining a new job and child rearing, her temporarily moving in with a friend, had all followed in the wake of a flight from a violent ex-partner (an episode which she subsequently recounted in greater detail and which added another 15 minutes to the account – off-the-record, unrecorded and accessible now only through field notes and a summary afterwards). These details not only make one wonder: (i) what did this mother see as lying inside/outside the scope of the stated interview topic: 'her experiences as a parent'; and (ii) did the on-record nature of the interview affect her decision-making in this area? The details obtained off-the-record also affect Table 15.1 very directly (they provide a basis for the claim that the 'case' is congruent with a particular set of features).

Actual beginnings of interviews are often accompanied by the interviewer stating the general purpose of the talk, and this is often a crucial step in the 'keying' of the encounter (Goffman 1981). In the case of interview 2, a professional couple in an affluent council estate, the father responded by signalling a difference in perception.

Excerpt 2 (interview 2) – translated into English
[FA:]   oh the way we see ourselves as parents
         but Mr Kloosters had said *our experiences with CLB erm CBJ*

The father was assuming that the interview would be about a particular institutional experience; in his response he initially mixes up the learner advisory centre (CLB, 'Centrum voor Leerlingenbegeleiding') with the district's juvenile care committee (CBJ, 'Comité Bijzondere Jeugdzorg'). In fact, both institutions played a major role in this particular case. The father's response takes us back to the moment where the counsellor negotiated the consent of these parents to be interviewed. It makes one wonder about the role which the letter of introduction, which also stated the topic of the interview, played in this earlier encounter (how it was possibly quite in the background, not particularly read in detail, interpretatively paraphrased by the counsellor). Another interpretative avenue presents itself here, one which does not necessarily rule out the first possibility: by framing the talk in terms of a client experience with an institution, these parents make it easier for themselves to maintain face; it allows them to maintain a particular 'line' during the interaction (Goffman 1967: 7), a distance from a painful experience which, as they will be well aware, can easily undermine their credibility as parents.

Interestingly, even though I cleared the misunderstanding, a kind of consumer-satisfaction talk continued to run through their account, for instance, particular comments which occurred in the margin of (or even framed) particular narrative episodes. Excerpt 3 offers an example of this. In this excerpt the father sums up the nature of the 'family problem' which resulted into a brief reception into residential care (a youngster's home, here referred to anonymously as 'de Eik', *the Oak*). The mother corroborates his view, stressing how their daughter's case did not come with 'loud alarm bells'. Playing down the seriousness of the case is one way in which parenthood can be redeemed in the face of the interviewer. Immediately next, the father shifts the talk from 'properties of the case' to 'institutional coordination and decision-making':

Excerpt 3 (interview 2) – translated into English

[FA:]   in our case it was a problem of authority and Sara's
          future and (not) sticking to agreed rules and the
          circles she was moving in
          while the youngsters she was confronted with there had
          been through a lot more than she had [IN: mm] and
[MO:]   indeed were facing more serious problems
[FA:]   I can very well imagine that inside the Eik they say
          well ok the others first [IN: yes yes]
          how they arrive at decisions in this erm how the
          decision-making happens there I have no idea
          [IN: mm]
          how they outline their policy there I don't know.
          we were always talking to a social worker or the scho_
          resident psychologist er.
          but apparently they don't communicate all that much
          and one has to guess
          and then check with the other one.
          really sit down together we didn't succeed in

In his second turn, the father lists as possible reasons for why their daughter's case was not 'high priority': a lack of communication among the professionals, a lack of communication with the parents, and a lack of transparency in the decision-making.

The above set of data-historical observations are important in two respects. First, this set of interviews may have a uniformly-stated topical focus, but it cannot be said to have resulted in a uniform range of interview topics and interpretative frames. To detect an angle of service-centred talk with a client-satisfaction angle in interview 2 forms part of understanding the specific data history for this specific interview. It helps us understand how the case is contextualised and how the narrative is entextualised. It cautions the researcher not to treat the individual interviews as interchangeable tokens of the same type. As Cicourel (2003) demonstrates in detail: informants who are faced with relative uncertainty about what a specific data event will be about – here: 'an interview about their experiences as parents' – will tend to fill the gaps and develop a frame for action by relying on readily available interpretations. Similarly, a counsellor who negotiates an interview on behalf of the researcher is also likely to engage in work of interpretative 'gap-filling' (you make up for the gaps by adding what is plausible). In this case, it may be that the counsellor was unsure about the exact scope of the pre-text stated in the letter and made up for this by suggesting to the parents that the interview would probably be about their experiences with the juvenile care committee (such is indeed suggested by Excerpt 2). Alternatively, the counsellor's addition to the pre-text stated in the letter may have been strategic: to win over these parents for an interview. Second, and more importantly still, an epistemological concern with ethnographic reflexivity adds to such observations that an analysis of the data histories bears directly on the main topic of research. Applied here: the father's slipping into service-oriented talk foregrounds his familiarity with and literacy about how institutions go about their business; in other words: it reveals his own professional-occupational status as a senior civil servant who is quite acquainted with coordinating talk and with the fact that institutional action is often directed by the accidental imponderables of such talk. Together with other details (e.g. the way in which the father presents the intervention as largely staged and coordinated by the parents; the way in which he cites particular legislative detail), this aspect of the talk brings out a specific dimension of the parents' middle classness.

Let me now turn to a second set of examples. Also in these cases, an interactional analysis of framing moves in the talk can be shown to add focus and scope to the distributional results listed in Table 15.1. At the beginning of the recorded parts, interviewees were offered a choice: just to tell me what happened or instead I could direct the talk by asking particular questions. The decision to offer a choice was informed by an anticipation of contradictory tendencies in the interviewees' responses to the occasion of interviewing. On the one hand, I had a clear interest in 'narrativity' (and my own preference was, initially, towards the uninterrupted narrative which unfolds quasi-monologically). I also expected some parents to be keen to tell their story in full. At the same time, I was also expecting some parents to be uncertain about what the interview was really about or reluctant to tell their story. Let us now look at how two parents, a cleaner (interview no. 4), and a secondary school teacher (interview no. 3), responded to the choice on offer. In the second case (middle-class parent), the mother responded by hinting at a coherent narrative to tell, but she matches her observation with an expressed uncertainty about how the larger narrative will tally with the researcher's expectations.

Excerpt 4 (interview 3) – translated into English
[MO:]   it's rather a lot the story
            and I wouldn't know where to begin
            perhaps it is better if you ask some questions
            then it will happen any way
            and if you think I'm leaving something out just tell me

This response is quite similar to the one given by the mother in interview 2. These two occurrences can be contrasted with interview 4 (working-class parent): here the mother opted for 'answers to specific questions', happy to abide by the authority of the interviewer.

Excerpt 5 (interview 4) – translated into English
[ND:]   I prefer you to ask questions .
            it makes things easy

This difference is not only important in its own right, it is also echoed in the sequences which followed. In as much as the mother in interview no. 4 stuck to the narrow thematic scope of individual questions (she gave little detail, she paused a lot, etc.) and showed various signs of unease with the 'interview game', the mother in interview no. 3 quite freely ventured beyond the thematic scope of individual questions and elaborated spontaneously on the individuals involved, with a delicate monitoring of voice, adding judgement and evaluative comment even when not invited to do so, etc. In so far as the mother in interview no. 4 cites the institutional categorisation and remedial recipe as also her own (see Excerpt 6), the mother in interview no. 3 engages dialogically with the institutional analysis (see Excerpt 7). She does so by acting out a dialogue in which she separates her own voice from that of the institutional representative, and by doing so, she adds qualification to the institutional analysis. Interviews no. 3 and 4 both concern cases of an adolescent son involved in small crime. Excerpt nos. 6 and 7 also show the different orientation in terms of who is problematised and where the causes are being located (the parents in interview 4; the adolescent son in interview 3).

Excerpt 6 (interview 4) – translated into English
[IN:]   or where did things go wrong (or how did things go
              wrong)
[MO:]   (I think that it erm) has to do with the way I
              was brought up erm er
            that I didn't know what you can do when you raise kids
              and what you can't do
            so I had so an extremely bad a very bad youth .
            and from there from there onwards er just about
              everything started going wrong
            and also the father who to some extent wouldn't take up
              his responsibilities .
            and who wouldn't look after him (0.4)
            but yes if you don't get the right upbringing at home
              and you are being neglected and you don't know
              just . how to do it all yes
            then [IN: uhuh] the problems begin don't they (0.2)
[IN:]   yeah uhuh a (0.2) and what would you have done differently
[MO:]   erm draw more boundaries for Karel because that I did
              not do (0.4)
[IN:]   yes

Excerpt 7 (interview 3) – translated into English
[MO:]   he was looking up to [IN: uhum] those who had the
              nerve to do these things .
            and then they say *yes bad friends*
            any of the schools he went to I pfff the principal
              the principal always said *it must be this friend of
              his*
            I began to think so too *yes I guess so*
            but he does know where to find them

[. . .] A key question raised by such comparative data is whether the mother's lack of displayed separation between her own voice and that of the institutional diagnosis and categorisation (interview 4) is a direct expression of a class-oriented coding tendency, because as a cleaner (and, unlike the professional couple, a senior civil servant and a teacher trainer, in interview 2 and the secondary school teacher in interview 3), she is in a low autonomy profession, more used to receiving orders and instructions rather than being required to negotiate the nature of her work. The underlying suggestion is thus that economic relations impact on the way the mother in interview no. 4 has received and accepted the institutional diagnosis and intervention as defining her own individual social reality as a parent. It is also in this light that Bourdieu's (1984) cautionary, reflexive note becomes very relevant: there may be a real class-bias in cross-class interviewing practice and working-class interviewees may be silenced as a result. Indeed, the mother in interview no. 4 also appears to abide by the authority of the interviewer's questions. She does not seek any initiative in directing the interview. She responds to the questions as well as she can, but she does not elaborate, qualify or rephrase. [. . .]

Conclusion: relevance to professionals in child protection

My research in this area is ongoing. But the analysis is quite suggestive of how social class may enter the picture of discourses of child protection and may be consequential in any decisions finally made.

Counsellors stress that child protection cases are spread statistically across social classes, but they also throw up their arms, sometimes in disbelief, about certain populations. Discourses of child protection found within institutions in Belgium often come with a difficult and uncomfortable balance. On the one hand, there is a committed policy of steering clear of, and actively fighting, stigma and prejudice, as well as a refusal to accept the irreversibility of any of the situations workers have to confront; and, on the other hand, there are tacit assumptions about certain families, populations, areas, neighbourhoods, etc. being predisposed in particular ways.

From the analysis of my preliminary interview data, social class relevance emerges not so much in the classist terms of susceptibility to particular problems, but class in terms of distinction of contact with the institution, in the explanations offered by the parents, in the parents' responses to institutional diagnosis and intervention. This is an agenda which so far I have not come across in the field. It is one which can be brought to the field, in the form of a set of hypotheses worth being tested and which may lead to a number of tangible implications for the institutional provision of intervention resources.

Notes

1   See however Slembrouck (2001) on the thematic impact of CDA on sociolinguistic, linguistic and discourse analytical enquiry, more generally.

2   'Triangulation' is originally a mathematical concept. It refers to a method for finding out the distance and position of a third point by measuring the distance between two other, fixed points and then measuring the angle from each of these to the third point. Here it is used metaphorically for a method of interpretation by which you relate findings from two separate data sources to determine the unknown or uncertain value of a third 'variable' (the term is used for instance in Gumperz (2003: 117)).

3   Compare also: 'Because ethnography traditionally has been associated with a potential critical mandate, distinct boundaries separating well-done ethnography from critical scholarship are often blurry. Critical ethnography is a style of analysis and discourse embedded within conventional ethnography' (Thomas 1993: 3).

References

Barton, D. and Hamilton, M. (2000) 'Literacy practices', in D. Barton, M. Hamilton and R. Ivanic (eds) *Situated Literacies* (pp. 7–15). London: Routledge.

Bourdieu, P. (1984) *Questions de Sociologie*. Paris: Les Éditions de Minuit.

Chouliaraki, L. and Fairclough, N. (1999) *Discourse in Late Modernity. Rethinking critical discourse analysis*. Edinburgh: Edinburgh University Press.

Cicourel, A. (2003) 'Reflections on Bourdieu'. Paper read at the 8th International Pragmatics Conference, Toronto.

Fairclough, N. (1989) *Language and Power*. London: Longman.

Fairclough, N. (ed.) (1992) *Critical Language Awareness*. London: Longman.

Goffman, E. (1967) 'On face-work', in E. Goffman (ed.) *Interaction Ritual, Essays on Face-to-Face Behaviour* (pp. 5–46). New York: Pantheon Books.

Goffman, E. (1974) *Frame Analysis. An essay on the organisation of experience*. New York: Harper & Row.

Goffman, E. (1981) 'Footing', in E. Goffman (ed.) *Interaction Ritual* (pp. 124–59). Philadelphia, PA: University of Pennsylvania Press.

Gumperz, J. (2003) 'Response essay', in S. Eerdmans, C. Prevignanon and P. Thibault (eds) *Language and Interaction. Discussions with John J. Gumperz* (pp. 104–26). Amsterdam: John Benjamins.

Halliday, M. and Martin, J. (1993) *Writing Science: Literacy and discursive power*. London: Falmer.

Haviland, J. (2003) 'Ideologies of language: some reflections on language and the US law'. *American Anthropologist* 105: 764–74.

Iedema, R., Feez, S. and White, P. (1994) *Media Literacy*. Sydney: Metropolitan East Region's Disadvantaged Schools Programme.

Kress, G., Jewitt, C., Ogborn, J. and Tsatsarelis, C. (2001) *Multimodal Teaching and Learning. The rhetorics of the science classroom*. London: Continuum.

Martin, J. (1992) *English Text*. Amsterdam: John Benjamins.

Martin, J. and Rose, D. (2002) *Working with Discourse. Meaning beyond the clause*. London: Continuum.

McElhinny, B. (2003) 'Three approaches to the study of language and gender'. *American Anthropologist* 105: 848–55.

O'Halloran, K.A. (2004) *Critical Discourse Analysis and Language Cognition*. Edinburgh: Edinburgh University Press.

Saville-Troike, M. (2003) *The Ethnography of Communication. An introduction* (3rd rev. edn, orig. 1982). Oxford: Blackwell.

Schleppegrell, M. (2004) *The Language of Schooling. A functional linguistics perspective*. Mahwah, NJ: Lawrence Erlbaum.

Slembrouck, S. (2001) 'Explanation, interpretation and critique in the analysis of discourse'. *Critique of Anthropology* 21: 33–57.

Slembrouck, S. and Hall, C. (2003) 'Caring but not coping: fashioning a legitimate parent identity', in C. Hall, K. Juhila, N. Parton and T. Pösö (eds) *Constructing Clienthood in Social Work and Human Services* (pp. 44–61). London: Jessica Kingsley.

Thomas, J. (1993) *Doing Critical Ethnography*. London: Sage.

Thompson, G. (1996) *Introducing Functional Grammar*. London: Arnold.

Van Maanen, J. (1995) 'An end to innocence. The ethnography of ethnography', in J. Van Maanen (ed.) *Representation in Ethnography* (pp. 1–35). London: Sage.

Vigouroux, C. (2004) 'Questioning our research practice in order to understand our subject matter: a case study'. Unpublished manuscript.

Watson, R. (1997) 'Ethnomethodology and textual analysis', in D. Silverman (ed.) *Qualitative Research: Theory, method and practice* (pp. 80–98). London: Sage.

Widdowson, H. (1995) 'Discourse analysis: a critical view'. *Language and Literature* 4: 157–72.

Index

In the following index, British English spelling conventions have been used, which may differ slightly from those in the text. As authors differ in their usage, terms in small capitals and with initial capitals have been collected together under general headings in lower case.